# THE AVENGERS

WRITER
**BRIAN MICHAEL BENDIS**

PENCILER
**JOHN ROMITA JR.**

INKER
**KLAUS JANSON**
WITH **TOM PALMER & SCOTT HANNA**

COLORIST
**DEAN WHITE**
WITH **PAUL MOUNTS, RAIN BEREDO, LAURA MARTIN, MORRY HOLLOWELL & MATT MILLA**

COVER ART
**JOHN ROMITA JR., KLAUS JANSON, DEAN WHITE & MORRY HOLLOWELL**



## ISSUE #12.1

PENCILER
**BRYAN HITCH**

INKER
**PAUL NEARY**

COLORIST
**PAUL MOUNTS**

COVER ART
**BRYAN HITCH, PAUL NEARY & PAUL MOUNTS**

LETTERER
**VC'S CORY PETIT**

ASSOCIATE EDITOR
**LAUREN SANKOVITCH**

EDITOR
**TOM BREVOORT**

ollection Editor: JENNIFER GRÜNWALD • Editorial Assistants: JAMES EMMETT & JOE HOCHSTEIN • Assistant Editors: ALEX STARBUCK & NELSON RIBEIRO
Editor, Special Projects: MARK D. BEAZLEY • Senior Editor, Special Projects: JEFF YOUNGQUIST • Senior Vice President of Sales: DAVID GABRIEL
SVP of Brand Planning & Communications: MICHAEL PASCIULLO • Book Design: JEFF POWELL

Editor in Chief: AXEL ALONSO • Chief Creative Officer: JOE QUESADA • Publisher: DAN BUCKLEY • Executive Producer: ALAN FINE

**VENGERS BY BRIAN MICHAEL BENDIS VOL. 2.** Contains material originally published in magazine form as AVENGERS #7-12 and #12.1. First printing 2011. Hardcover ISBN# 978-0-7851-4504-2. Softcover BN# 978-0-7851-4505-9. Published by MARVEL WORLDWIDE, INC., a subsidiary of MARVEL ENTERTAINMENT, LLC. OFFICE OF PUBLICATION: 135 West 50th Street, New York, NY 10020.  Hardcover: $24.99 per copy in the U.S. and $27.99 in Canada (GST #R127032852). Softcover: $19.99 per copy in the U.S. and $21.99 in Canada (GST 127032852). Canadian Agreement #40668537.  **Printed in the U.S.A.** ALAN FINE, EVP - Office of the President, Marvel Worldwide, Inc. and EVP & CMO Marvel Characters B.V.; DAN BUCKLEY, Publisher & President - Print, Animation & Digital sions; JOE QUESADA, Chief Creative Officer; JIM SOKOLOWSKI, Chief Operating Officer; DAVID BOGART, SVP of Business Affairs & Talent Management; TOM BREVOORT, SVP of Publishing; C.B. CEBULSKI, P of Creator & Content Development; DAVID GABRIEL, SVP of Publishing Sales & Circulation; MICHAEL PASCIULLO, SVP of Brand Planning & Communications; JIM O'KEEFE, VP of Operations & Logistics; N CARR, Executive Director of Publishing Technology; JUSTIN F. GABRIE, Director of Publishing & Editorial Operations; SUSAN CRESPI, Editorial Operations Manager; ALEX MORALES, Publishing Operations nager; STAN LEE, Chairman Emeritus. For information regarding advertising in Marvel Comics or on Marvel.com, please contact John Dokes, SVP Integrated Sales and Marketing, at jdokes@marvel.com. For vel subscription inquiries, please call 800-217-9158. **Manufactured between 5/30/11 and 6/27/2011 (hardcover), and 5/30/11 and 12/26/2011 (softcover), by R.R. DONNELLEY, INC., SALEM, VA, USA.**

87654321

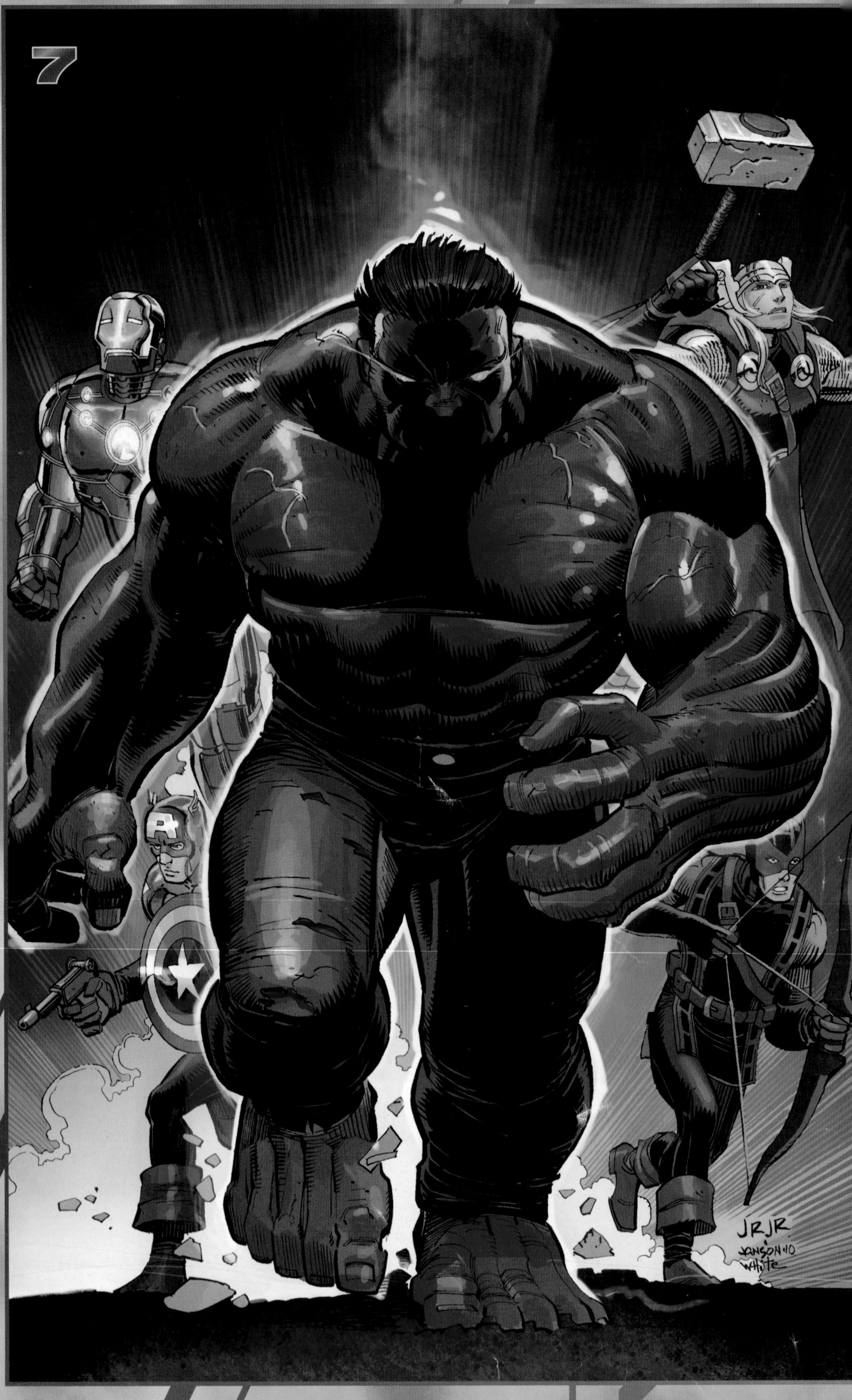
7
JRJR
JANSON '10
WHITE

And there came a day, a day unlike any other, when Earth's Mightiest Heroes found themselves united against a common threat! On that day, the Avengers were born, to fight the foes no single super hero could withstand!

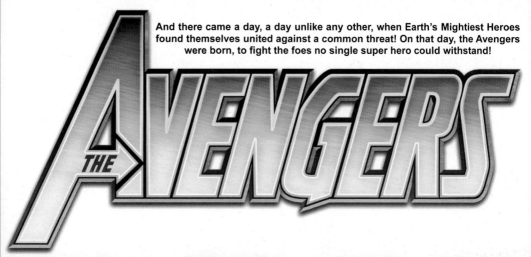

# THE AVENGERS

THE AVENGERS! WOLVERINE, IRON MAN, SPIDER-MAN, THOR, CAPTAIN AMERICA, SPIDER-WOMAN, THE PROTECTOR AND HAWKEYE ARE HAND-PICKED BY STEVE ROGERS TO LEAD THE PREMIERE AVENGERS TEAM!

AFTER AN AMAZING POWER-PLAY FOR CONTROL OF THE CRIMINAL EMPIRES OF THE MARVEL UNIVERSE, PARKER ROBBINS, A.K.A. THE HOOD, WAS DEPOWERED AND IMPRISONED BY THE AVENGERS.

LONGTIME HULK NEMESIS GENERAL THUNDERBOLT ROSS WAS IRRADIATED AND TRANSFORMED INTO THE RED HULK. NO ONE KNOWS WHO HE REALLY IS OR WHAT HE PLANS TO DO NEXT.

FORMER AVENGER WONDER MAN HAS TAKEN A SURPRISINGLY ANTI-AVENGERS STANCE AND HAS GONE SO FAR AS TO ATTACK THEM.

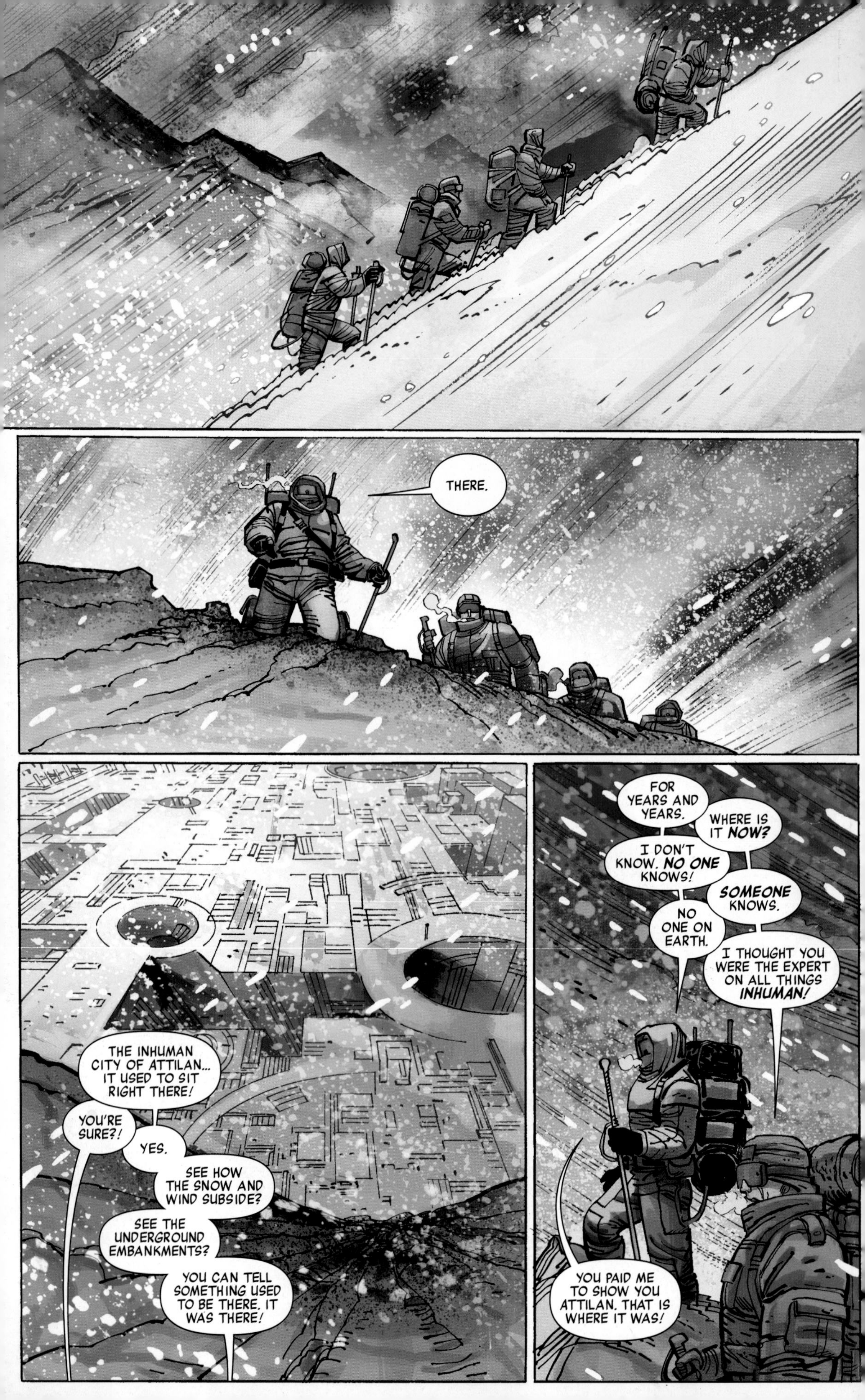
THERE.
THE INHUMAN CITY OF ATTILAN... IT USED TO SIT RIGHT THERE!
YOU'RE SURE?!
YES.
SEE HOW THE SNOW AND WIND SUBSIDE?
SEE THE UNDERGROUND EMBANKMENTS?
YOU CAN TELL SOMETHING USED TO BE THERE. IT WAS THERE!
FOR YEARS AND YEARS.
WHERE IS IT NOW?
I DON'T KNOW. NO ONE KNOWS!
SOMEONE KNOWS.
NO ONE ON EARTH.
I THOUGHT YOU WERE THE EXPERT ON ALL THINGS INHUMAN!
YOU PAID ME TO SHOW YOU ATTILAN. THAT IS WHERE IT WAS!

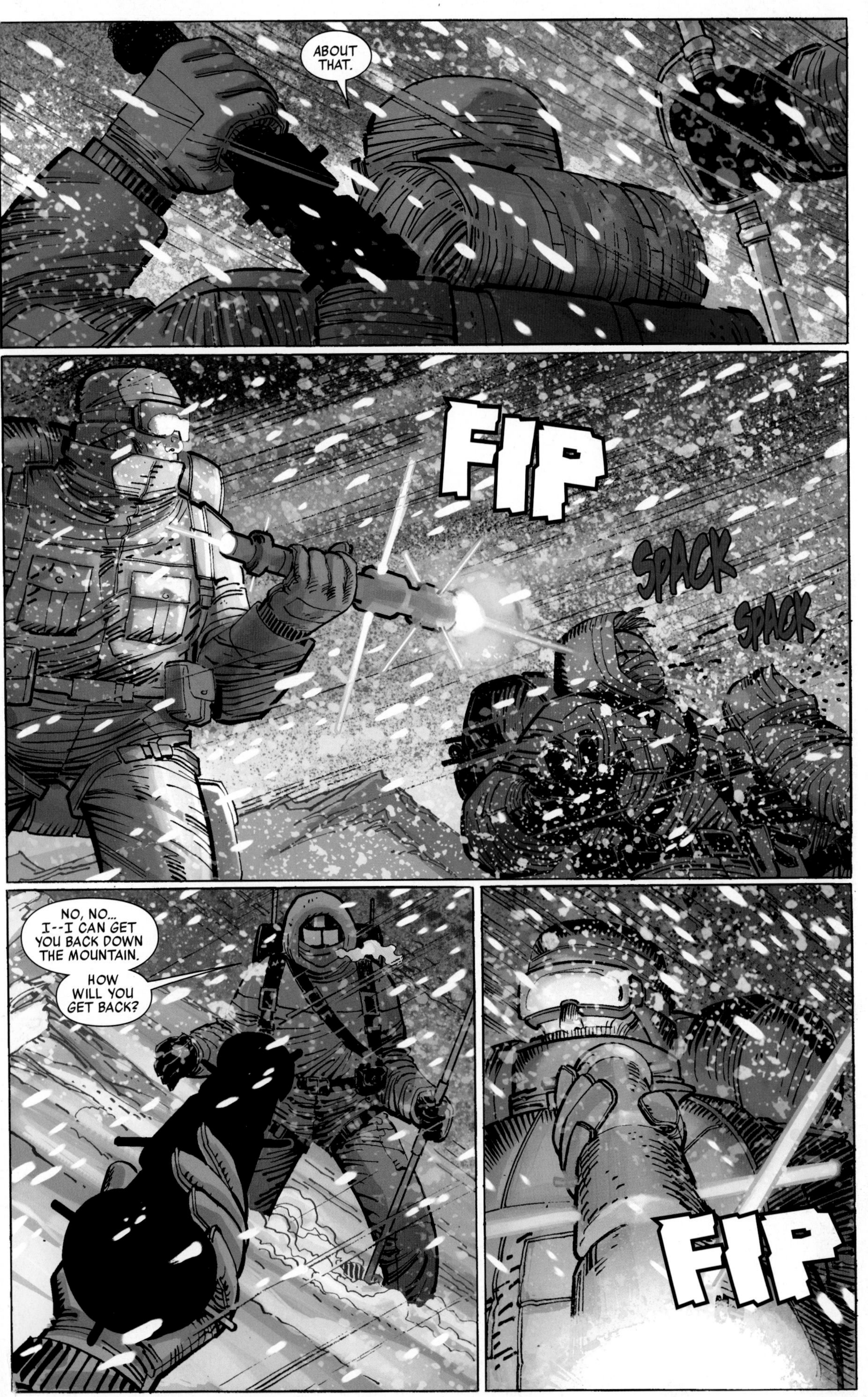
ABOUT THAT.
FIP
SPACK
SPACK
NO, NO... I--I CAN GET YOU BACK DOWN THE MOUNTAIN.
HOW WILL YOU GET BACK?
FIP

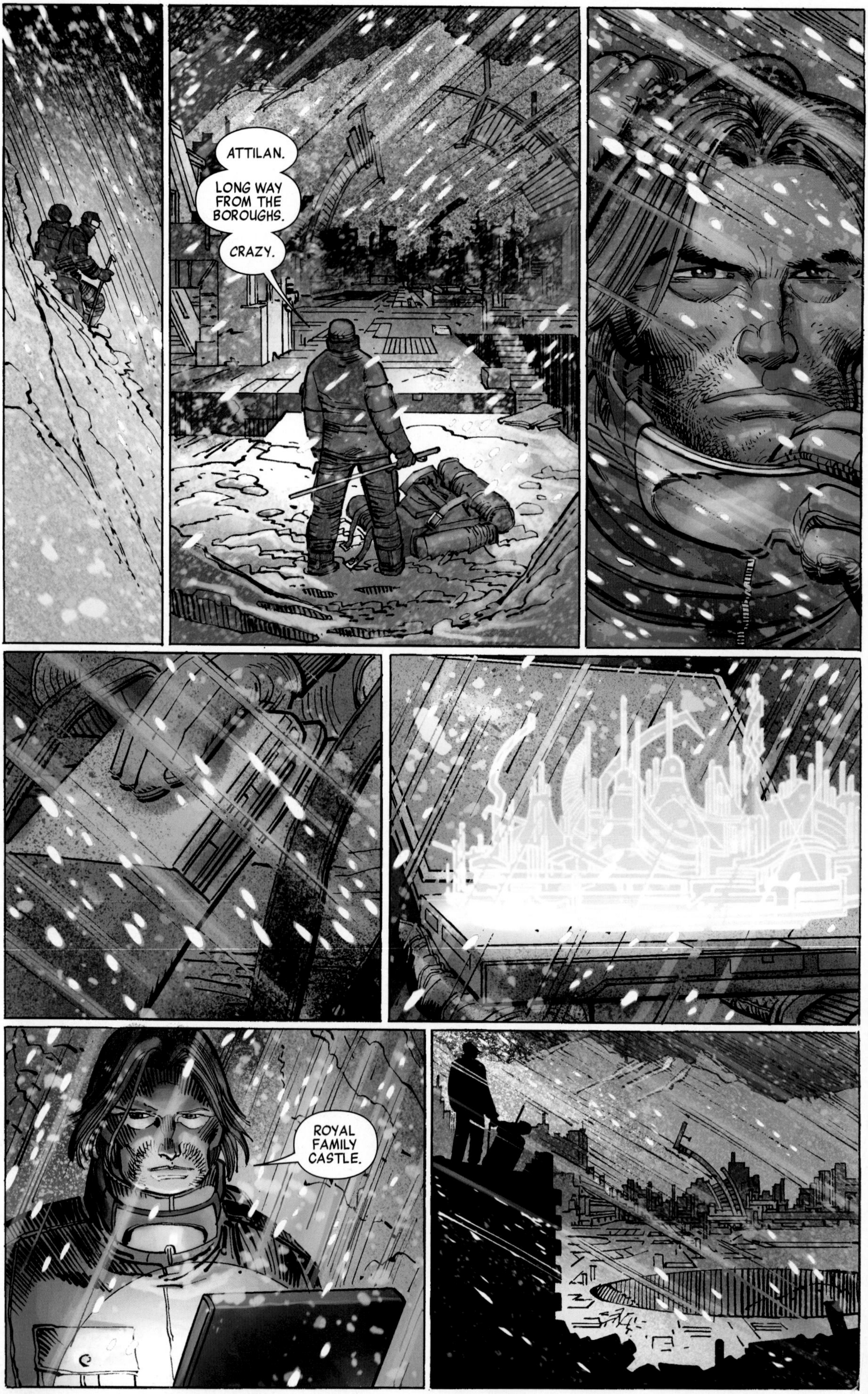
ATTILAN.
LONG WAY FROM THE BOROUGHS.
CRAZY.
ROYAL FAMILY CASTLE.

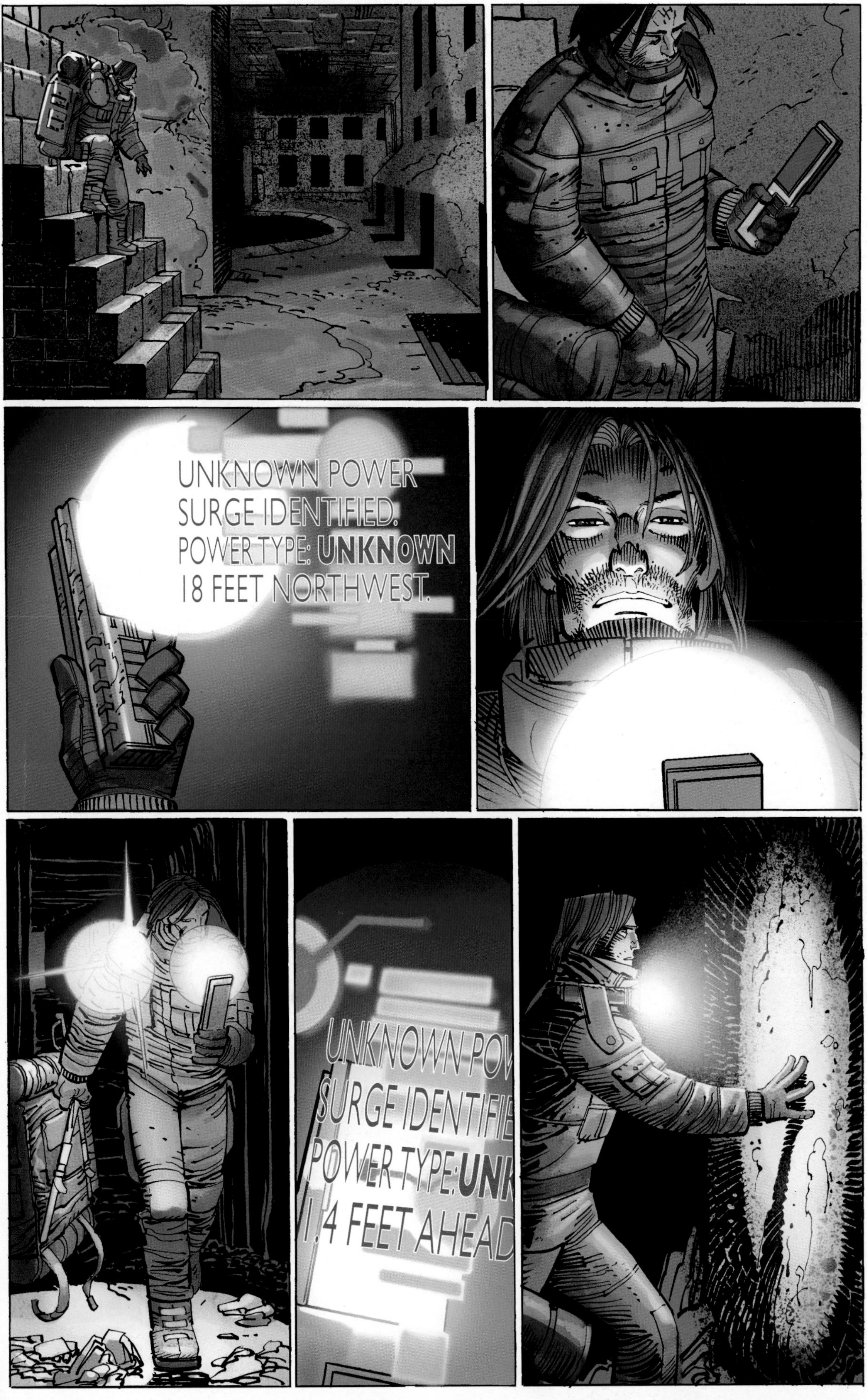
UNKNOWN POWER
SURGE IDENTIFIED.
POWER TYPE: **UNKNOWN**
18 FEET NORTHWEST.
UNKNOWN POW
SURGE IDENTIFIE
POWER TYPE:**UNK**
1.4 FEET AHEAD

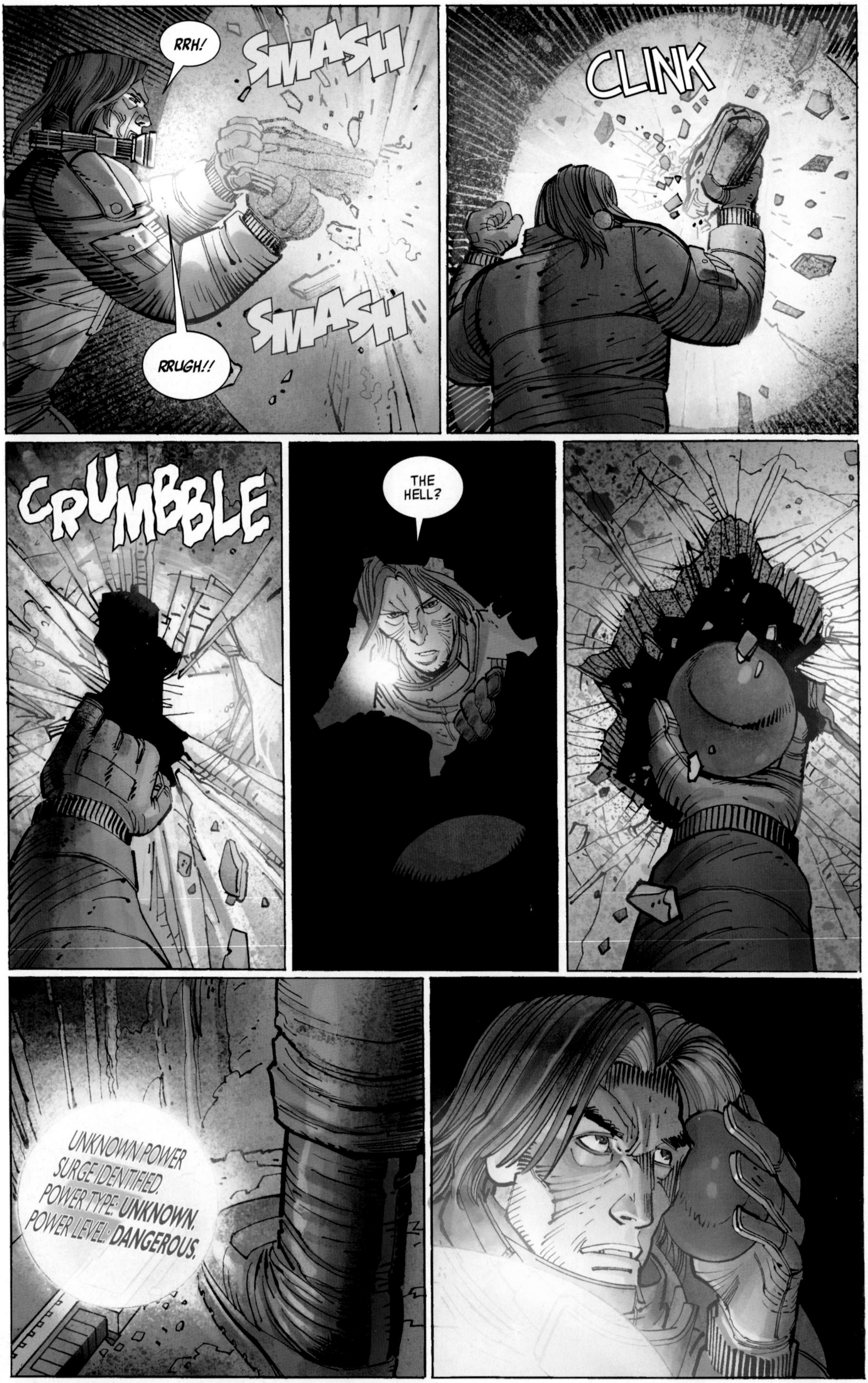
RRH!
SMASH
SMASH
RRUGH!!
CLINK
CRUMBBLE
THE HELL?
UNKNOWN POWER SURGE IDENTIFIED. POWER TYPE: UNKNOWN. POWER LEVEL: DANGEROUS.

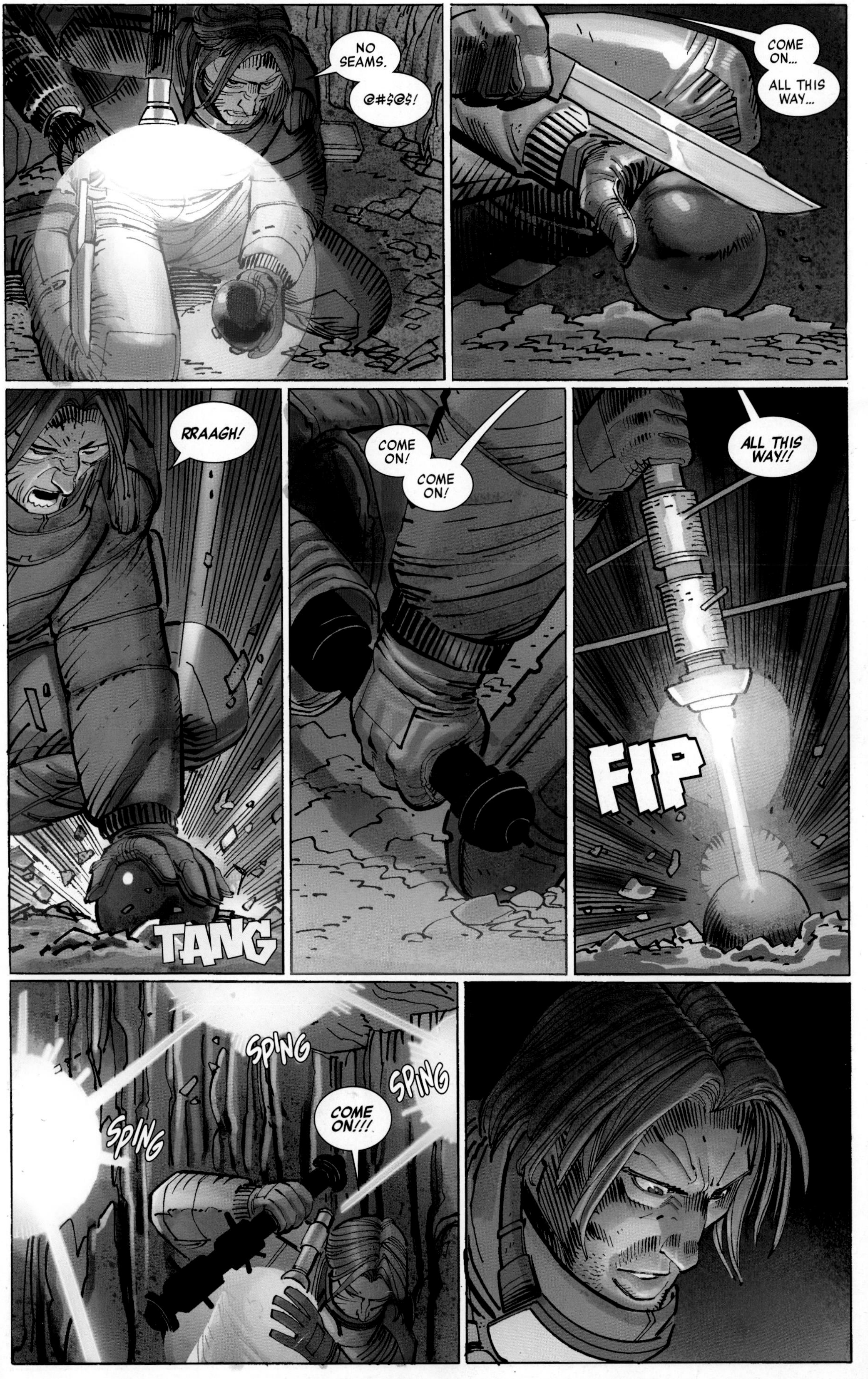
NO SEAMS.
@#$@$!
COME ON...
ALL THIS WAY...
RRAAGH!
TANG
COME ON!
COME ON!
ALL THIS WAY!!
FIP
SPING
SPING
SPING
COME ON!!!

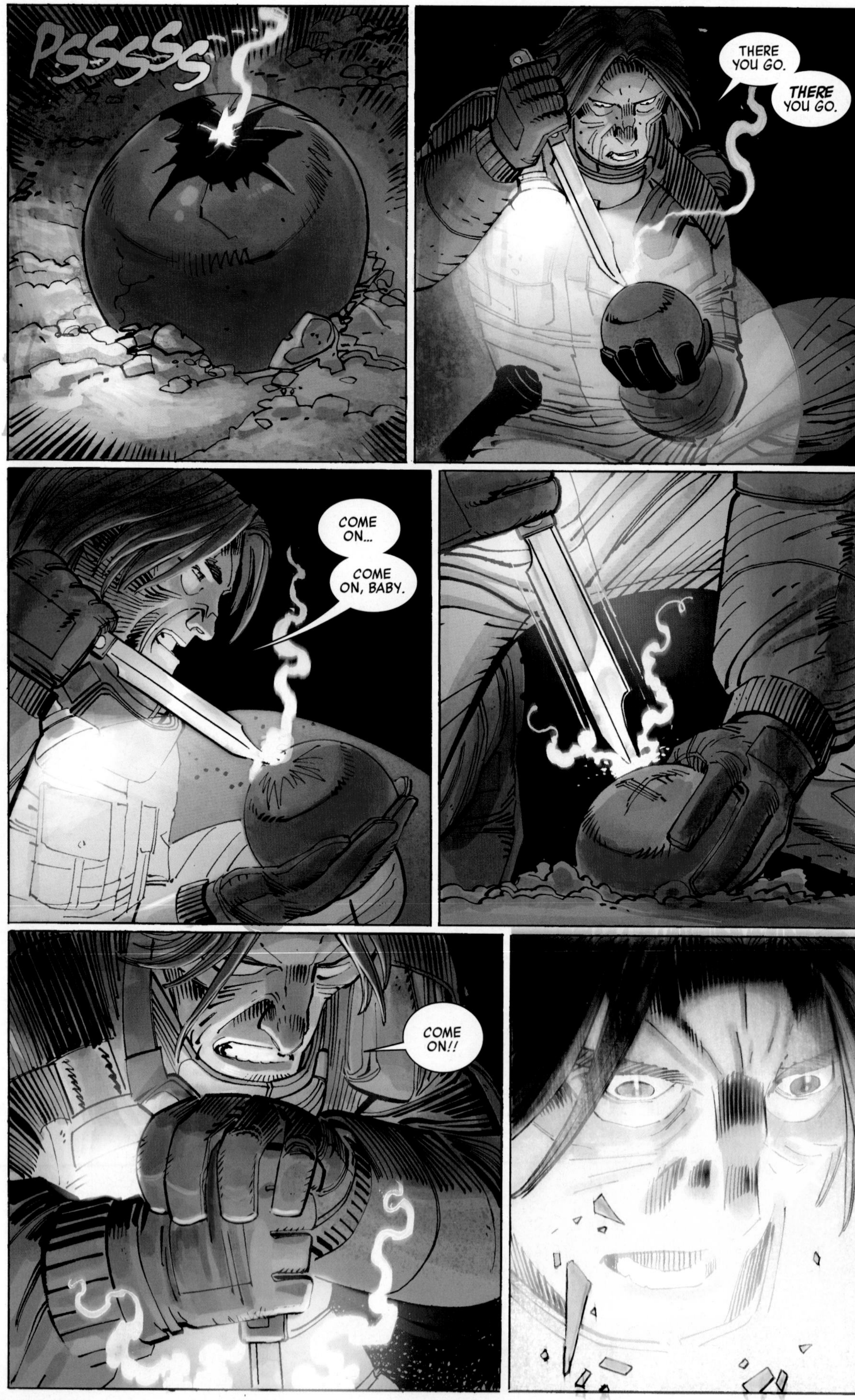
PSSSSS
THERE YOU GO.
THERE YOU GO.
COME ON...
COME ON, BABY.
COME ON!!

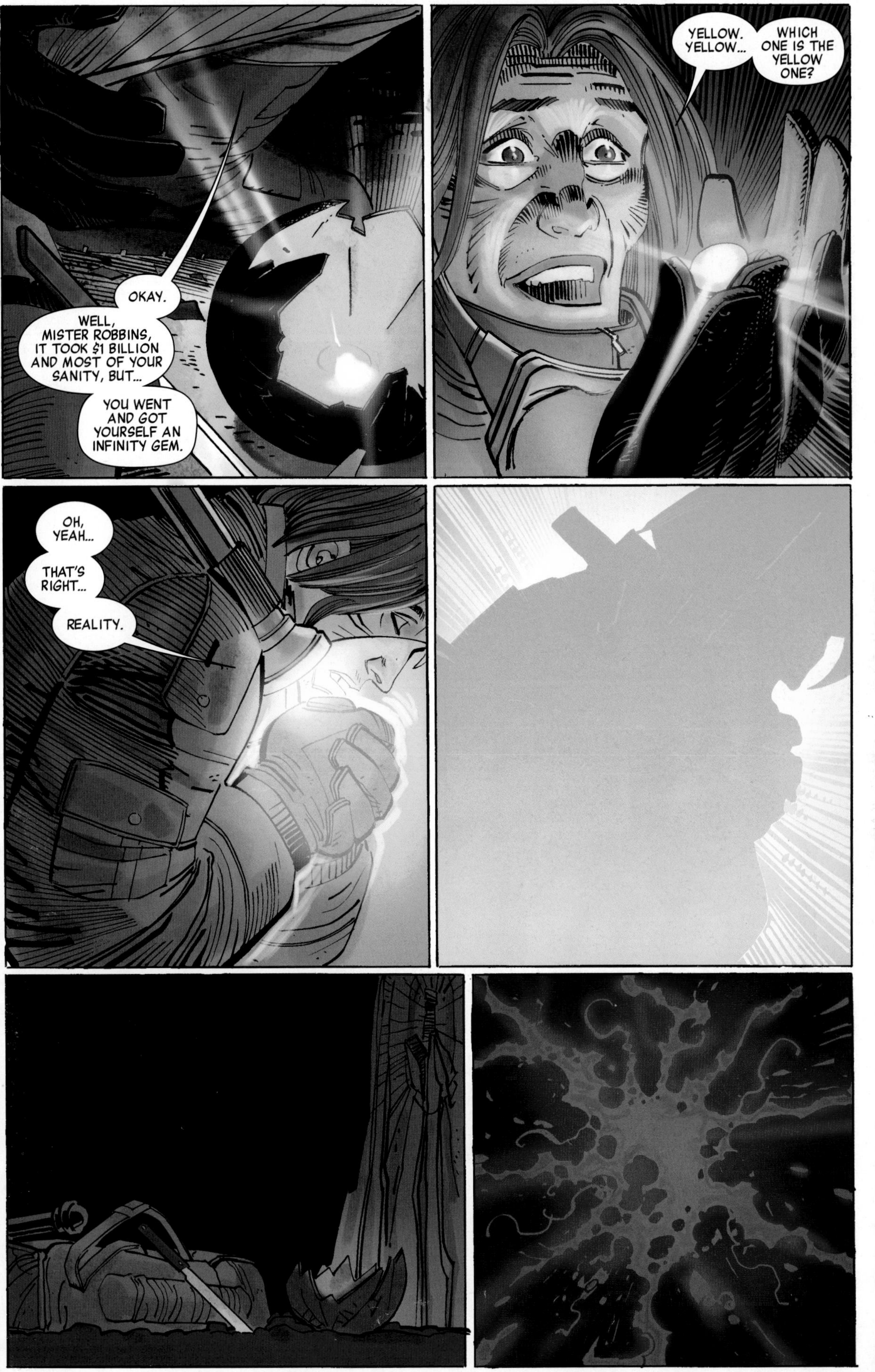
OKAY.
WELL, MISTER ROBBINS, IT TOOK $1 BILLION AND MOST OF YOUR SANITY, BUT...
YOU WENT AND GOT YOURSELF AN INFINITY GEM.
YELLOW. YELLOW...
WHICH ONE IS THE YELLOW ONE?
OH, YEAH...
THAT'S RIGHT...
REALITY.

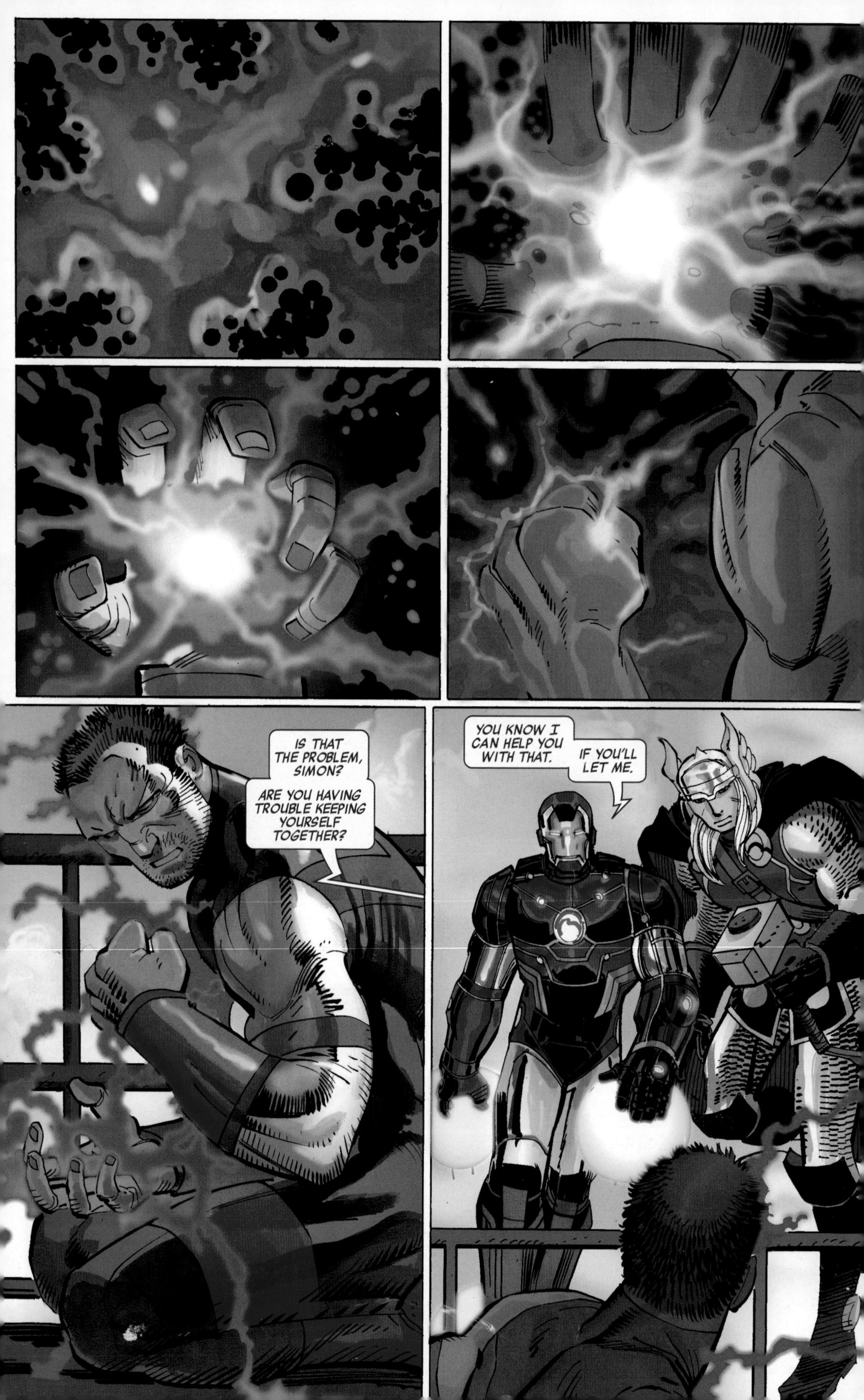
IS THAT THE PROBLEM, SIMON?
ARE YOU HAVING TROUBLE KEEPING YOURSELF TOGETHER?
YOU KNOW I CAN HELP YOU WITH THAT.
IF YOU'LL LET ME.

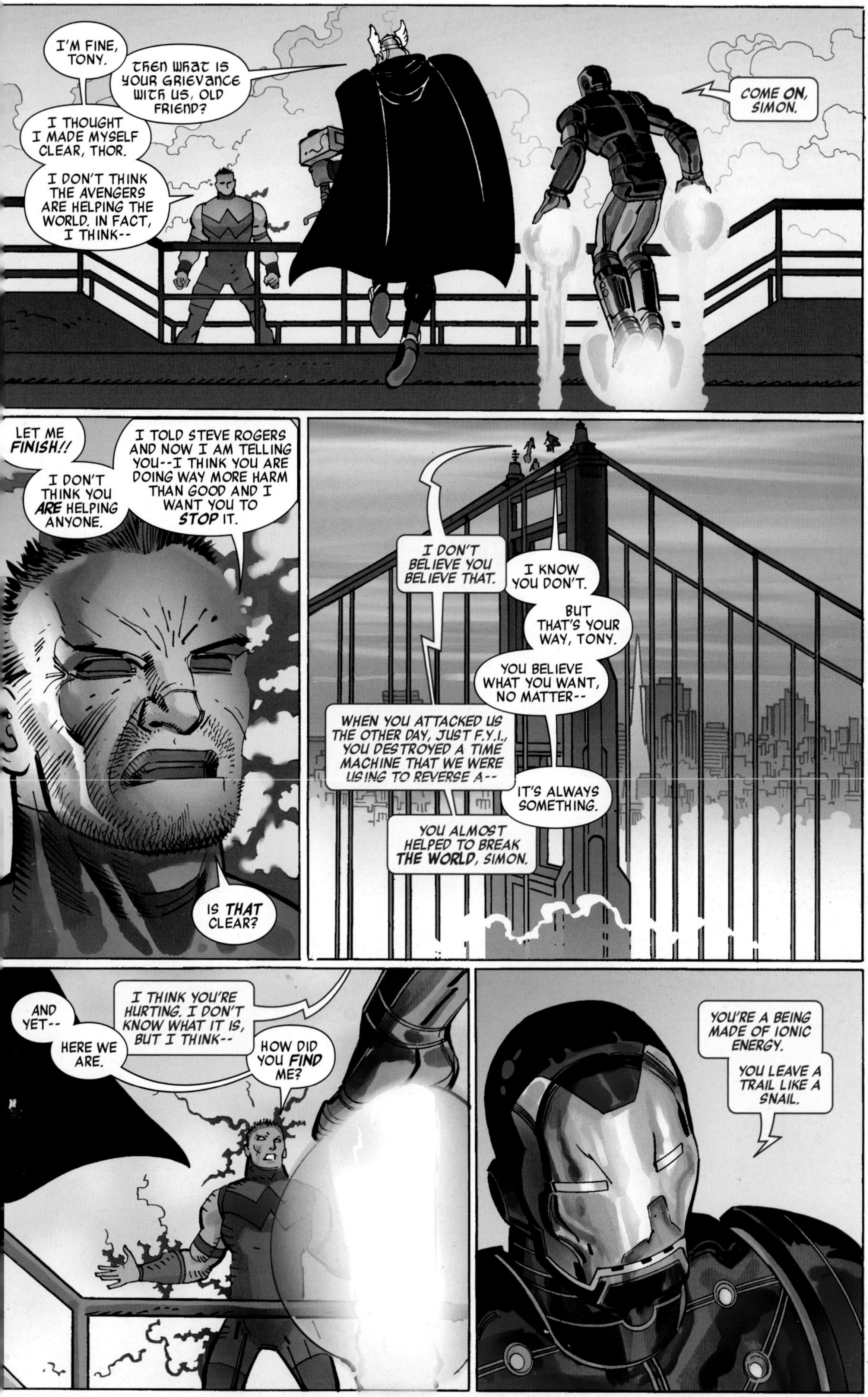
I'M FINE, TONY.
THEN WHAT IS YOUR GRIEVANCE WITH US, OLD FRIEND?
I THOUGHT I MADE MYSELF CLEAR, THOR.
I DON'T THINK THE AVENGERS ARE HELPING THE WORLD. IN FACT, I THINK--
COME ON, SIMON.
LET ME FINISH!!
I DON'T THINK YOU ARE HELPING ANYONE.
I TOLD STEVE ROGERS AND NOW I AM TELLING YOU--I THINK YOU ARE DOING WAY MORE HARM THAN GOOD AND I WANT YOU TO STOP IT.
IS THAT CLEAR?
I DON'T BELIEVE YOU BELIEVE THAT.
I KNOW YOU DON'T.
BUT THAT'S YOUR WAY, TONY.
YOU BELIEVE WHAT YOU WANT, NO MATTER--
WHEN YOU ATTACKED US THE OTHER DAY, JUST F.Y.I., YOU DESTROYED A TIME MACHINE THAT WE WERE USING TO REVERSE A--
IT'S ALWAYS SOMETHING.
YOU ALMOST HELPED TO BREAK THE WORLD, SIMON.
AND YET--
HERE WE ARE.
I THINK YOU'RE HURTING. I DON'T KNOW WHAT IT IS, BUT I THINK--
HOW DID YOU FIND ME?
YOU'RE A BEING MADE OF IONIC ENERGY.
YOU LEAVE A TRAIL LIKE A SNAIL.

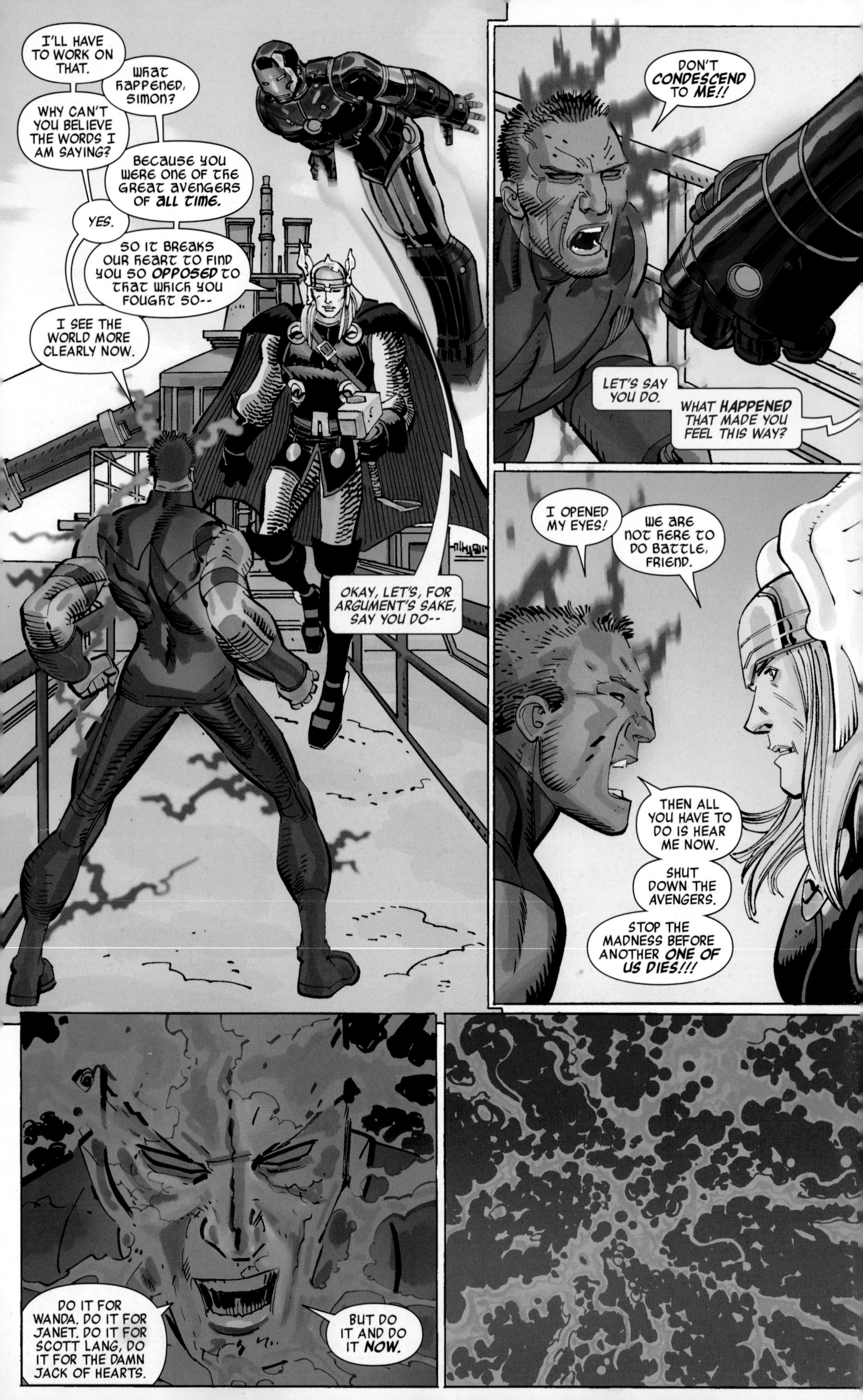
I'LL HAVE TO WORK ON THAT.
WHAT HAPPENED, SIMON?
WHY CAN'T YOU BELIEVE THE WORDS I AM SAYING?
BECAUSE YOU WERE ONE OF THE GREAT AVENGERS OF ALL TIME.
YES.
SO IT BREAKS OUR HEART TO FIND YOU SO OPPOSED TO THAT WHICH YOU FOUGHT SO--
I SEE THE WORLD MORE CLEARLY NOW.
OKAY, LET'S, FOR ARGUMENT'S SAKE, SAY YOU DO--
DON'T CONDESCEND TO ME!!
LET'S SAY YOU DO.
WHAT HAPPENED THAT MADE YOU FEEL THIS WAY?
I OPENED MY EYES!
WE ARE NOT HERE TO DO BATTLE, FRIEND.
THEN ALL YOU HAVE TO DO IS HEAR ME NOW.
SHUT DOWN THE AVENGERS.
STOP THE MADNESS BEFORE ANOTHER ONE OF US DIES!!!
DO IT FOR WANDA. DO IT FOR JANET. DO IT FOR SCOTT LANG, DO IT FOR THE DAMN JACK OF HEARTS.
BUT DO IT AND DO IT NOW.

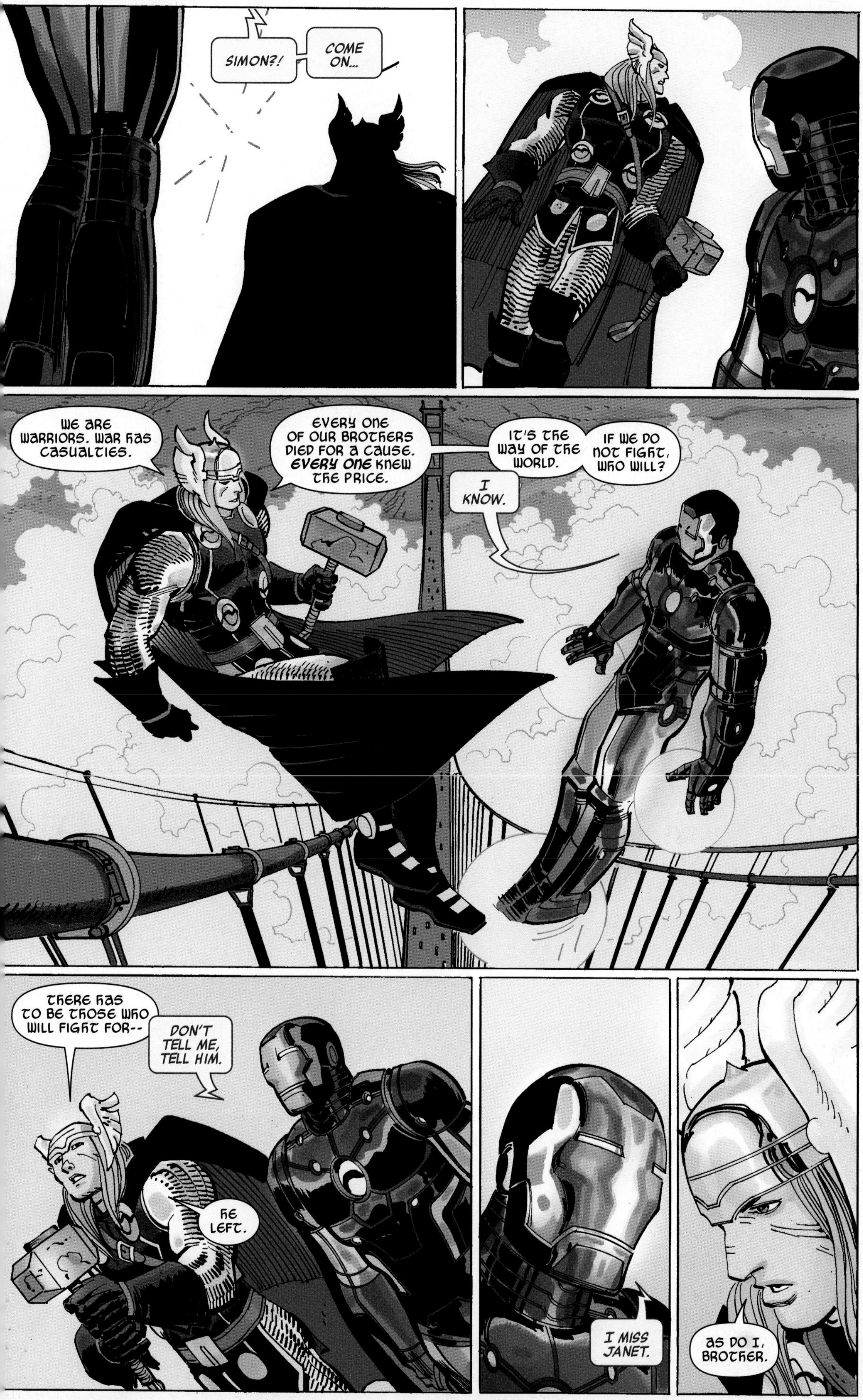
SIMON?!
COME ON...
WE ARE WARRIORS. WAR HAS CASUALTIES.
EVERY ONE OF OUR BROTHERS DIED FOR A CAUSE. EVERY ONE KNEW THE PRICE.
IT'S THE WAY OF THE WORLD.
IF WE DO NOT FIGHT, WHO WILL?
I KNOW.
THERE HAS TO BE THOSE WHO WILL FIGHT FOR--
DON'T TELL ME, TELL HIM.
HE LEFT.
I MISS JANET.
AS DO I, BROTHER.

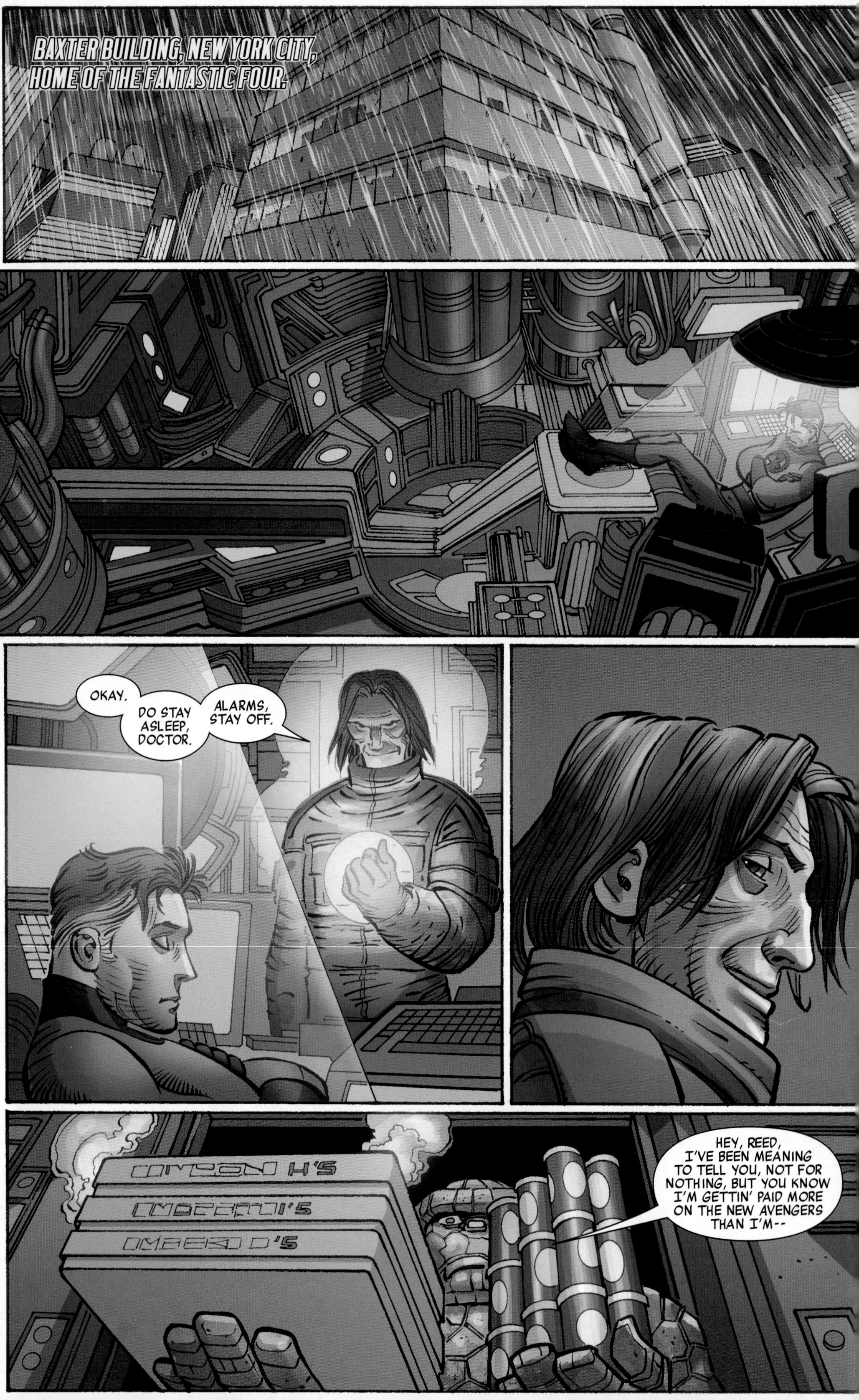
BAXTER BUILDING, NEW YORK CITY, HOME OF THE FANTASTIC FOUR.
OKAY.
DO STAY ASLEEP, DOCTOR.
ALARMS, STAY OFF.
HEY, REED, I'VE BEEN MEANING TO TELL YOU, NOT FOR NOTHING, BUT YOU KNOW I'M GETTIN' PAID MORE ON THE NEW AVENGERS THAN I'M--

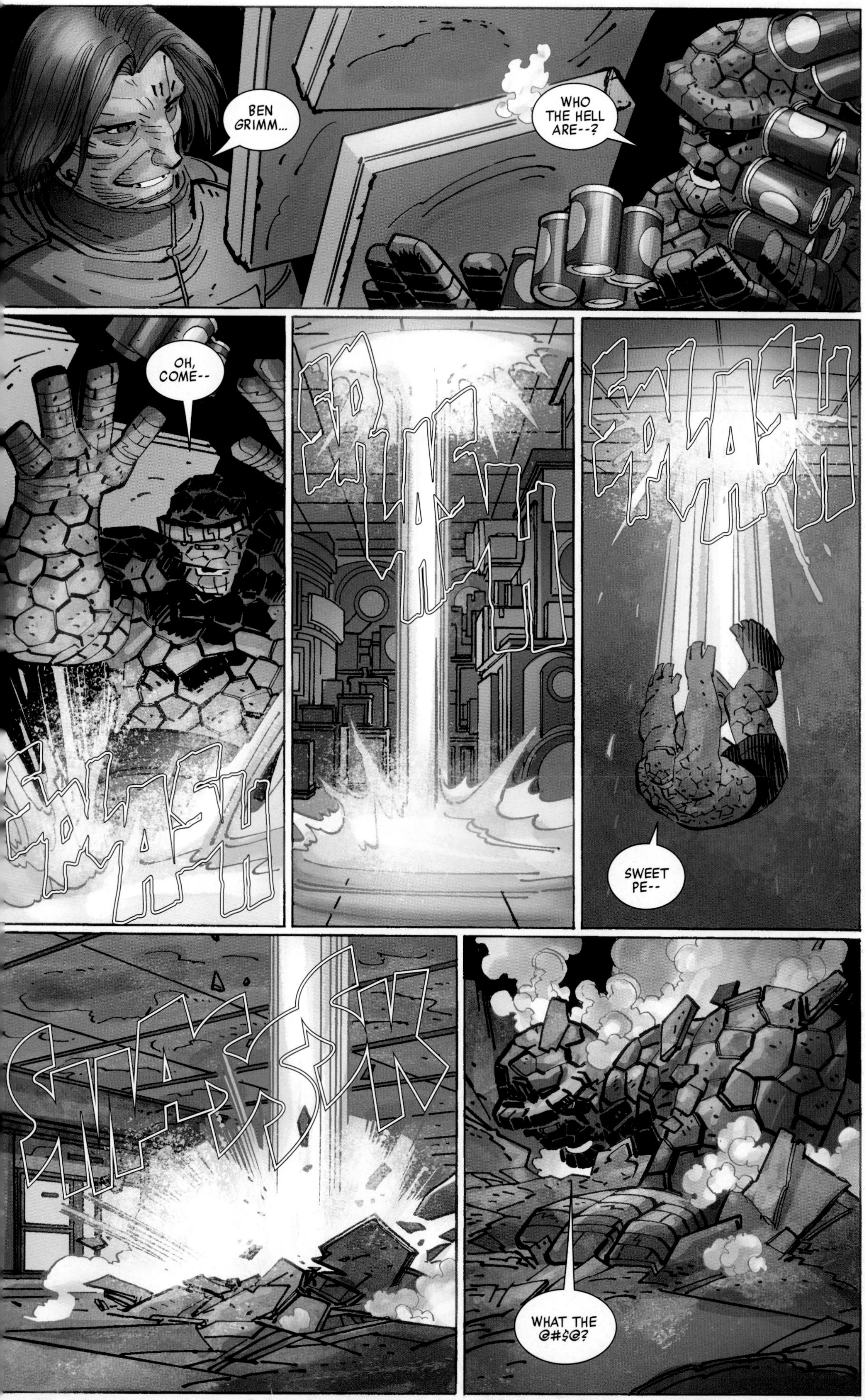
BEN GRIMM...
WHO THE HELL ARE--?
OH, COME--
SWEET PE--
WHAT THE @#$@?

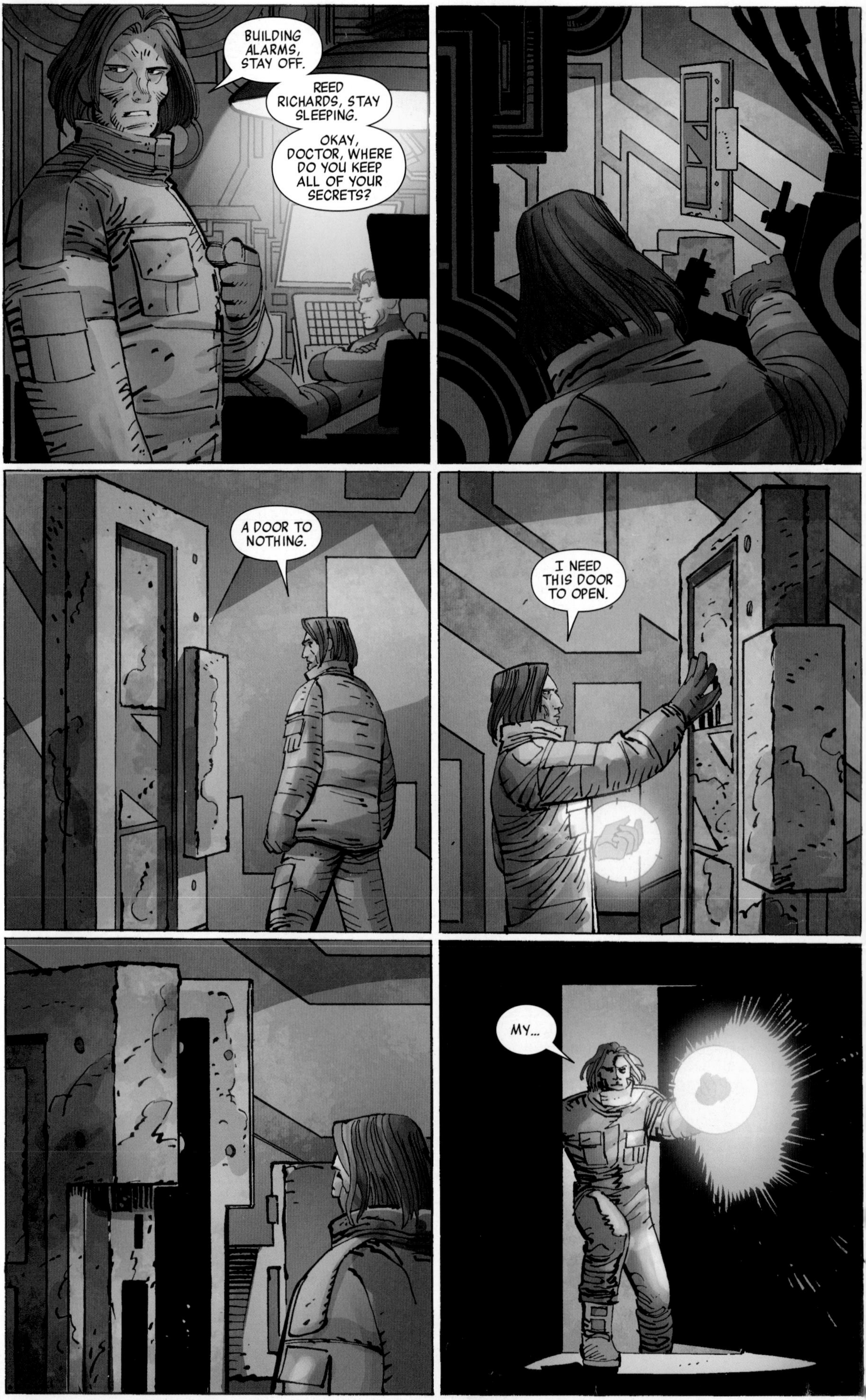

BUILDING ALARMS, STAY OFF.
REED RICHARDS, STAY SLEEPING.
OKAY, DOCTOR, WHERE DO YOU KEEP ALL OF YOUR SECRETS?
A DOOR TO NOTHING.
I NEED THIS DOOR TO OPEN.
MY...

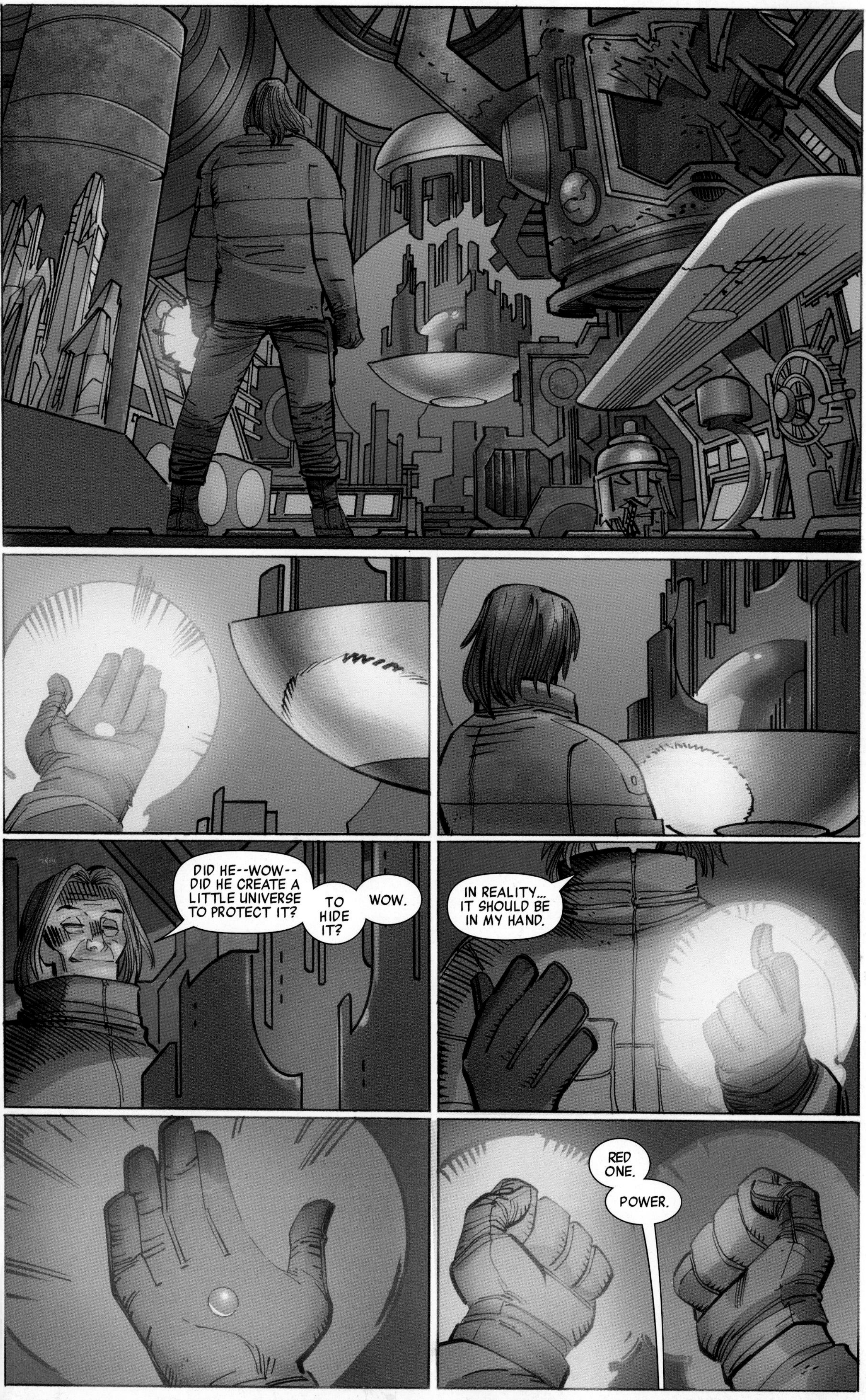
DID HE--WOW--DID HE CREATE A LITTLE UNIVERSE TO PROTECT IT?
TO HIDE IT?
WOW.
IN REALITY... IT SHOULD BE IN MY HAND.
RED ONE.
POWER.

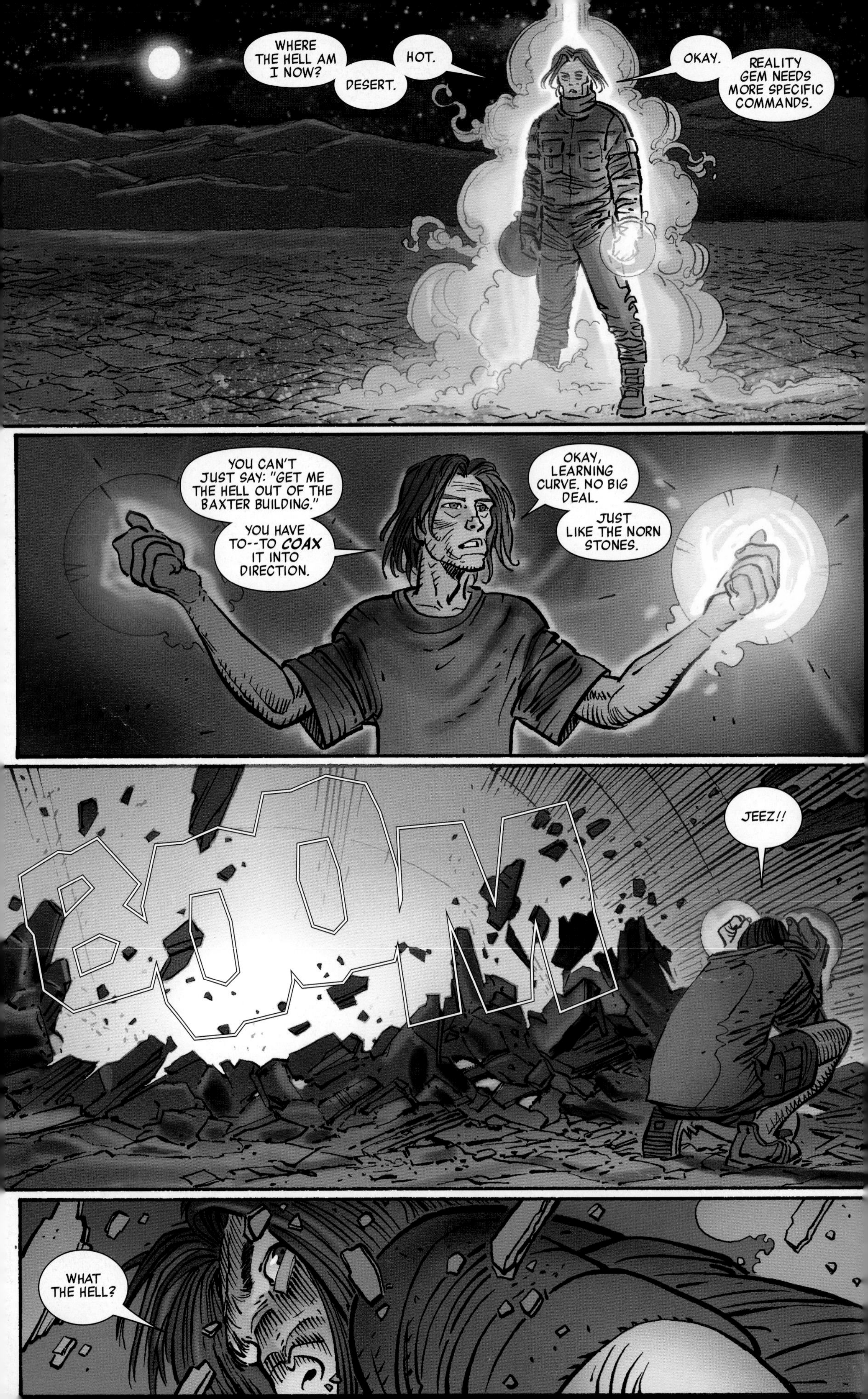
WHERE THE HELL AM I NOW?
HOT.
DESERT.
OKAY.
REALITY GEM NEEDS MORE SPECIFIC COMMANDS.
YOU CAN'T JUST SAY: "GET ME THE HELL OUT OF THE BAXTER BUILDING."
YOU HAVE TO--TO COAX IT INTO DIRECTION.
OKAY, LEARNING CURVE. NO BIG DEAL.
JUST LIKE THE NORN STONES.
BOOM
JEEZ!!
WHAT THE HELL?

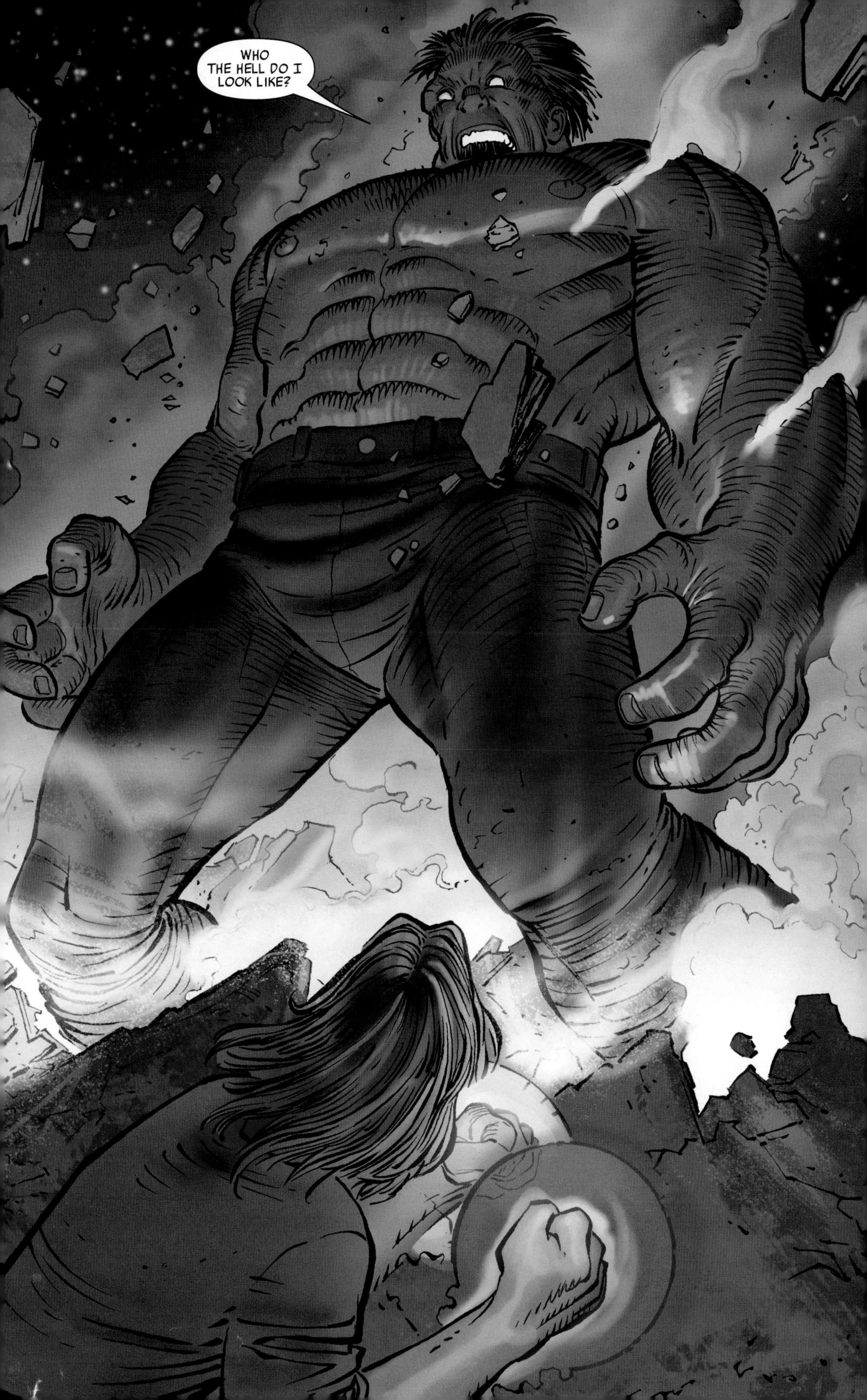
WHO THE HELL DO I LOOK LIKE?

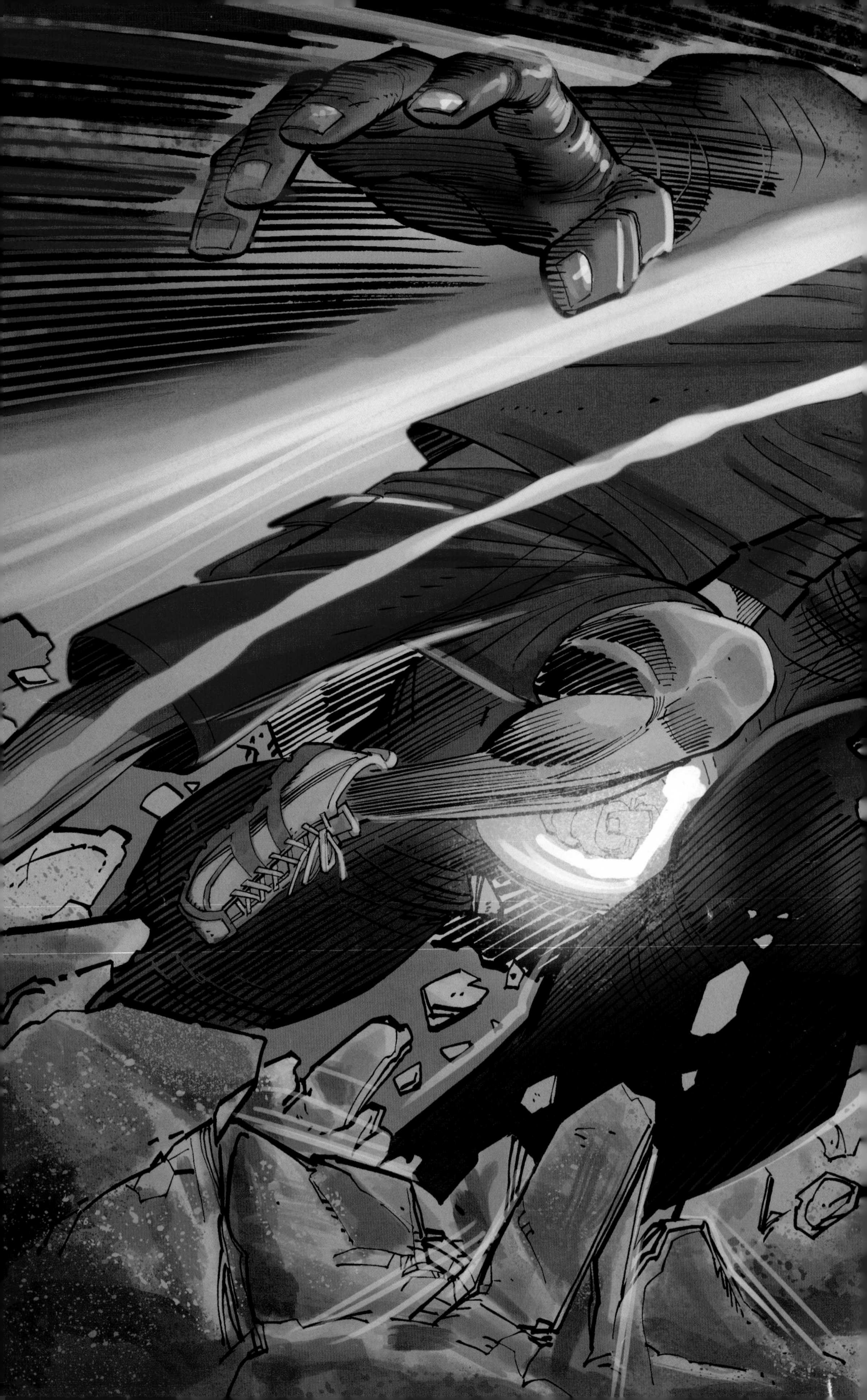

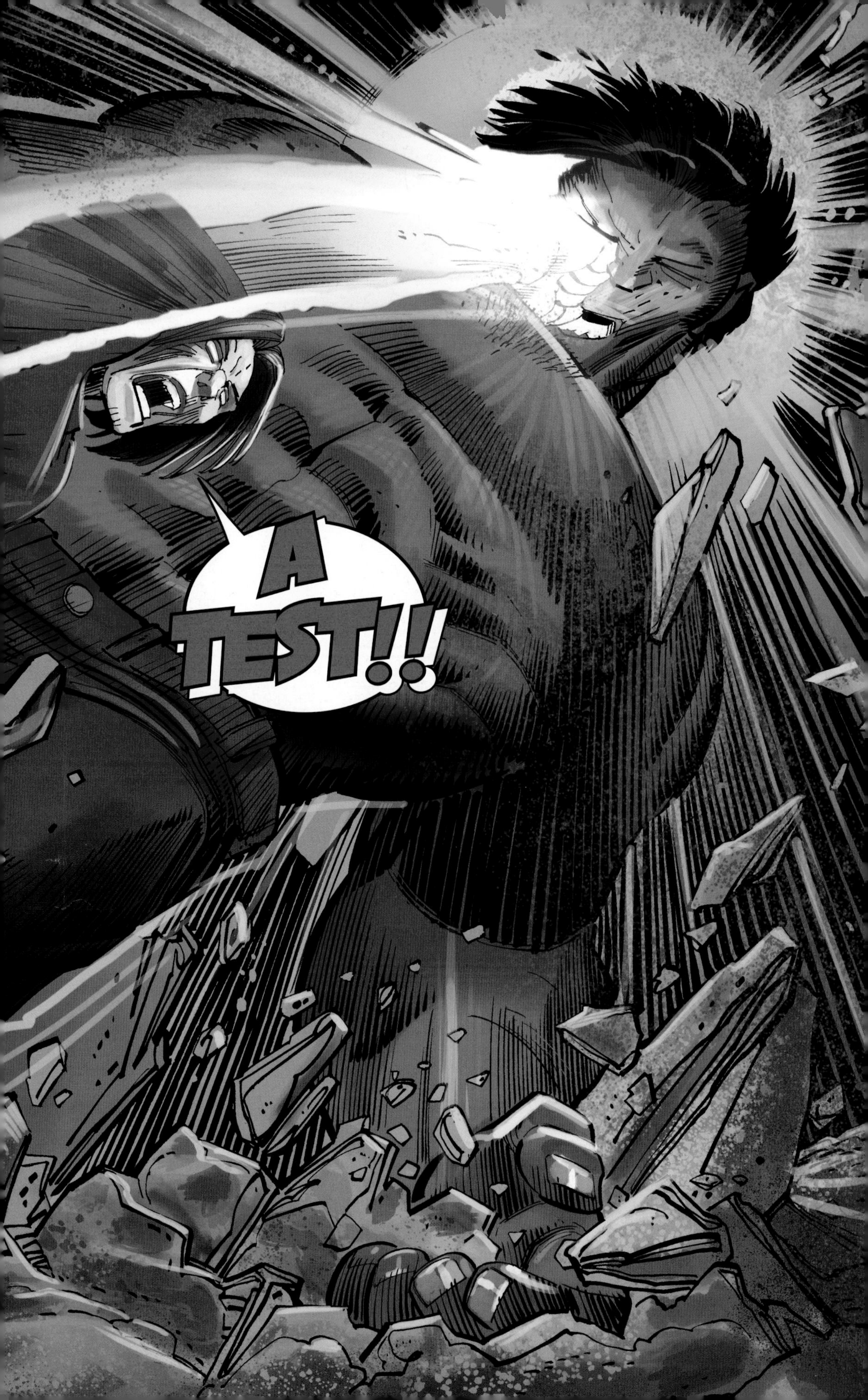
A TEST!!

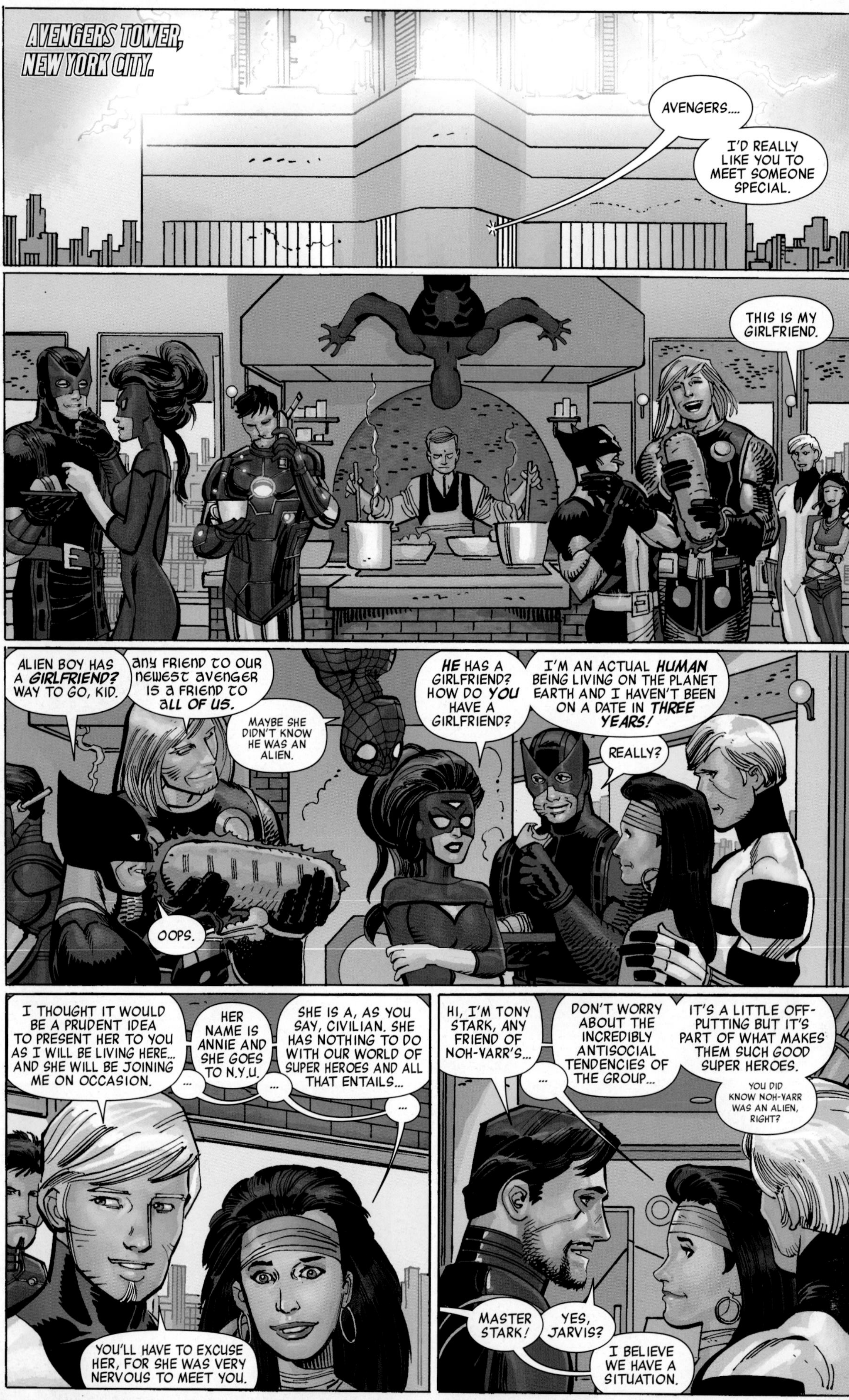
AVENGERS TOWER, NEW YORK CITY.
AVENGERS....
I'D REALLY LIKE YOU TO MEET SOMEONE SPECIAL.
THIS IS MY GIRLFRIEND.
ALIEN BOY HAS A GIRLFRIEND? WAY TO GO, KID.
ANY FRIEND TO OUR NEWEST AVENGER IS A FRIEND TO ALL OF US.
MAYBE SHE DIDN'T KNOW HE WAS AN ALIEN.
OOPS.
HE HAS A GIRLFRIEND? HOW DO YOU HAVE A GIRLFRIEND?
I'M AN ACTUAL HUMAN BEING LIVING ON THE PLANET EARTH AND I HAVEN'T BEEN ON A DATE IN THREE YEARS!
REALLY?
I THOUGHT IT WOULD BE A PRUDENT IDEA TO PRESENT HER TO YOU AS I WILL BE LIVING HERE... AND SHE WILL BE JOINING ME ON OCCASION.
...
HER NAME IS ANNIE AND SHE GOES TO N.Y.U.
...
SHE IS A, AS YOU SAY, CIVILIAN. SHE HAS NOTHING TO DO WITH OUR WORLD OF SUPER HEROES AND ALL THAT ENTAILS...
...
YOU'LL HAVE TO EXCUSE HER, FOR SHE WAS VERY NERVOUS TO MEET YOU.
HI, I'M TONY STARK, ANY FRIEND OF NOH-VARR'S...
...
DON'T WORRY ABOUT THE INCREDIBLY ANTISOCIAL TENDENCIES OF THE GROUP...
IT'S A LITTLE OFF-PUTTING BUT IT'S PART OF WHAT MAKES THEM SUCH GOOD SUPER HEROES.
YOU DID KNOW NOH-VARR WAS AN ALIEN, RIGHT?
MASTER STARK!
YES, JARVIS?
I BELIEVE WE HAVE A SITUATION.

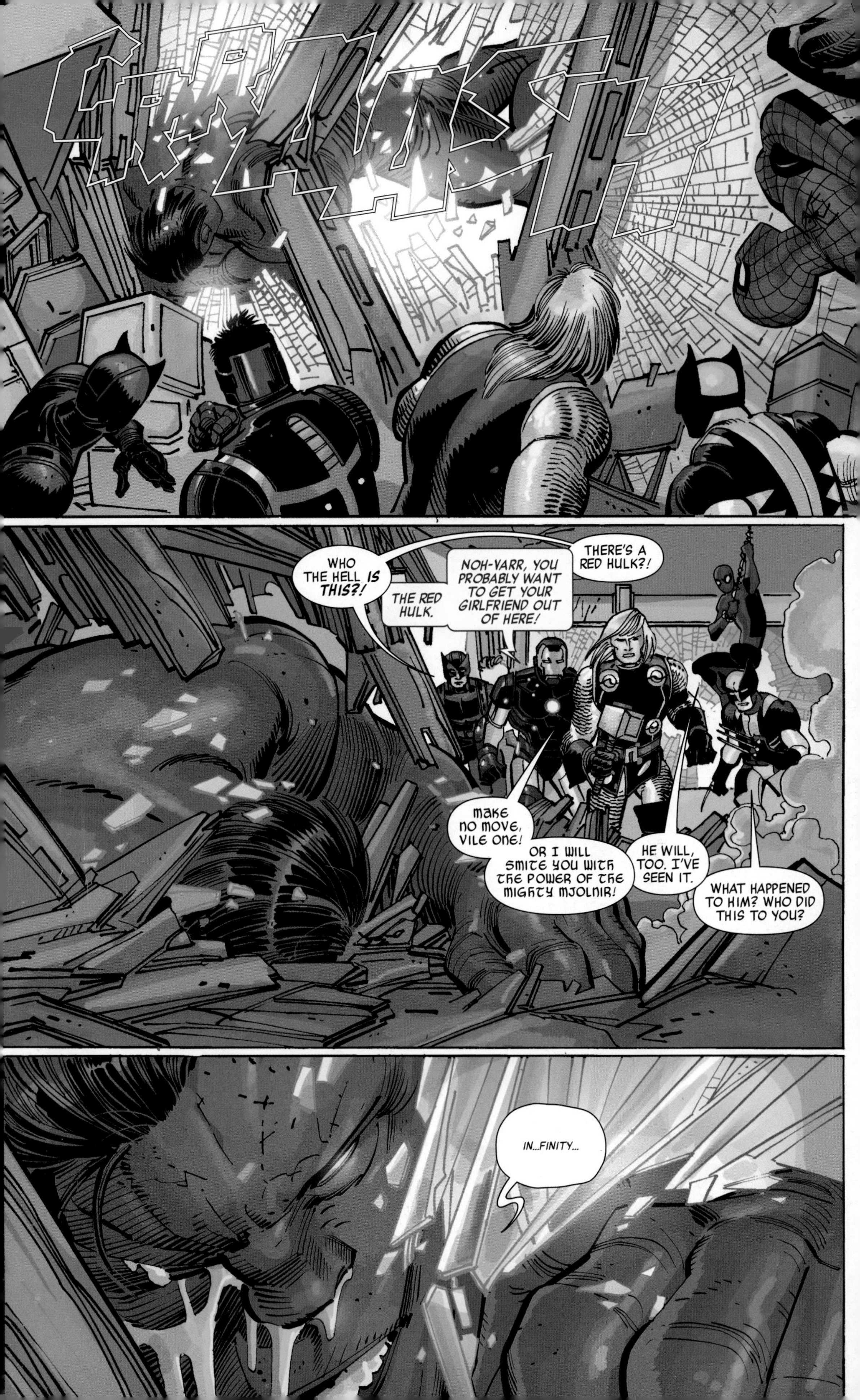
WHO THE HELL IS THIS?!
THE RED HULK.
NOH-VARR, YOU PROBABLY WANT TO GET YOUR GIRLFRIEND OUT OF HERE!
THERE'S A RED HULK?!
MAKE NO MOVE, VILE ONE!
OR I WILL SMITE YOU WITH THE POWER OF THE MIGHTY MJOLNIR!
HE WILL, TOO. I'VE SEEN IT.
WHAT HAPPENED TO HIM? WHO DID THIS TO YOU?
IN...FINITY...

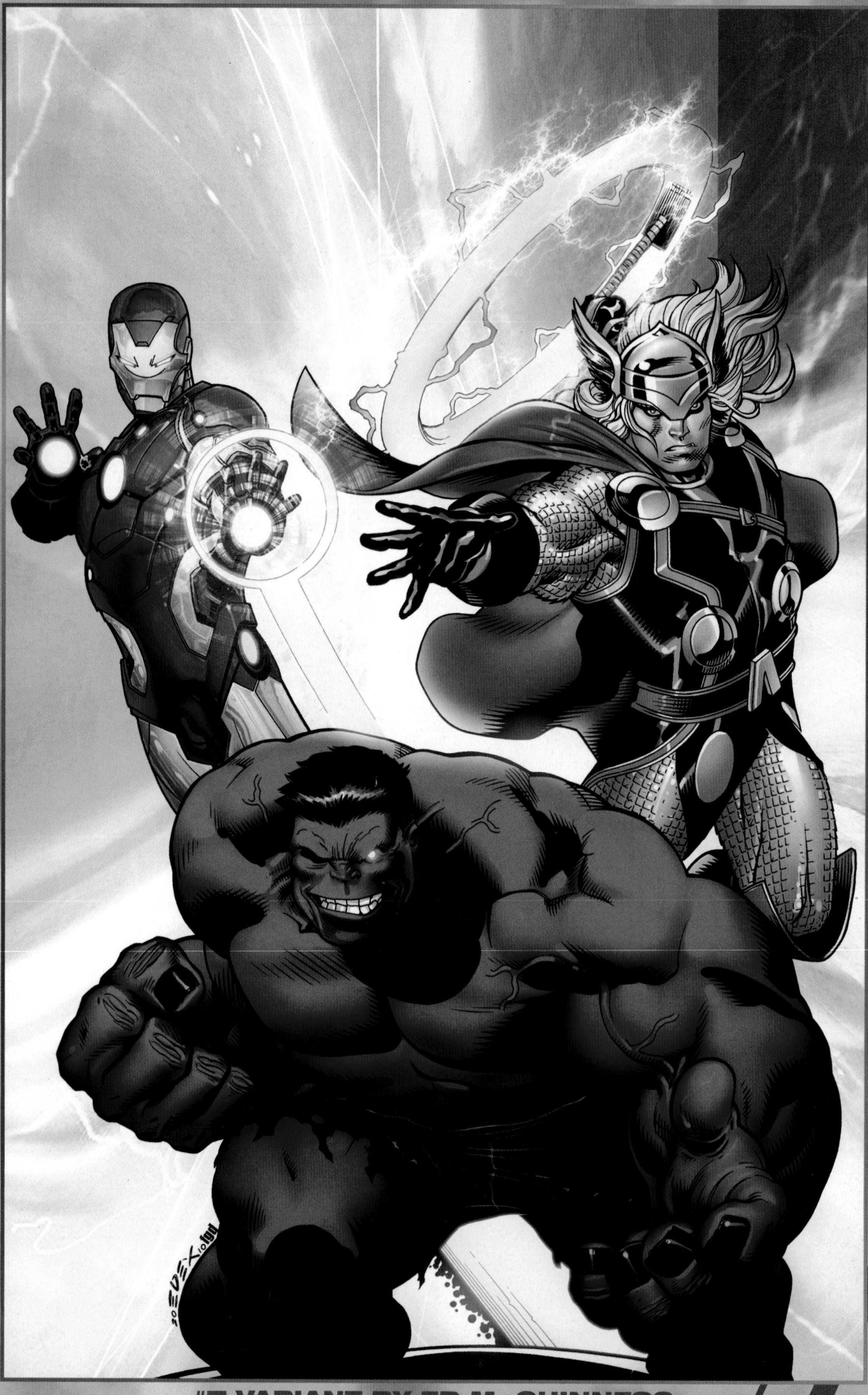

#7 VARIANT BY ED McGUINNESS

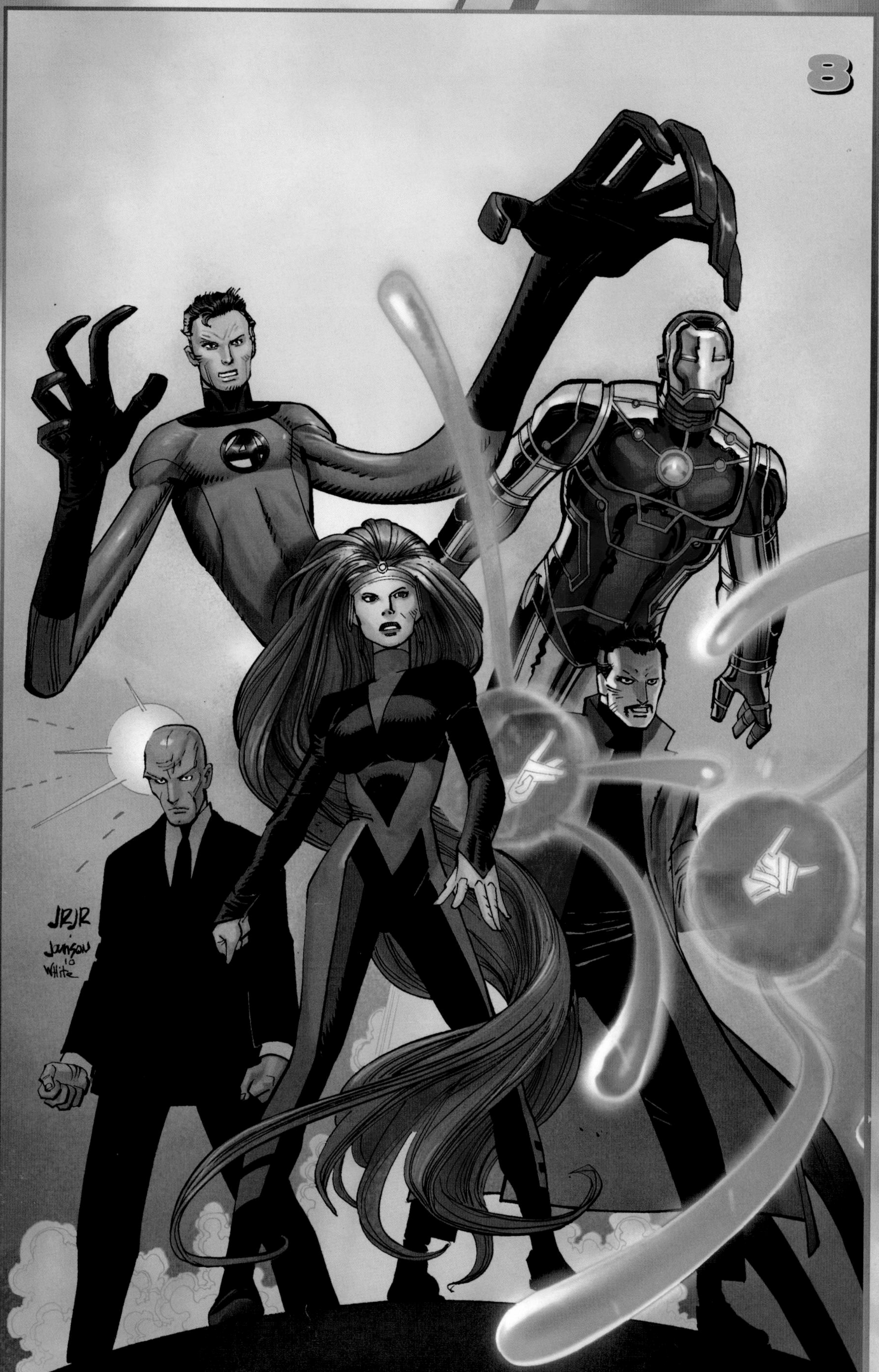
8

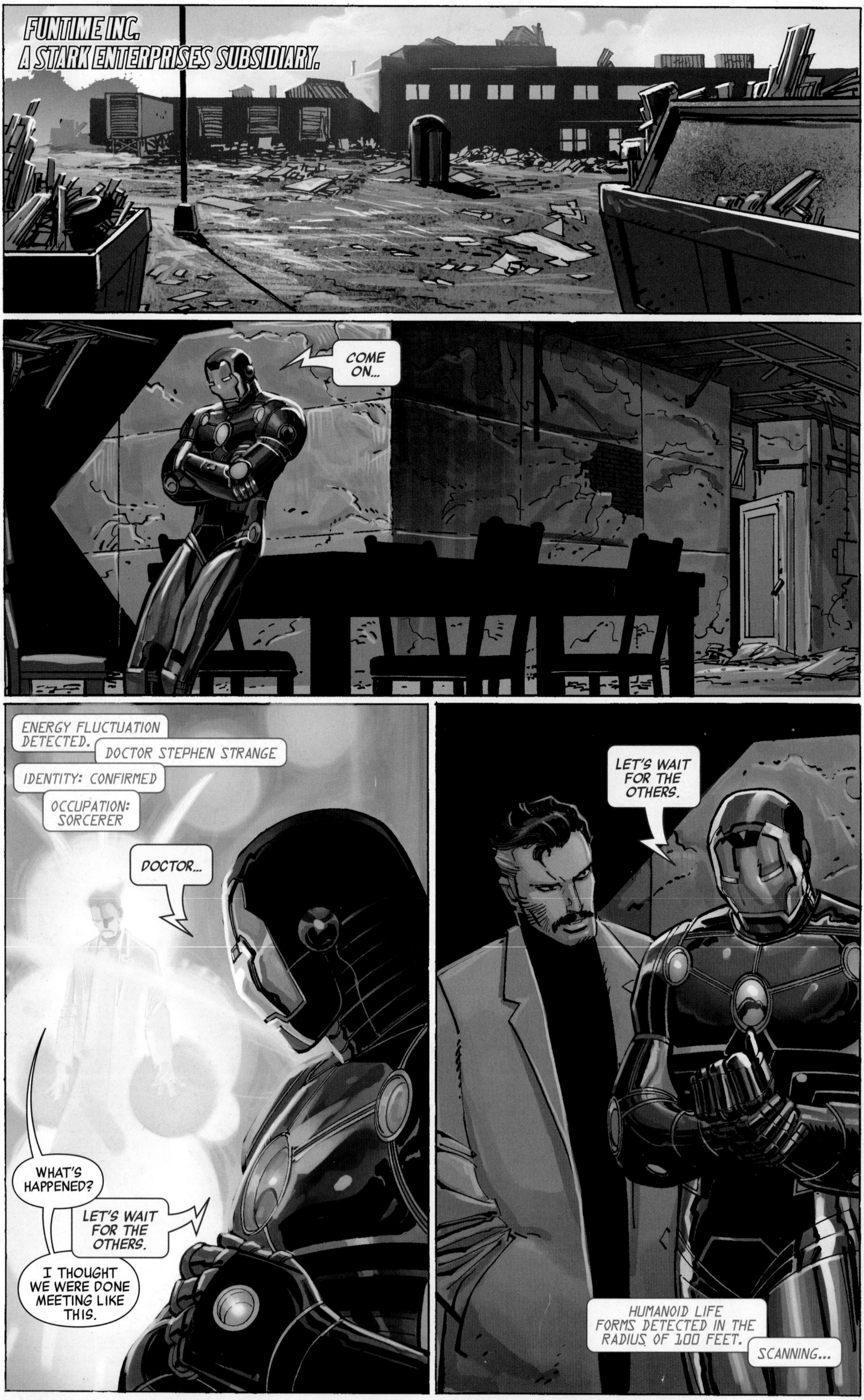
FUNTIME INC.
A STARK ENTERPRISES SUBSIDIARY.
COME ON...
ENERGY FLUCTUATION DETECTED.
DOCTOR STEPHEN STRANGE
IDENTITY: CONFIRMED
OCCUPATION: SORCERER
DOCTOR...
WHAT'S HAPPENED?
LET'S WAIT FOR THE OTHERS.
I THOUGHT WE WERE DONE MEETING LIKE THIS.
LET'S WAIT FOR THE OTHERS.
HUMANOID LIFE FORMS DETECTED IN THE RADIUS OF 100 FEET.
SCANNING...

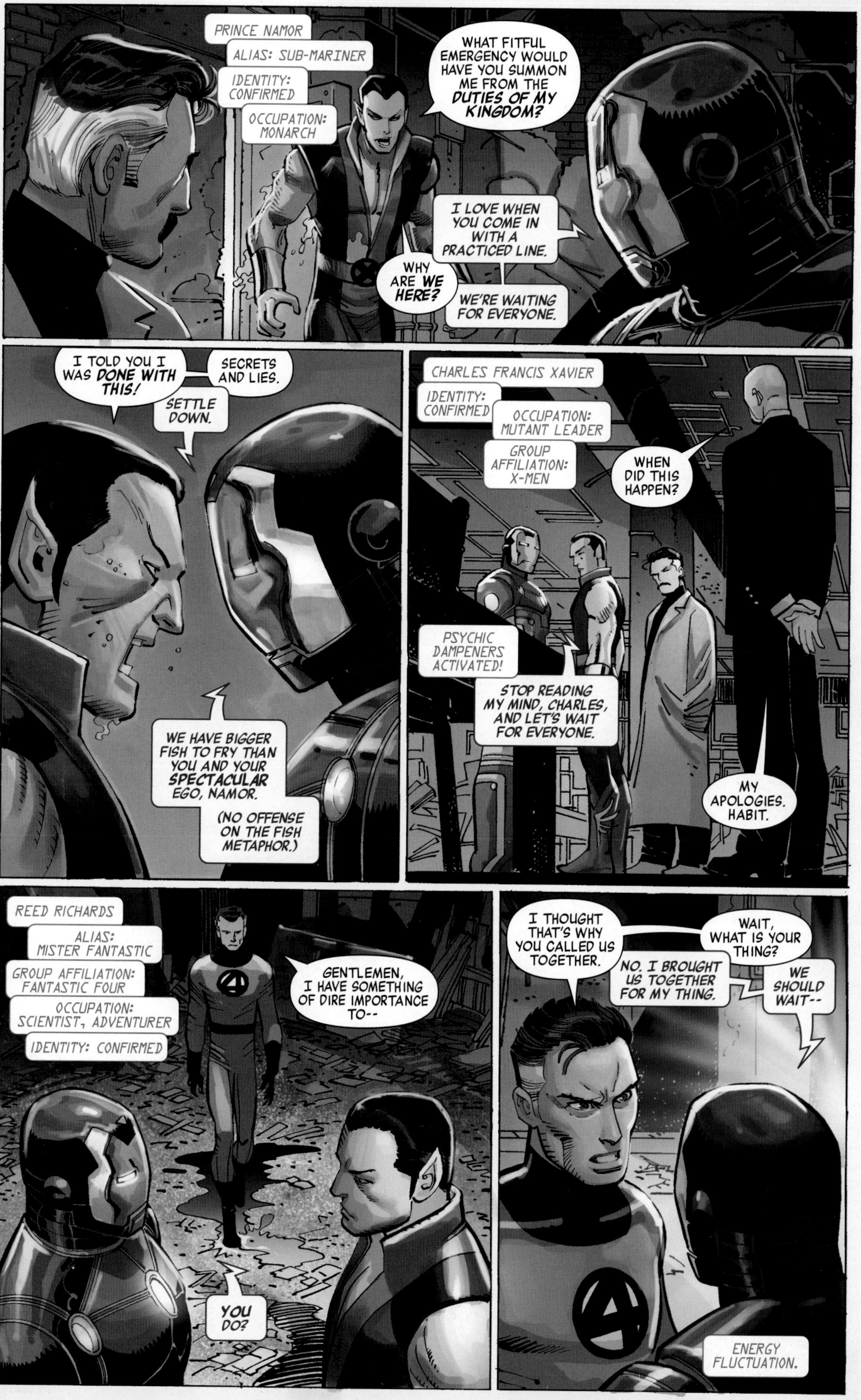
PRINCE NAMOR
ALIAS: SUB-MARINER
IDENTITY: CONFIRMED
OCCUPATION: MONARCH
WHAT FITFUL EMERGENCY WOULD HAVE YOU SUMMON ME FROM THE DUTIES OF MY KINGDOM?
I LOVE WHEN YOU COME IN WITH A PRACTICED LINE.
WHY ARE WE HERE?
WE'RE WAITING FOR EVERYONE.
I TOLD YOU I WAS DONE WITH THIS!
SECRETS AND LIES.
SETTLE DOWN.
WE HAVE BIGGER FISH TO FRY THAN YOU AND YOUR SPECTACULAR EGO, NAMOR.
(NO OFFENSE ON THE FISH METAPHOR.)
CHARLES FRANCIS XAVIER
IDENTITY: CONFIRMED
OCCUPATION: MUTANT LEADER
GROUP AFFILIATION: X-MEN
WHEN DID THIS HAPPEN?
PSYCHIC DAMPENERS ACTIVATED!
STOP READING MY MIND, CHARLES, AND LET'S WAIT FOR EVERYONE.
MY APOLOGIES. HABIT.
REED RICHARDS
ALIAS: MISTER FANTASTIC
GROUP AFFILIATION: FANTASTIC FOUR
OCCUPATION: SCIENTIST, ADVENTURER
IDENTITY: CONFIRMED
GENTLEMEN, I HAVE SOMETHING OF DIRE IMPORTANCE TO--
YOU DO?
I THOUGHT THAT'S WHY YOU CALLED US TOGETHER.
WAIT, WHAT IS YOUR THING?
NO. I BROUGHT US TOGETHER FOR MY THING.
WE SHOULD WAIT--
ENERGY FLUCTUATION.

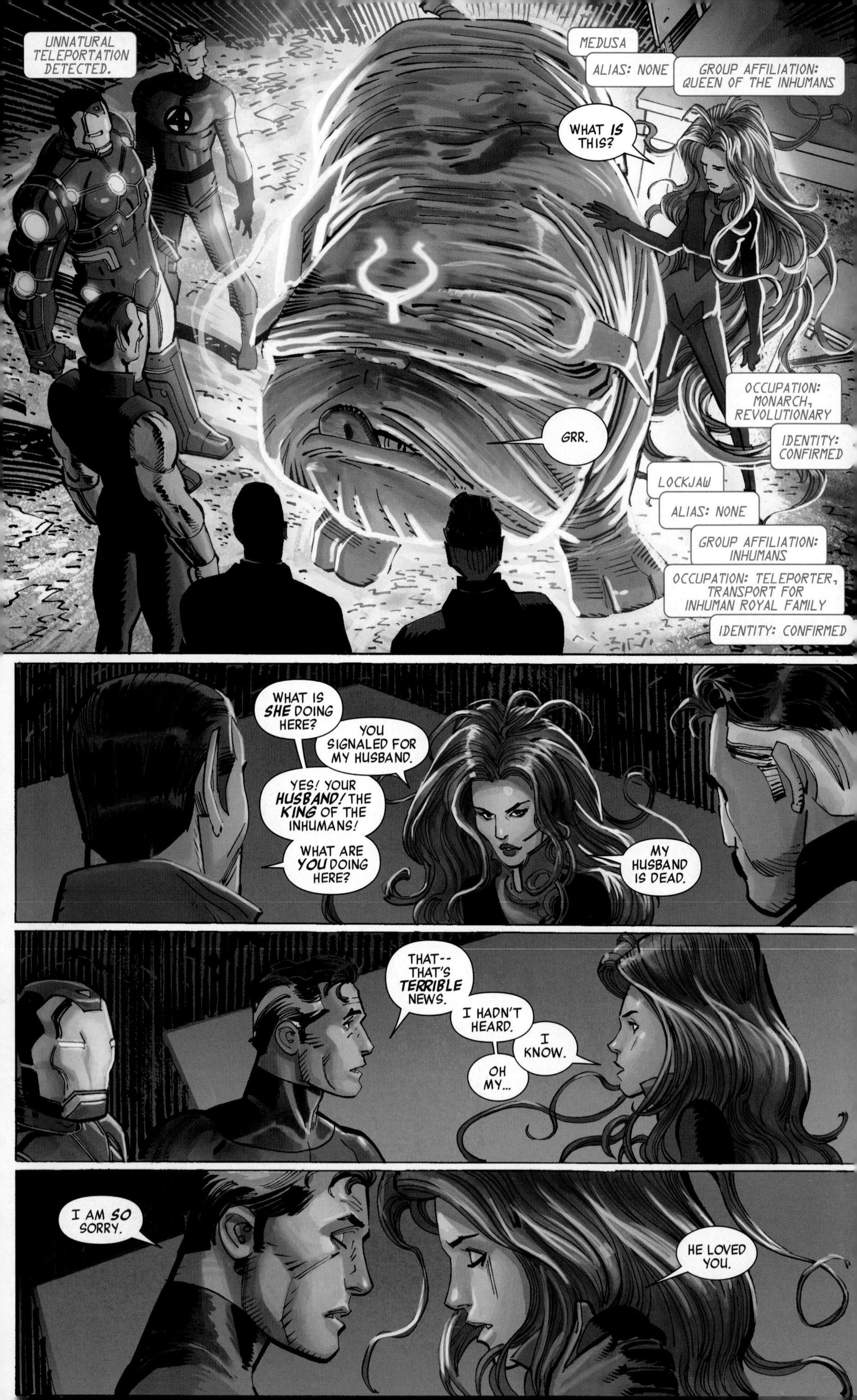

UNNATURAL TELEPORTATION DETECTED.
MEDUSA
ALIAS: NONE
GROUP AFFILIATION: QUEEN OF THE INHUMANS
WHAT IS THIS?
OCCUPATION: MONARCH, REVOLUTIONARY
IDENTITY: CONFIRMED
GRR.
LOCKJAW
ALIAS: NONE
GROUP AFFILIATION: INHUMANS
OCCUPATION: TELEPORTER, TRANSPORT FOR INHUMAN ROYAL FAMILY
IDENTITY: CONFIRMED
WHAT IS SHE DOING HERE?
YOU SIGNALED FOR MY HUSBAND.
YES! YOUR HUSBAND! THE KING OF THE INHUMANS!
WHAT ARE YOU DOING HERE?
MY HUSBAND IS DEAD.
THAT-- THAT'S TERRIBLE NEWS.
I HADN'T HEARD.
I KNOW.
OH MY...
I AM SO SORRY.
HE LOVED YOU.

HOW OFTEN WOULD YOU MEN MEET IN SECRET LIKE THIS?

WE DON'T HAVE TIME FOR THAT RIGHT NOW, MEDUSA.

PLEASE, DO YOU KNOW--DO YOU KNOW WHERE YOUR HUSBAND HAD KEPT A--A GEM?

A JEWEL?

WHAT HAS HAPPENED?

THE INFINITY GEMS.

YOU DO KNOW.

WHAT HAS HAPPENED?

I THINK-- I THINK SOMEONE MAY HAVE STOLEN BLACK BOLT'S GEM.

NO.

NO?

NO.

HE STOLE MINE.

WHEN DID THIS HAPPEN?

LAST NIGHT. JUST LAST NIGHT.

WHICH ONE DID YOU HAVE?

RED. POWER.

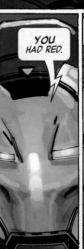

YOU HAD RED.

WHAT IS GOING ON HERE?

THIS GROUP... WE GATHERED IN SECRET.

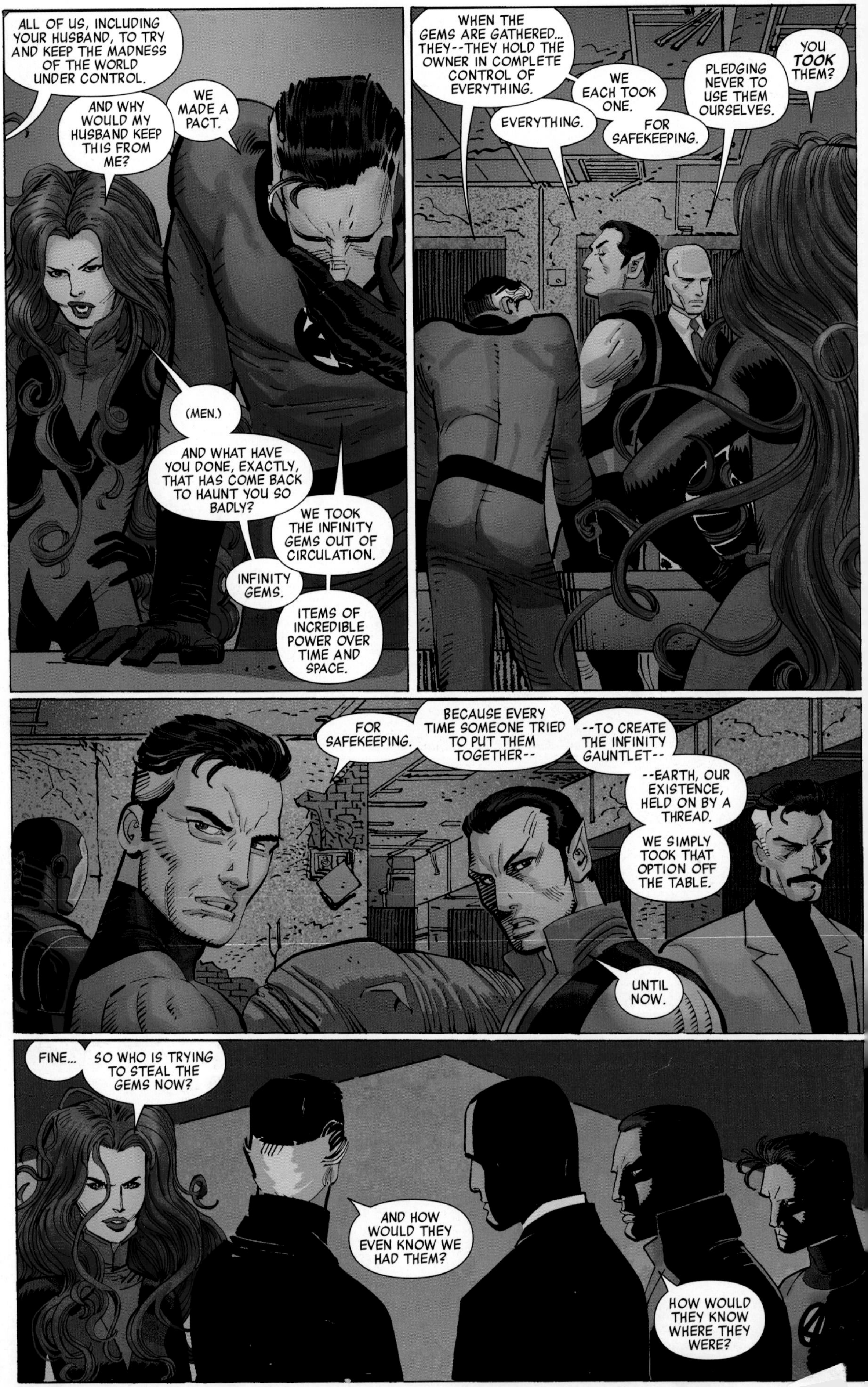
ALL OF US, INCLUDING YOUR HUSBAND, TO TRY AND KEEP THE MADNESS OF THE WORLD UNDER CONTROL.
AND WHY WOULD MY HUSBAND KEEP THIS FROM ME?
WE MADE A PACT.
(MEN.)
AND WHAT HAVE YOU DONE, EXACTLY, THAT HAS COME BACK TO HAUNT YOU SO BADLY?
WE TOOK THE INFINITY GEMS OUT OF CIRCULATION.
INFINITY GEMS.
ITEMS OF INCREDIBLE POWER OVER TIME AND SPACE.
WHEN THE GEMS ARE GATHERED... THEY--THEY HOLD THE OWNER IN COMPLETE CONTROL OF EVERYTHING.
EVERYTHING.
WE EACH TOOK ONE.
FOR SAFEKEEPING.
PLEDGING NEVER TO USE THEM OURSELVES.
YOU TOOK THEM?
FOR SAFEKEEPING.
BECAUSE EVERY TIME SOMEONE TRIED TO PUT THEM TOGETHER--
--TO CREATE THE INFINITY GAUNTLET--
--EARTH, OUR EXISTENCE, HELD ON BY A THREAD.
WE SIMPLY TOOK THAT OPTION OFF THE TABLE.
UNTIL NOW.
FINE...
SO WHO IS TRYING TO STEAL THE GEMS NOW?
AND HOW WOULD THEY EVEN KNOW WE HAD THEM?
HOW WOULD THEY KNOW WHERE THEY WERE?

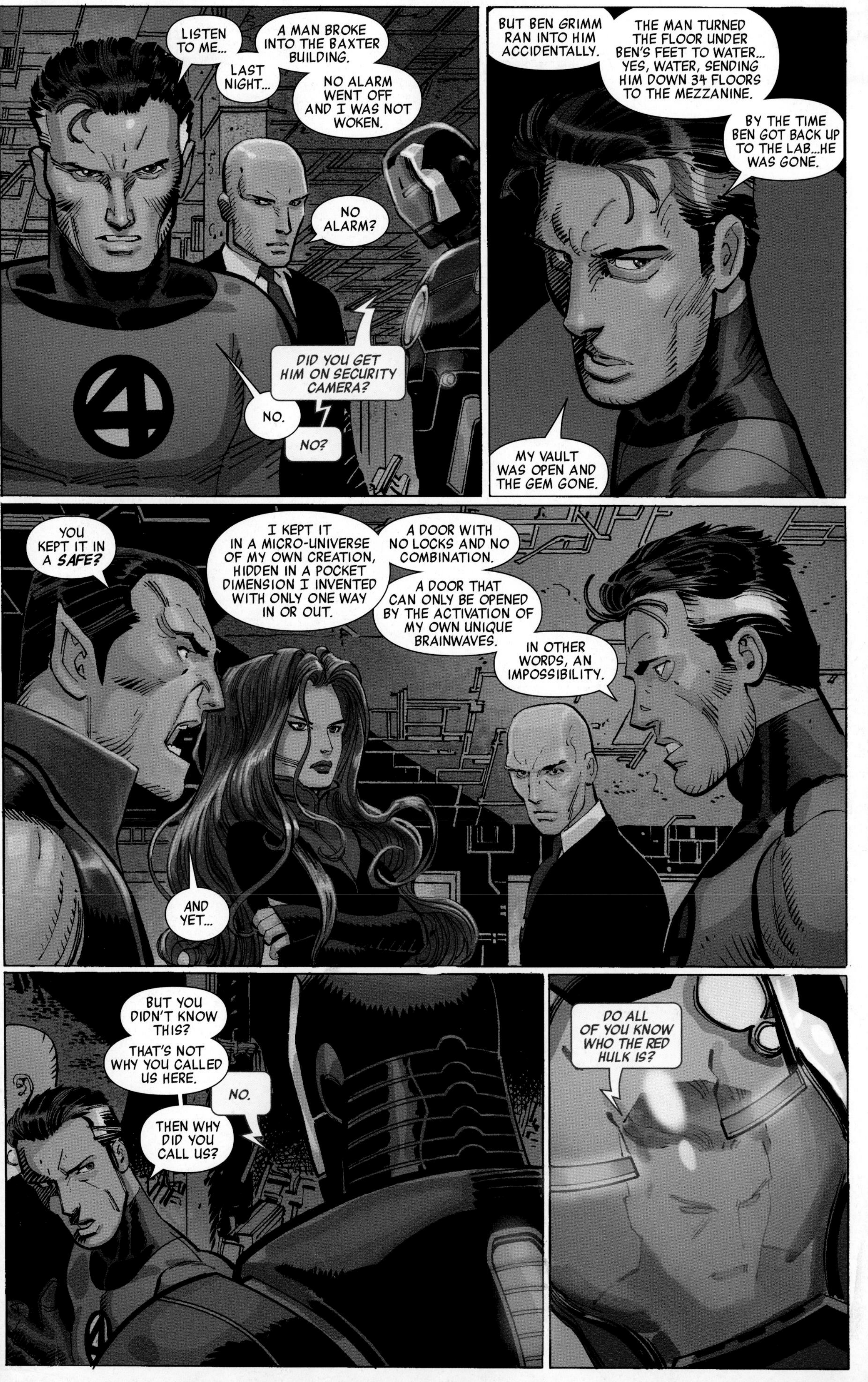

LISTEN TO ME...
A MAN BROKE INTO THE BAXTER BUILDING.
LAST NIGHT...
NO ALARM WENT OFF AND I WAS NOT WOKEN.
NO ALARM?
DID YOU GET HIM ON SECURITY CAMERA?
NO.
NO?
BUT BEN GRIMM RAN INTO HIM ACCIDENTALLY.
THE MAN TURNED THE FLOOR UNDER BEN'S FEET TO WATER... YES, WATER, SENDING HIM DOWN 34 FLOORS TO THE MEZZANINE.
BY THE TIME BEN GOT BACK UP TO THE LAB...HE WAS GONE.
MY VAULT WAS OPEN AND THE GEM GONE.
YOU KEPT IT IN A SAFE?
I KEPT IT IN A MICRO-UNIVERSE OF MY OWN CREATION, HIDDEN IN A POCKET DIMENSION I INVENTED WITH ONLY ONE WAY IN OR OUT.
A DOOR WITH NO LOCKS AND NO COMBINATION.
A DOOR THAT CAN ONLY BE OPENED BY THE ACTIVATION OF MY OWN UNIQUE BRAINWAVES.
IN OTHER WORDS, AN IMPOSSIBILITY.
AND YET...
BUT YOU DIDN'T KNOW THIS?
THAT'S NOT WHY YOU CALLED US HERE.
NO.
THEN WHY DID YOU CALL US?
DO ALL OF YOU KNOW WHO THE RED HULK IS?

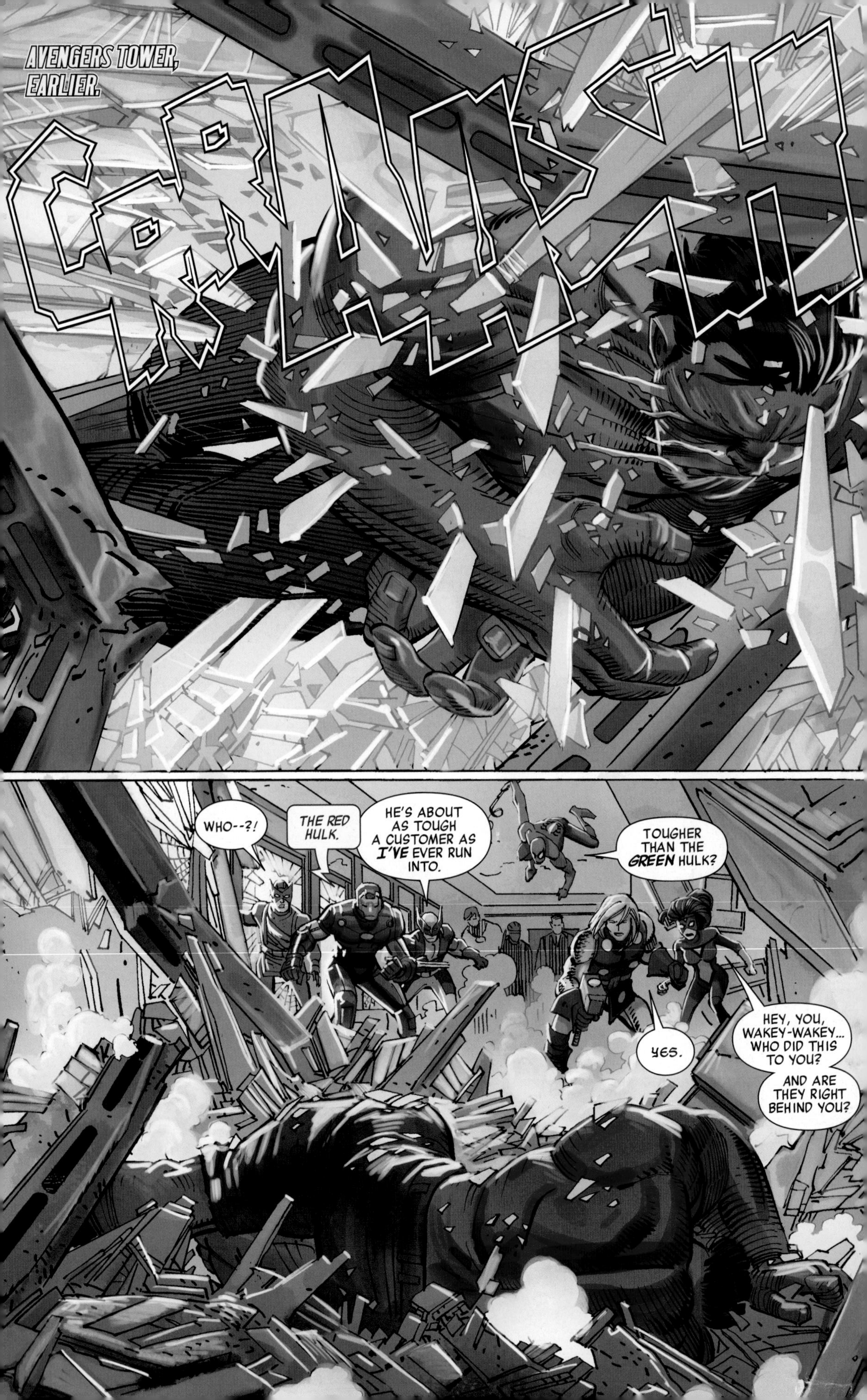
AVENGERS TOWER, EARLIER.
WHO--?!
THE RED HULK.
HE'S ABOUT AS TOUGH A CUSTOMER AS I'VE EVER RUN INTO.
TOUGHER THAN THE GREEN HULK?
YES.
HEY, YOU, WAKEY-WAKEY... WHO DID THIS TO YOU?
AND ARE THEY RIGHT BEHIND YOU?

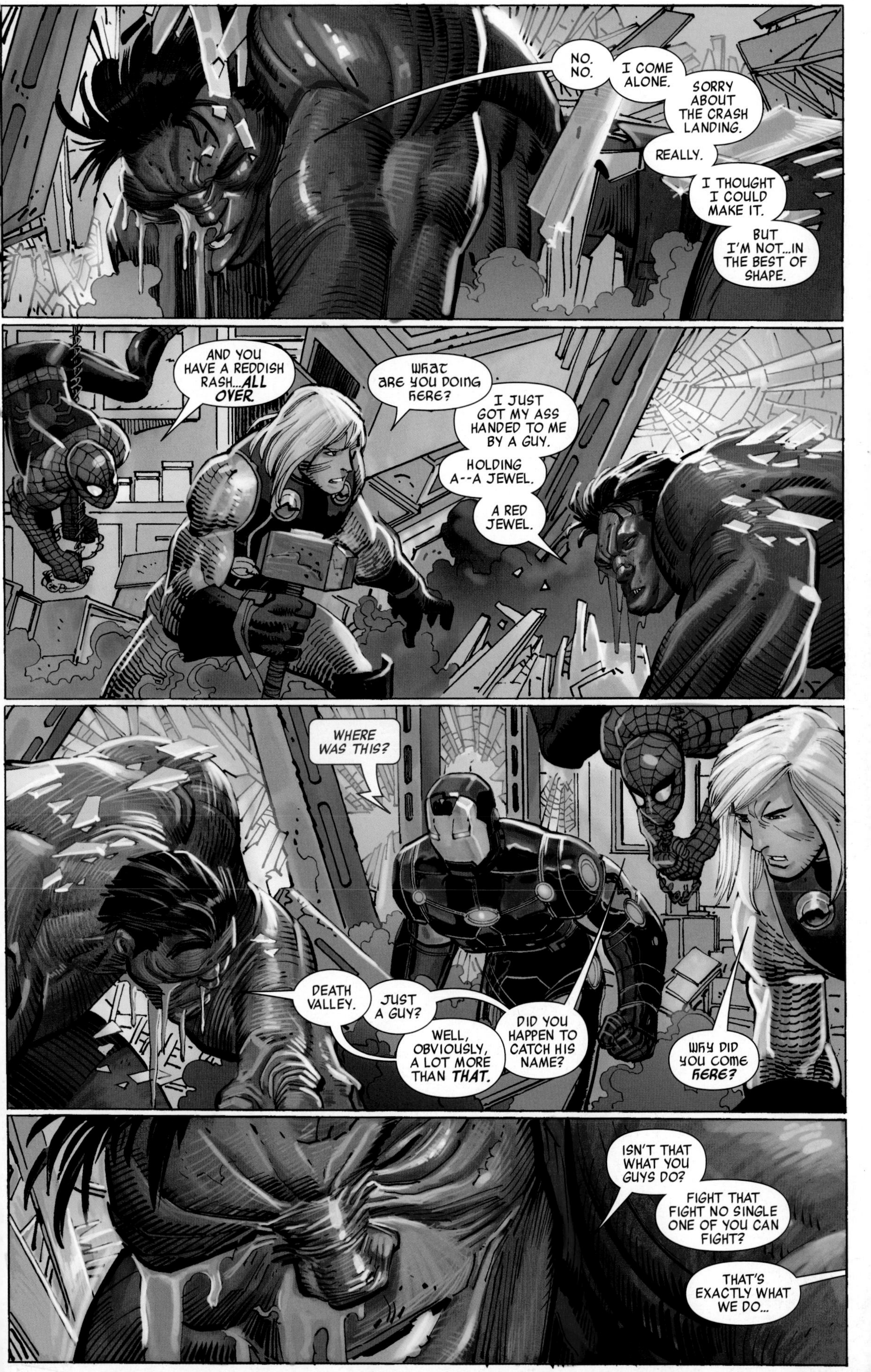

NO. NO.
I COME ALONE.
SORRY ABOUT THE CRASH LANDING.
REALLY.
I THOUGHT I COULD MAKE IT.
BUT I'M NOT...IN THE BEST OF SHAPE.
AND YOU HAVE A REDDISH RASH...ALL OVER.
WHAT ARE YOU DOING HERE?
I JUST GOT MY ASS HANDED TO ME BY A GUY.
HOLDING A--A JEWEL.
A RED JEWEL.
WHERE WAS THIS?
DEATH VALLEY.
JUST A GUY?
WELL, OBVIOUSLY, A LOT MORE THAN THAT.
DID YOU HAPPEN TO CATCH HIS NAME?
WHY DID YOU COME HERE?
ISN'T THAT WHAT YOU GUYS DO?
FIGHT THAT FIGHT NO SINGLE ONE OF YOU CAN FIGHT?
THAT'S EXACTLY WHAT WE DO...

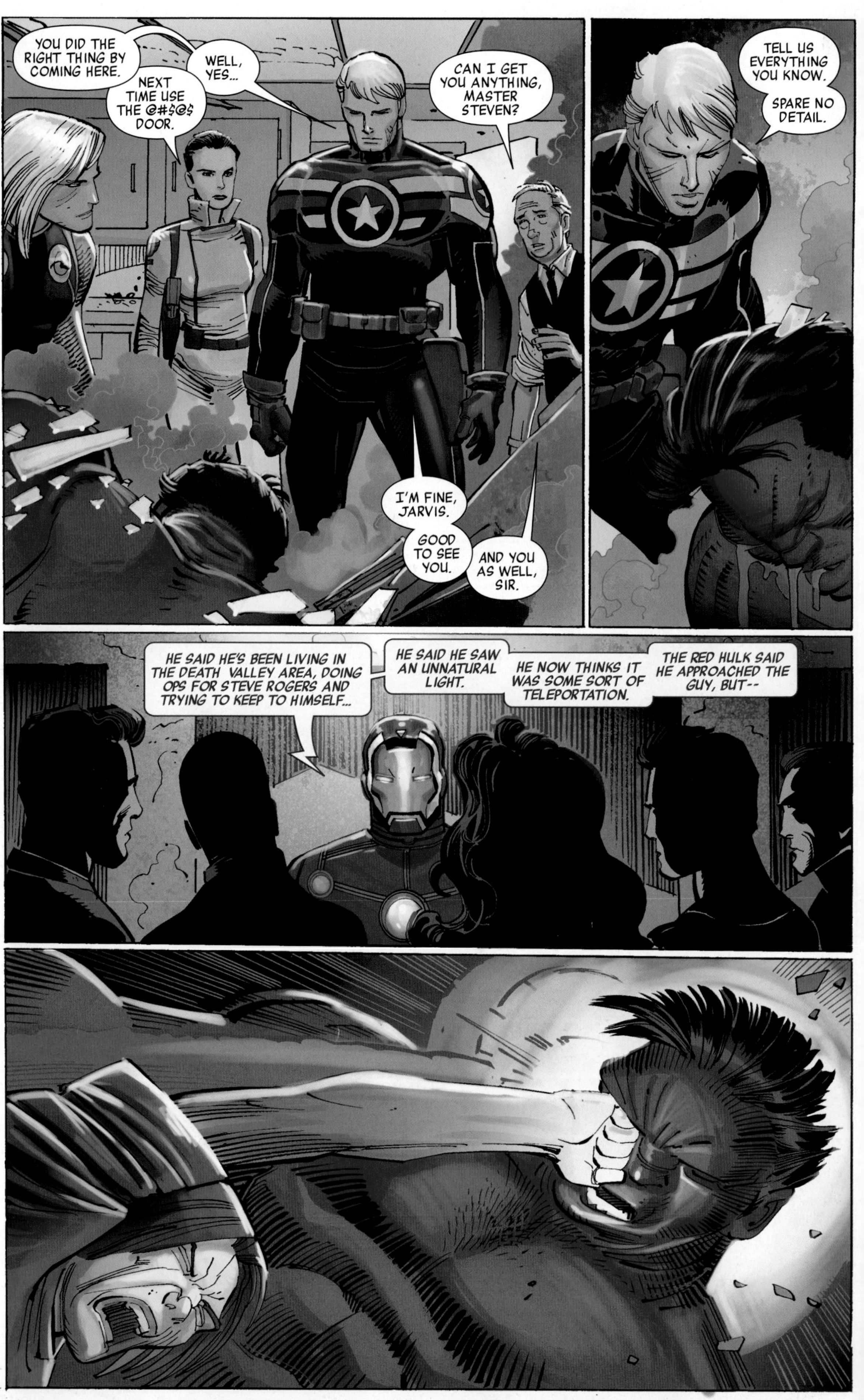

YOU DID THE RIGHT THING BY COMING HERE.
WELL, YES...
NEXT TIME USE THE @#$@$ DOOR.
CAN I GET YOU ANYTHING, MASTER STEVEN?
I'M FINE, JARVIS.
GOOD TO SEE YOU.
AND YOU AS WELL, SIR.
TELL US EVERYTHING YOU KNOW.
SPARE NO DETAIL.
HE SAID HE'S BEEN LIVING IN THE DEATH VALLEY AREA, DOING OPS FOR STEVE ROGERS AND TRYING TO KEEP TO HIMSELF...
HE SAID HE SAW AN UNNATURAL LIGHT.
HE NOW THINKS IT WAS SOME SORT OF TELEPORTATION.
THE RED HULK SAID HE APPROACHED THE GUY, BUT--

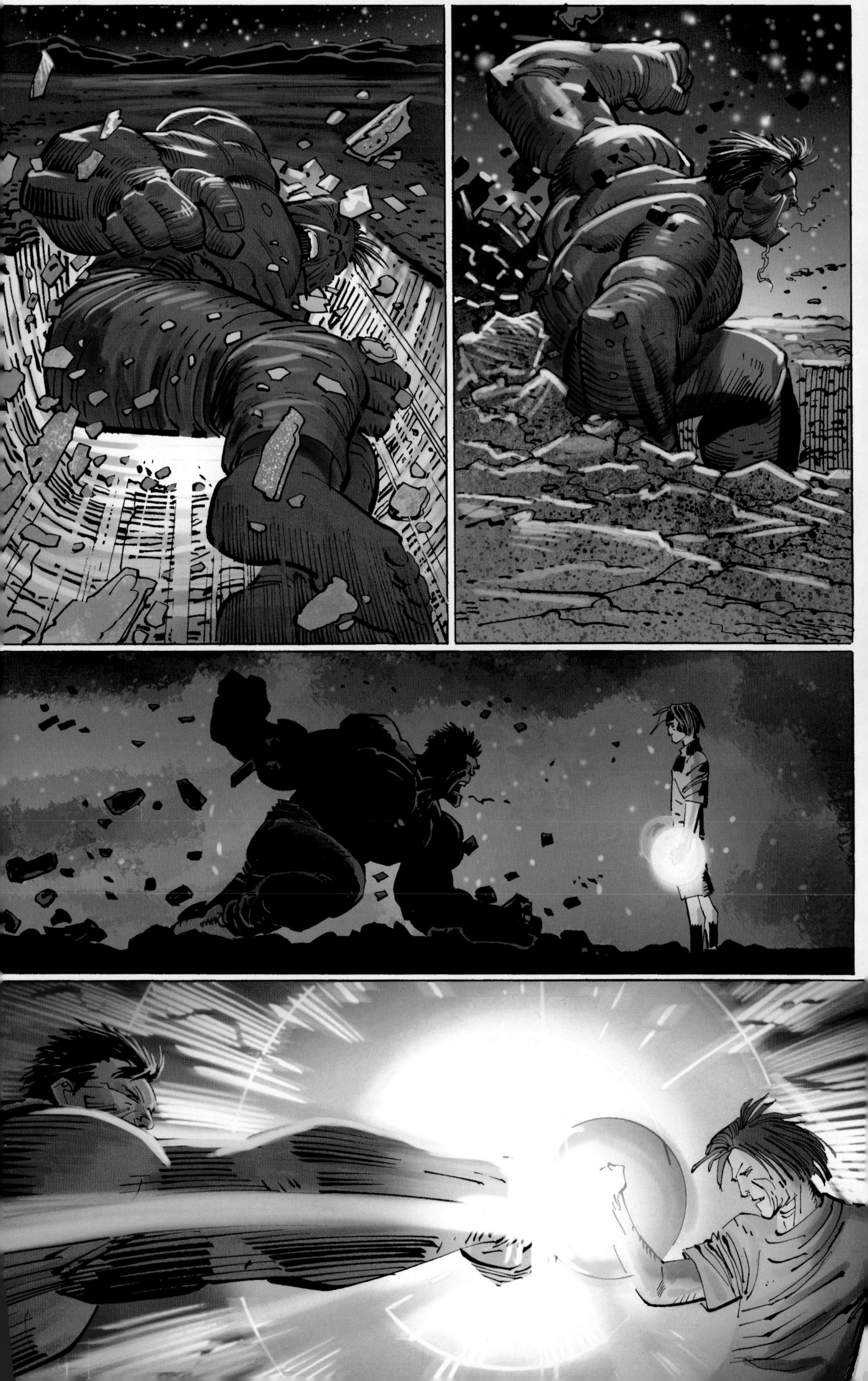

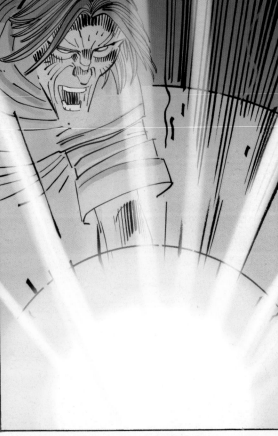

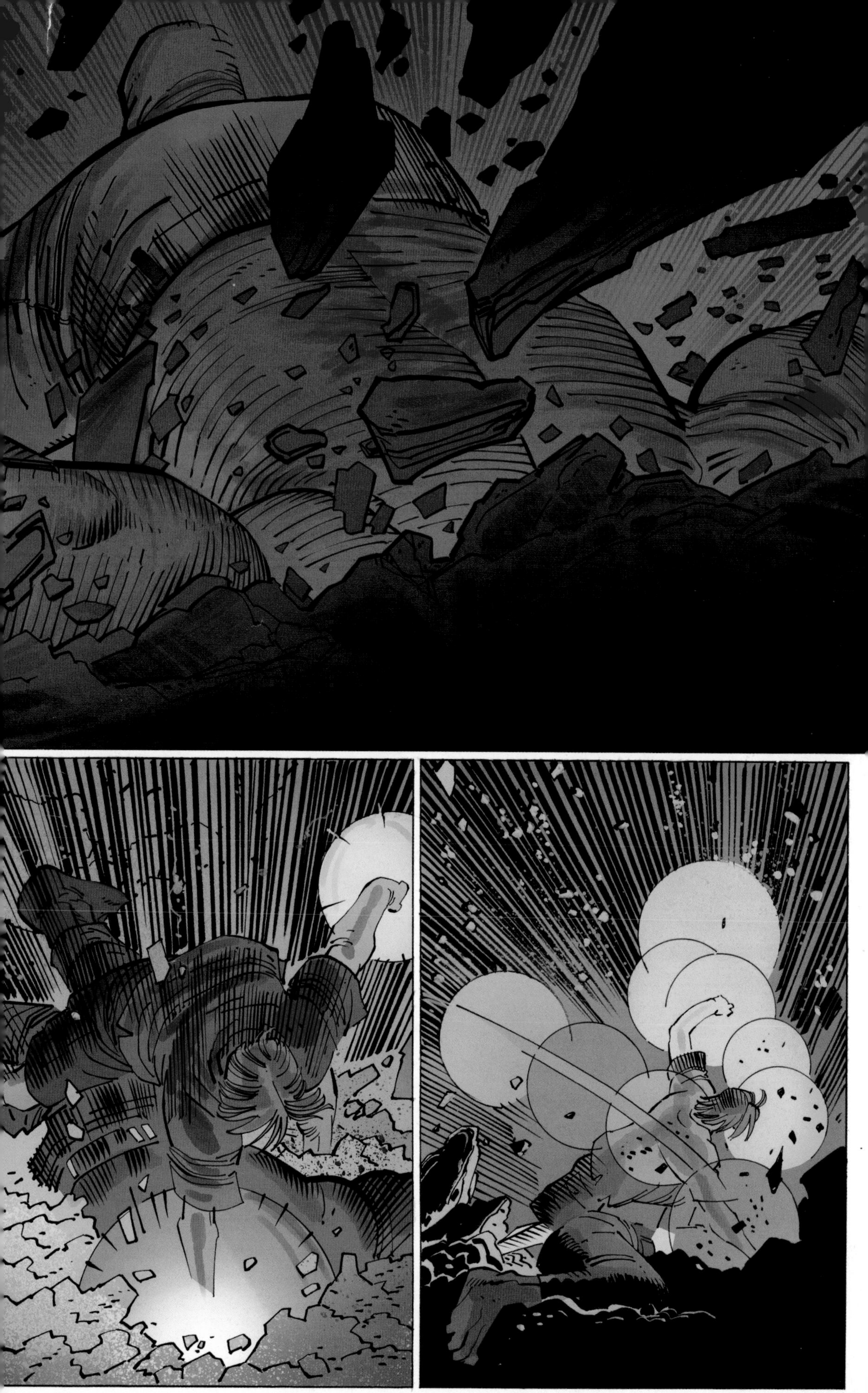

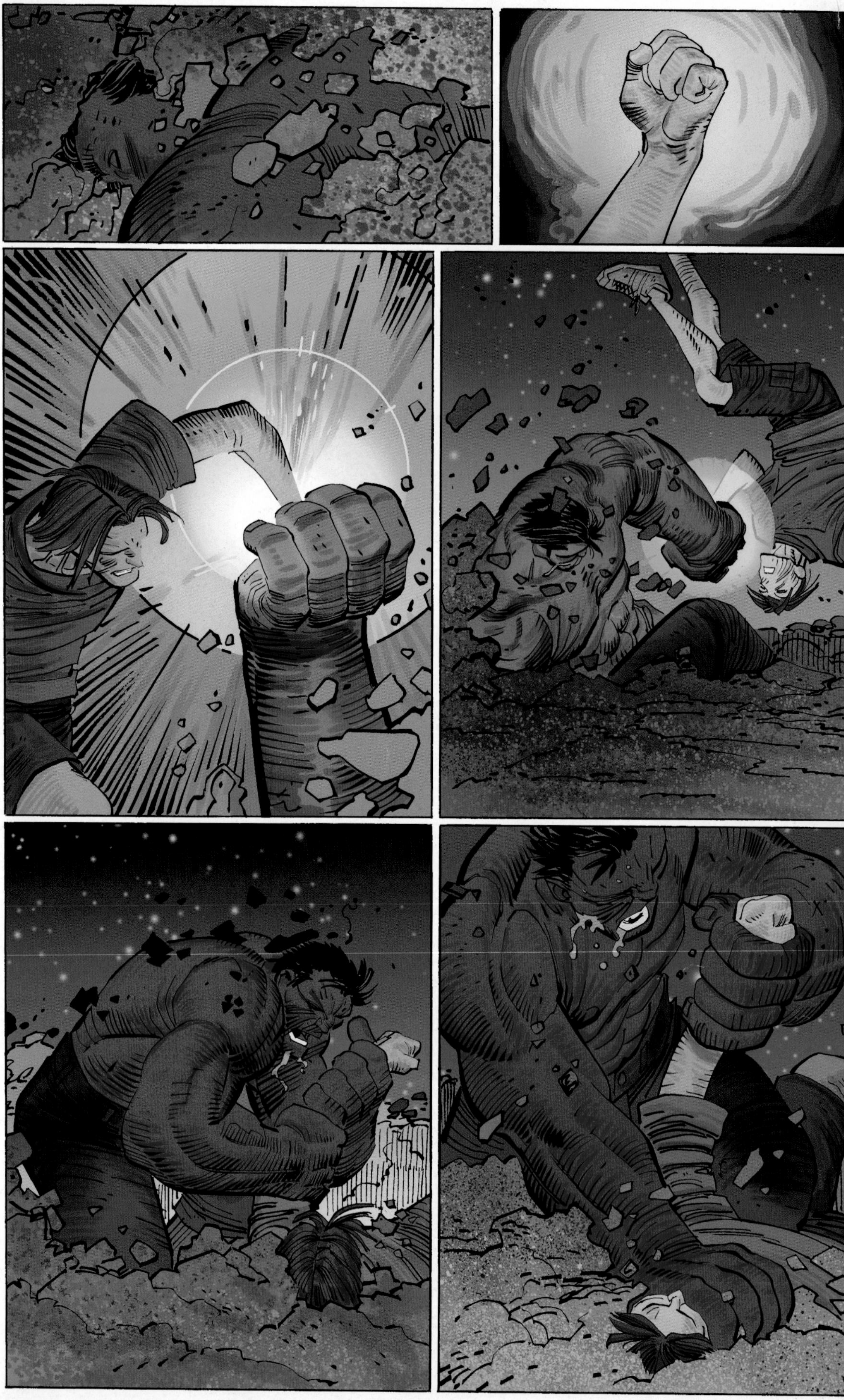

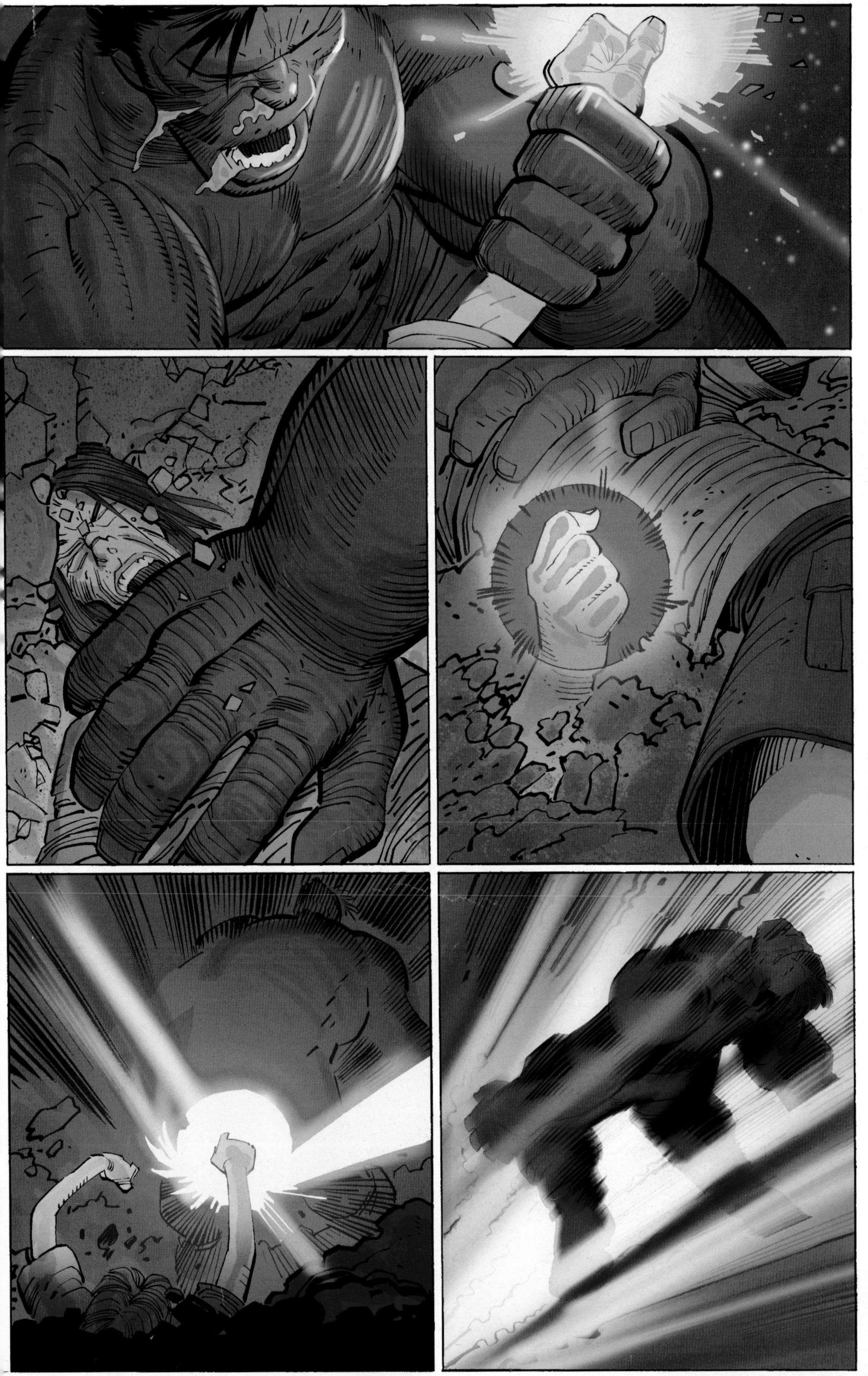

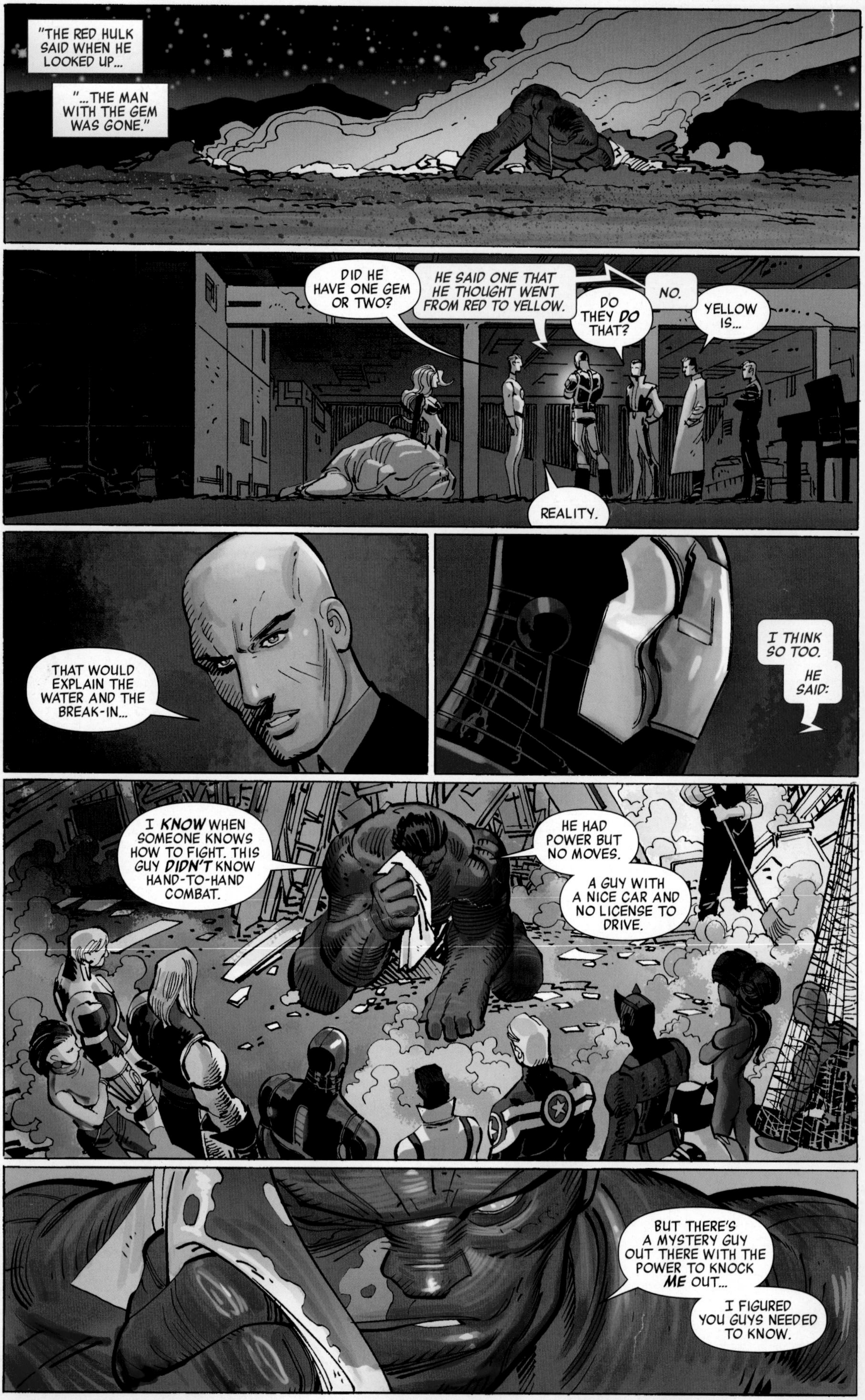
"THE RED HULK SAID WHEN HE LOOKED UP...
"...THE MAN WITH THE GEM WAS GONE."
DID HE HAVE ONE GEM OR TWO?
HE SAID ONE THAT HE THOUGHT WENT FROM RED TO YELLOW.
DO THEY DO THAT?
NO.
YELLOW IS...
REALITY.
THAT WOULD EXPLAIN THE WATER AND THE BREAK-IN...
I THINK SO TOO.
HE SAID:
I KNOW WHEN SOMEONE KNOWS HOW TO FIGHT. THIS GUY DIDN'T KNOW HAND-TO-HAND COMBAT.
HE HAD POWER BUT NO MOVES.
A GUY WITH A NICE CAR AND NO LICENSE TO DRIVE.
BUT THERE'S A MYSTERY GUY OUT THERE WITH THE POWER TO KNOCK ME OUT...
I FIGURED YOU GUYS NEEDED TO KNOW.

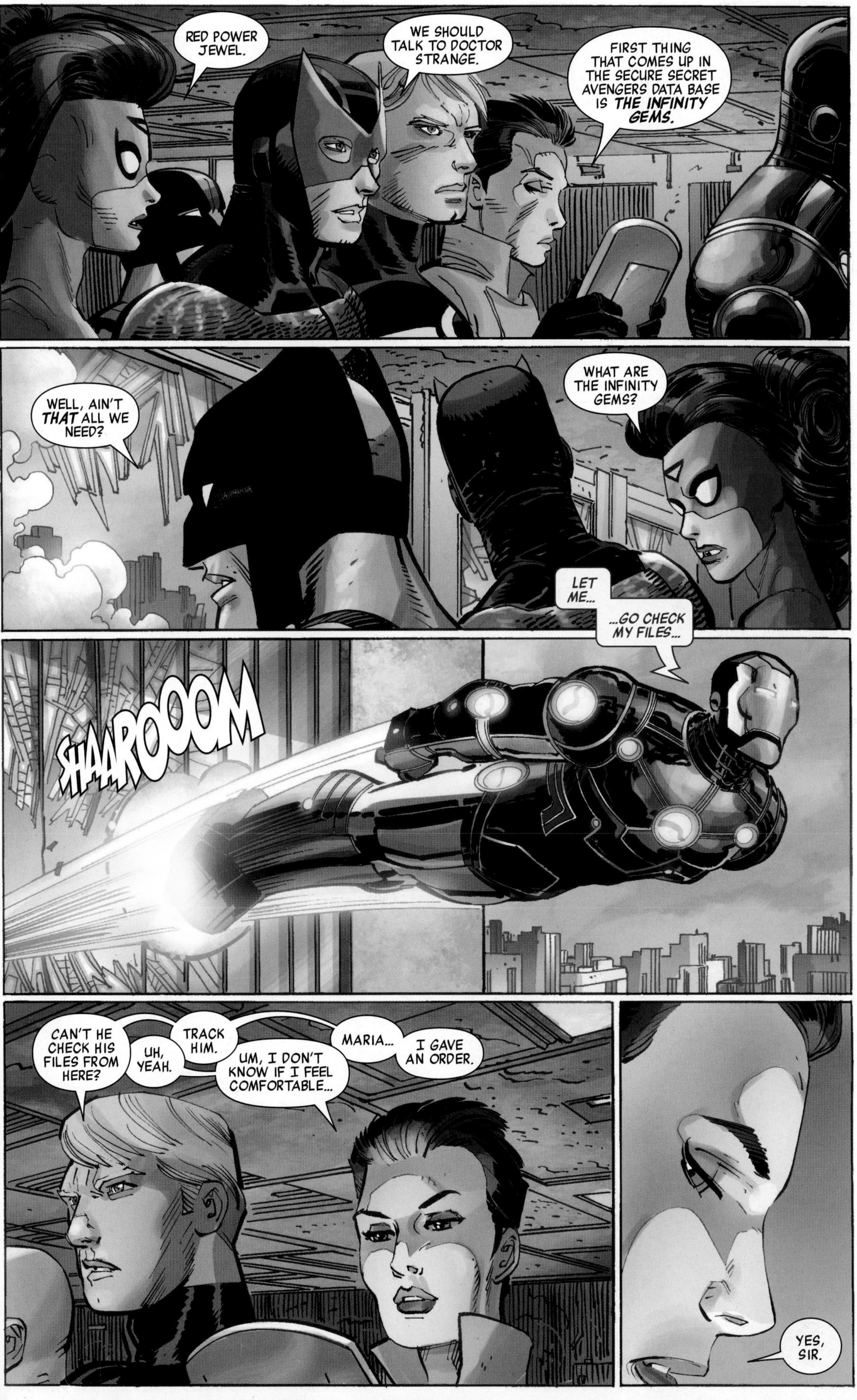
RED POWER JEWEL.
WE SHOULD TALK TO DOCTOR STRANGE.
FIRST THING THAT COMES UP IN THE SECURE SECRET AVENGERS DATA BASE IS **THE INFINITY GEMS.**
WELL, AIN'T *THAT* ALL WE NEED?
WHAT ARE THE INFINITY GEMS?
LET ME...
...GO CHECK MY FILES...
SHAAROOOM
CAN'T HE CHECK HIS FILES FROM HERE?
UH, YEAH.
TRACK HIM.
UM, I DON'T KNOW IF I FEEL COMFORTABLE...
MARIA...
I GAVE AN ORDER.
YES, SIR.

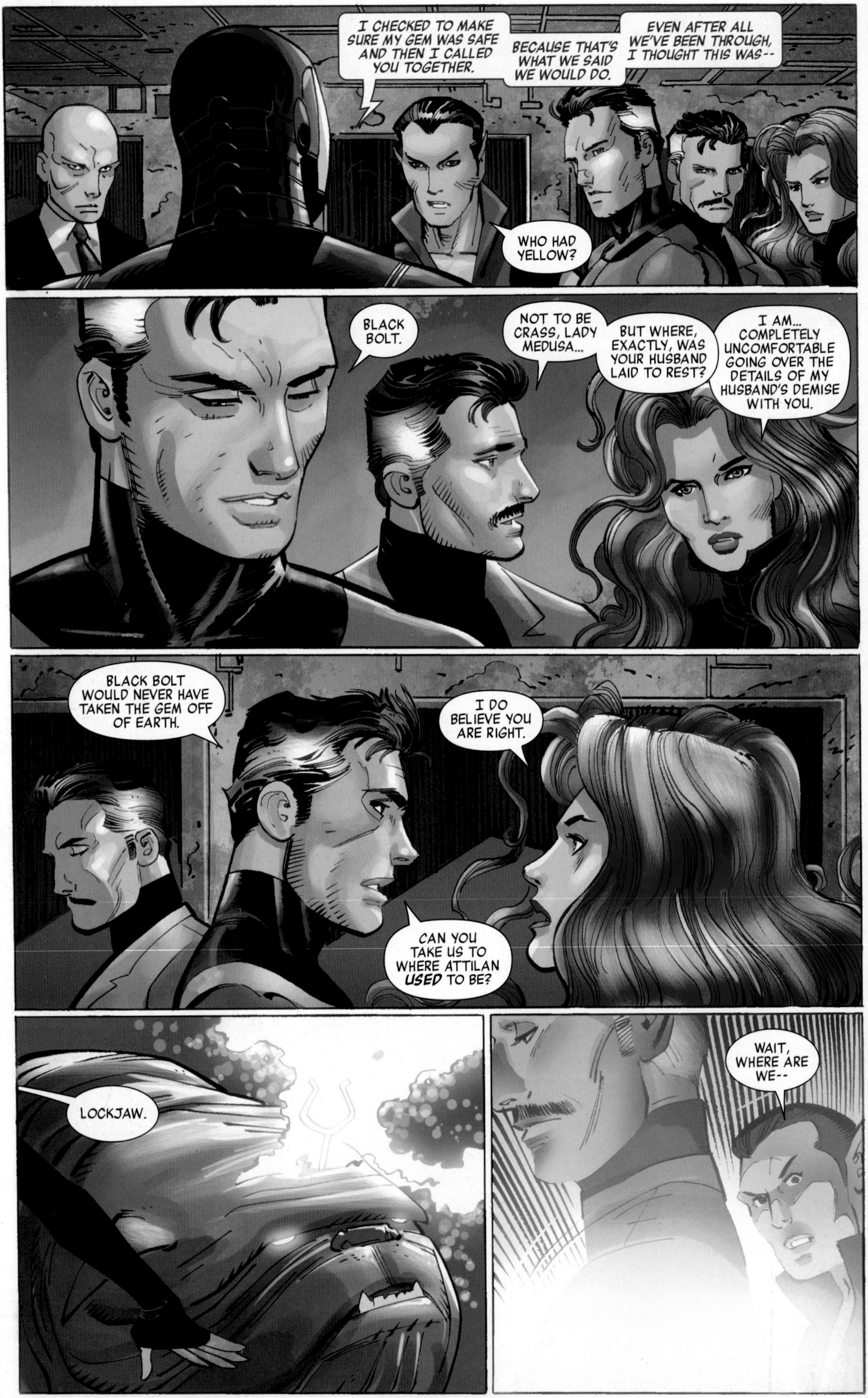
I CHECKED TO MAKE SURE MY GEM WAS SAFE AND THEN I CALLED YOU TOGETHER.
BECAUSE THAT'S WHAT WE SAID WE WOULD DO.
EVEN AFTER ALL WE'VE BEEN THROUGH, I THOUGHT THIS WAS--
WHO HAD YELLOW?
BLACK BOLT.
NOT TO BE CRASS, LADY MEDUSA...
BUT WHERE, EXACTLY, WAS YOUR HUSBAND LAID TO REST?
I AM... COMPLETELY UNCOMFORTABLE GOING OVER THE DETAILS OF MY HUSBAND'S DEMISE WITH YOU.
BLACK BOLT WOULD NEVER HAVE TAKEN THE GEM OFF OF EARTH.
I DO BELIEVE YOU ARE RIGHT.
CAN YOU TAKE US TO WHERE ATTILAN USED TO BE?
LOCKJAW.
WAIT, WHERE ARE WE--

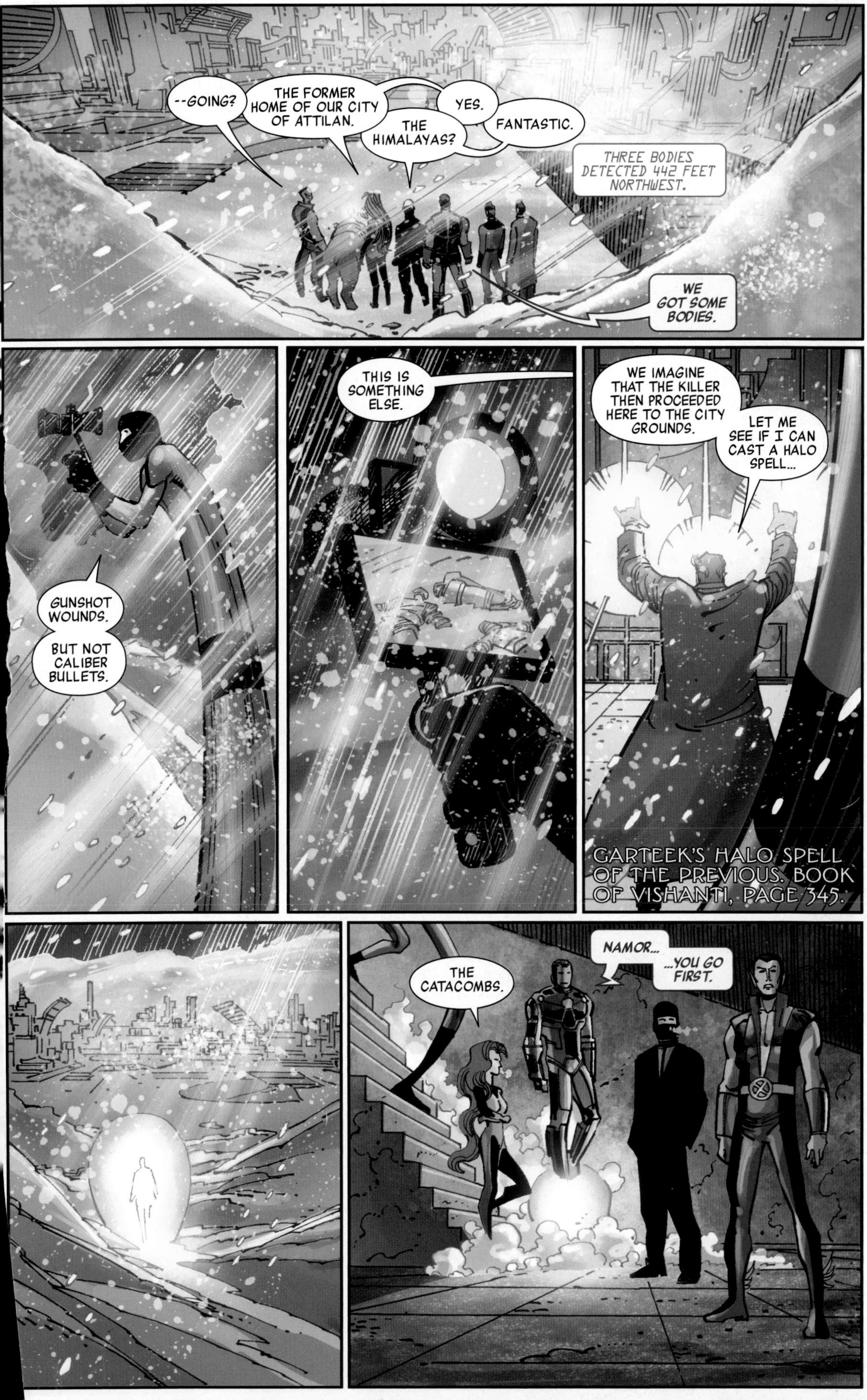
--GOING?
THE FORMER HOME OF OUR CITY OF ATTILAN.
THE HIMALAYAS?
YES.
FANTASTIC.
THREE BODIES DETECTED 442 FEET NORTHWEST.
WE GOT SOME BODIES.
GUNSHOT WOUNDS.
BUT NOT CALIBER BULLETS.
THIS IS SOMETHING ELSE.
WE IMAGINE THAT THE KILLER THEN PROCEEDED HERE TO THE CITY GROUNDS.
LET ME SEE IF I CAN CAST A HALO SPELL...
GARTEEK'S HALO SPELL OF THE PREVIOUS. BOOK OF VISHANTI, PAGE 345.
THE CATACOMBS.
NAMOR...
...YOU GO FIRST.

THERE ARE NO MIND WAVES DOWN HERE. ANIMAL, HUMAN OR INHUMAN...

I KNOW. I WAS MAKING A BAD JOKE.

(I CAN'T REMEMBER YOU MAKING ANY OTHER KIND.)

THIS IS WHERE THE ROYAL FAMILY WOULD JAIL ITS INSURGENTS.

THIS WAY.

WELL...

WE HAVE ANOTHER CRIME SCENE.

SCANNING...

MMRRFF...

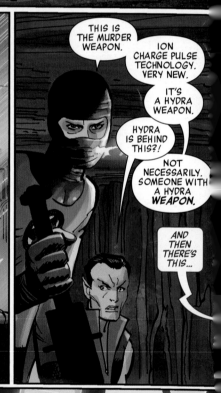

THIS IS THE MURDER WEAPON. ION CHARGE PULSE TECHNOLOGY. VERY NEW.

IT'S A HYDRA WEAPON.

HYDRA IS BEHIND THIS?!

NOT NECESSARILY. SOMEONE WITH A HYDRA WEAPON.

AND THEN THERE'S THIS...

THIS IS A.I.M. TECHNOLOGY. THIS IS AN ENVIRONMENTAL ENERGY SOURCE SCANNER.

WHICH MEANS?

A SUPER-HIGH-TECH PIECE OF EQUIPMENT-- LIKE--LIKE THE THING YOU USE TO LOOK FOR METAL ON THE BEACH.

WHO MAKES THEM? WHERE CAN YOU GET ONE?

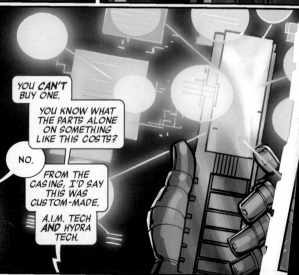

YOU CAN'T BUY ONE.

YOU KNOW WHAT THE PARTS ALONE ON SOMETHING LIKE THIS COSTS?

NO.

FROM THE CASING, I'D SAY THIS WAS CUSTOM-MADE.

A.I.M. TECH AND HYDRA TECH.

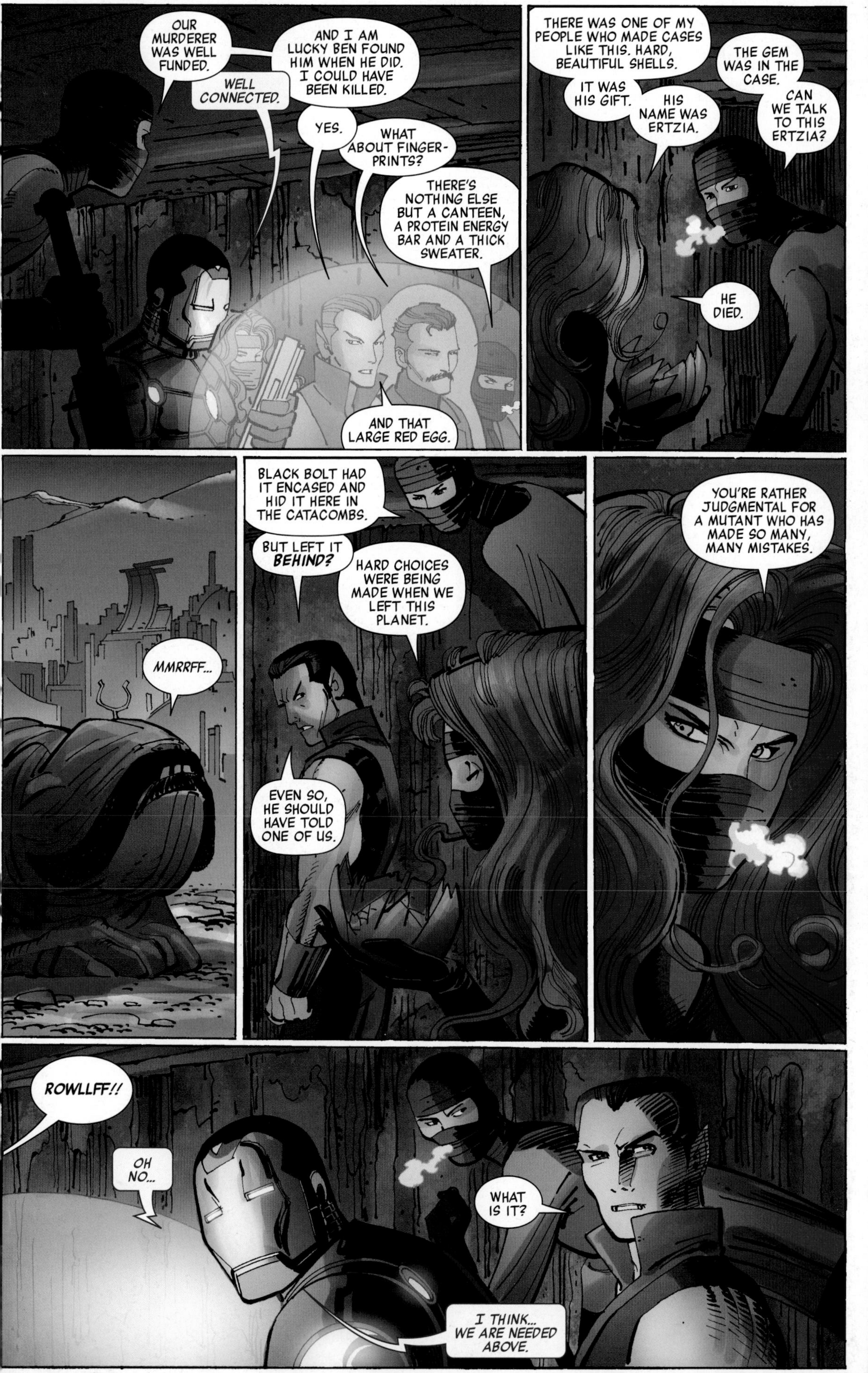
OUR MURDERER WAS WELL FUNDED.
WELL CONNECTED.
AND I AM LUCKY BEN FOUND HIM WHEN HE DID. I COULD HAVE BEEN KILLED.
YES.
WHAT ABOUT FINGER-PRINTS?
THERE'S NOTHING ELSE BUT A CANTEEN, A PROTEIN ENERGY BAR AND A THICK SWEATER.
AND THAT LARGE RED EGG.
THERE WAS ONE OF MY PEOPLE WHO MADE CASES LIKE THIS. HARD, BEAUTIFUL SHELLS.
IT WAS HIS GIFT.
HIS NAME WAS ERTZIA.
THE GEM WAS IN THE CASE.
CAN WE TALK TO THIS ERTZIA?
HE DIED.
MMRRFF...
BLACK BOLT HAD IT ENCASED AND HID IT HERE IN THE CATACOMBS.
BUT LEFT IT BEHIND?
HARD CHOICES WERE BEING MADE WHEN WE LEFT THIS PLANET.
EVEN SO, HE SHOULD HAVE TOLD ONE OF US.
YOU'RE RATHER JUDGMENTAL FOR A MUTANT WHO HAS MADE SO MANY, MANY MISTAKES.
ROWLLFF!!
OH NO...
WHAT IS IT?
I THINK... WE ARE NEEDED ABOVE.

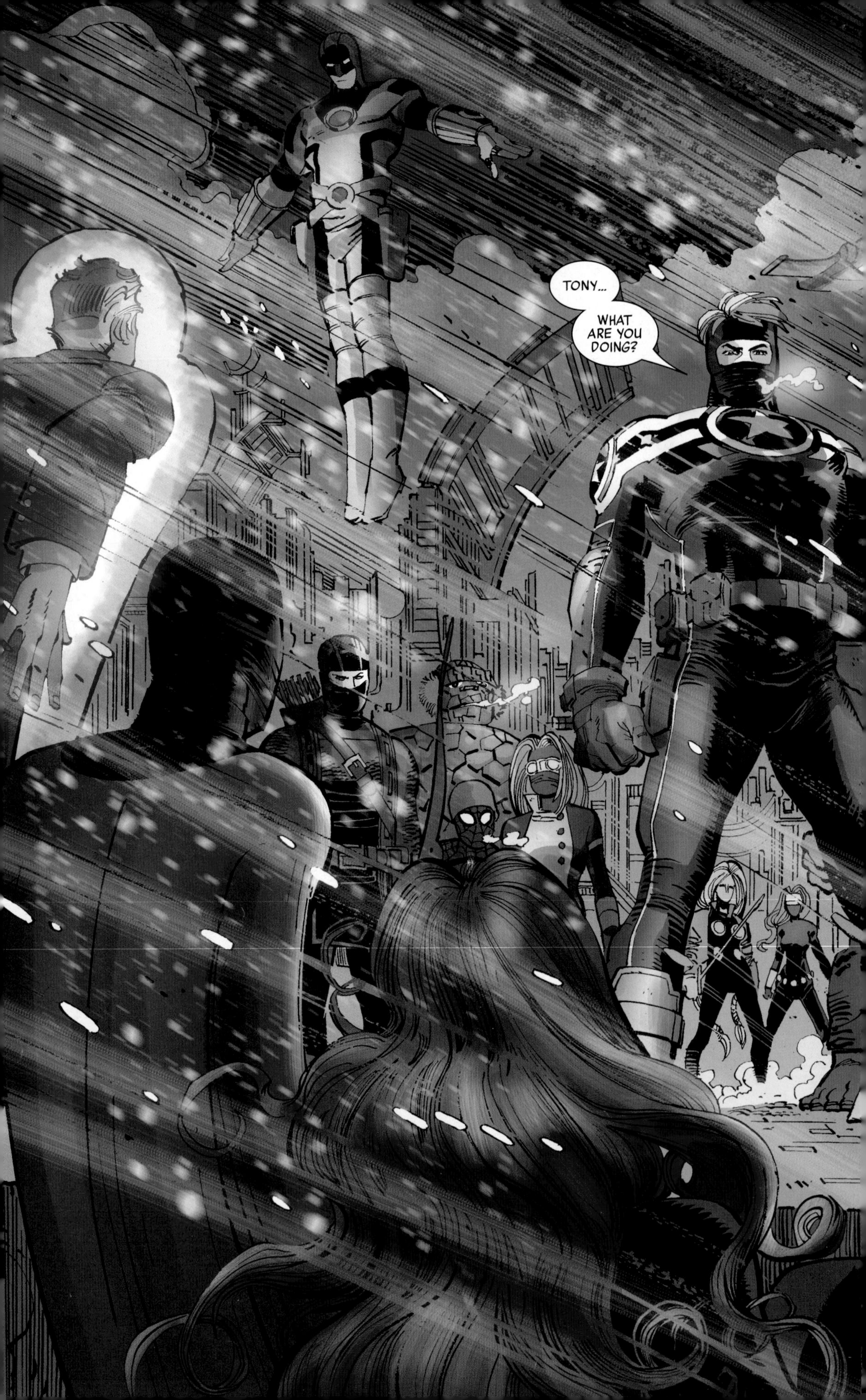
TONY...
WHAT ARE YOU DOING?

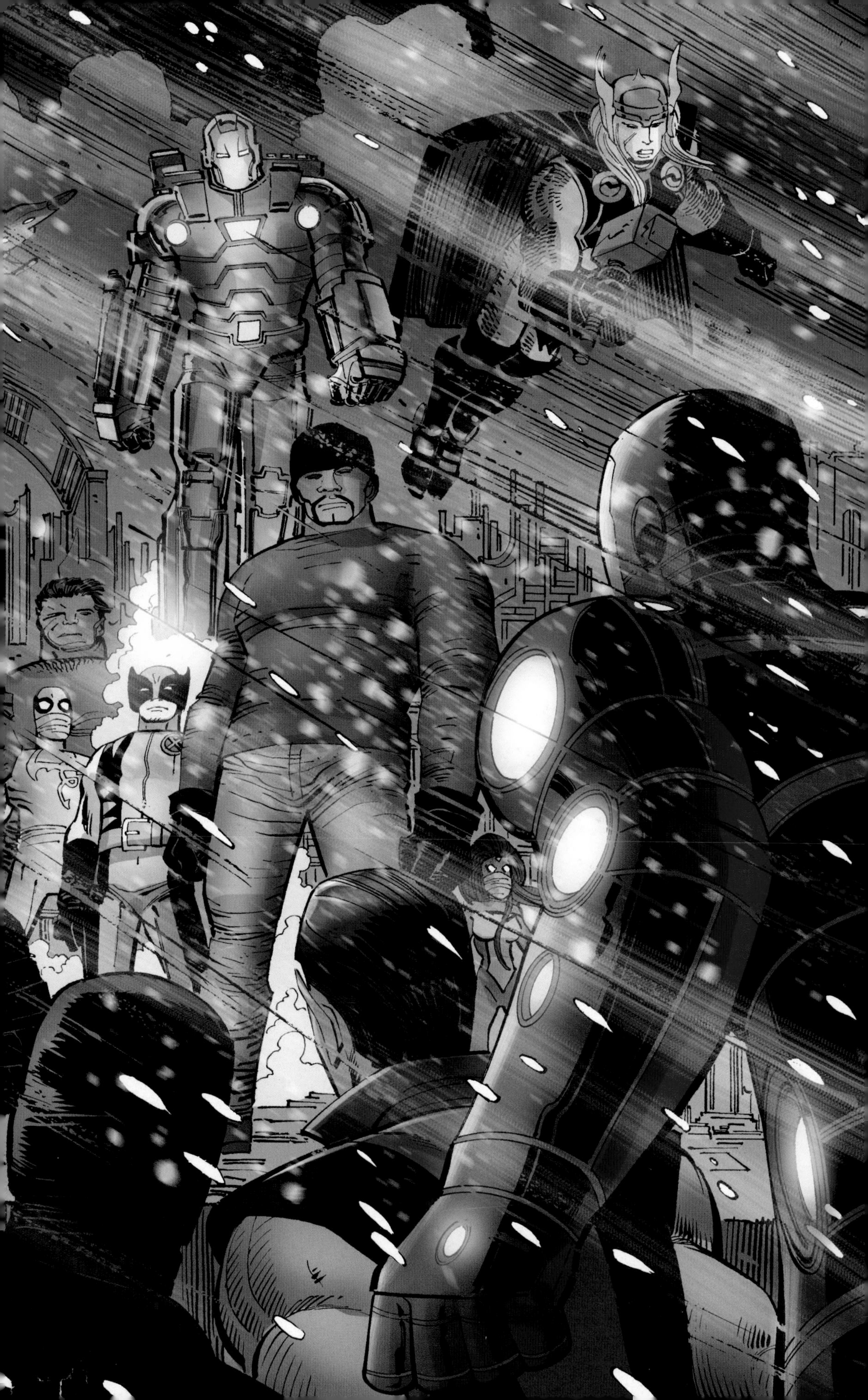

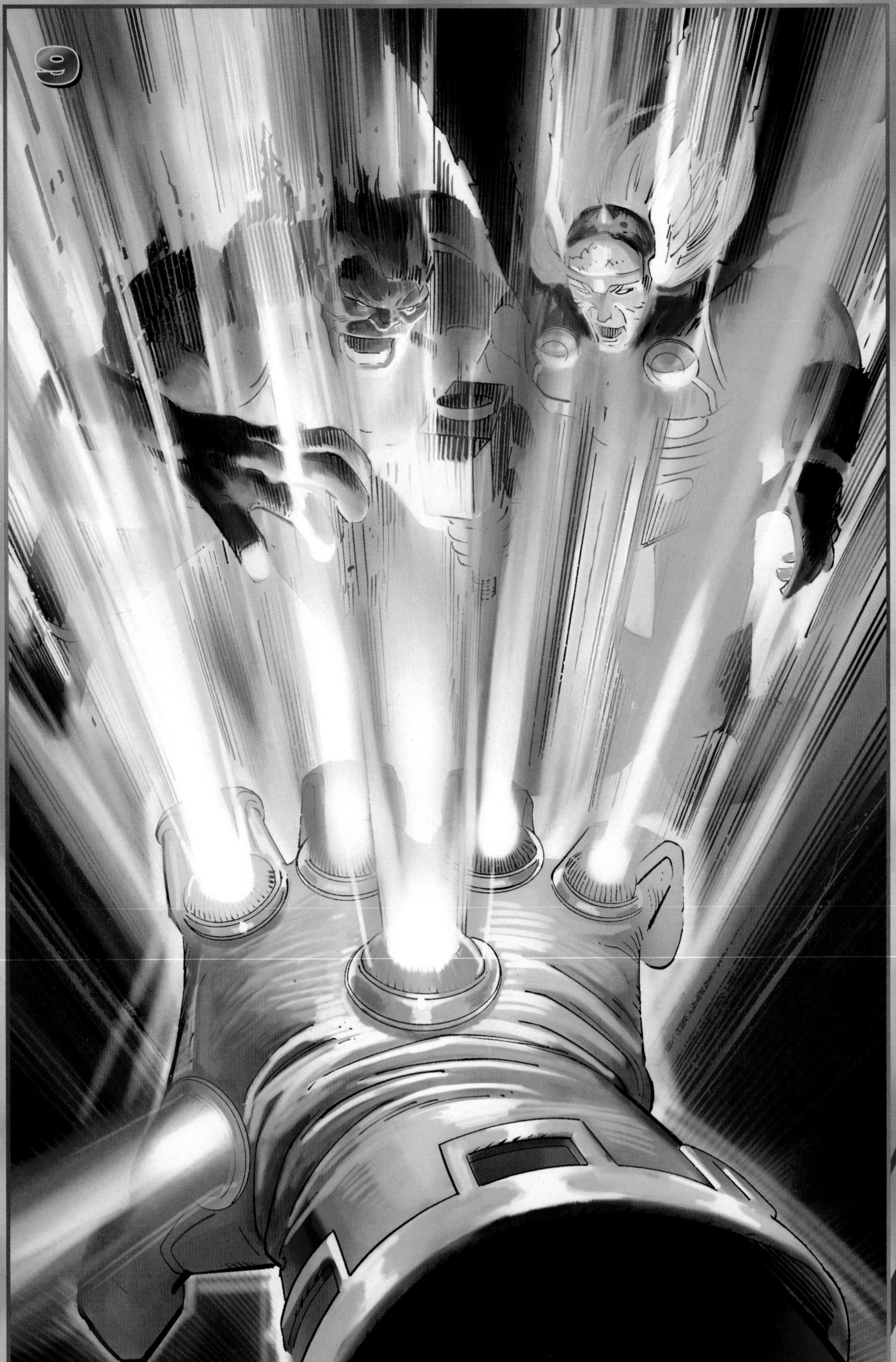
9

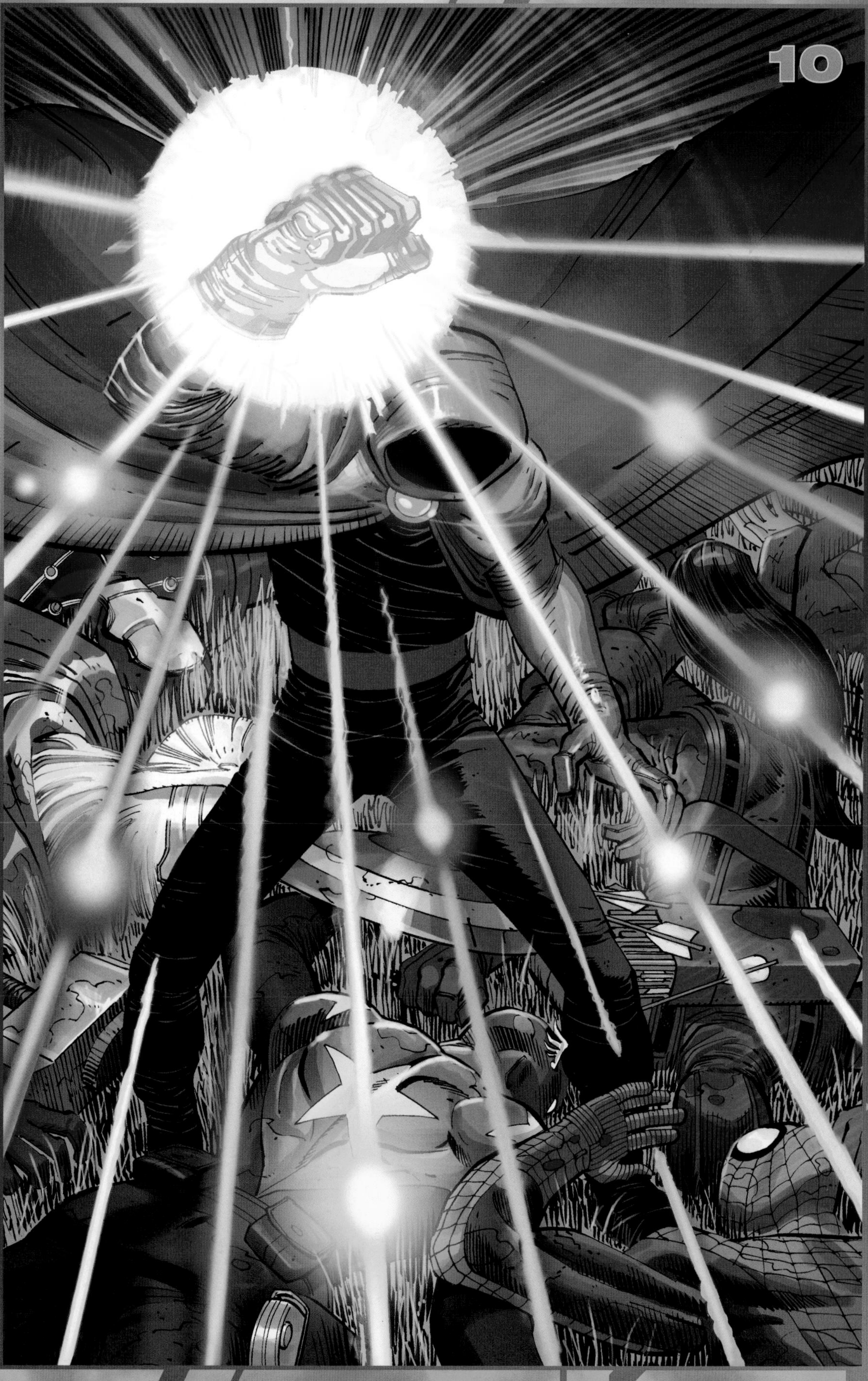
10

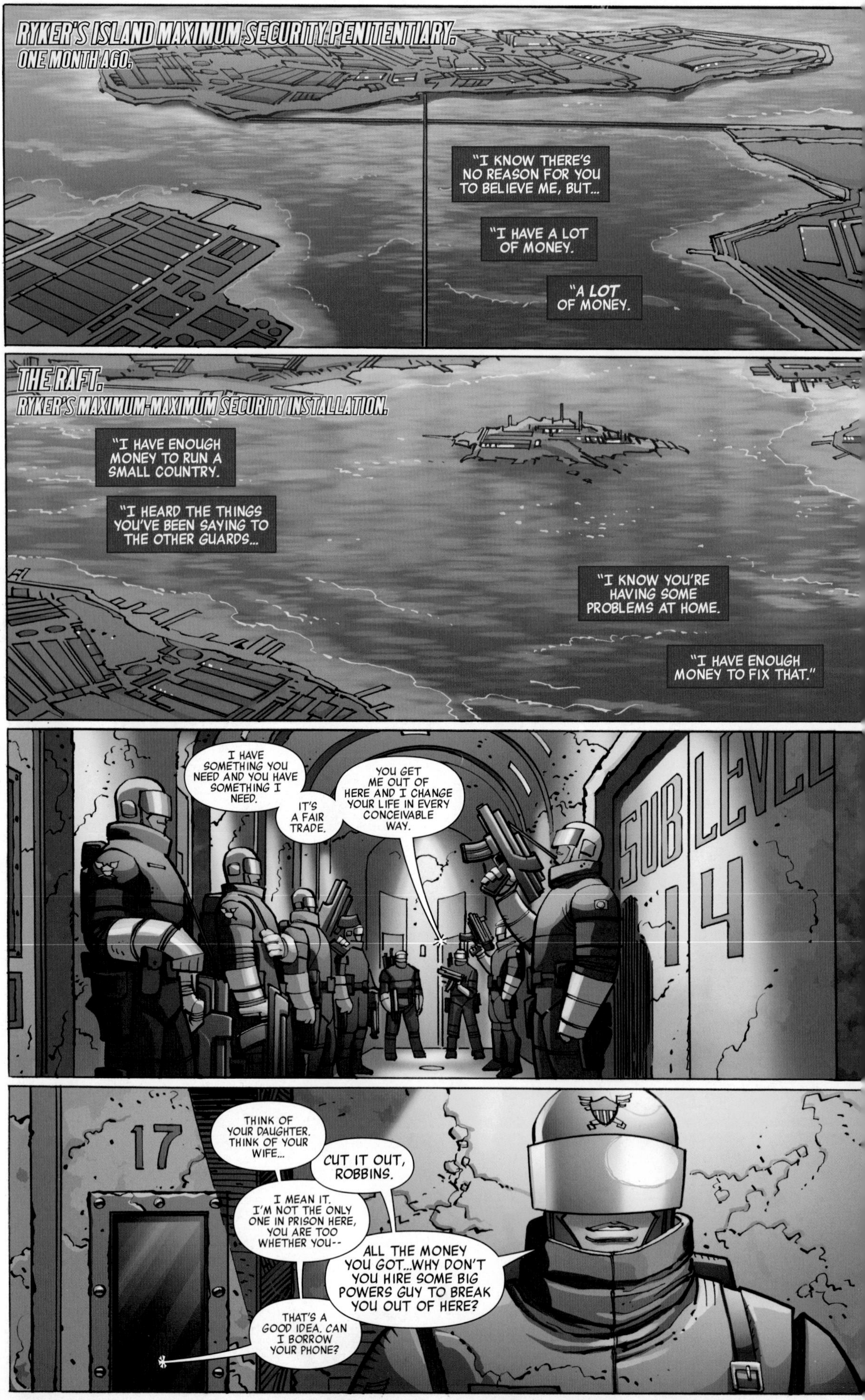
RYKER'S ISLAND MAXIMUM-SECURITY PENITENTIARY.
ONE MONTH AGO.
"I KNOW THERE'S NO REASON FOR YOU TO BELIEVE ME, BUT...
"I HAVE A LOT OF MONEY.
"A LOT OF MONEY.
THE RAFT.
RYKER'S MAXIMUM-MAXIMUM SECURITY INSTALLATION.
"I HAVE ENOUGH MONEY TO RUN A SMALL COUNTRY.
"I HEARD THE THINGS YOU'VE BEEN SAYING TO THE OTHER GUARDS...
"I KNOW YOU'RE HAVING SOME PROBLEMS AT HOME.
"I HAVE ENOUGH MONEY TO FIX THAT."
I HAVE SOMETHING YOU NEED AND YOU HAVE SOMETHING I NEED.
IT'S A FAIR TRADE.
YOU GET ME OUT OF HERE AND I CHANGE YOUR LIFE IN EVERY CONCEIVABLE WAY.
SUB LEVEL 14
17
THINK OF YOUR DAUGHTER. THINK OF YOUR WIFE...
CUT IT OUT, ROBBINS.
I MEAN IT. I'M NOT THE ONLY ONE IN PRISON HERE, YOU ARE TOO WHETHER YOU--
ALL THE MONEY YOU GOT...WHY DON'T YOU HIRE SOME BIG POWERS GUY TO BREAK YOU OUT OF HERE?
THAT'S A GOOD IDEA. CAN I BORROW YOUR PHONE?

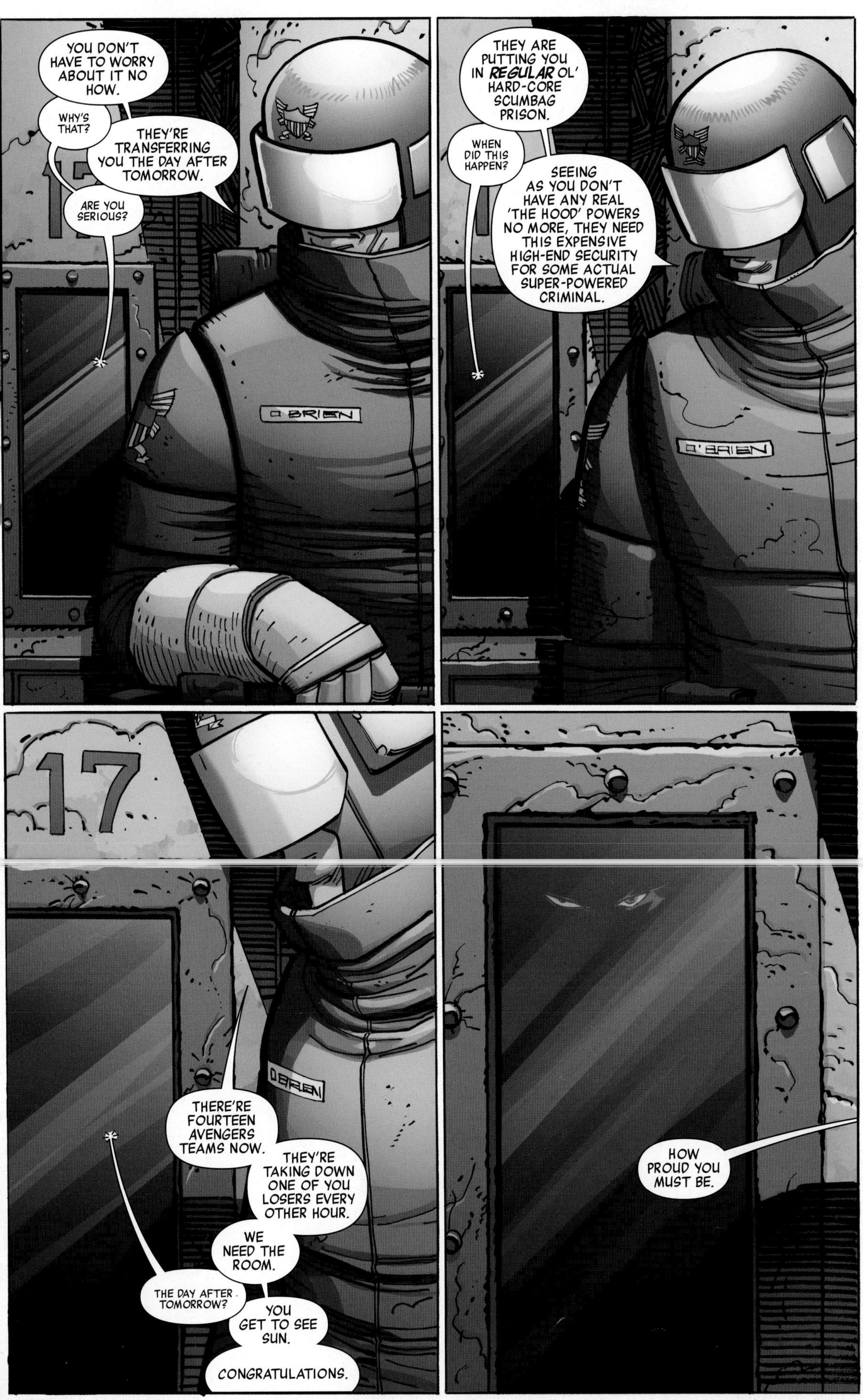
YOU DON'T HAVE TO WORRY ABOUT IT NO HOW.
WHY'S THAT?
THEY'RE TRANSFERRING YOU THE DAY AFTER TOMORROW.
ARE YOU SERIOUS?
O'BRIEN
THEY ARE PUTTING YOU IN REGULAR OL' HARD-CORE SCUMBAG PRISON.
WHEN DID THIS HAPPEN?
SEEING AS YOU DON'T HAVE ANY REAL 'THE HOOD' POWERS NO MORE, THEY NEED THIS EXPENSIVE HIGH-END SECURITY FOR SOME ACTUAL SUPER-POWERED CRIMINAL.
O'BRIEN
17
O'BRIEN
THERE'RE FOURTEEN AVENGERS TEAMS NOW.
THEY'RE TAKING DOWN ONE OF YOU LOSERS EVERY OTHER HOUR.
WE NEED THE ROOM.
THE DAY AFTER TOMORROW?
YOU GET TO SEE SUN.
CONGRATULATIONS.
HOW PROUD YOU MUST BE.

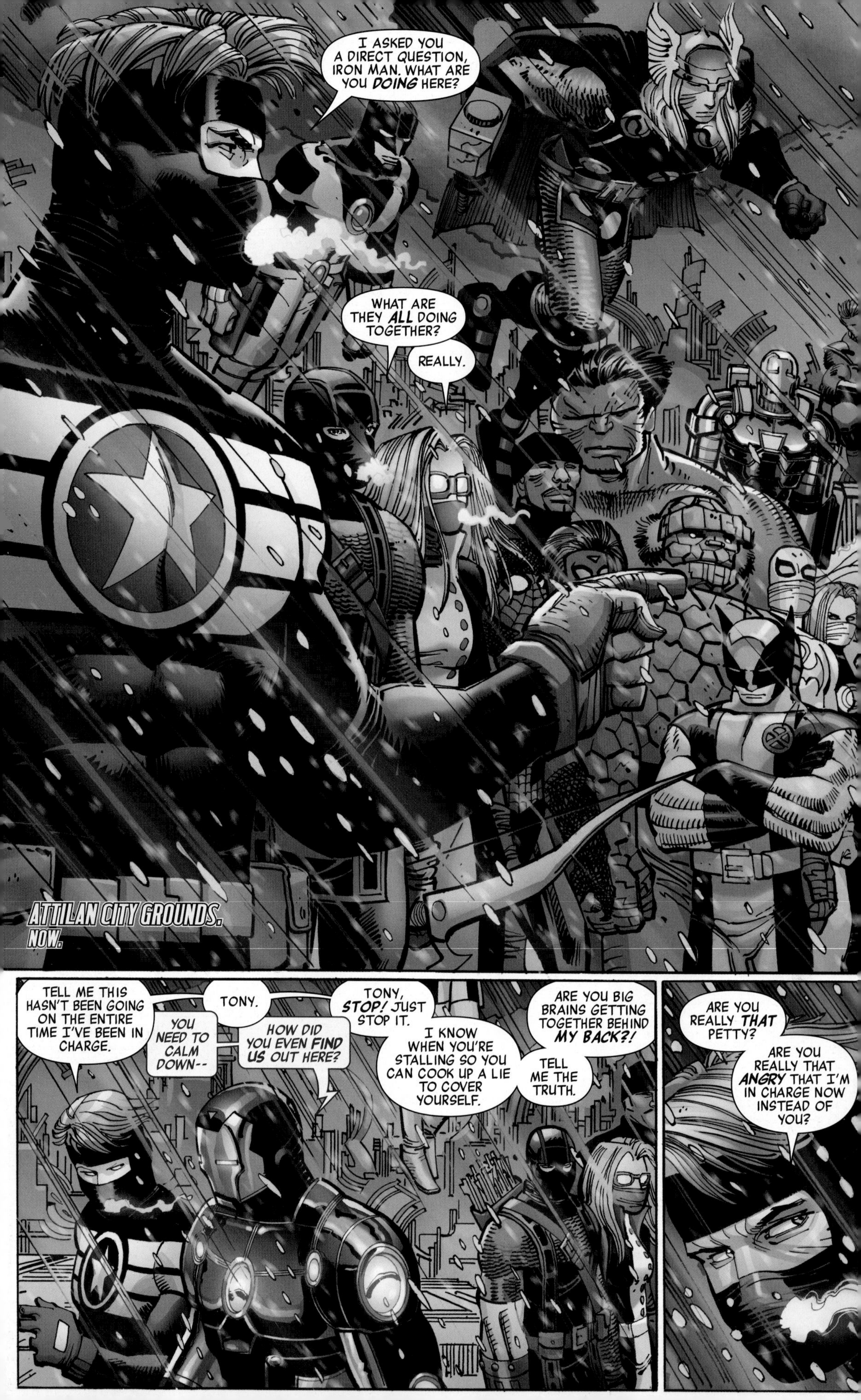

I ASKED YOU A DIRECT QUESTION, IRON MAN. WHAT ARE YOU DOING HERE?
WHAT ARE THEY ALL DOING TOGETHER?
REALLY.
ATTILAN CITY GROUNDS. NOW.
TELL ME THIS HASN'T BEEN GOING ON THE ENTIRE TIME I'VE BEEN IN CHARGE.
TONY.
YOU NEED TO CALM DOWN--
HOW DID YOU EVEN FIND US OUT HERE?
TONY, STOP! JUST STOP IT.
I KNOW WHEN YOU'RE STALLING SO YOU CAN COOK UP A LIE TO COVER YOURSELF.
ARE YOU BIG BRAINS GETTING TOGETHER BEHIND MY BACK?!
TELL ME THE TRUTH.
ARE YOU REALLY THAT PETTY?
ARE YOU REALLY THAT ANGRY THAT I'M IN CHARGE NOW INSTEAD OF YOU?

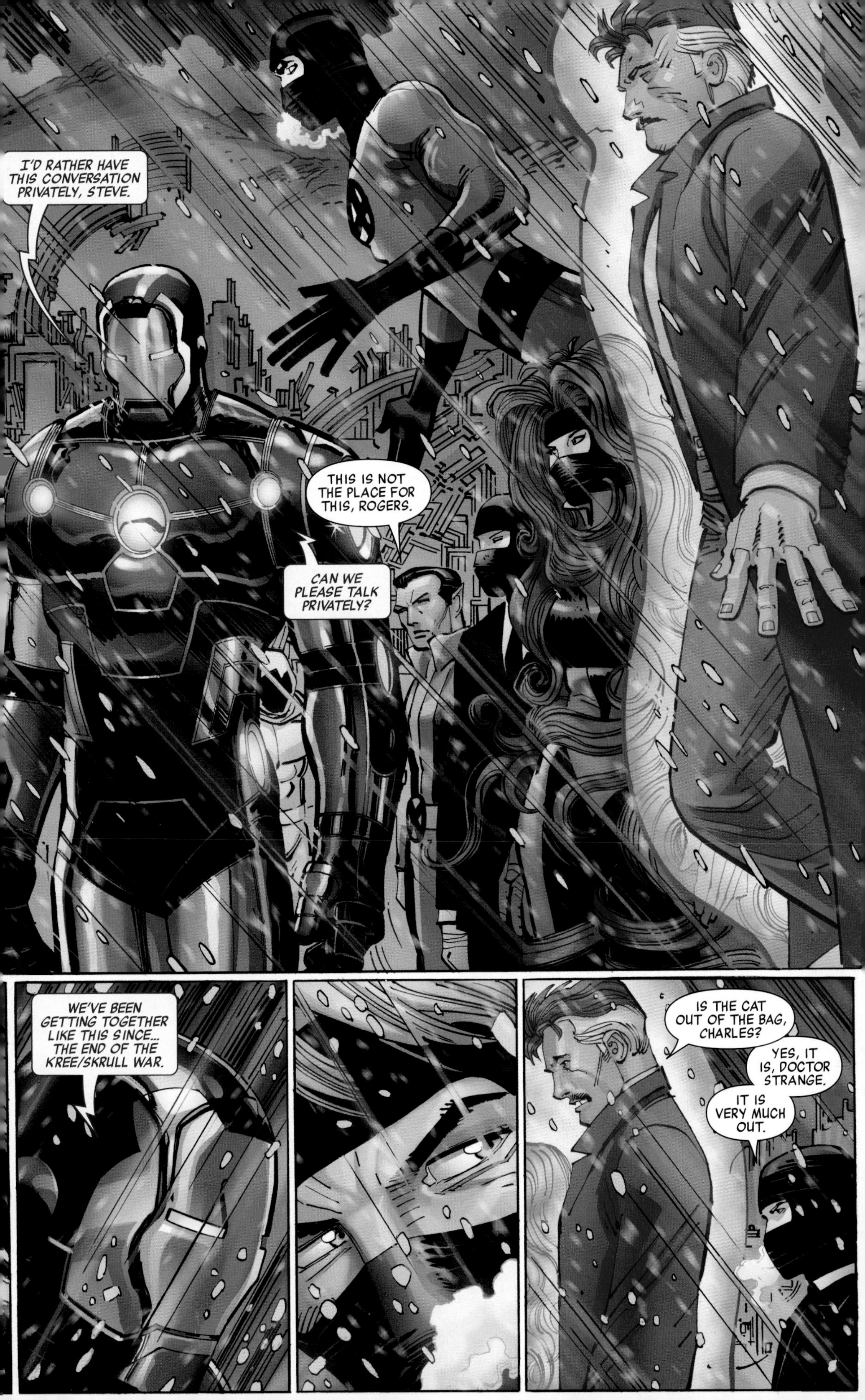
I'D RATHER HAVE THIS CONVERSATION PRIVATELY, STEVE.
THIS IS NOT THE PLACE FOR THIS, ROGERS.
CAN WE PLEASE TALK PRIVATELY?
WE'VE BEEN GETTING TOGETHER LIKE THIS SINCE... THE END OF THE KREE/SKRULL WAR.
IS THE CAT OUT OF THE BAG, CHARLES?
YES, IT IS, DOCTOR STRANGE.
IT IS VERY MUCH OUT.

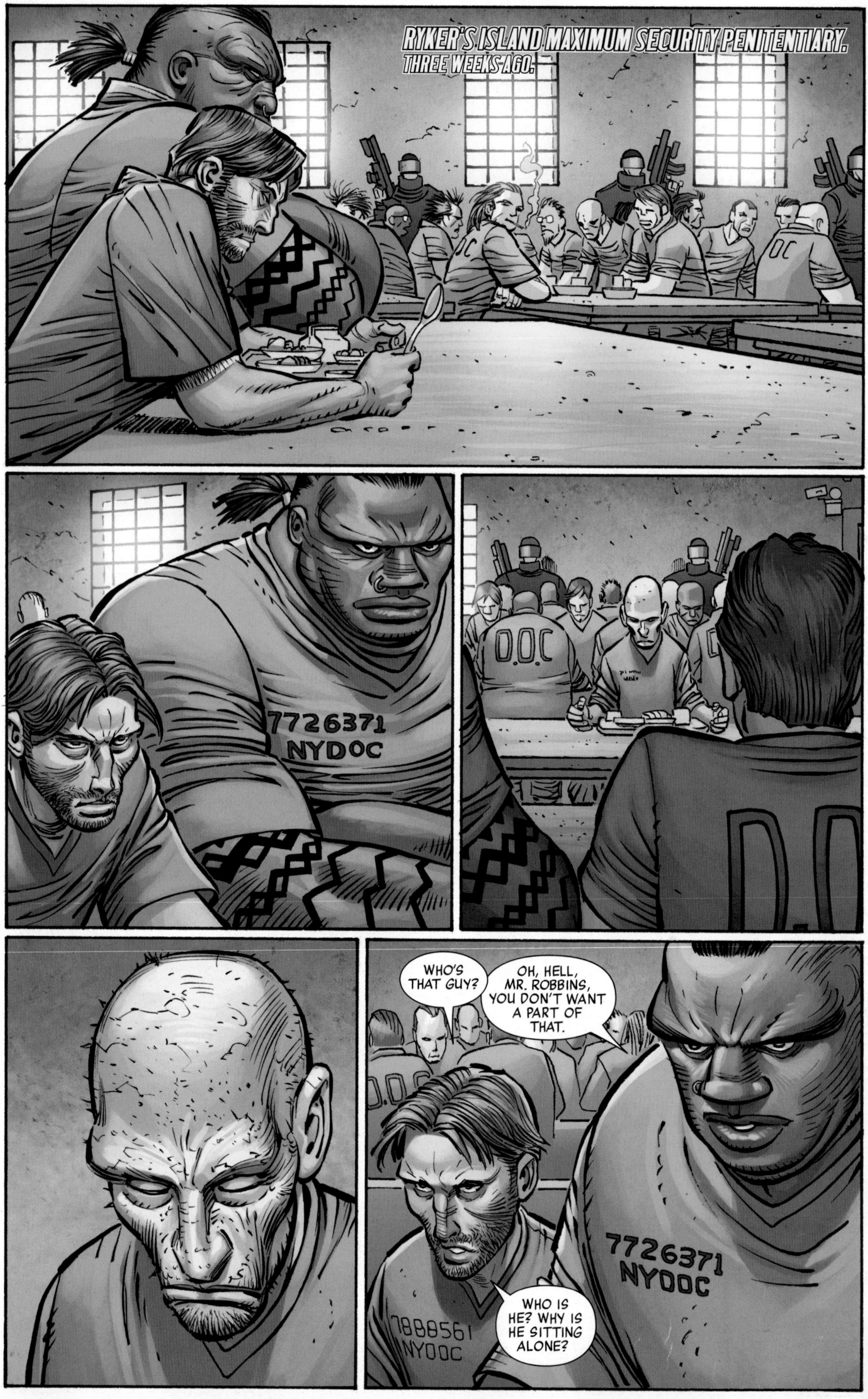
RYKER'S ISLAND MAXIMUM SECURITY PENITENTIARY.
THREE WEEKS AGO.
7726371 NYDOC
WHO'S THAT GUY?
OH, HELL, MR. ROBBINS, YOU DON'T WANT A PART OF THAT.
7726371 NYDOC
7888561 NYDOC
WHO IS HE? WHY IS HE SITTING ALONE?

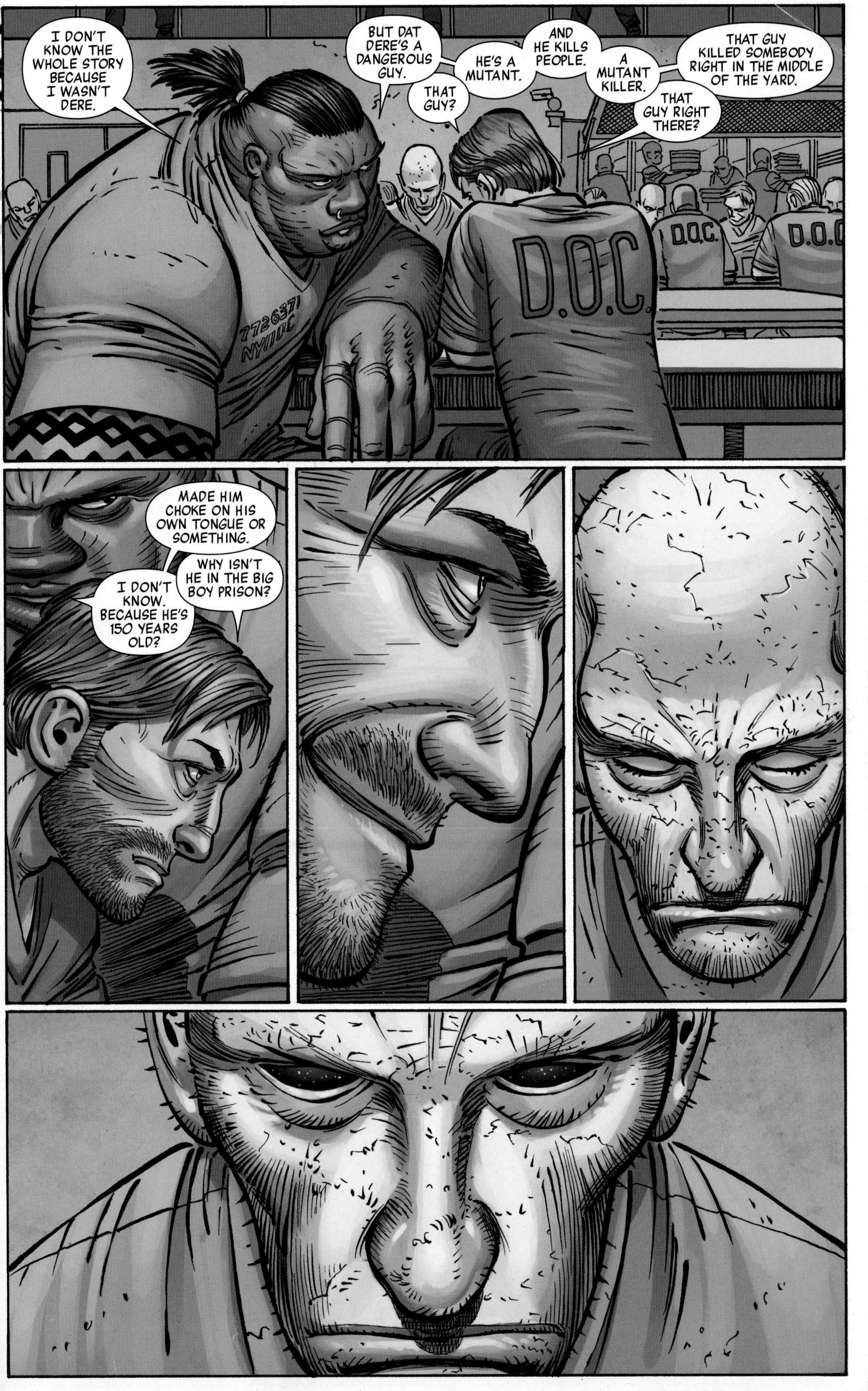
I DON'T KNOW THE WHOLE STORY BECAUSE I WASN'T DERE.
BUT DAT DERE'S A DANGEROUS GUY.
THAT GUY?
HE'S A MUTANT.
AND HE KILLS PEOPLE.
A MUTANT KILLER.
THAT GUY KILLED SOMEBODY RIGHT IN THE MIDDLE OF THE YARD.
THAT GUY RIGHT THERE?
MADE HIM CHOKE ON HIS OWN TONGUE OR SOMETHING.
WHY ISN'T HE IN THE BIG BOY PRISON?
I DON'T KNOW. BECAUSE HE'S 150 YEARS OLD?

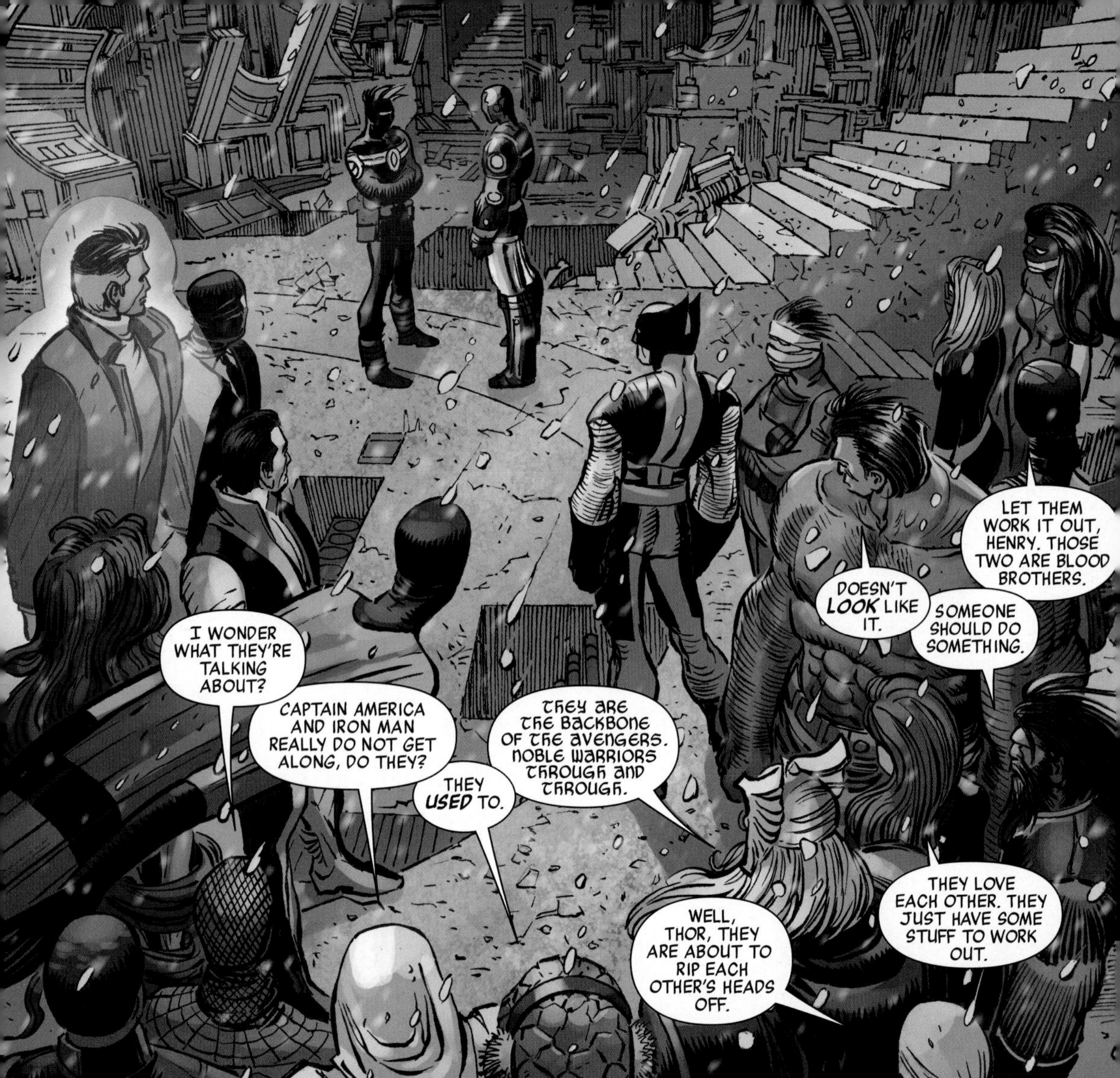
I WONDER WHAT THEY'RE TALKING ABOUT?
CAPTAIN AMERICA AND IRON MAN REALLY DO NOT GET ALONG, DO THEY?
THEY *USED* TO.
THEY ARE THE BACKBONE OF THE AVENGERS. NOBLE WARRIORS THROUGH AND THROUGH.
WELL, THOR, THEY ARE ABOUT TO RIP EACH OTHER'S HEADS OFF.
LET THEM WORK IT OUT, HENRY. THOSE TWO ARE BLOOD BROTHERS.
DOESN'T *LOOK* LIKE IT.
SOMEONE SHOULD DO SOMETHING.
THEY LOVE EACH OTHER. THEY JUST HAVE SOME STUFF TO WORK OUT.

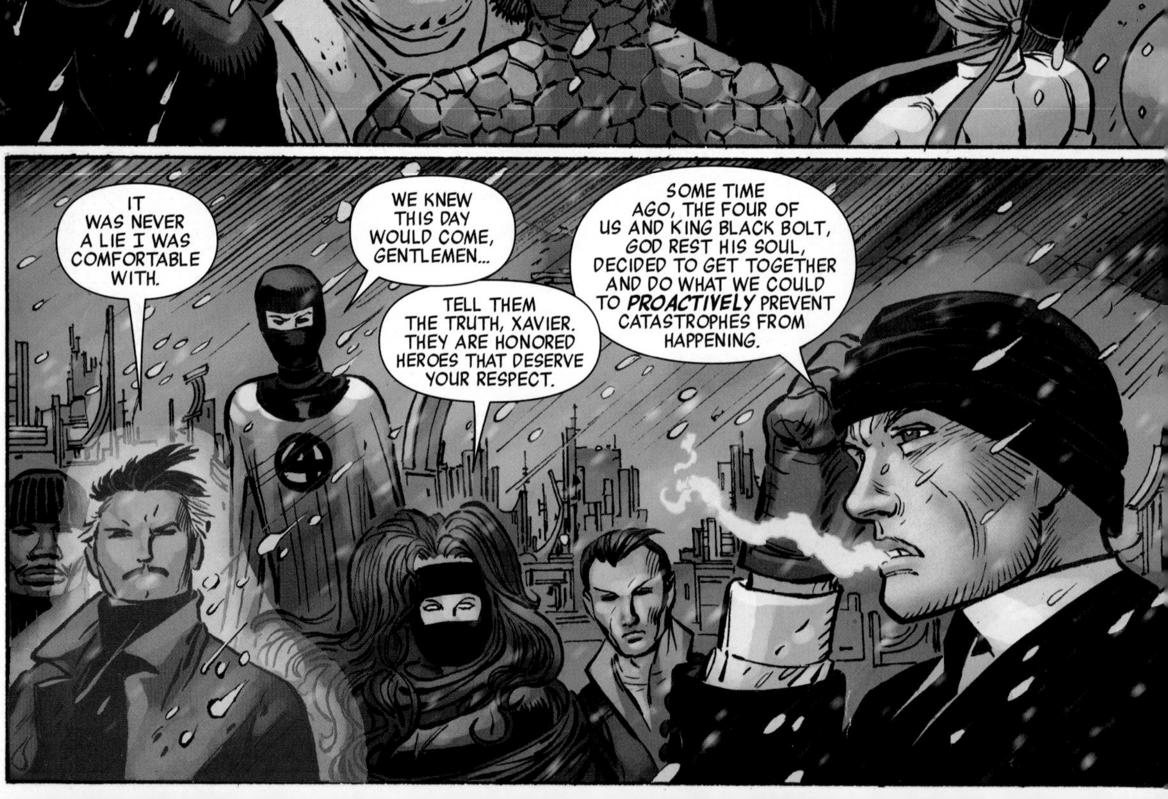
IT WAS NEVER A LIE I WAS COMFORTABLE WITH.
WE KNEW THIS DAY WOULD COME, GENTLEMEN...
TELL THEM THE TRUTH, XAVIER. THEY ARE HONORED HEROES THAT DESERVE YOUR RESPECT.
SOME TIME AGO, THE FOUR OF US AND KING BLACK BOLT, GOD REST HIS SOUL, DECIDED TO GET TOGETHER AND DO WHAT WE COULD TO *PROACTIVELY* PREVENT CATASTROPHES FROM HAPPENING.

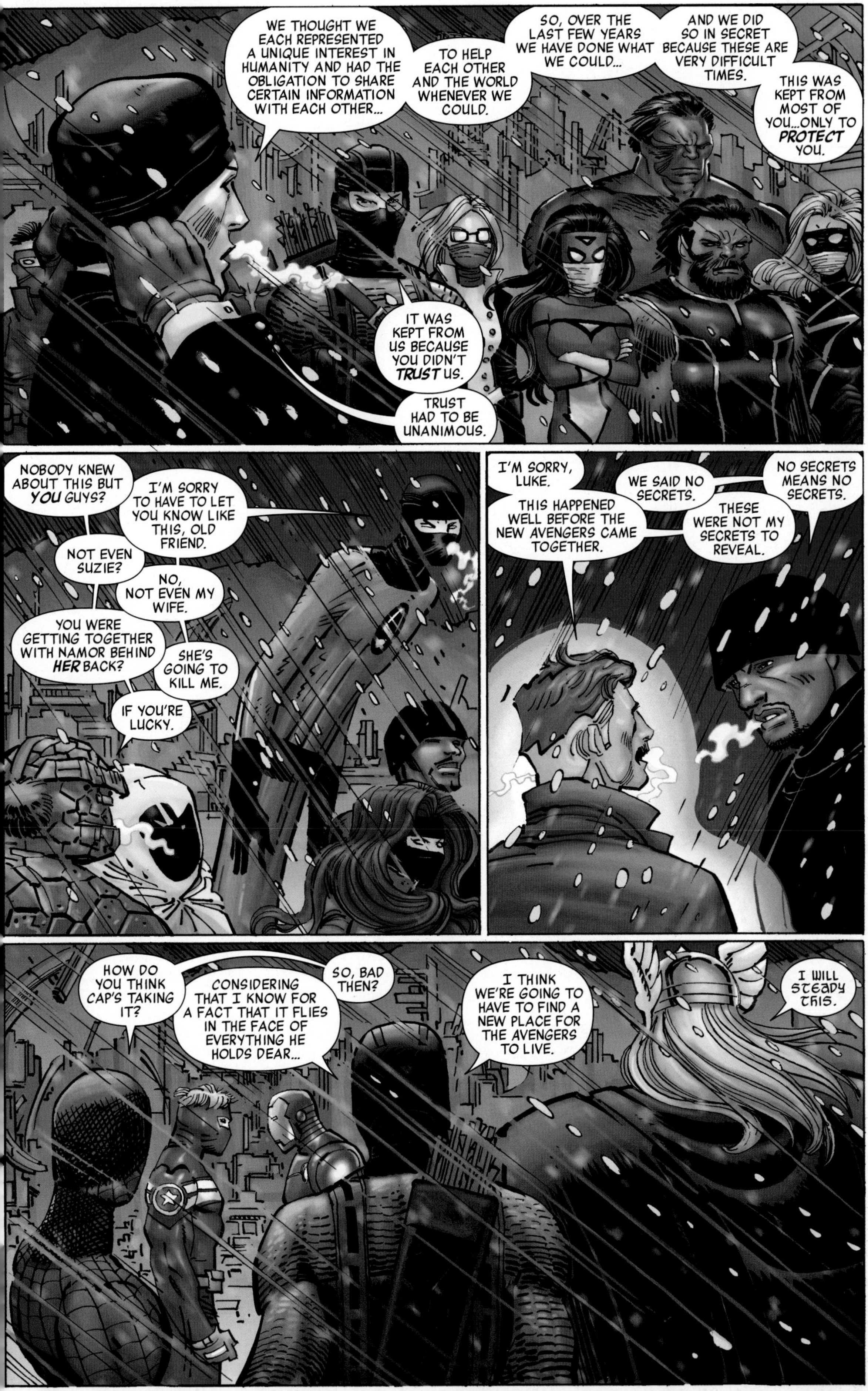

WE THOUGHT WE EACH REPRESENTED A UNIQUE INTEREST IN HUMANITY AND HAD THE OBLIGATION TO SHARE CERTAIN INFORMATION WITH EACH OTHER...
TO HELP EACH OTHER AND THE WORLD WHENEVER WE COULD.
SO, OVER THE LAST FEW YEARS WE HAVE DONE WHAT WE COULD...
AND WE DID SO IN SECRET BECAUSE THESE ARE VERY DIFFICULT TIMES.
THIS WAS KEPT FROM MOST OF YOU...ONLY TO PROTECT YOU.
IT WAS KEPT FROM US BECAUSE YOU DIDN'T TRUST US.
TRUST HAD TO BE UNANIMOUS.
NOBODY KNEW ABOUT THIS BUT YOU GUYS?
I'M SORRY TO HAVE TO LET YOU KNOW LIKE THIS, OLD FRIEND.
NOT EVEN SUZIE?
NO, NOT EVEN MY WIFE.
YOU WERE GETTING TOGETHER WITH NAMOR BEHIND HER BACK?
SHE'S GOING TO KILL ME.
IF YOU'RE LUCKY.
I'M SORRY, LUKE.
THIS HAPPENED WELL BEFORE THE NEW AVENGERS CAME TOGETHER.
WE SAID NO SECRETS.
NO SECRETS MEANS NO SECRETS.
THESE WERE NOT MY SECRETS TO REVEAL.
HOW DO YOU THINK CAP'S TAKING IT?
CONSIDERING THAT I KNOW FOR A FACT THAT IT FLIES IN THE FACE OF EVERYTHING HE HOLDS DEAR...
SO, BAD THEN?
I THINK WE'RE GOING TO HAVE TO FIND A NEW PLACE FOR THE AVENGERS TO LIVE.
I WILL STEADY THIS.

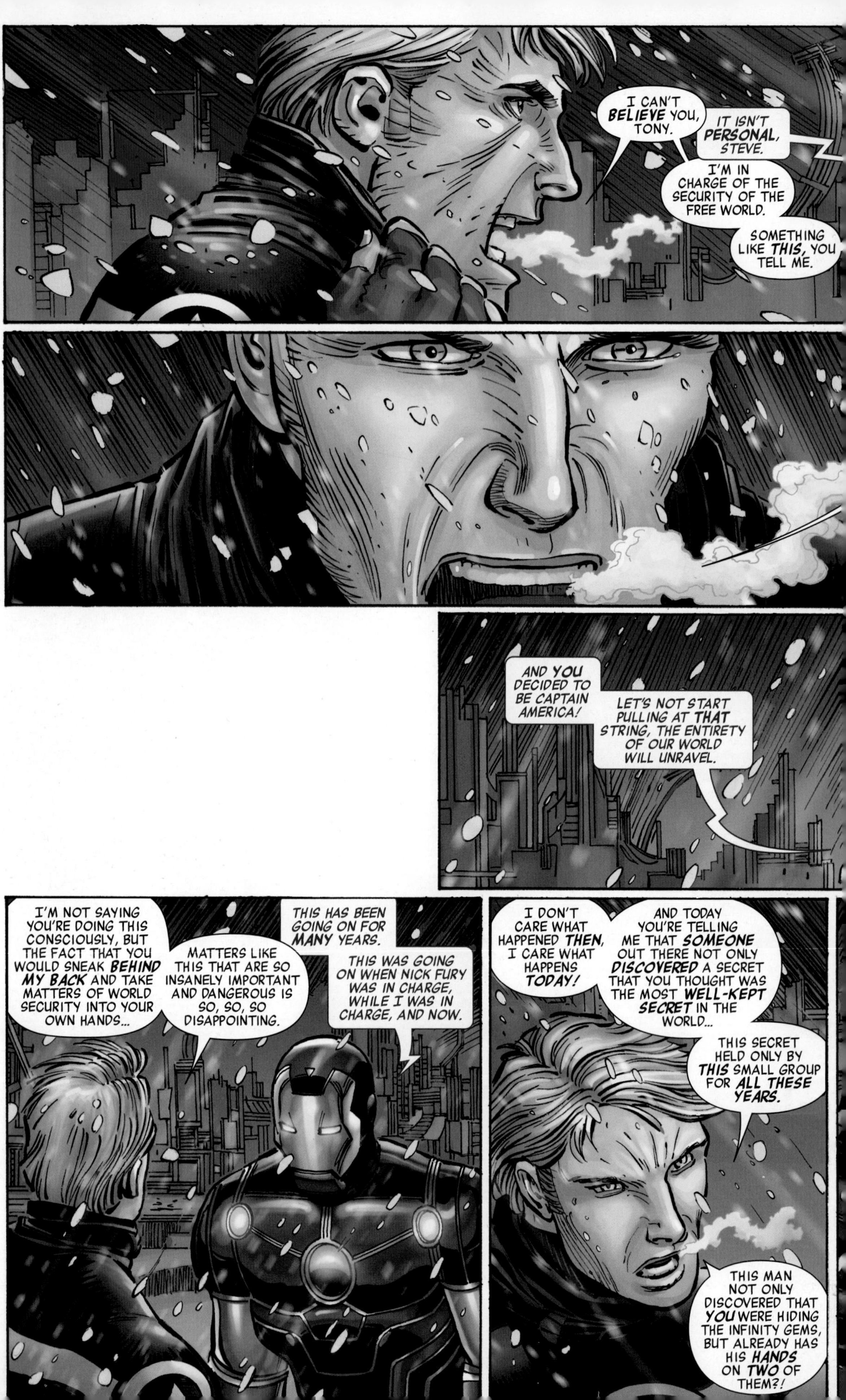
I CAN'T BELIEVE YOU, TONY.
IT ISN'T PERSONAL, STEVE.
I'M IN CHARGE OF THE SECURITY OF THE FREE WORLD.
SOMETHING LIKE THIS, YOU TELL ME.
AND YOU DECIDED TO BE CAPTAIN AMERICA!
LET'S NOT START PULLING AT THAT STRING, THE ENTIRETY OF OUR WORLD WILL UNRAVEL.
I'M NOT SAYING YOU'RE DOING THIS CONSCIOUSLY, BUT THE FACT THAT YOU WOULD SNEAK BEHIND MY BACK AND TAKE MATTERS OF WORLD SECURITY INTO YOUR OWN HANDS...
MATTERS LIKE THIS THAT ARE SO INSANELY IMPORTANT AND DANGEROUS IS SO, SO, SO DISAPPOINTING.
THIS HAS BEEN GOING ON FOR MANY YEARS.
THIS WAS GOING ON WHEN NICK FURY WAS IN CHARGE, WHILE I WAS IN CHARGE, AND NOW.
I DON'T CARE WHAT HAPPENED THEN, I CARE WHAT HAPPENS TODAY!
AND TODAY YOU'RE TELLING ME THAT SOMEONE OUT THERE NOT ONLY DISCOVERED A SECRET THAT YOU THOUGHT WAS THE MOST WELL-KEPT SECRET IN THE WORLD...
THIS SECRET HELD ONLY BY THIS SMALL GROUP FOR ALL THESE YEARS.
THIS MAN NOT ONLY DISCOVERED THAT YOU WERE HIDING THE INFINITY GEMS, BUT ALREADY HAS HIS HANDS ON TWO OF THEM?!

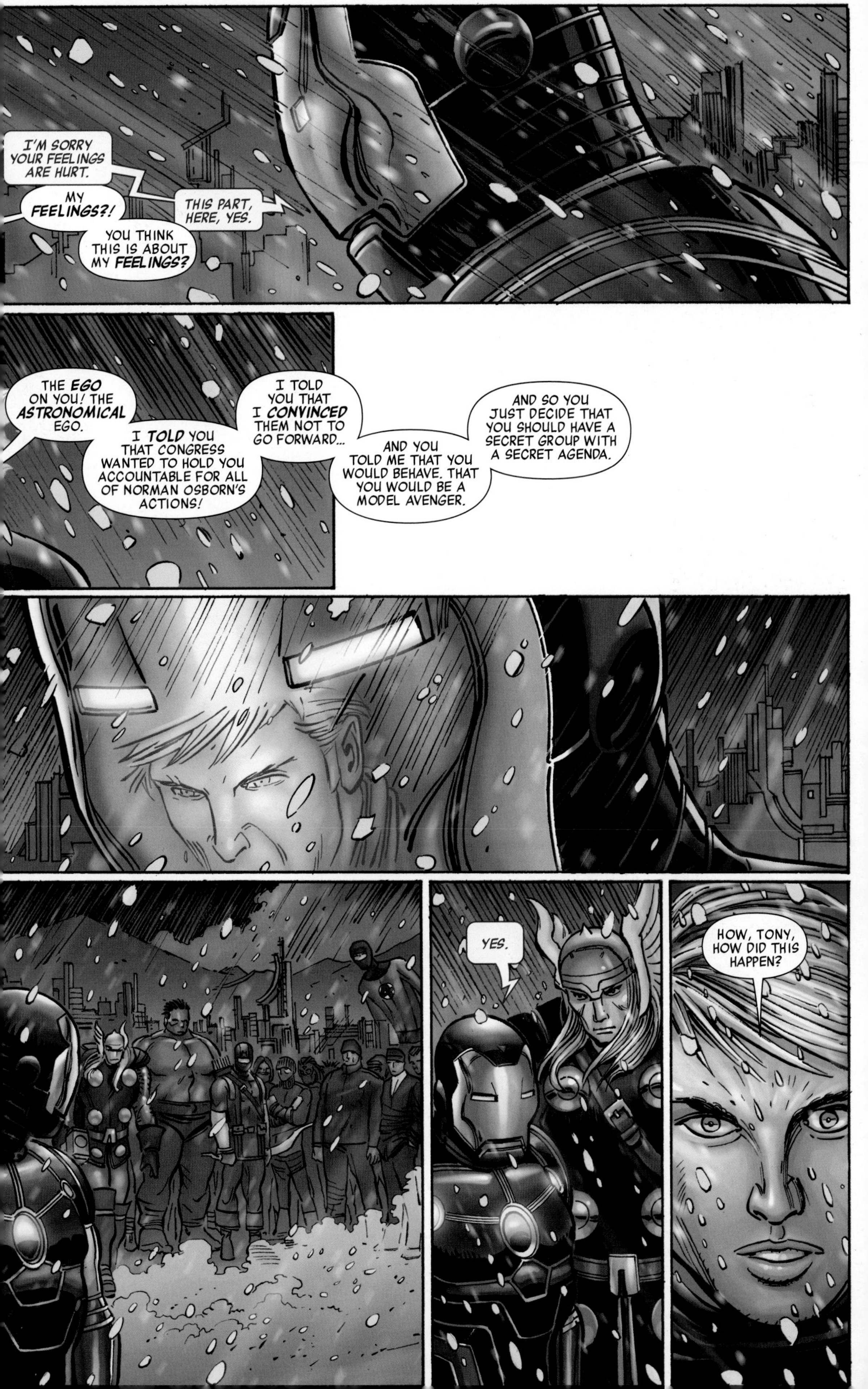

I'M SORRY YOUR FEELINGS ARE HURT.
MY FEELINGS?!
THIS PART, HERE, YES.
YOU THINK THIS IS ABOUT MY FEELINGS?
THE EGO ON YOU! THE ASTRONOMICAL EGO.
I TOLD YOU THAT CONGRESS WANTED TO HOLD YOU ACCOUNTABLE FOR ALL OF NORMAN OSBORN'S ACTIONS!
I TOLD YOU THAT I CONVINCED THEM NOT TO GO FORWARD...
AND YOU TOLD ME THAT YOU WOULD BEHAVE. THAT YOU WOULD BE A MODEL AVENGER.
AND SO YOU JUST DECIDE THAT YOU SHOULD HAVE A SECRET GROUP WITH A SECRET AGENDA.
YES.
HOW, TONY, HOW DID THIS HAPPEN?

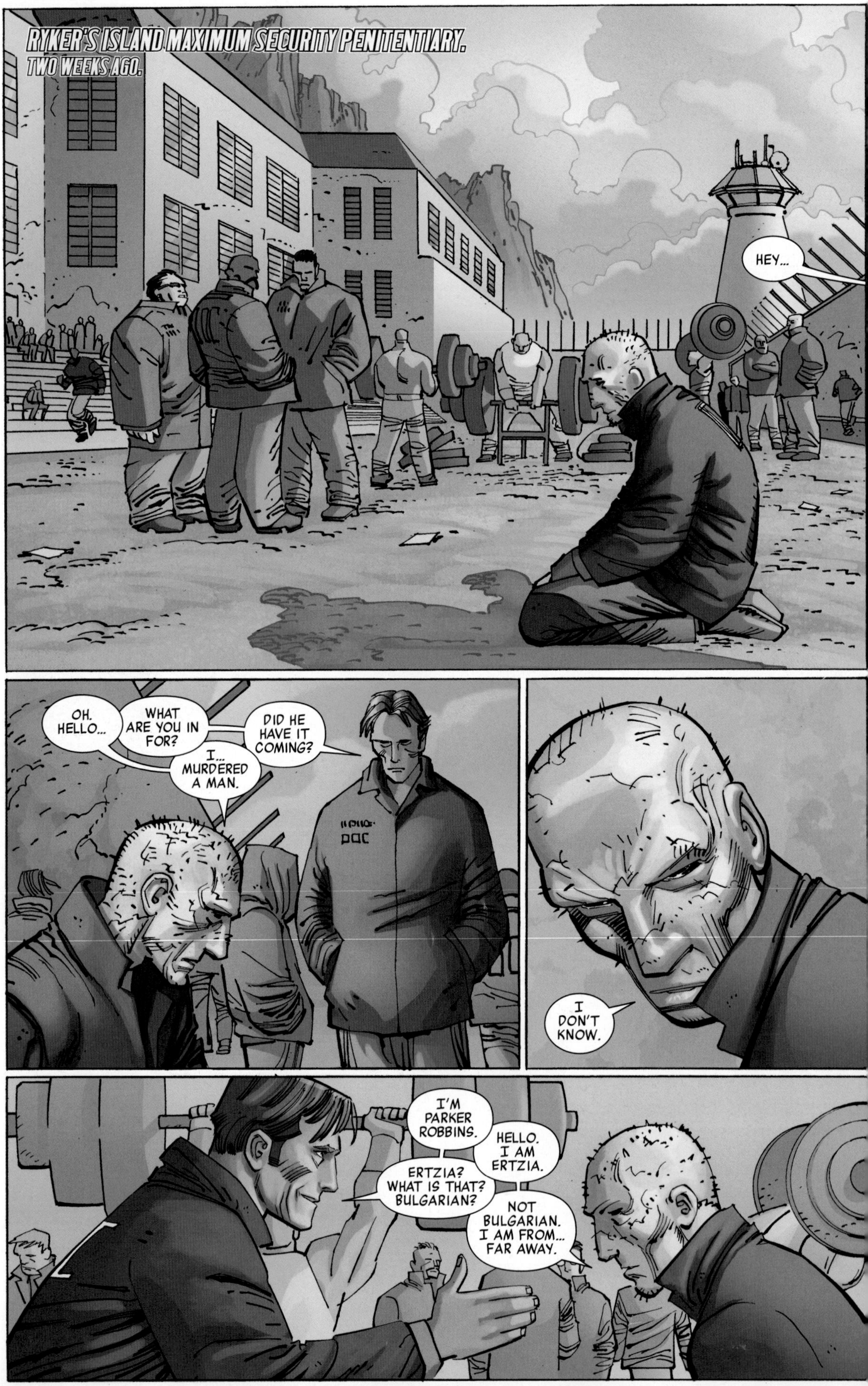
RYKER'S ISLAND MAXIMUM SECURITY PENITENTIARY.
TWO WEEKS AGO.
HEY...
OH. HELLO...
WHAT ARE YOU IN FOR?
I... MURDERED A MAN.
DID HE HAVE IT COMING?
I DON'T KNOW.
I'M PARKER ROBBINS.
HELLO. I AM ERTZIA.
ERTZIA? WHAT IS THAT? BULGARIAN?
NOT BULGARIAN. I AM FROM... FAR AWAY.

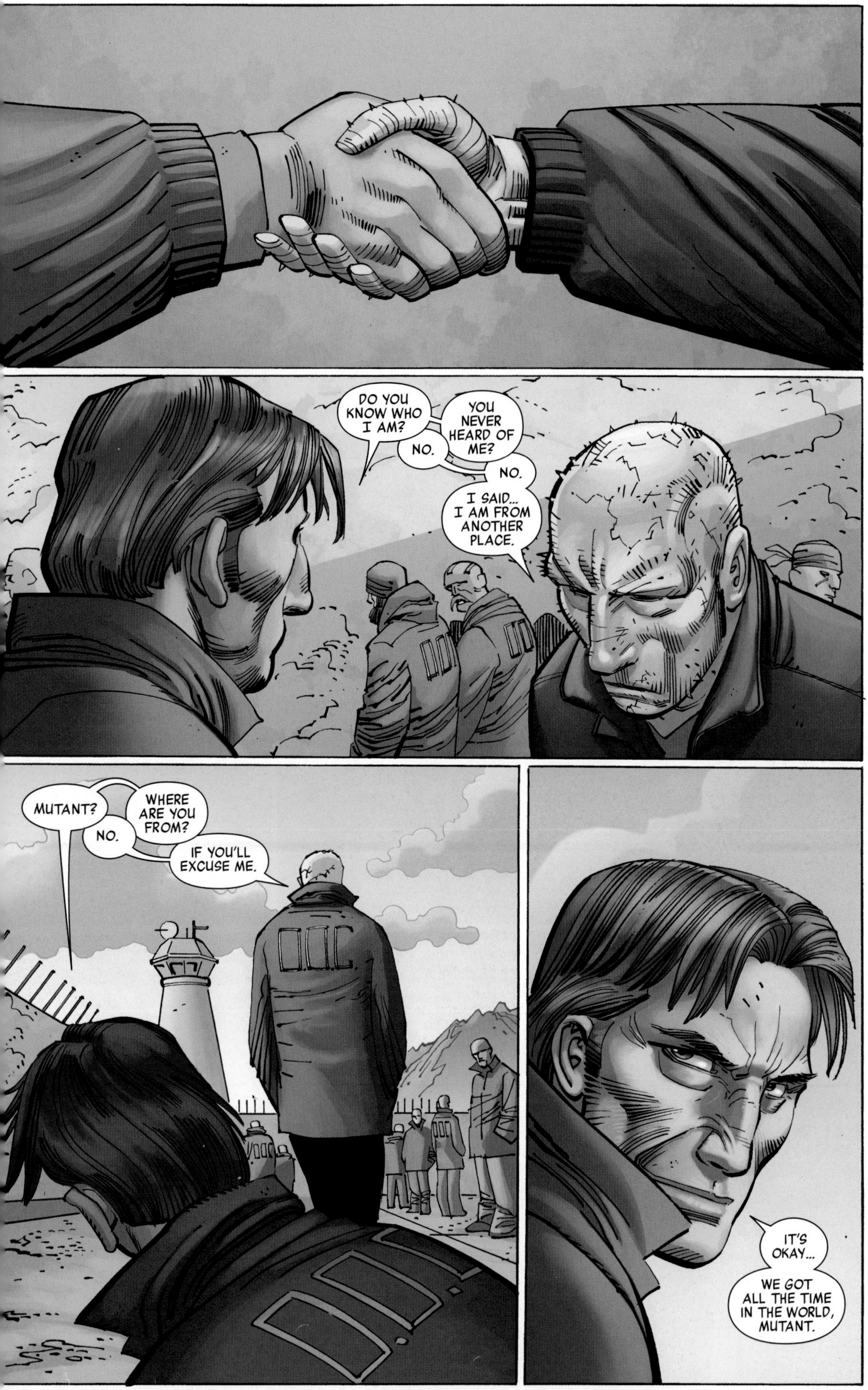
DO YOU KNOW WHO I AM?
NO.
YOU NEVER HEARD OF ME?
NO.
I SAID... I AM FROM ANOTHER PLACE.
MUTANT?
NO.
WHERE ARE YOU FROM?
IF YOU'LL EXCUSE ME.
IT'S OKAY...
WE GOT ALL THE TIME IN THE WORLD, MUTANT.

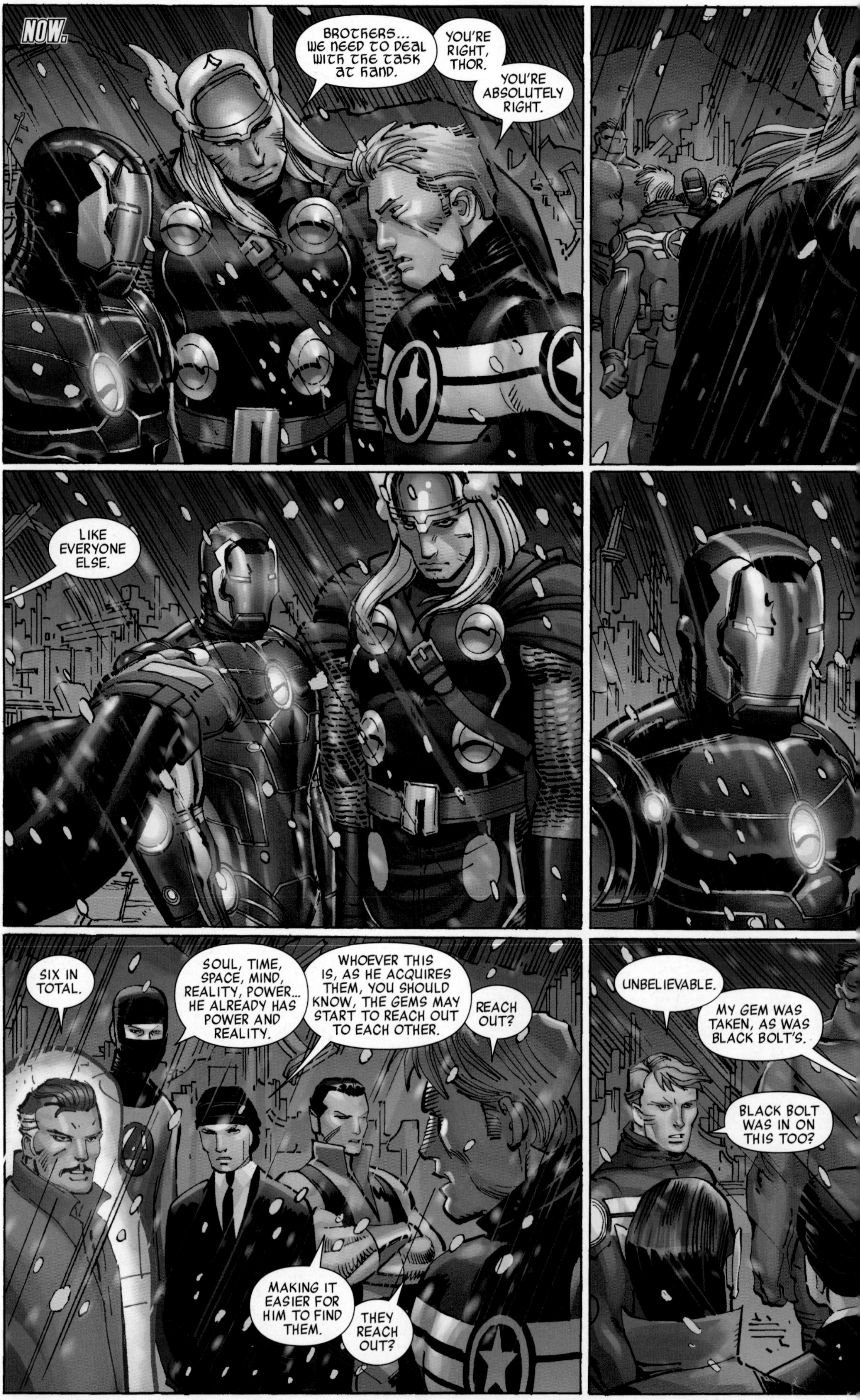
NOW.
BROTHERS... WE NEED TO DEAL WITH THE TASK AT HAND.
YOU'RE RIGHT, THOR.
YOU'RE ABSOLUTELY RIGHT.
LIKE EVERYONE ELSE.
SIX IN TOTAL.
SOUL, TIME, SPACE, MIND, REALITY, POWER... HE ALREADY HAS POWER AND REALITY.
WHOEVER THIS IS, AS HE ACQUIRES THEM, YOU SHOULD KNOW, THE GEMS MAY START TO REACH OUT TO EACH OTHER.
REACH OUT?
MAKING IT EASIER FOR HIM TO FIND THEM.
THEY REACH OUT?
UNBELIEVABLE.
MY GEM WAS TAKEN, AS WAS BLACK BOLT'S.
BLACK BOLT WAS IN ON THIS TOO?

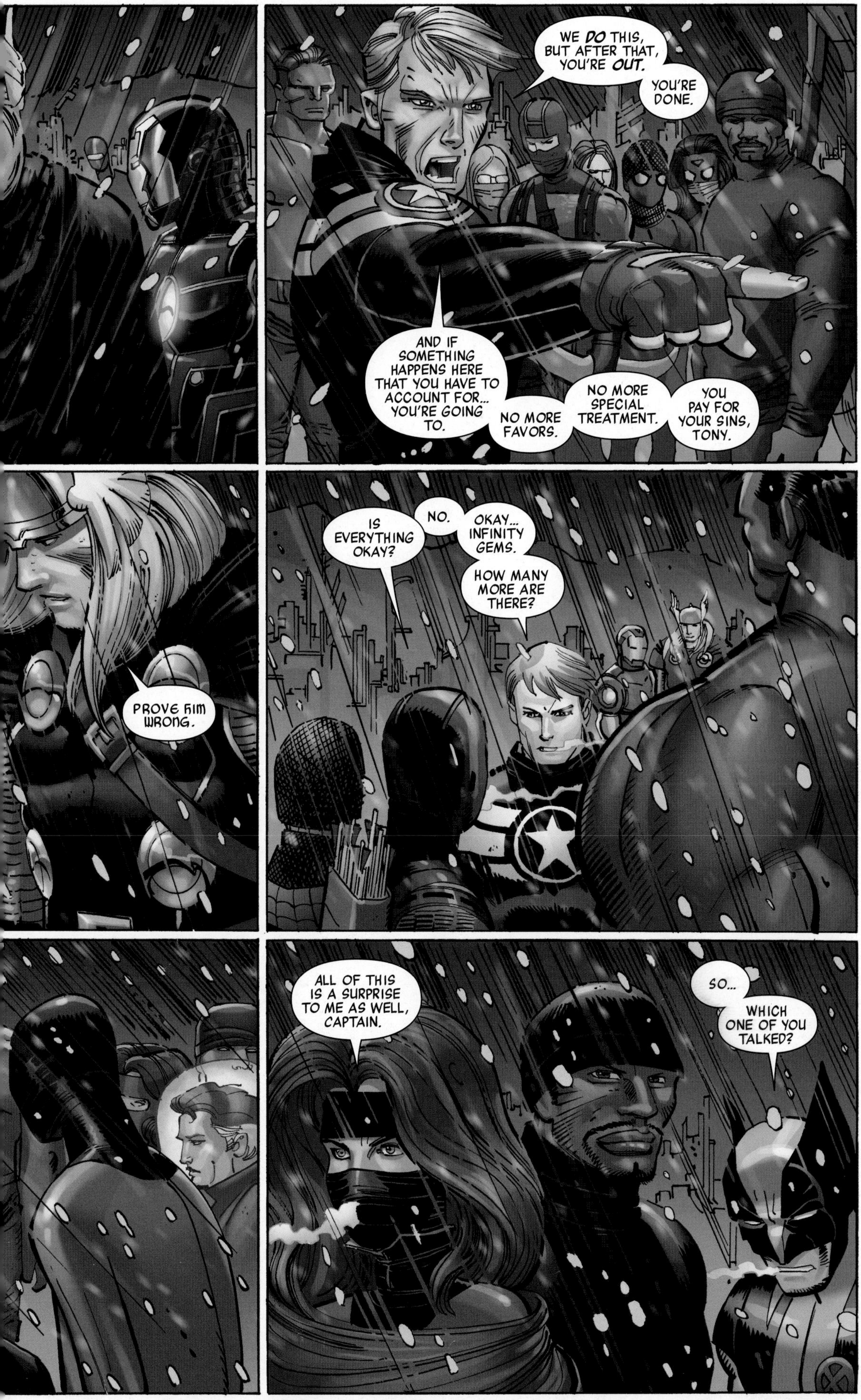
WE DO THIS, BUT AFTER THAT, YOU'RE OUT.
YOU'RE DONE.
AND IF SOMETHING HAPPENS HERE THAT YOU HAVE TO ACCOUNT FOR... YOU'RE GOING TO.
NO MORE FAVORS.
NO MORE SPECIAL TREATMENT.
YOU PAY FOR YOUR SINS, TONY.
PROVE HIM WRONG.
IS EVERYTHING OKAY?
NO.
OKAY... INFINITY GEMS.
HOW MANY MORE ARE THERE?
ALL OF THIS IS A SURPRISE TO ME AS WELL, CAPTAIN.
SO...
WHICH ONE OF YOU TALKED?

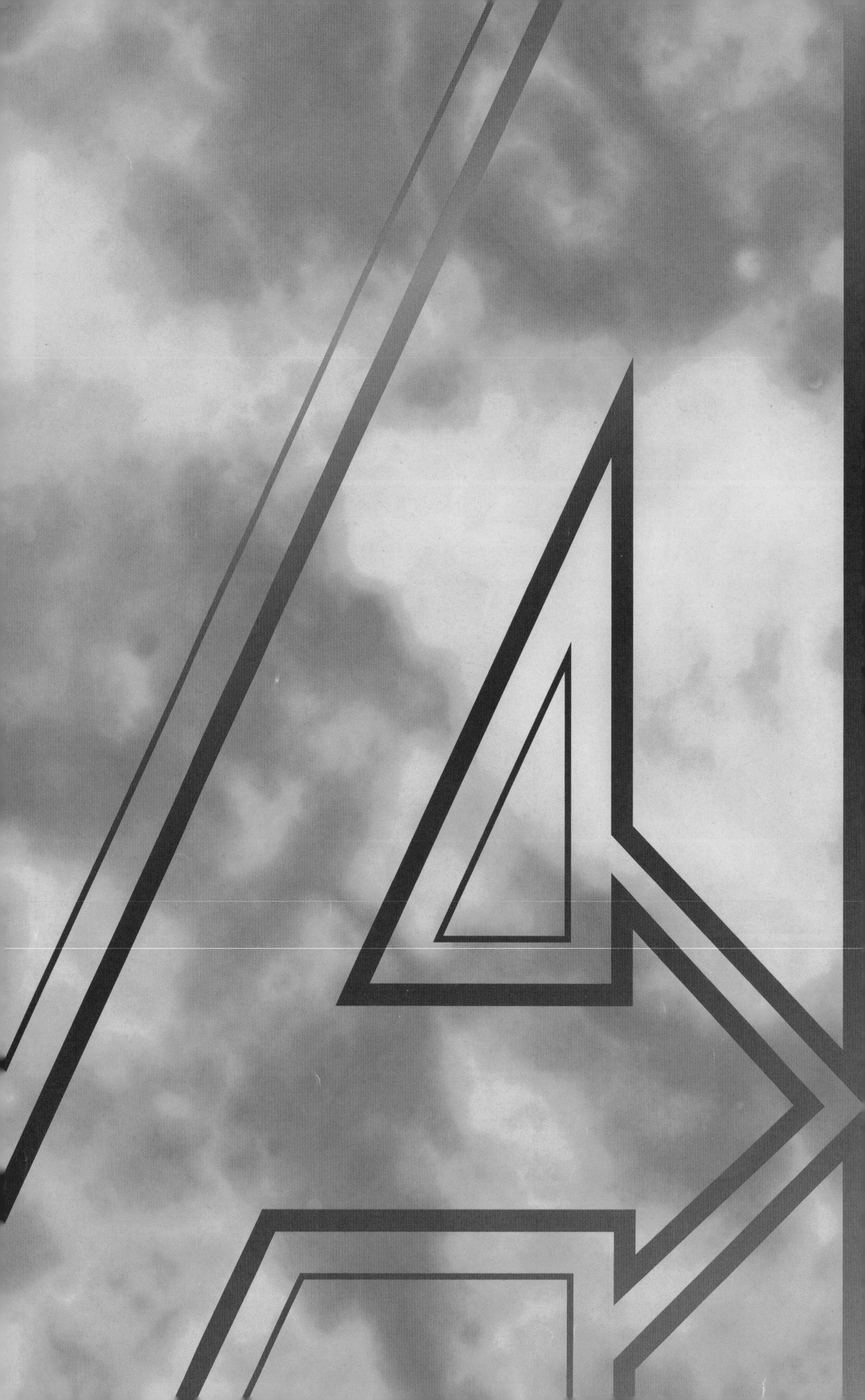

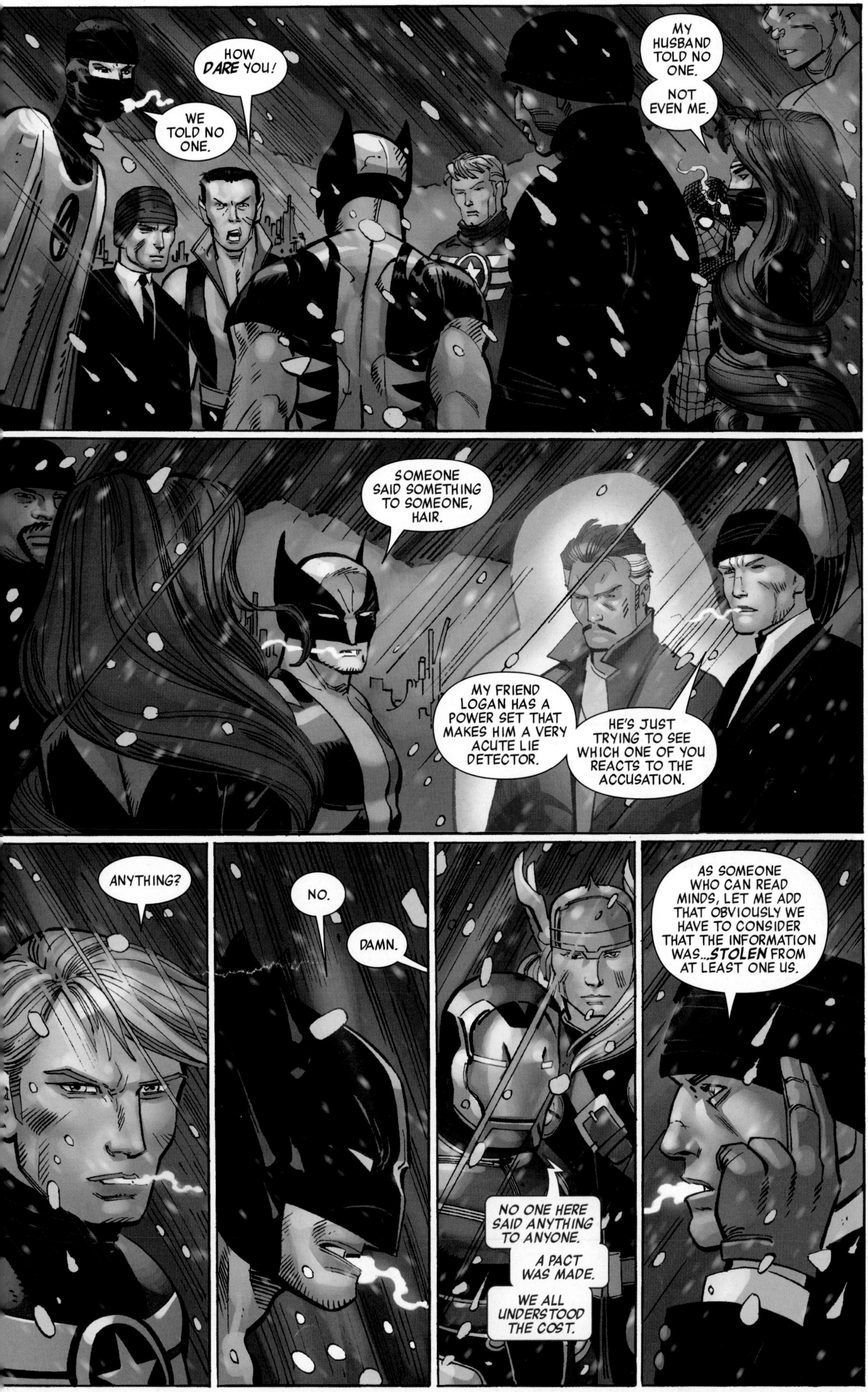
HOW DARE YOU!
WE TOLD NO ONE.
MY HUSBAND TOLD NO ONE.
NOT EVEN ME.
SOMEONE SAID SOMETHING TO SOMEONE, HAIR.
MY FRIEND LOGAN HAS A POWER SET THAT MAKES HIM A VERY ACUTE LIE DETECTOR.
HE'S JUST TRYING TO SEE WHICH ONE OF YOU REACTS TO THE ACCUSATION.
ANYTHING?
NO.
DAMN.
NO ONE HERE SAID ANYTHING TO ANYONE.
A PACT WAS MADE.
WE ALL UNDERSTOOD THE COST.
AS SOMEONE WHO CAN READ MINDS, LET ME ADD THAT OBVIOUSLY WE HAVE TO CONSIDER THAT THE INFORMATION WAS...STOLEN FROM AT LEAST ONE US.

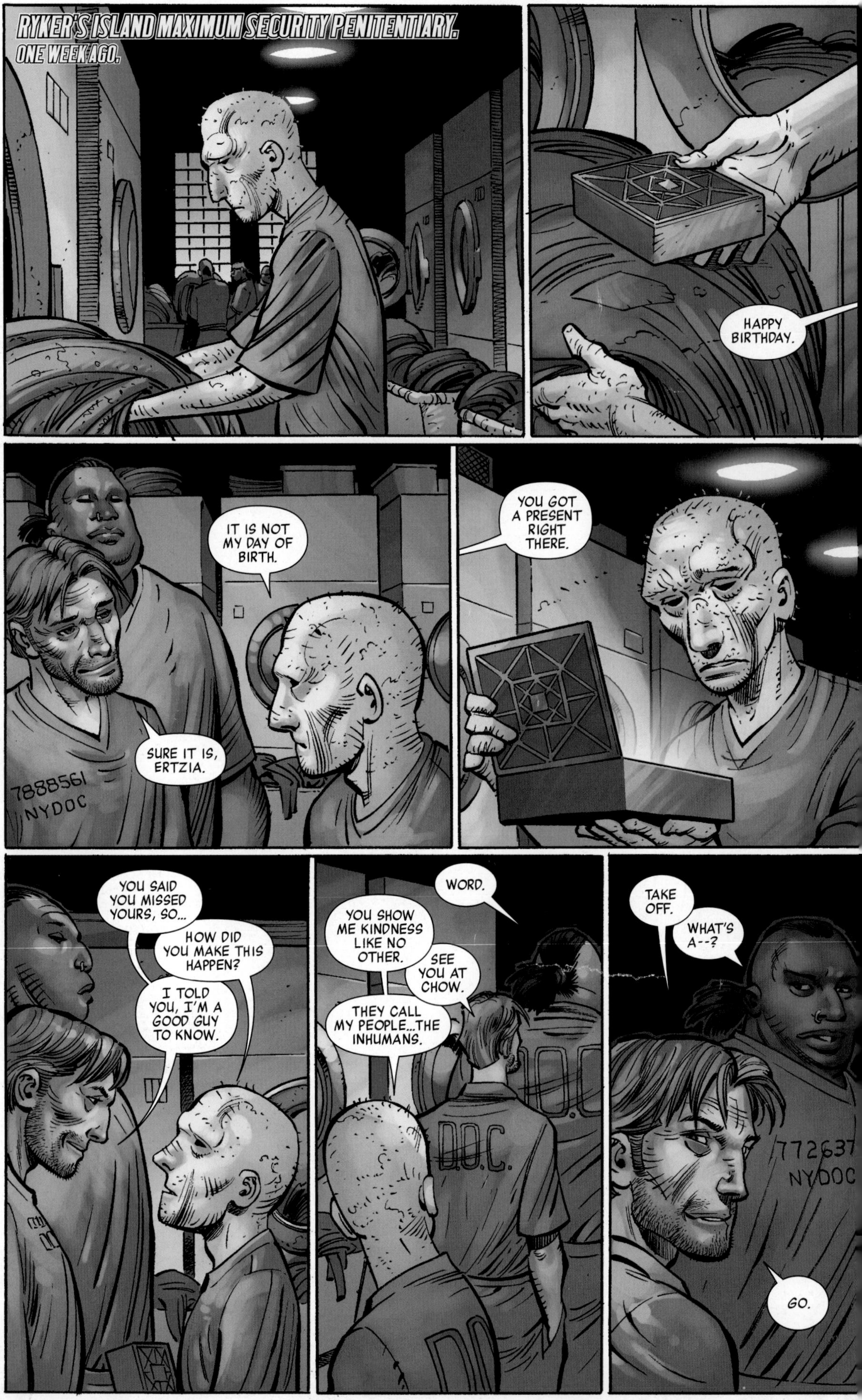
RYKER'S ISLAND MAXIMUM SECURITY PENITENTIARY.
ONE WEEK AGO.
HAPPY BIRTHDAY.
IT IS NOT MY DAY OF BIRTH.
SURE IT IS, ERTZIA.
7888561 NYDOC
YOU GOT A PRESENT RIGHT THERE.
YOU SAID YOU MISSED YOURS, SO...
HOW DID YOU MAKE THIS HAPPEN?
I TOLD YOU, I'M A GOOD GUY TO KNOW.
YOU SHOW ME KINDNESS LIKE NO OTHER.
WORD.
SEE YOU AT CHOW.
THEY CALL MY PEOPLE...THE INHUMANS.
D.O.C.
TAKE OFF.
WHAT'S A--?
GO.

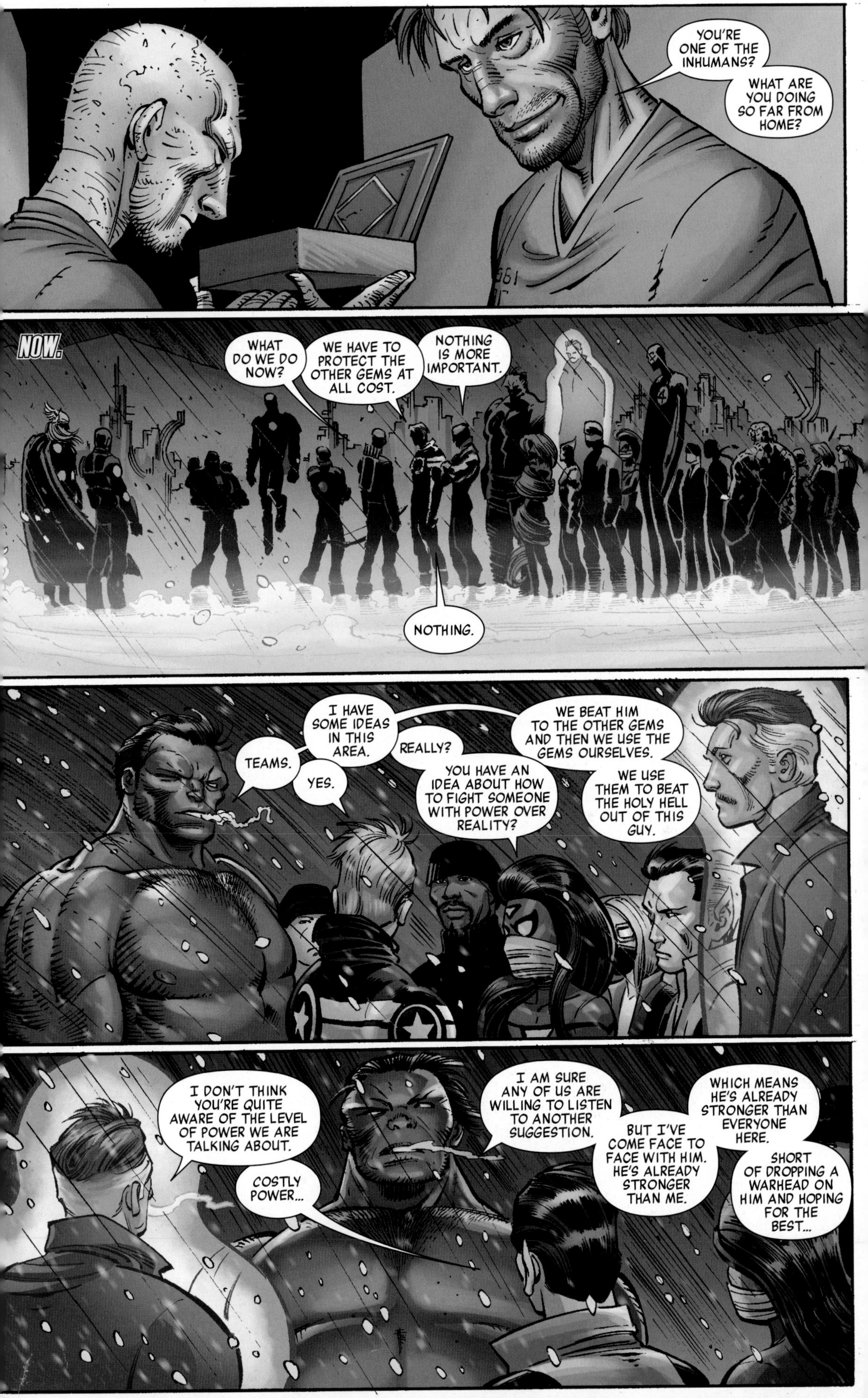
YOU'RE ONE OF THE INHUMANS?
WHAT ARE YOU DOING SO FAR FROM HOME?
NOW.
WHAT DO WE DO NOW?
WE HAVE TO PROTECT THE OTHER GEMS AT ALL COST.
NOTHING IS MORE IMPORTANT.
NOTHING.
TEAMS.
I HAVE SOME IDEAS IN THIS AREA.
YES.
REALLY?
YOU HAVE AN IDEA ABOUT HOW TO FIGHT SOMEONE WITH POWER OVER REALITY?
WE BEAT HIM TO THE OTHER GEMS AND THEN WE USE THE GEMS OURSELVES.
WE USE THEM TO BEAT THE HOLY HELL OUT OF THIS GUY.
I DON'T THINK YOU'RE QUITE AWARE OF THE LEVEL OF POWER WE ARE TALKING ABOUT.
COSTLY POWER...
I AM SURE ANY OF US ARE WILLING TO LISTEN TO ANOTHER SUGGESTION.
BUT I'VE COME FACE TO FACE WITH HIM. HE'S ALREADY STRONGER THAN ME.
WHICH MEANS HE'S ALREADY STRONGER THAN EVERYONE HERE.
SHORT OF DROPPING A WARHEAD ON HIM AND HOPING FOR THE BEST...

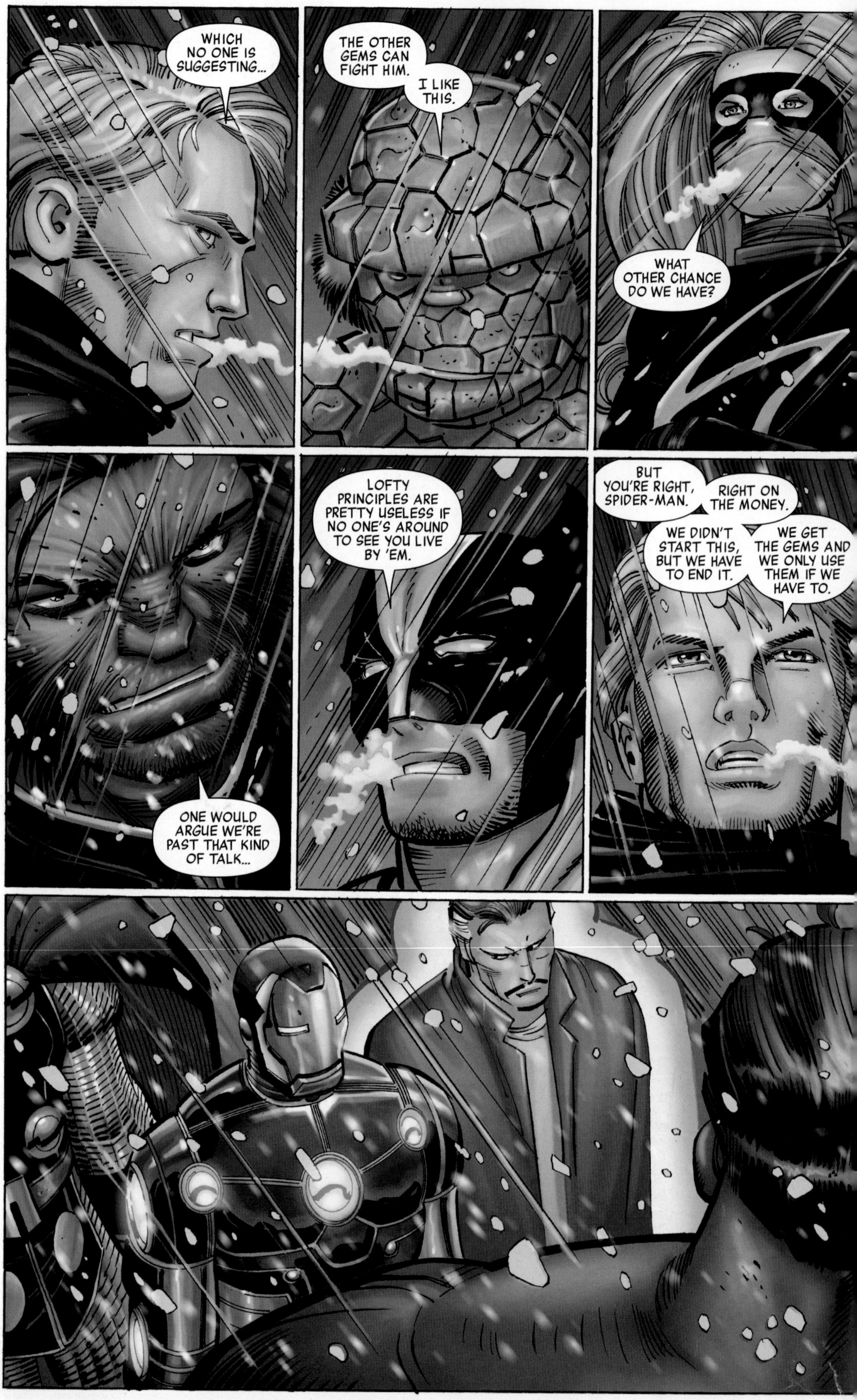
WHICH NO ONE IS SUGGESTING...
THE OTHER GEMS CAN FIGHT HIM.
I LIKE THIS.
WHAT OTHER CHANCE DO WE HAVE?
ONE WOULD ARGUE WE'RE PAST THAT KIND OF TALK...
LOFTY PRINCIPLES ARE PRETTY USELESS IF NO ONE'S AROUND TO SEE YOU LIVE BY 'EM.
BUT YOU'RE RIGHT, SPIDER-MAN.
RIGHT ON THE MONEY.
WE DIDN'T START THIS, BUT WE HAVE TO END IT.
WE GET THE GEMS AND WE ONLY USE THEM IF WE HAVE TO.

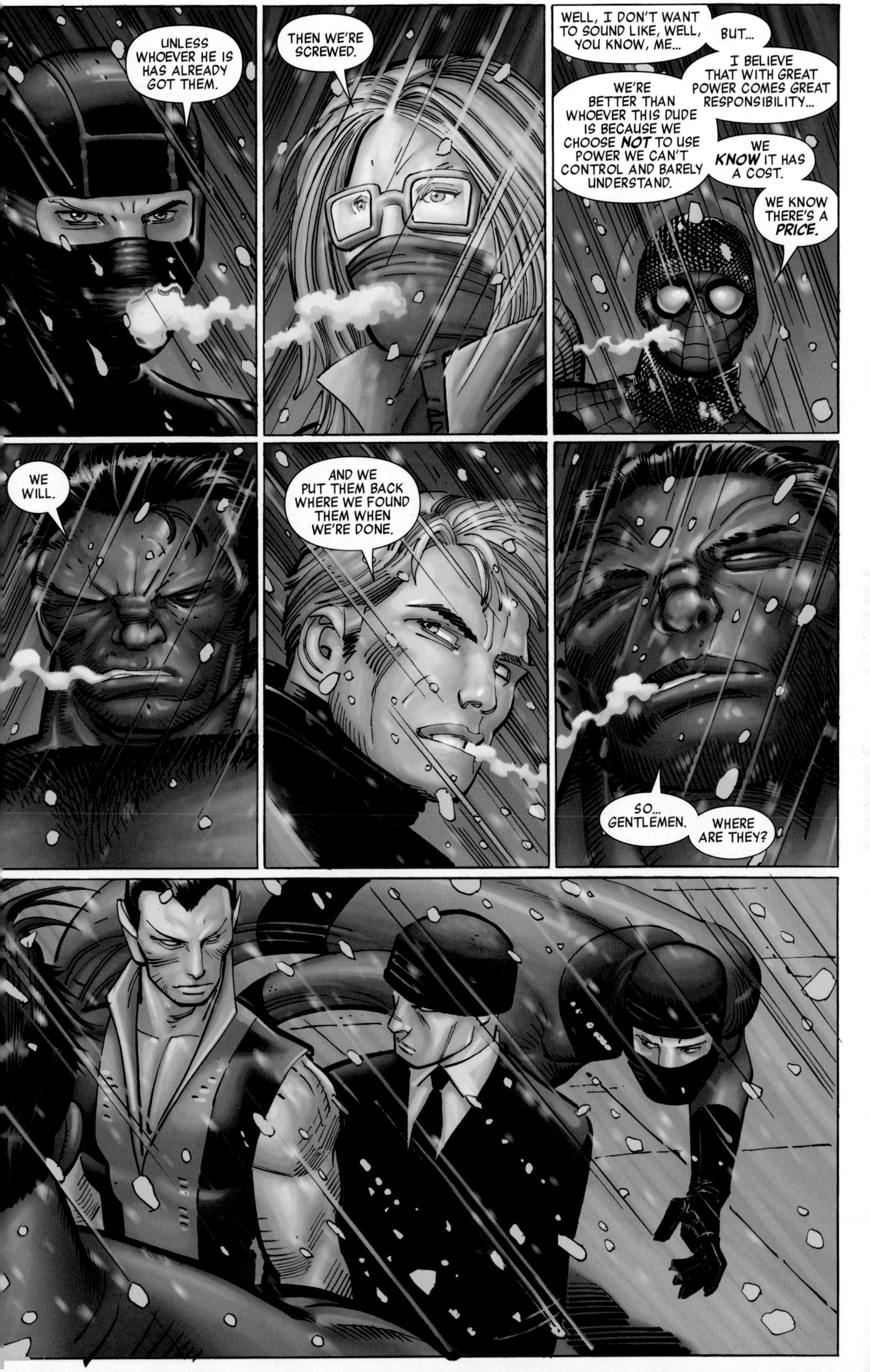
UNLESS WHOEVER HE IS HAS ALREADY GOT THEM.
THEN WE'RE SCREWED.
WELL, I DON'T WANT TO SOUND LIKE, WELL, YOU KNOW, ME...
BUT...
I BELIEVE THAT WITH GREAT POWER COMES GREAT RESPONSIBILITY...
WE'RE BETTER THAN WHOEVER THIS DUDE IS BECAUSE WE CHOOSE NOT TO USE POWER WE CAN'T CONTROL AND BARELY UNDERSTAND.
WE KNOW IT HAS A COST.
WE KNOW THERE'S A PRICE.
WE WILL.
AND WE PUT THEM BACK WHERE WE FOUND THEM WHEN WE'RE DONE.
SO... GENTLEMEN.
WHERE ARE THEY?

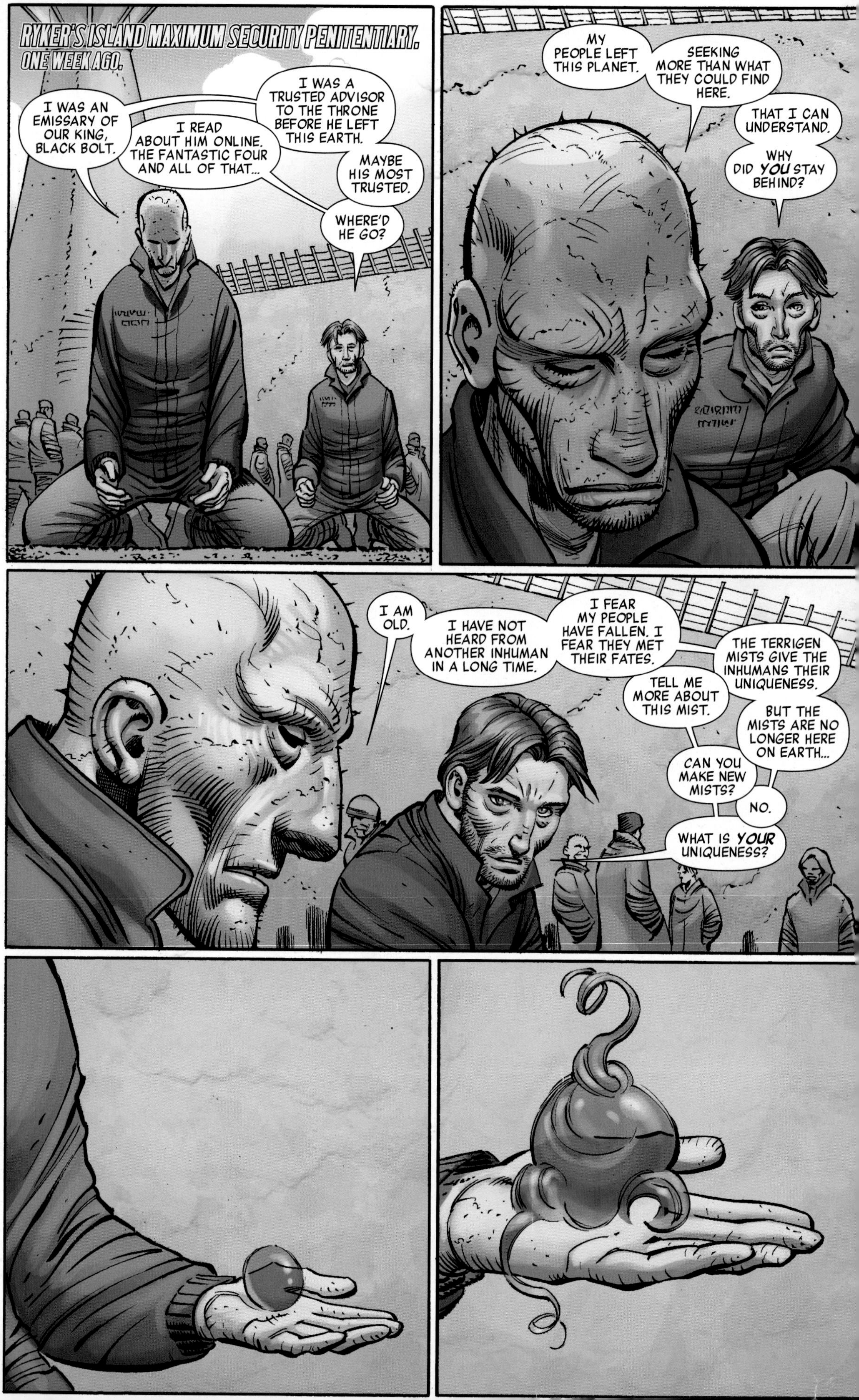
RYKER'S ISLAND MAXIMUM SECURITY PENITENTIARY. ONE WEEK AGO.
I WAS AN EMISSARY OF OUR KING, BLACK BOLT.
I READ ABOUT HIM ONLINE. THE FANTASTIC FOUR AND ALL OF THAT...
I WAS A TRUSTED ADVISOR TO THE THRONE BEFORE HE LEFT THIS EARTH.
MAYBE HIS MOST TRUSTED.
WHERE'D HE GO?
MY PEOPLE LEFT THIS PLANET.
SEEKING MORE THAN WHAT THEY COULD FIND HERE.
THAT I CAN UNDERSTAND.
WHY DID YOU STAY BEHIND?
I AM OLD.
I HAVE NOT HEARD FROM ANOTHER INHUMAN IN A LONG TIME.
I FEAR MY PEOPLE HAVE FALLEN. I FEAR THEY MET THEIR FATES.
THE TERRIGEN MISTS GIVE THE INHUMANS THEIR UNIQUENESS.
TELL ME MORE ABOUT THIS MIST.
BUT THE MISTS ARE NO LONGER HERE ON EARTH...
CAN YOU MAKE NEW MISTS?
NO.
WHAT IS YOUR UNIQUENESS?

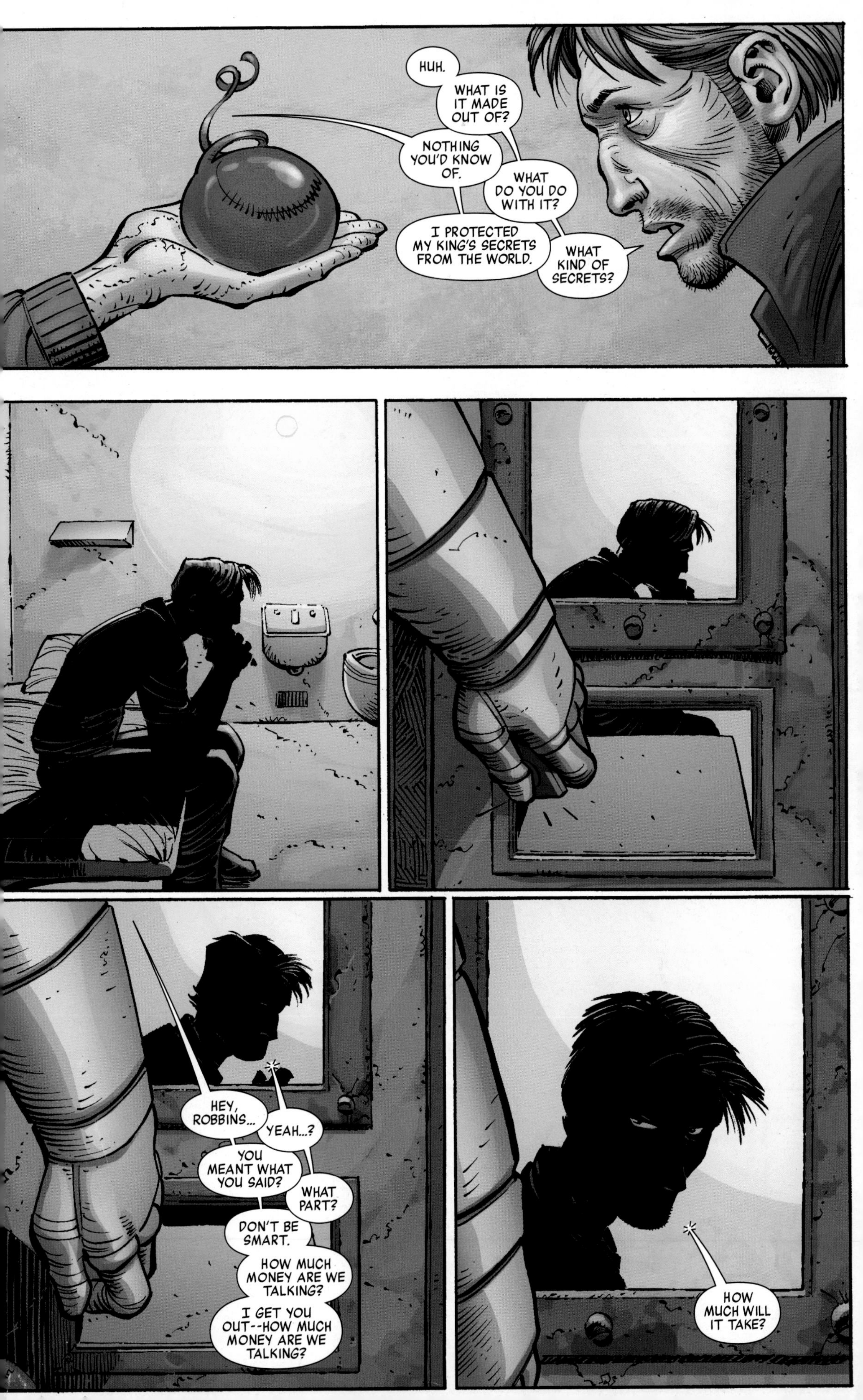
HUH.
WHAT IS IT MADE OUT OF?
NOTHING YOU'D KNOW OF.
WHAT DO YOU DO WITH IT?
I PROTECTED MY KING'S SECRETS FROM THE WORLD.
WHAT KIND OF SECRETS?
HEY, ROBBINS...
YEAH...?
YOU MEANT WHAT YOU SAID?
WHAT PART?
DON'T BE SMART.
HOW MUCH MONEY ARE WE TALKING?
I GET YOU OUT--HOW MUCH MONEY ARE WE TALKING?
HOW MUCH WILL IT TAKE?

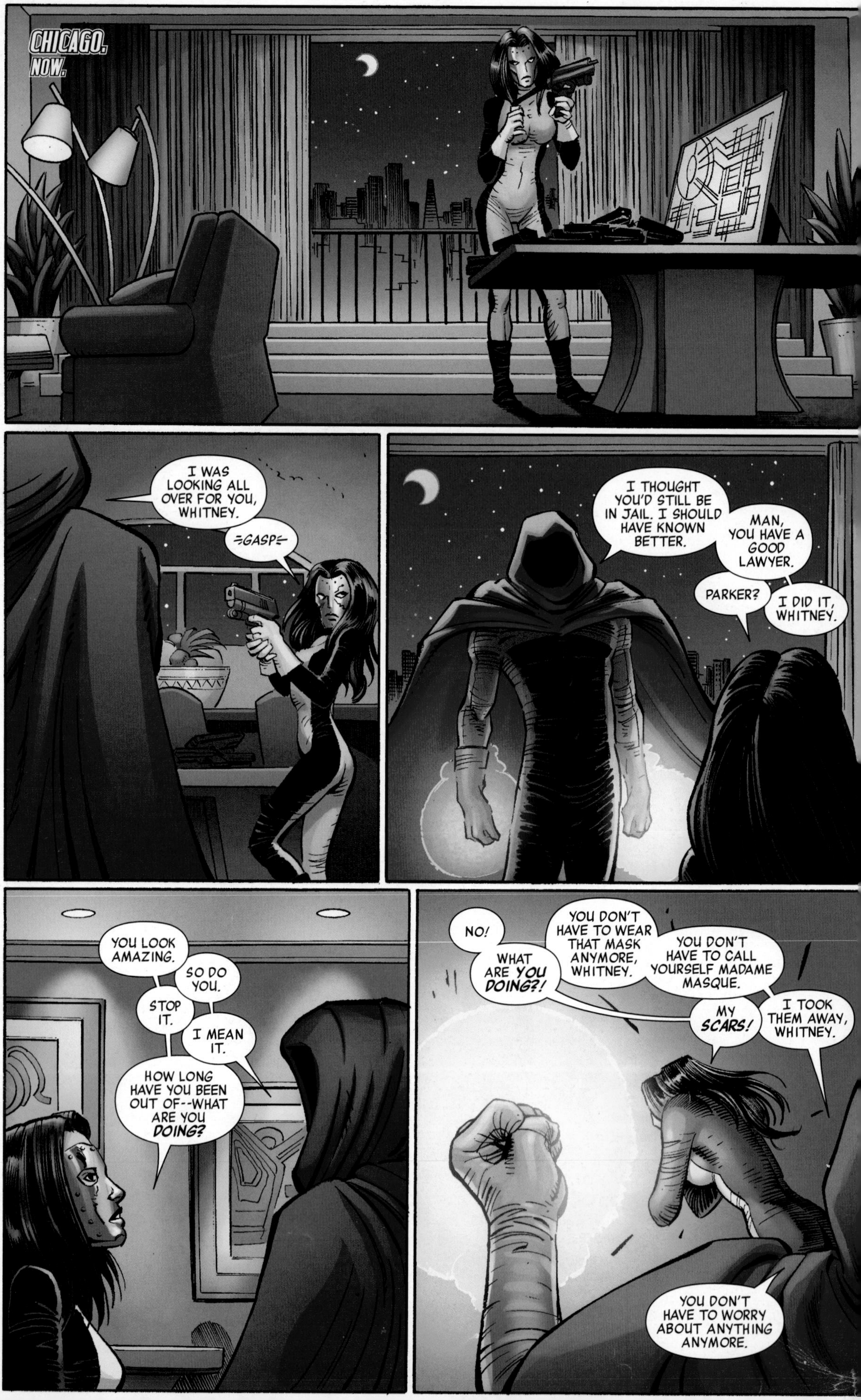
CHICAGO. NOW.
I WAS LOOKING ALL OVER FOR YOU, WHITNEY.
GASP
I THOUGHT YOU'D STILL BE IN JAIL. I SHOULD HAVE KNOWN BETTER.
MAN, YOU HAVE A GOOD LAWYER.
PARKER?
I DID IT, WHITNEY.
YOU LOOK AMAZING.
SO DO YOU.
STOP IT.
I MEAN IT.
HOW LONG HAVE YOU BEEN OUT OF--WHAT ARE YOU DOING?
NO!
WHAT ARE YOU DOING?!
YOU DON'T HAVE TO WEAR THAT MASK ANYMORE, WHITNEY.
YOU DON'T HAVE TO CALL YOURSELF MADAME MASQUE.
MY SCARS!
I TOOK THEM AWAY, WHITNEY.
YOU DON'T HAVE TO WORRY ABOUT ANYTHING ANYMORE.

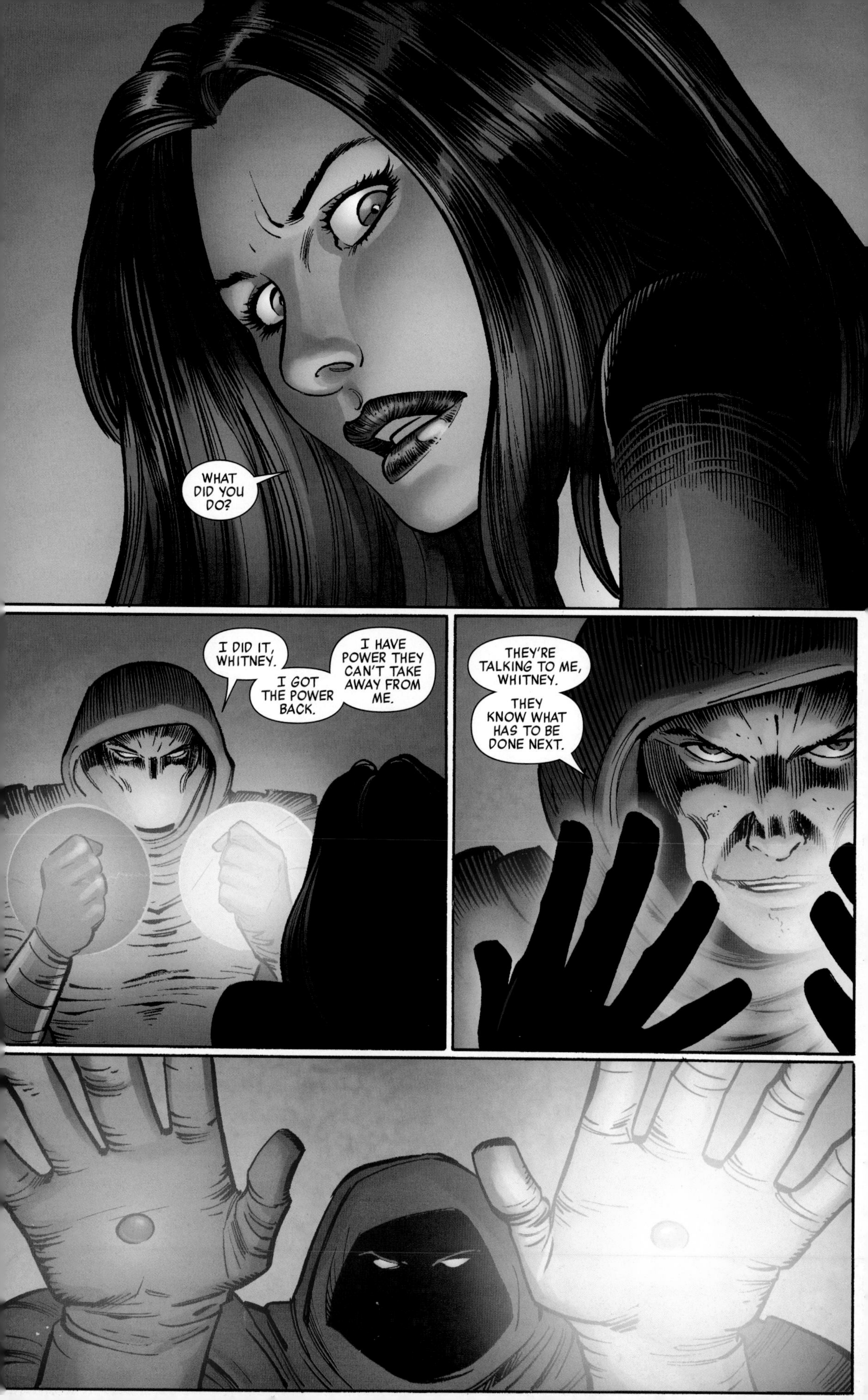

WHAT DID YOU DO?
I DID IT, WHITNEY.
I GOT THE POWER BACK.
I HAVE POWER THEY CAN'T TAKE AWAY FROM ME.
THEY'RE TALKING TO ME, WHITNEY.
THEY KNOW WHAT HAS TO BE DONE NEXT.

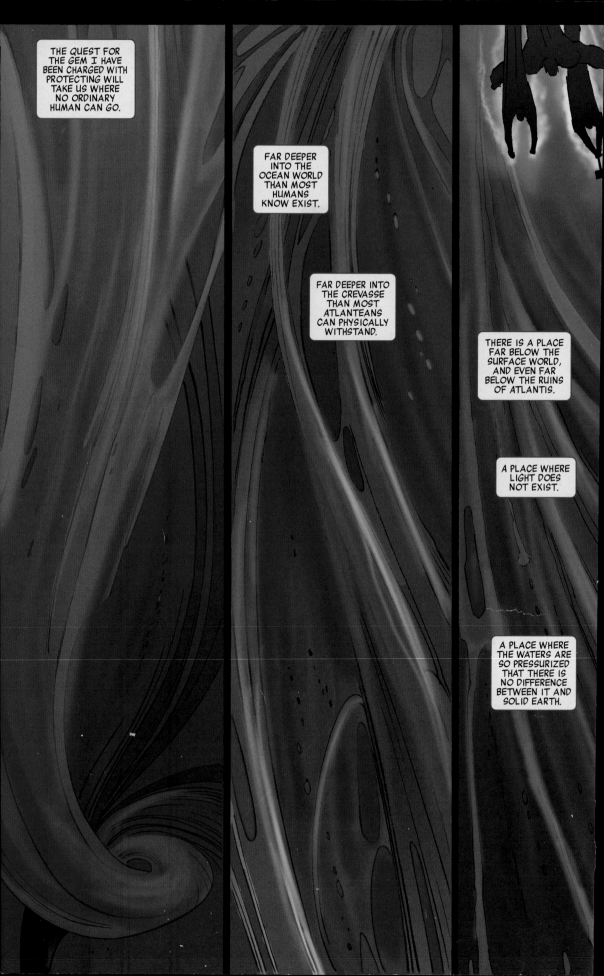

THE QUEST FOR THE GEM I HAVE BEEN CHARGED WITH PROTECTING WILL TAKE US WHERE NO ORDINARY HUMAN CAN GO.

FAR DEEPER INTO THE OCEAN WORLD THAN MOST HUMANS KNOW EXIST.

FAR DEEPER INTO THE CREVASSE THAN MOST ATLANTEANS CAN PHYSICALLY WITHSTAND.

THERE IS A PLACE FAR BELOW THE SURFACE WORLD, AND EVEN FAR BELOW THE RUINS OF ATLANTIS.

A PLACE WHERE LIGHT DOES NOT EXIST.

A PLACE WHERE THE WATERS ARE SO PRESSURIZED THAT THERE IS NO DIFFERENCE BETWEEN IT AND SOLID EARTH.

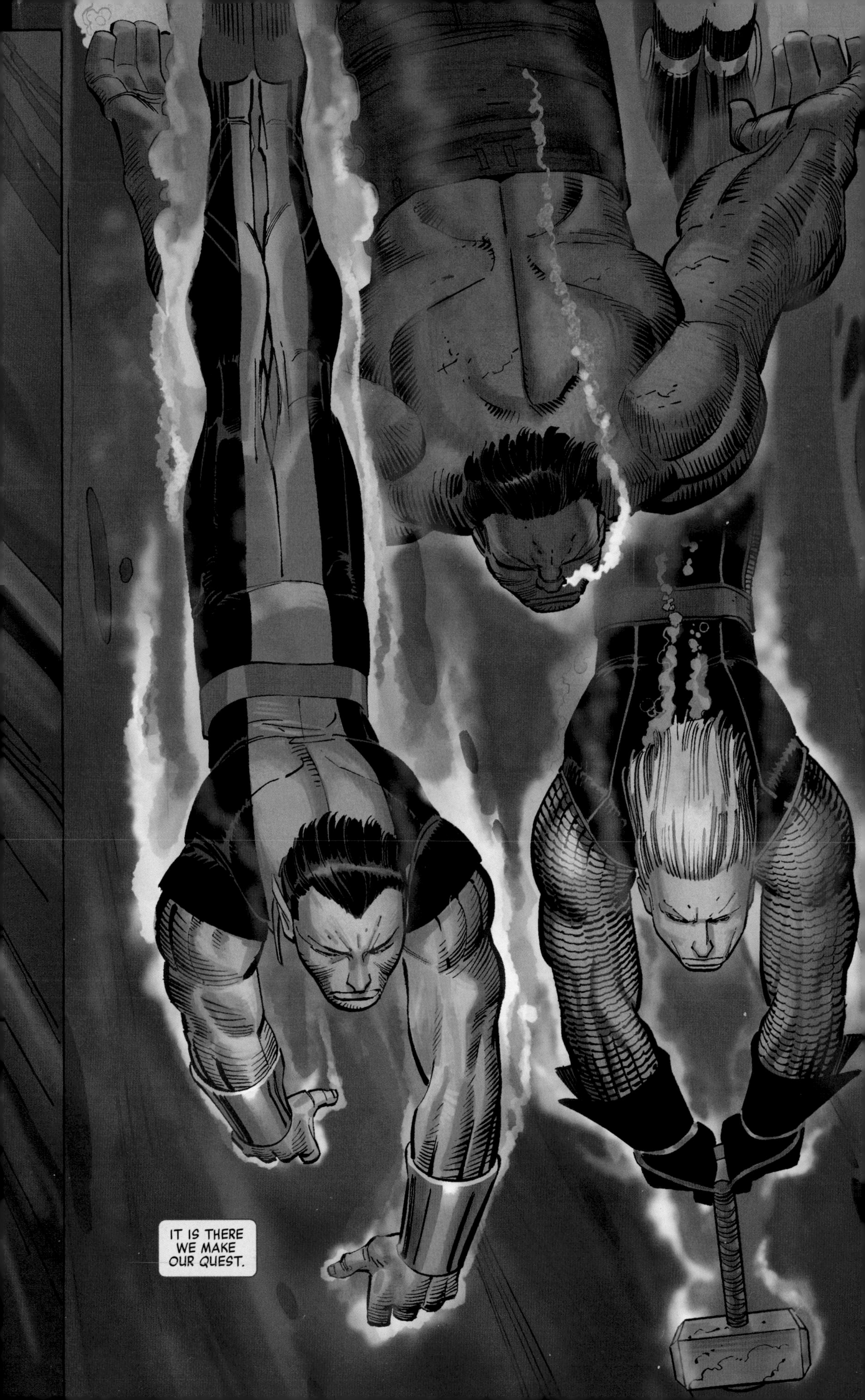
IT IS THERE
WE MAKE
OUR QUEST.

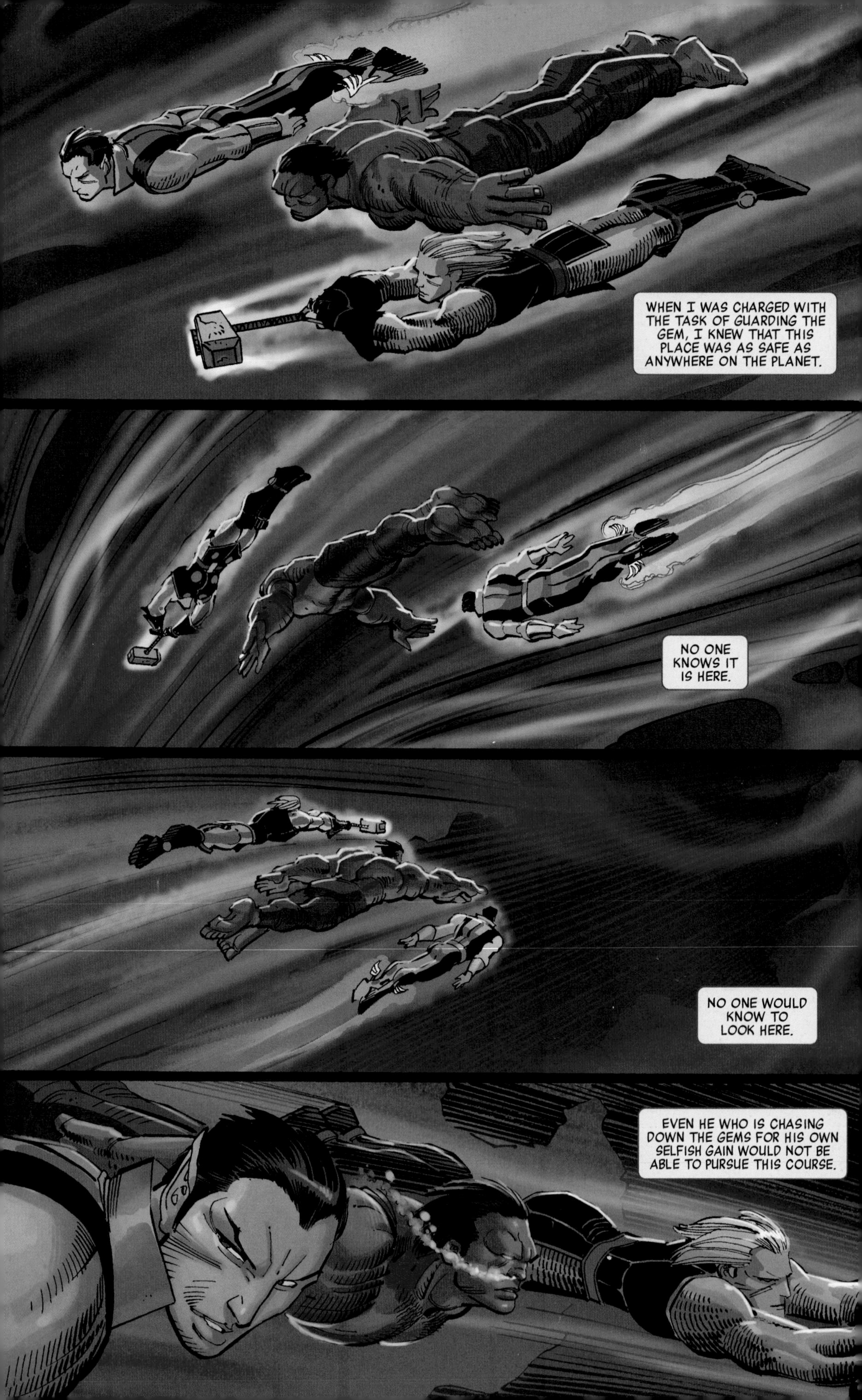

WHEN I WAS CHARGED WITH THE TASK OF GUARDING THE GEM, I KNEW THAT THIS PLACE WAS AS SAFE AS ANYWHERE ON THE PLANET.
NO ONE KNOWS IT IS HERE.
NO ONE WOULD KNOW TO LOOK HERE.
EVEN HE WHO IS CHASING DOWN THE GEMS FOR HIS OWN SELFISH GAIN WOULD NOT BE ABLE TO PURSUE THIS COURSE.

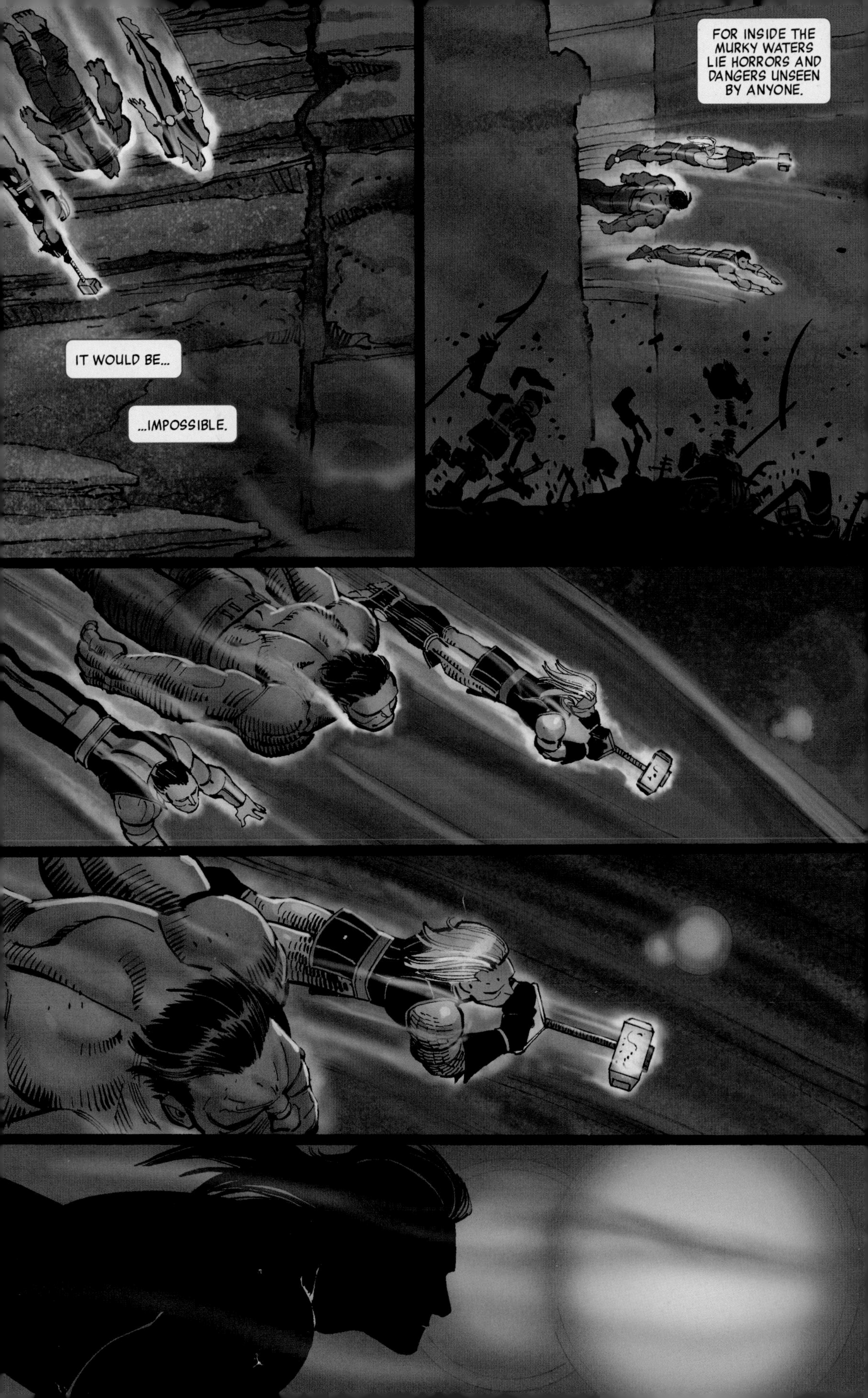
IT WOULD BE...
...IMPOSSIBLE.
FOR INSIDE THE MURKY WATERS LIE HORRORS AND DANGERS UNSEEN BY ANYONE.

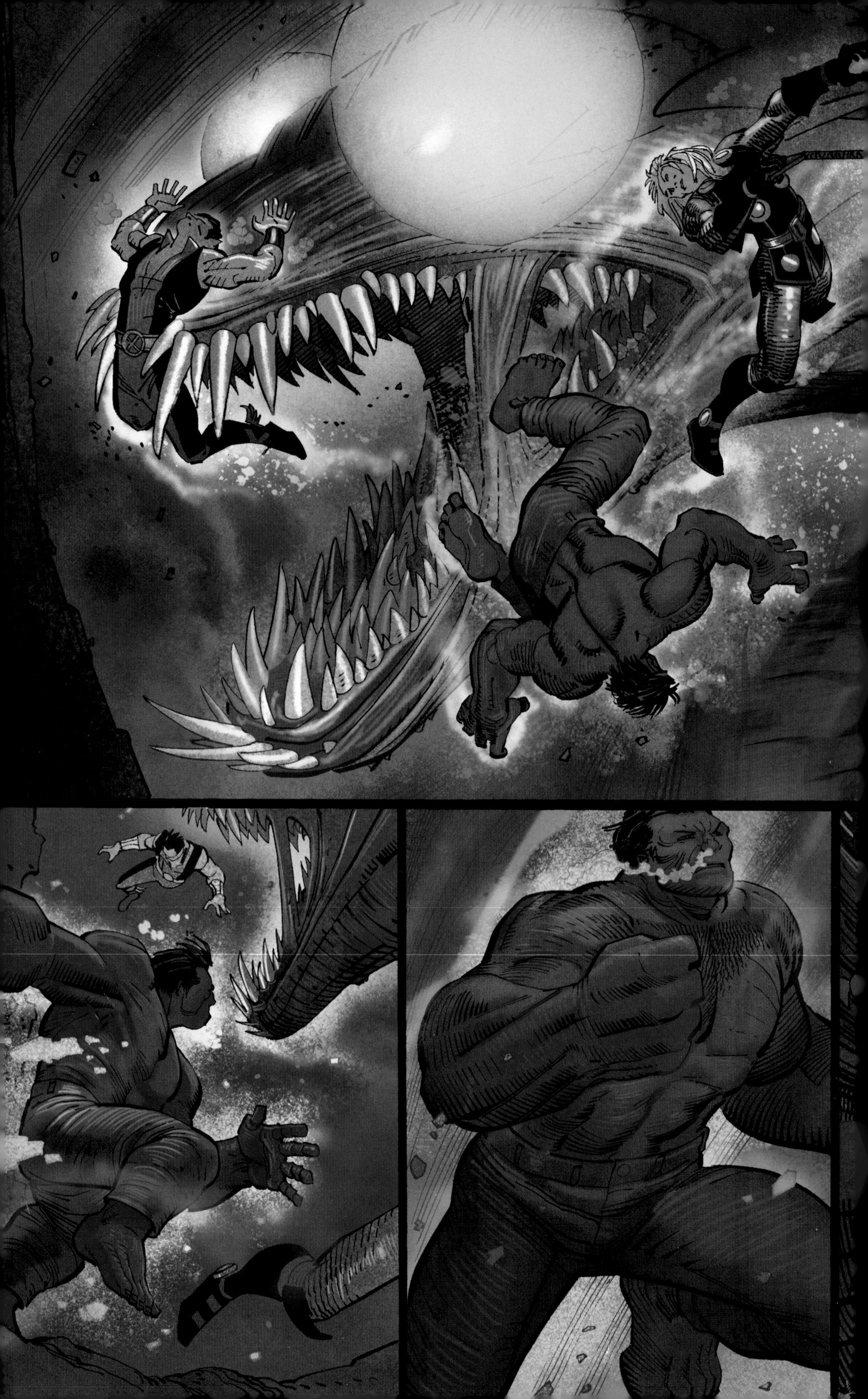

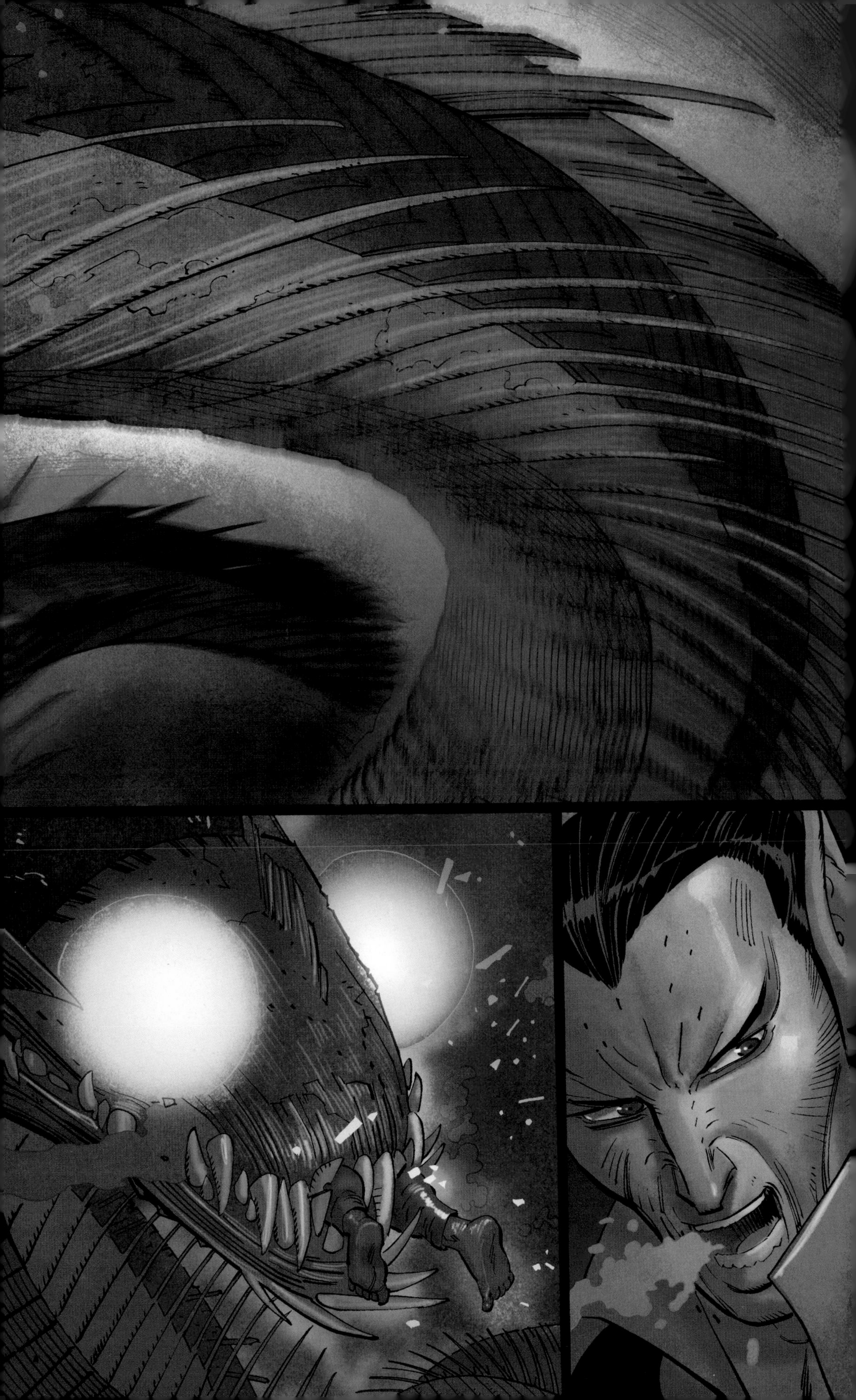

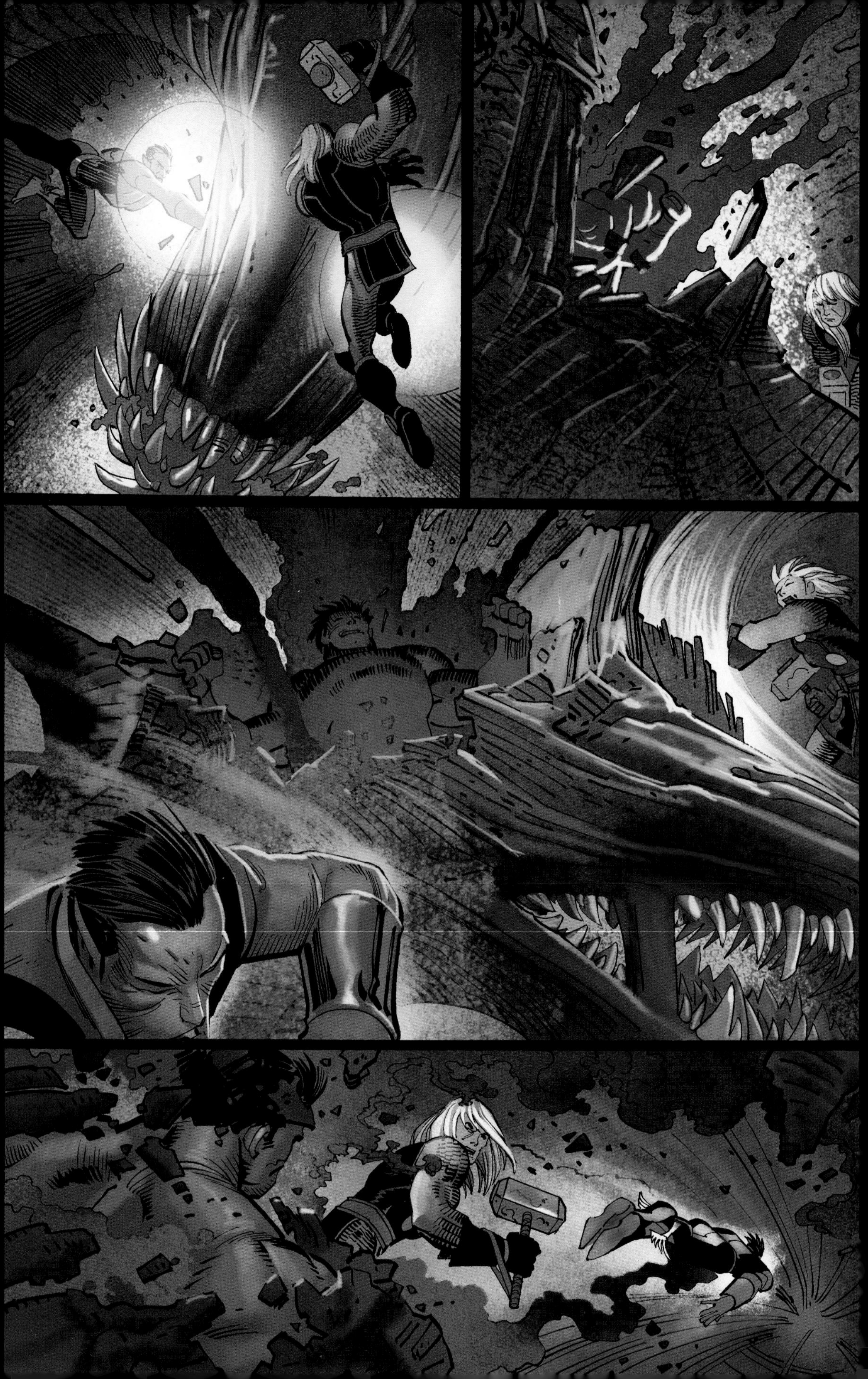

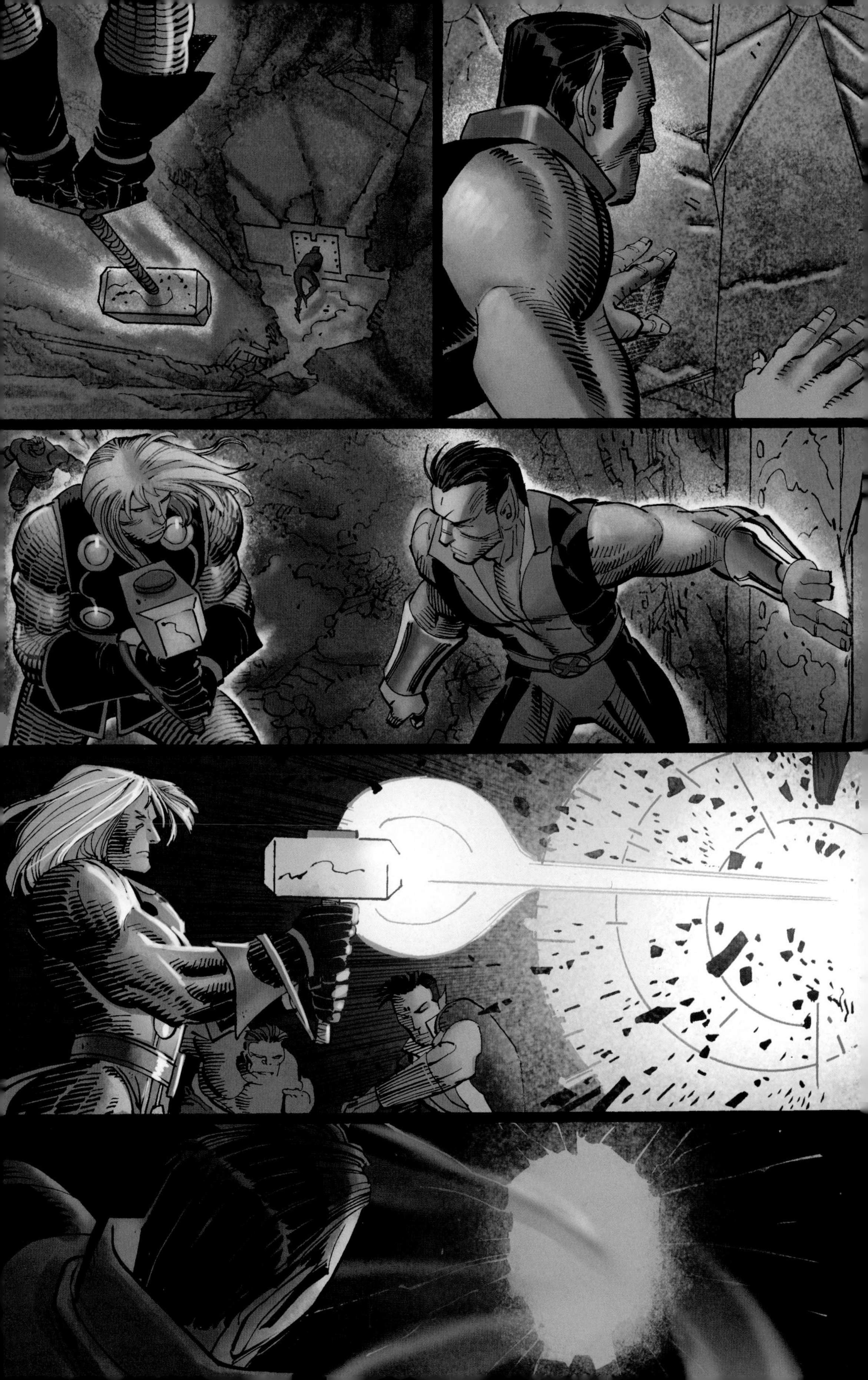

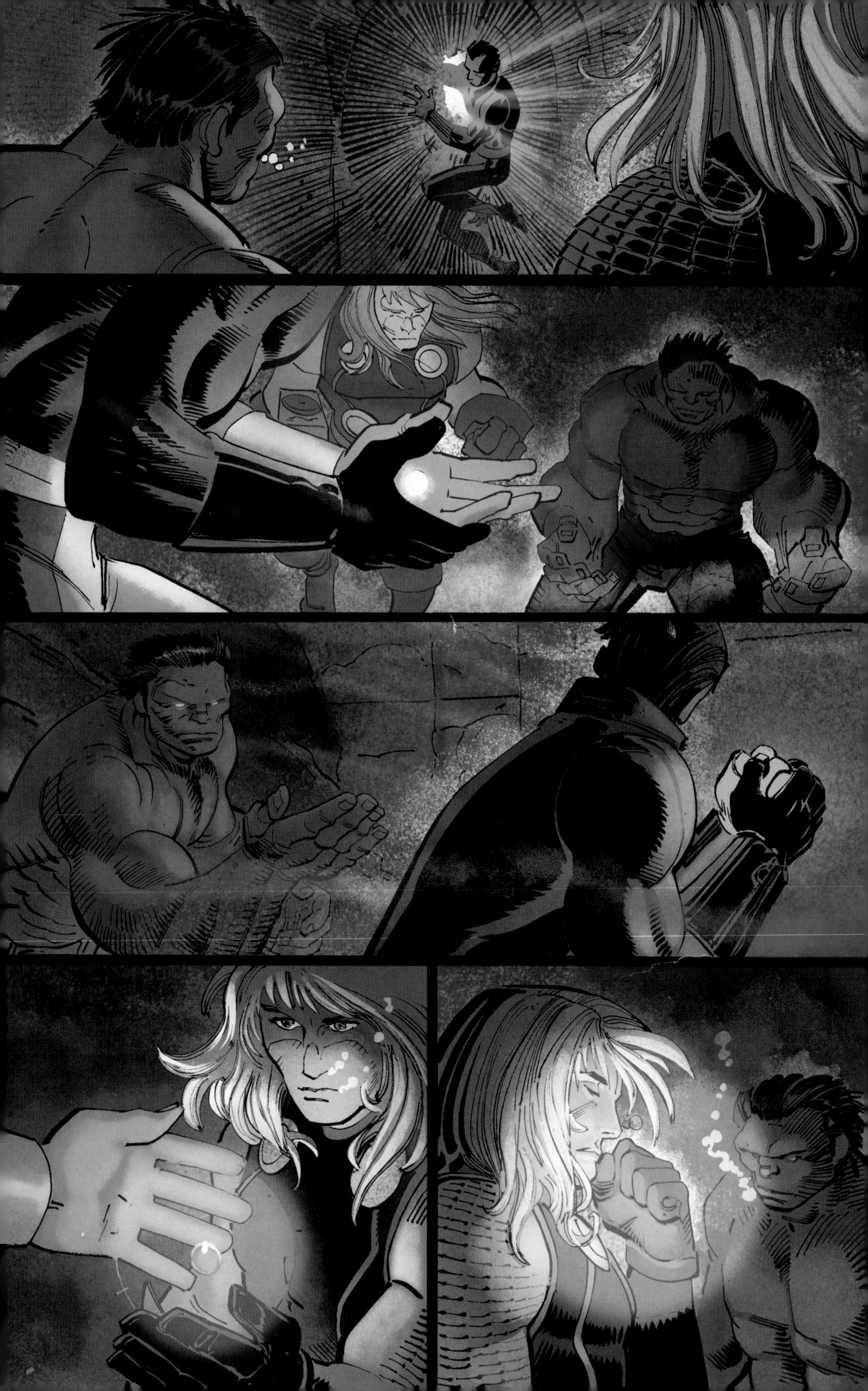

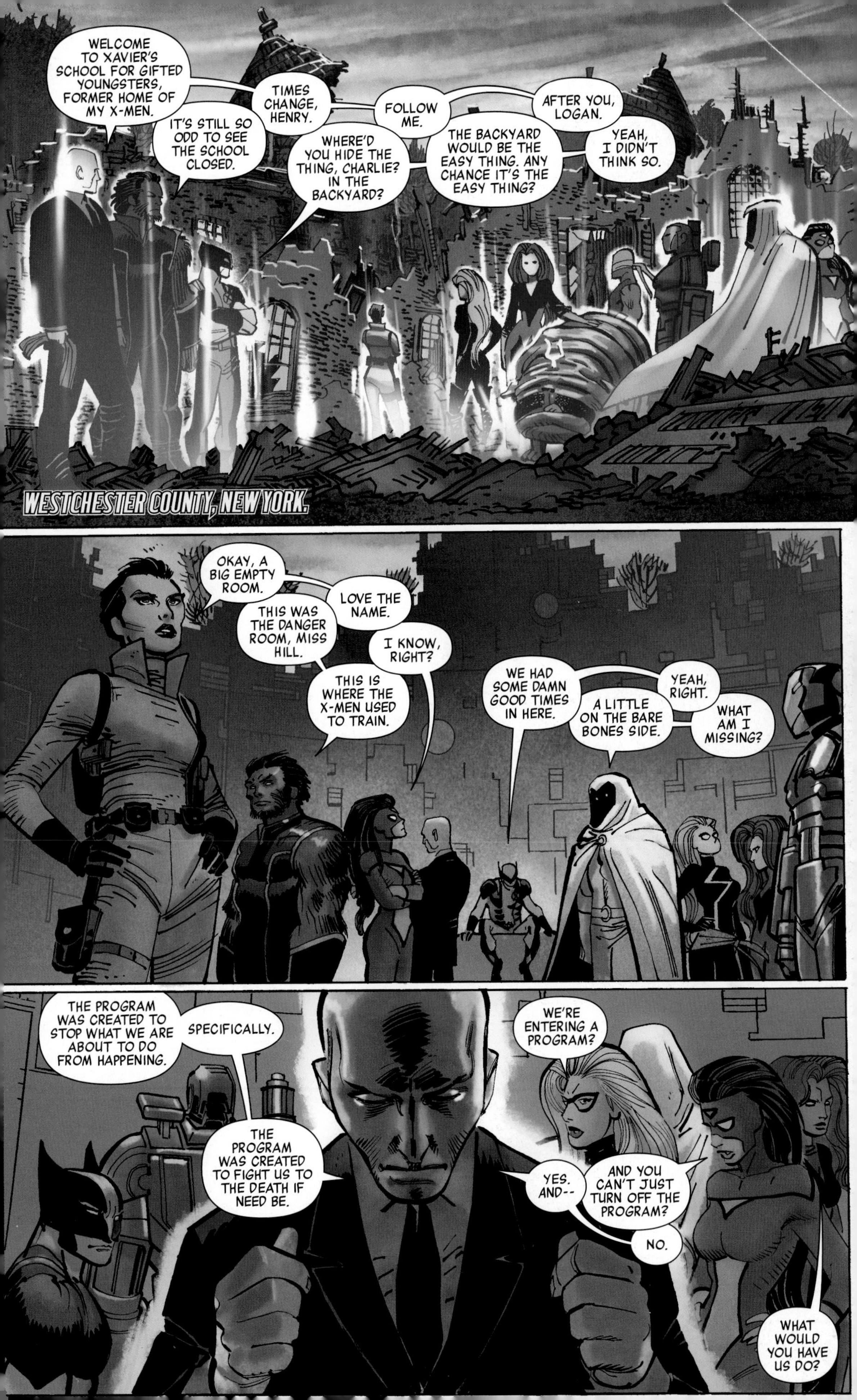
WELCOME TO XAVIER'S SCHOOL FOR GIFTED YOUNGSTERS, FORMER HOME OF MY X-MEN.
IT'S STILL SO ODD TO SEE THE SCHOOL CLOSED.
TIMES CHANGE, HENRY.
WHERE'D YOU HIDE THE THING, CHARLIE? IN THE BACKYARD?
FOLLOW ME.
THE BACKYARD WOULD BE THE EASY THING. ANY CHANCE IT'S THE EASY THING?
AFTER YOU, LOGAN.
YEAH, I DIDN'T THINK SO.
WESTCHESTER COUNTY, NEW YORK.
OKAY, A BIG EMPTY ROOM.
LOVE THE NAME.
THIS WAS THE DANGER ROOM, MISS HILL.
I KNOW, RIGHT?
THIS IS WHERE THE X-MEN USED TO TRAIN.
WE HAD SOME DAMN GOOD TIMES IN HERE.
YEAH, RIGHT.
A LITTLE ON THE BARE BONES SIDE.
WHAT AM I MISSING?
THE PROGRAM WAS CREATED TO STOP WHAT WE ARE ABOUT TO DO FROM HAPPENING.
SPECIFICALLY.
THE PROGRAM WAS CREATED TO FIGHT US TO THE DEATH IF NEED BE.
WE'RE ENTERING A PROGRAM?
YES. AND--
AND YOU CAN'T JUST TURN OFF THE PROGRAM?
NO.
WHAT WOULD YOU HAVE US DO?

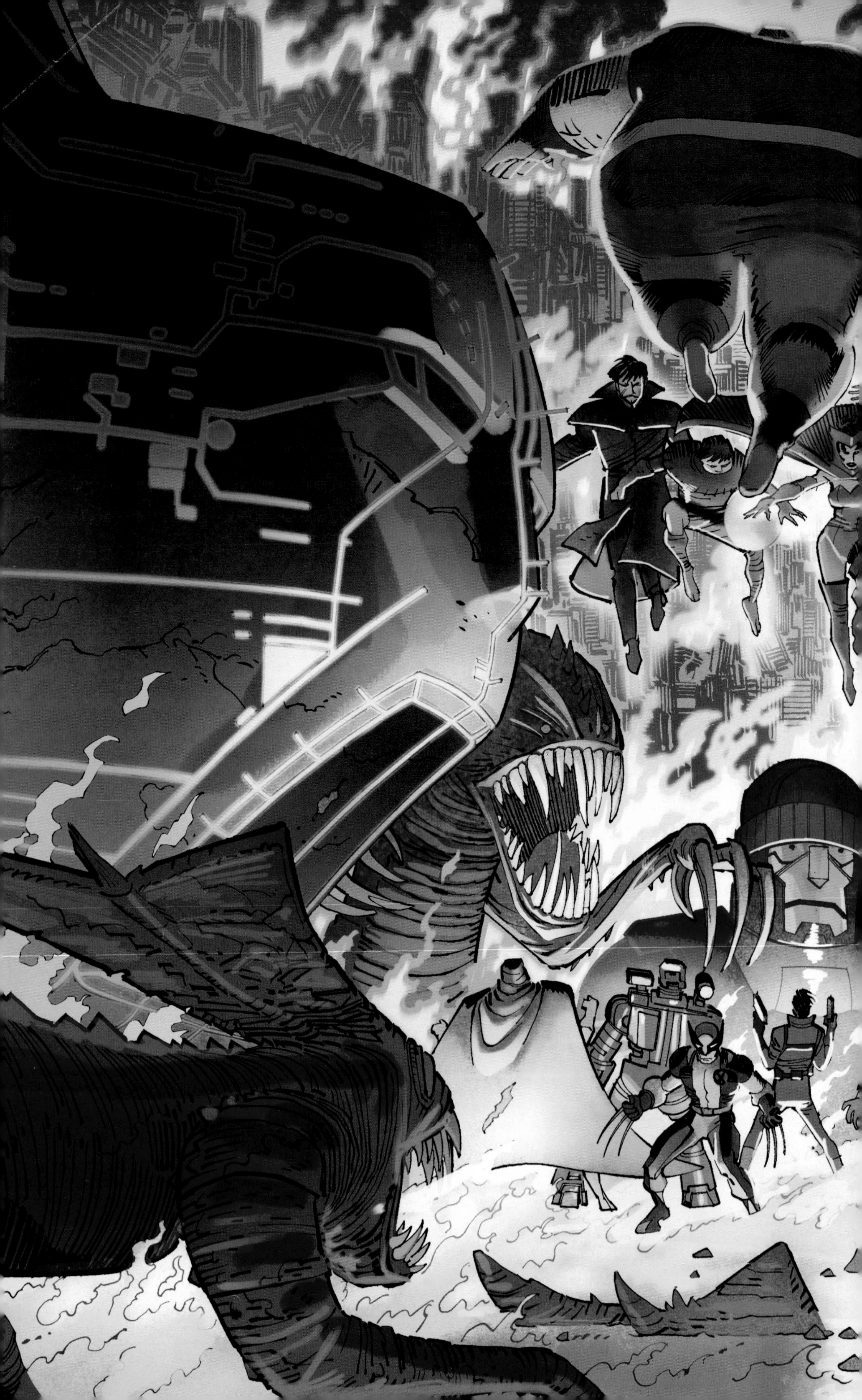

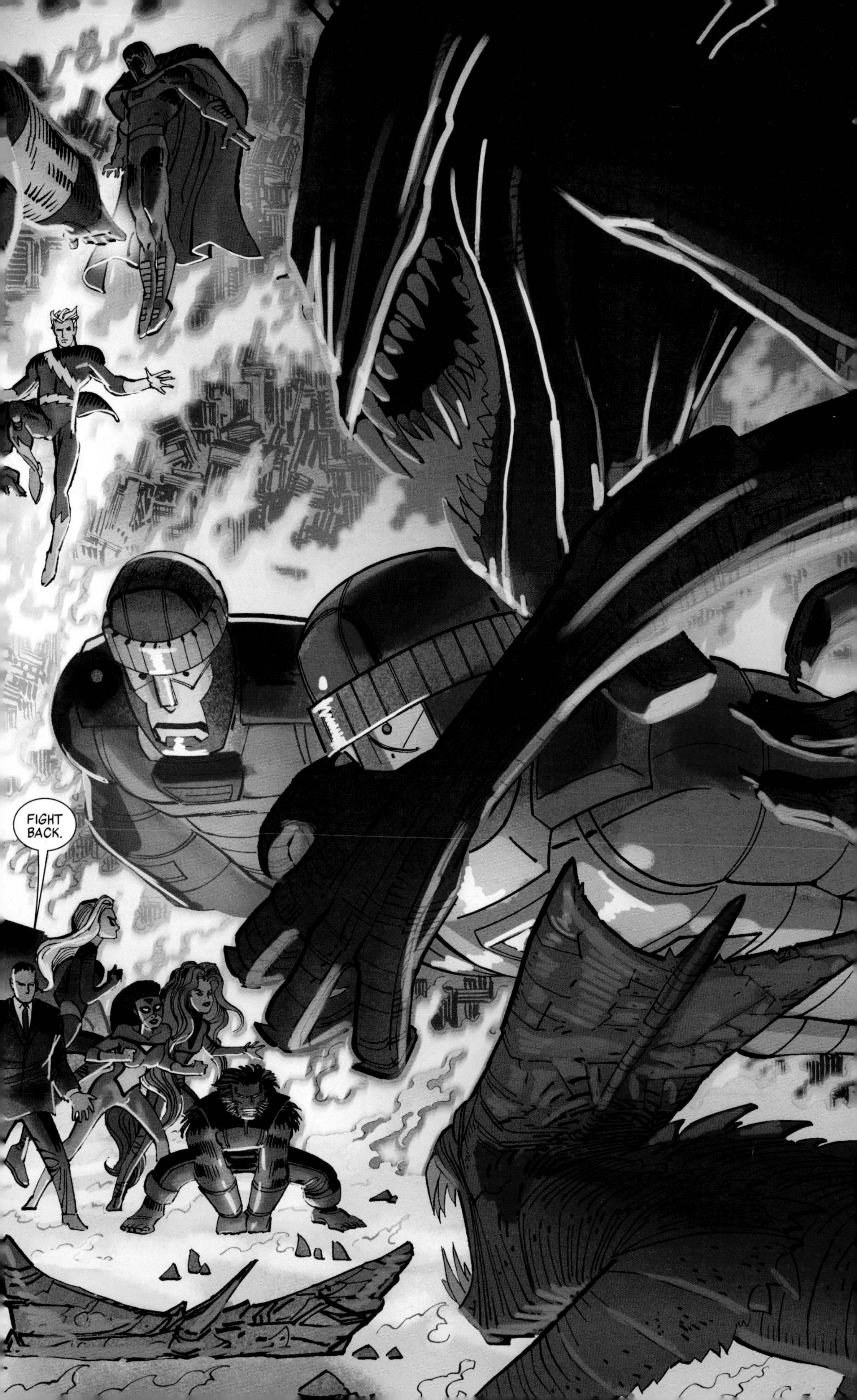
FIGHT BACK.

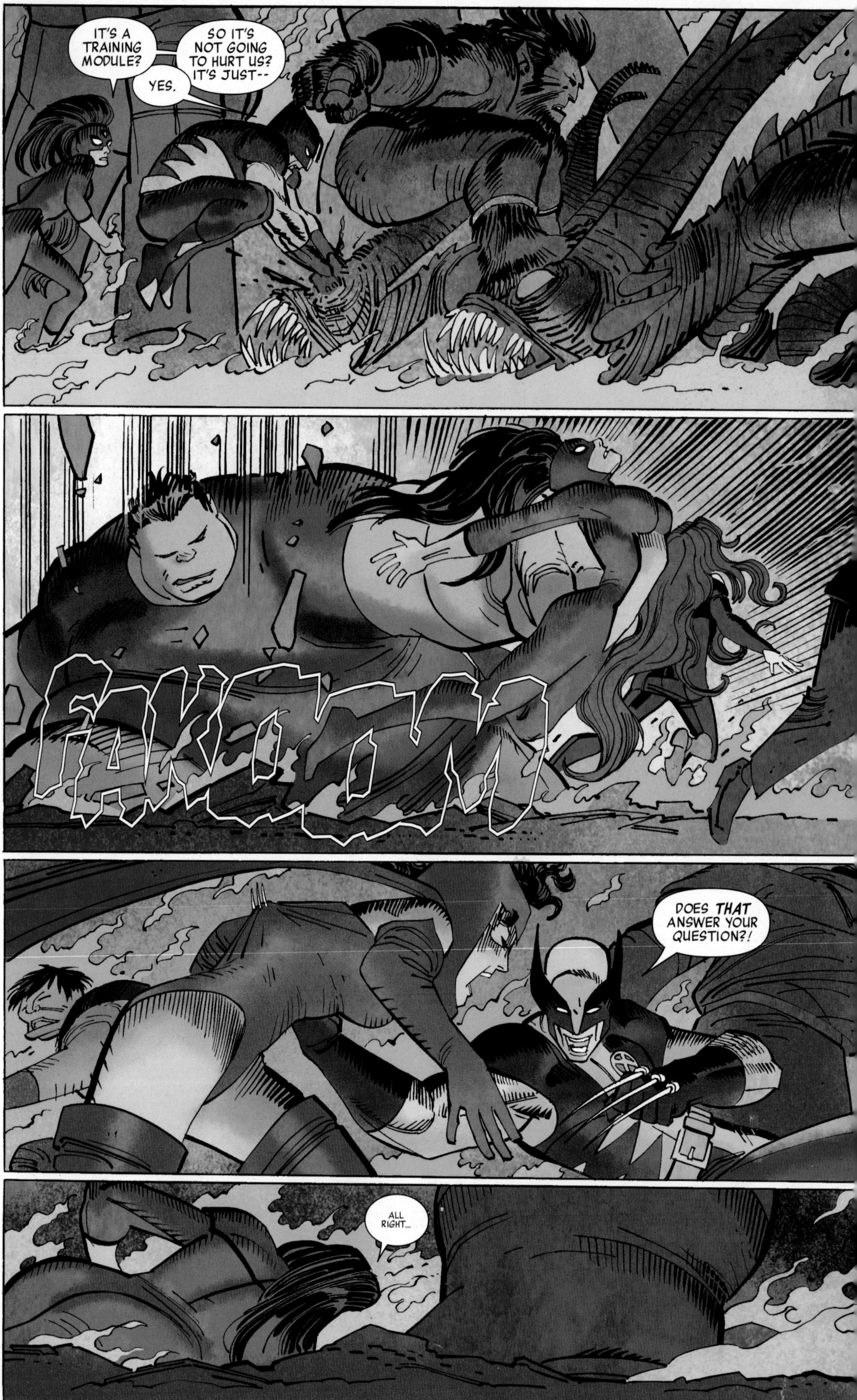
IT'S A TRAINING MODULE?
SO IT'S NOT GOING TO HURT US? IT'S JUST--
YES.
DOES THAT ANSWER YOUR QUESTION?!
ALL RIGHT...

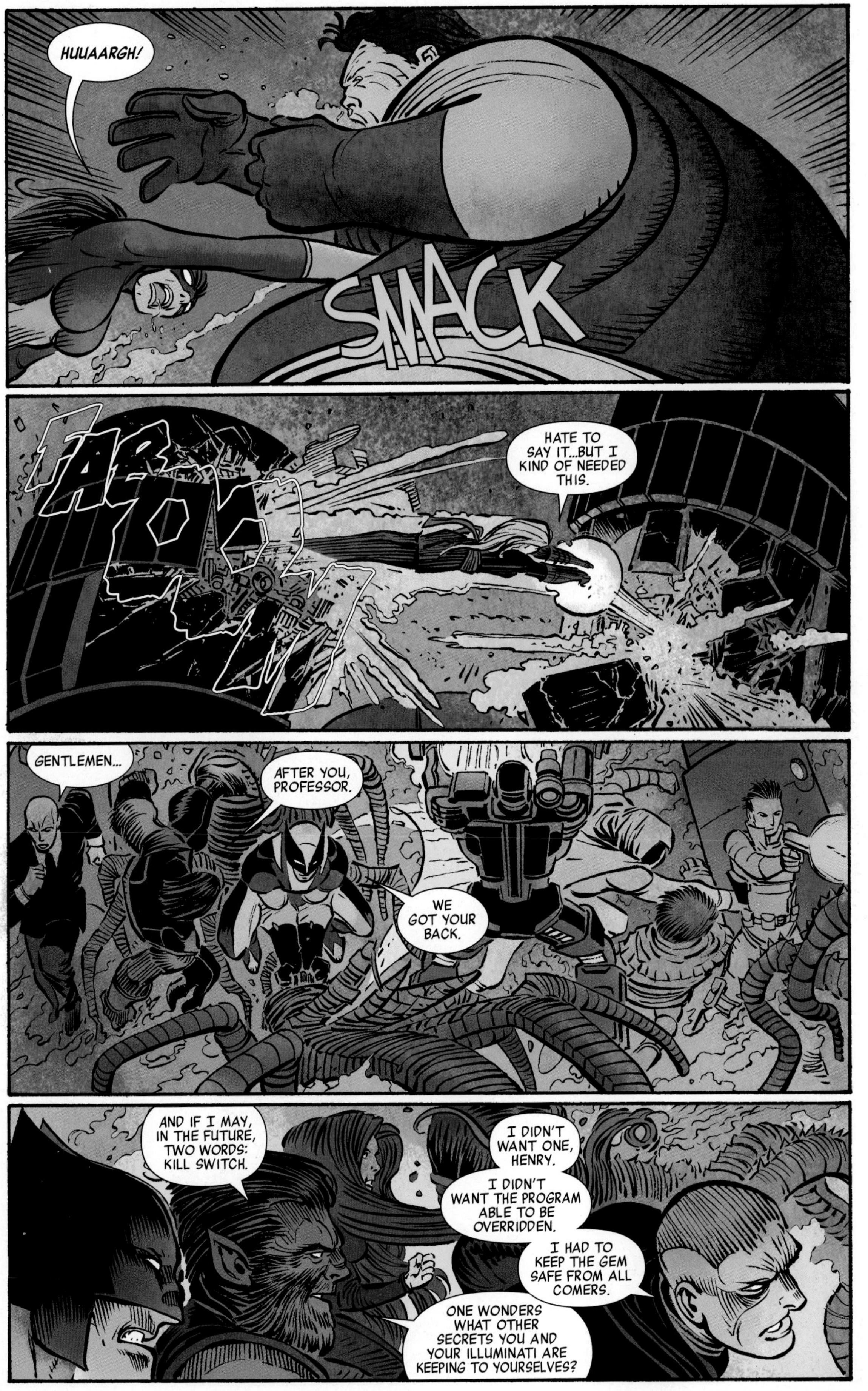
HUUAARGH!
SMACK
HATE TO SAY IT...BUT I KIND OF NEEDED THIS.
GENTLEMEN...
AFTER YOU, PROFESSOR.
WE GOT YOUR BACK.
AND IF I MAY, IN THE FUTURE, TWO WORDS: KILL SWITCH.
I DIDN'T WANT ONE, HENRY.
I DIDN'T WANT THE PROGRAM ABLE TO BE OVERRIDDEN.
I HAD TO KEEP THE GEM SAFE FROM ALL COMERS.
ONE WONDERS WHAT OTHER SECRETS YOU AND YOUR ILLUMINATI ARE KEEPING TO YOURSELVES?

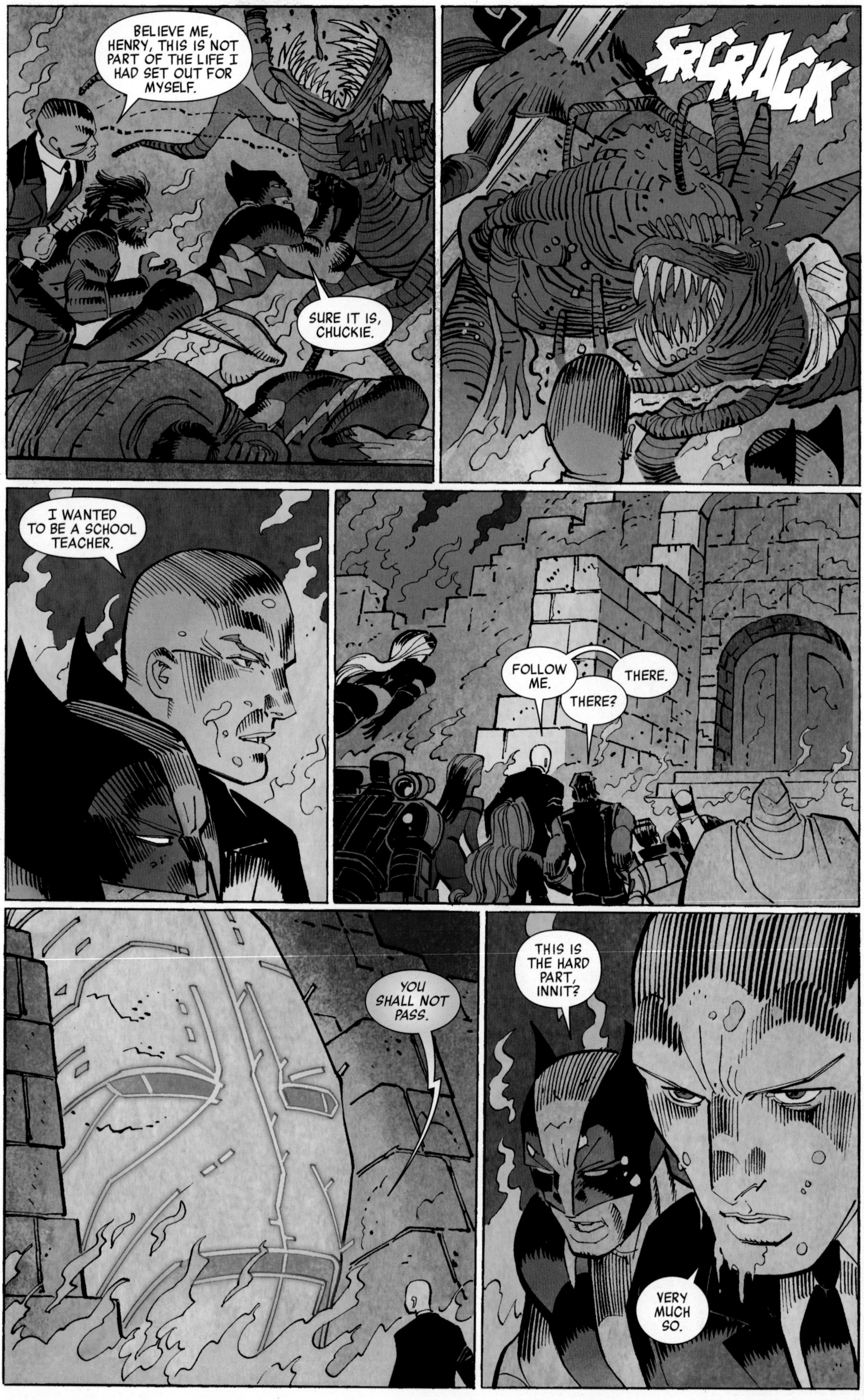
BELIEVE ME, HENRY, THIS IS NOT PART OF THE LIFE I HAD SET OUT FOR MYSELF.
SHAKT!!
SURE IT IS, CHUCKIE.
SRCRACK
I WANTED TO BE A SCHOOL TEACHER.
FOLLOW ME.
THERE?
THERE.
YOU SHALL NOT PASS.
THIS IS THE HARD PART, INNIT?
VERY MUCH SO.

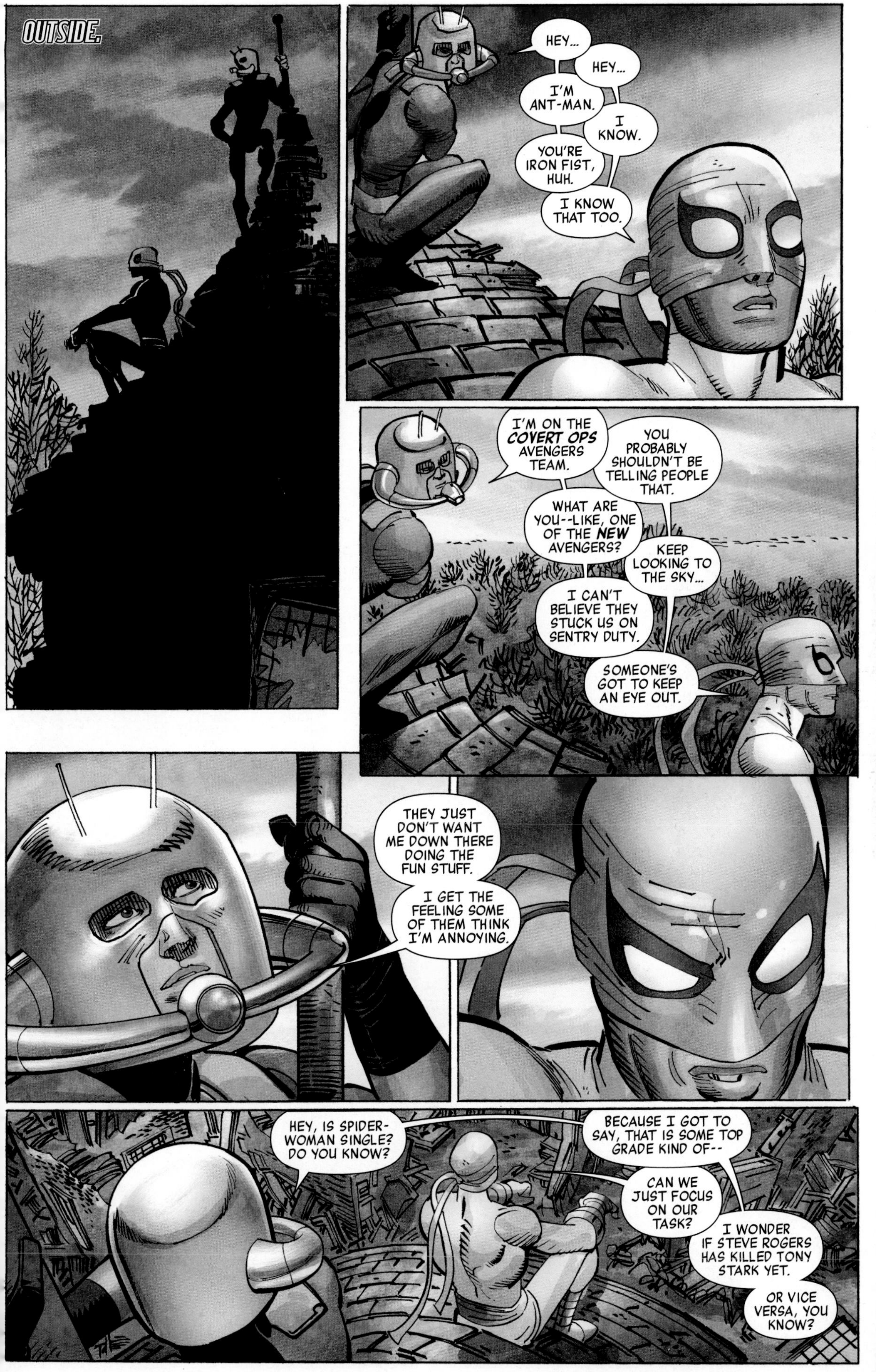
OUTSIDE.
HEY...
HEY...
I'M ANT-MAN.
I KNOW.
YOU'RE IRON FIST, HUH.
I KNOW THAT TOO.
I'M ON THE COVERT OPS AVENGERS TEAM.
YOU PROBABLY SHOULDN'T BE TELLING PEOPLE THAT.
WHAT ARE YOU--LIKE, ONE OF THE NEW AVENGERS?
KEEP LOOKING TO THE SKY...
I CAN'T BELIEVE THEY STUCK US ON SENTRY DUTY.
SOMEONE'S GOT TO KEEP AN EYE OUT.
THEY JUST DON'T WANT ME DOWN THERE DOING THE FUN STUFF.
I GET THE FEELING SOME OF THEM THINK I'M ANNOYING.
HEY, IS SPIDER-WOMAN SINGLE? DO YOU KNOW?
BECAUSE I GOT TO SAY, THAT IS SOME TOP GRADE KIND OF--
CAN WE JUST FOCUS ON OUR TASK?
I WONDER IF STEVE ROGERS HAS KILLED TONY STARK YET.
OR VICE VERSA, YOU KNOW?

WELL, THIS IS COMFORTABLE.

IT IS A LITTLE CROWDED.

NO, I WAS TALKING ABOUT MOMMY AND DADDY FIGHTING.

I HEAR THAT.

WHAT ARE YOU SAYING, SPIDER-MAN?

DON'T WORRY ABOUT IT, NOH-VARR.

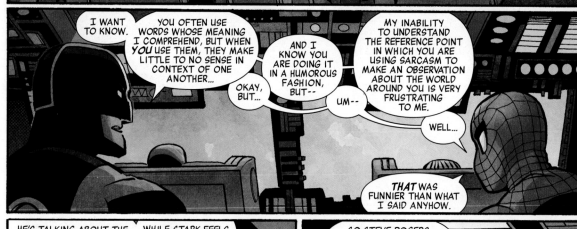

I WANT TO KNOW.

YOU OFTEN USE WORDS WHOSE MEANING I COMPREHEND, BUT WHEN *YOU* USE THEM, THEY MAKE LITTLE TO NO SENSE IN CONTEXT OF ONE ANOTHER...

AND I KNOW YOU ARE DOING IT IN A HUMOROUS FASHION, BUT--

OKAY, BUT...

MY INABILITY TO UNDERSTAND THE REFERENCE POINT IN WHICH YOU ARE USING SARCASM TO MAKE AN OBSERVATION ABOUT THE WORLD AROUND YOU IS VERY FRUSTRATING TO ME.

UM--

WELL...

*THAT* WAS FUNNIER THAN WHAT I SAID ANYHOW.

HE'S TALKING ABOUT THE FACT THAT STEVE ROGERS AND TONY STARK ARE IN THE MIDDLE OF WORLD WAR THREE BECAUSE ROGERS FEELS STARK'S DOING STUFF BEHIND HIS BACK...

WHILE STARK FEELS HE WAS JUST DOING WHAT WAS BEST FOR THE WORLD AT THE TIME HE DID IT.

LIKE HIDING THE INFINITY GEMS.

EXACTLY.

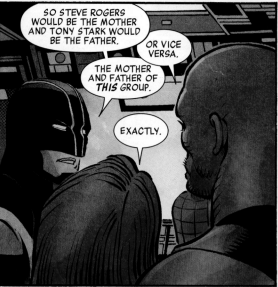

SO STEVE ROGERS WOULD BE THE MOTHER AND TONY STARK WOULD BE THE FATHER.

OR VICE VERSA.

THE MOTHER AND FATHER OF *THIS* GROUP.

EXACTLY.

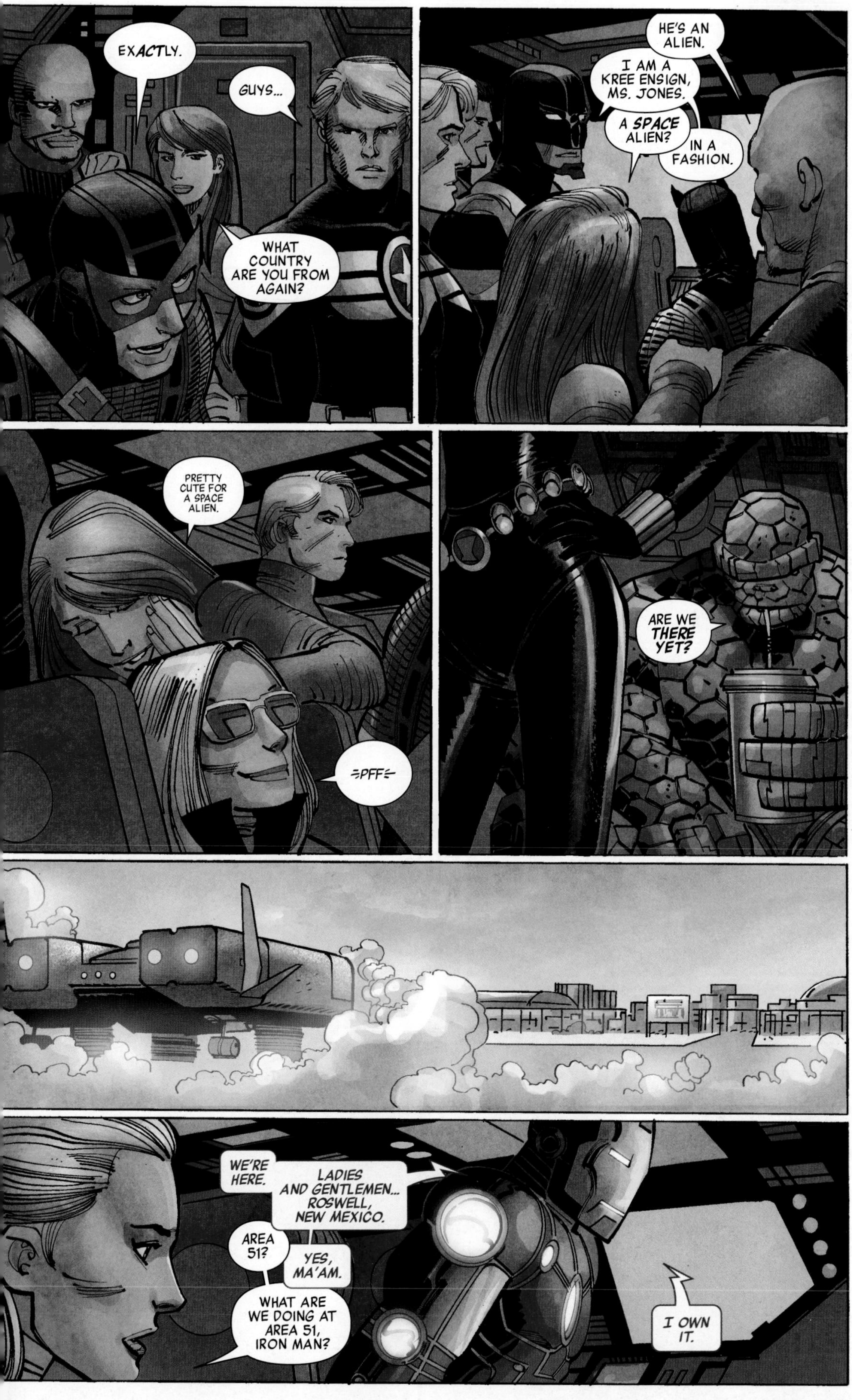

EXACTLY.
GUYS...
WHAT COUNTRY ARE YOU FROM AGAIN?
HE'S AN ALIEN.
I AM A KREE ENSIGN, MS. JONES.
A SPACE ALIEN?
IN A FASHION.
PRETTY CUTE FOR A SPACE ALIEN.
=PFF=
ARE WE THERE YET?
WE'RE HERE.
LADIES AND GENTLEMEN... ROSWELL, NEW MEXICO.
AREA 51?
YES, MA'AM.
WHAT ARE WE DOING AT AREA 51, IRON MAN?
I OWN IT.

YOU **OWN** AREA 51?

SINCE WHEN?

THE GOVERNMENT QUIETLY PUT IT UP FOR SALE AND I BOUGHT IT.

I THOUGHT YOU WERE BROKE.

**MY** BROKE IS NOT THE SAME AS **YOUR** BROKE.

AND THIS WAS YEARS AGO.

LET'S JUST GET THIS OVER WITH.

YOU KNOW, I'LL TELL YOU WHAT'S BOTHERING ME ABOUT THIS WHOLE THING.

WHAT'S BOTHERING YOU IS THAT I'M RIGHT.

WHAT'S BOTHERING ME IS THAT I THINK YOU'RE MORE MAD AT **YOU** THAN YOU ARE AT ME.

WE'VE MADE HARD CHOICES IN OUR LIVES.

WE'VE **ALL** MADE HARD CHOICES.

THIS LIFE THAT WE'VE CHOSEN--THIS LIFE--IT COMES WITH **INSANE** CHOICES THAT WE HAVE TO MAKE EVERY DAY.

TONY STARK VOICE PRINT IDENTIFIED.

WELCOME, TONY.

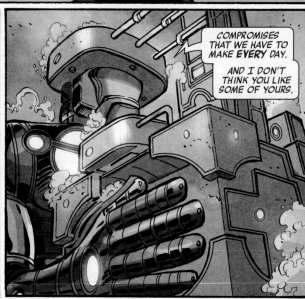

COMPROMISES THAT WE HAVE TO MAKE **EVERY** DAY.

AND I DON'T THINK YOU LIKE SOME OF YOURS.

WELL, THAT IS JUST--

HOLD ON--WE SHOULD LEAVE SOME SURFACE LEVEL RECON. KEEP AN EYE OUT FOR OUR MYSTERY GUEST.

YES.

HAWKEYE, MOCKINGBIRD, THING. YOU STAY TOP-SIDE.

BOO.

I MEAN, YES, SIR.

I'M JUST HAPPY FER THE QUIET.

GUESS I'LL HEAD TO THE ROOF.

HAVE FUN, DEAR.

YOU'RE COMING TOO.

IT'S CUTE THAT YOU THINK SO.

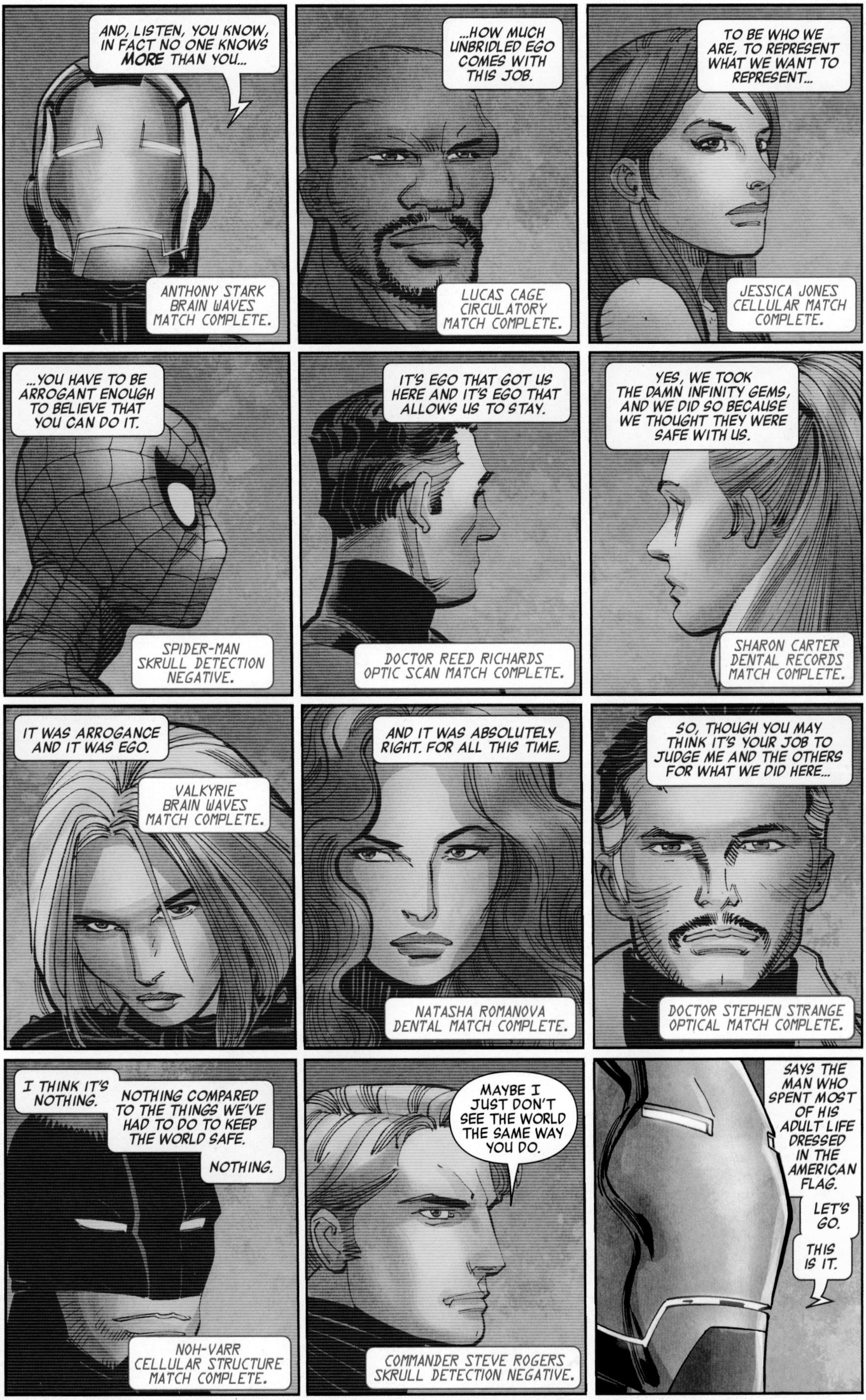
AND, LISTEN, YOU KNOW, IN FACT NO ONE KNOWS MORE THAN YOU...
ANTHONY STARK BRAIN WAVES MATCH COMPLETE.
...HOW MUCH UNBRIDLED EGO COMES WITH THIS JOB.
LUCAS CAGE CIRCULATORY MATCH COMPLETE.
TO BE WHO WE ARE, TO REPRESENT WHAT WE WANT TO REPRESENT...
JESSICA JONES CELLULAR MATCH COMPLETE.
...YOU HAVE TO BE ARROGANT ENOUGH TO BELIEVE THAT YOU CAN DO IT.
SPIDER-MAN SKRULL DETECTION NEGATIVE.
IT'S EGO THAT GOT US HERE AND IT'S EGO THAT ALLOWS US TO STAY.
DOCTOR REED RICHARDS OPTIC SCAN MATCH COMPLETE.
YES, WE TOOK THE DAMN INFINITY GEMS, AND WE DID SO BECAUSE WE THOUGHT THEY WERE SAFE WITH US.
SHARON CARTER DENTAL RECORDS MATCH COMPLETE.
IT WAS ARROGANCE AND IT WAS EGO.
VALKYRIE BRAIN WAVES MATCH COMPLETE.
AND IT WAS ABSOLUTELY RIGHT. FOR ALL THIS TIME.
NATASHA ROMANOVA DENTAL MATCH COMPLETE.
SO, THOUGH YOU MAY THINK IT'S YOUR JOB TO JUDGE ME AND THE OTHERS FOR WHAT WE DID HERE...
DOCTOR STEPHEN STRANGE OPTICAL MATCH COMPLETE.
I THINK IT'S NOTHING.
NOTHING COMPARED TO THE THINGS WE'VE HAD TO DO TO KEEP THE WORLD SAFE.
NOTHING.
NOH-VARR CELLULAR STRUCTURE MATCH COMPLETE.
MAYBE I JUST DON'T SEE THE WORLD THE SAME WAY YOU DO.
COMMANDER STEVE ROGERS SKRULL DETECTION NEGATIVE.
SAYS THE MAN WHO SPENT MOST OF HIS ADULT LIFE DRESSED IN THE AMERICAN FLAG.
LET'S GO.
THIS IS IT.

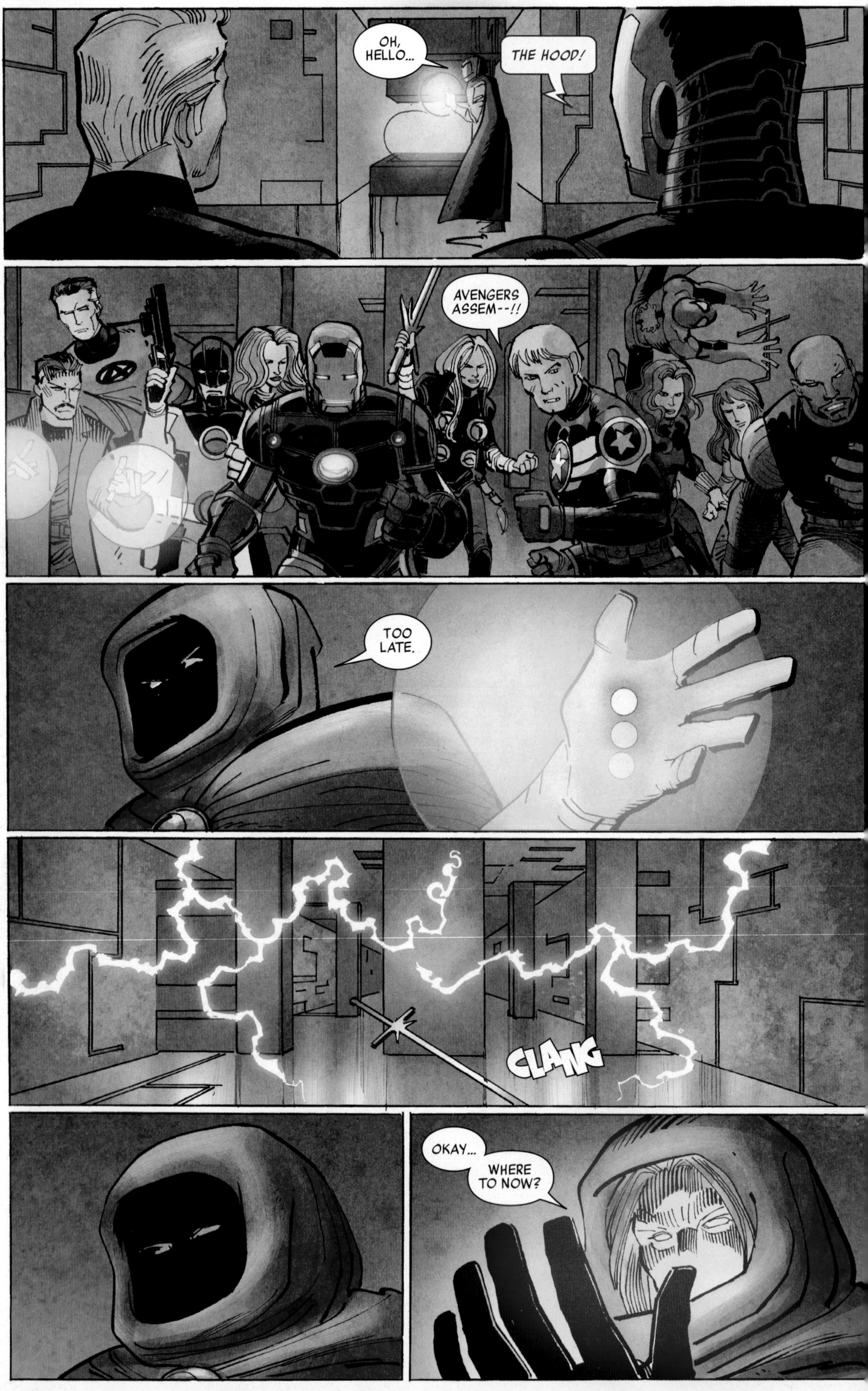
OH, HELLO...
THE HOOD!
AVENGERS ASSEM--!!
TOO LATE.
CLANG
OKAY... WHERE TO NOW?

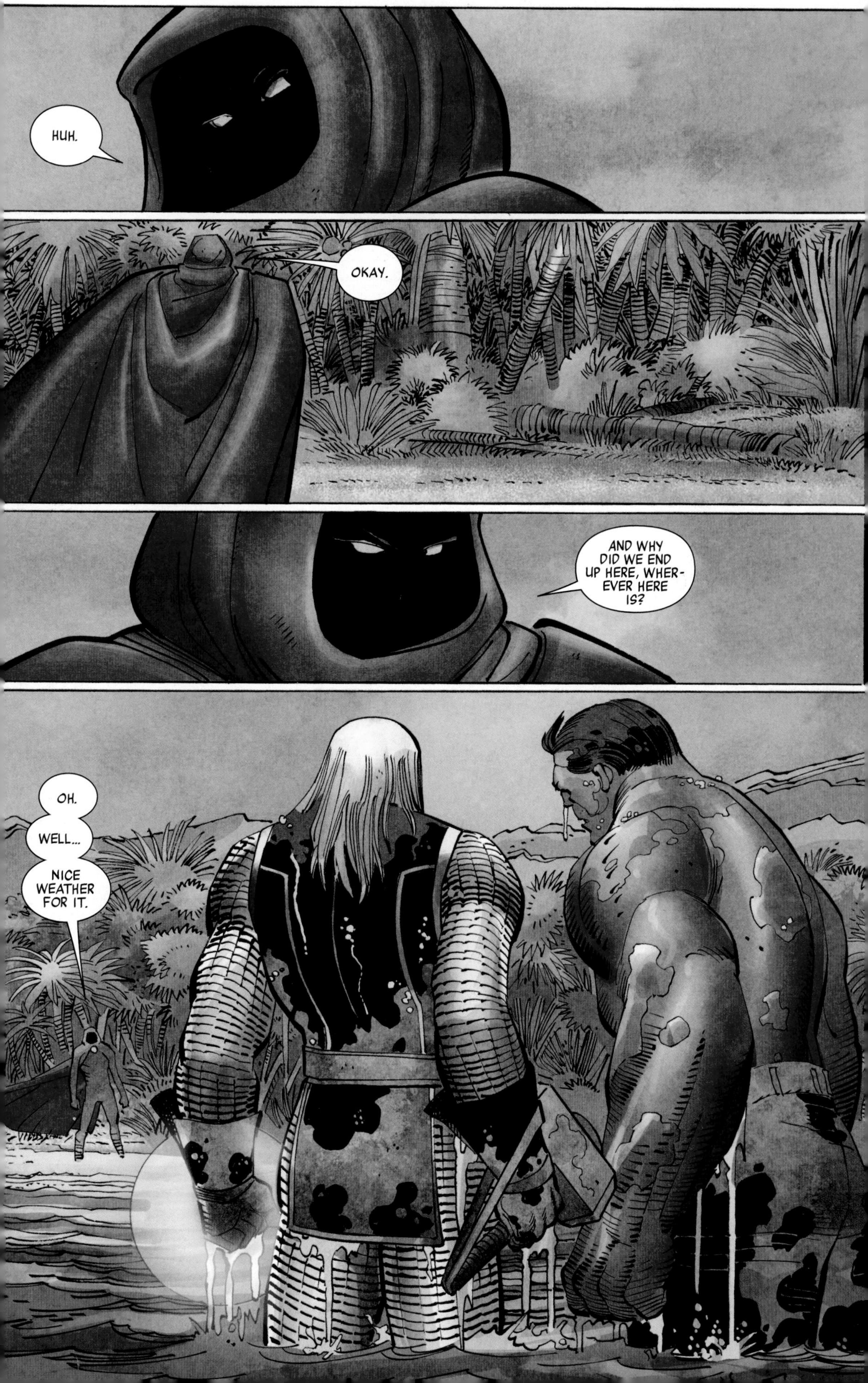
HUH.
OKAY.
AND WHY DID WE END UP HERE, WHER-EVER HERE IS?
OH.
WELL...
NICE WEATHER FOR IT.

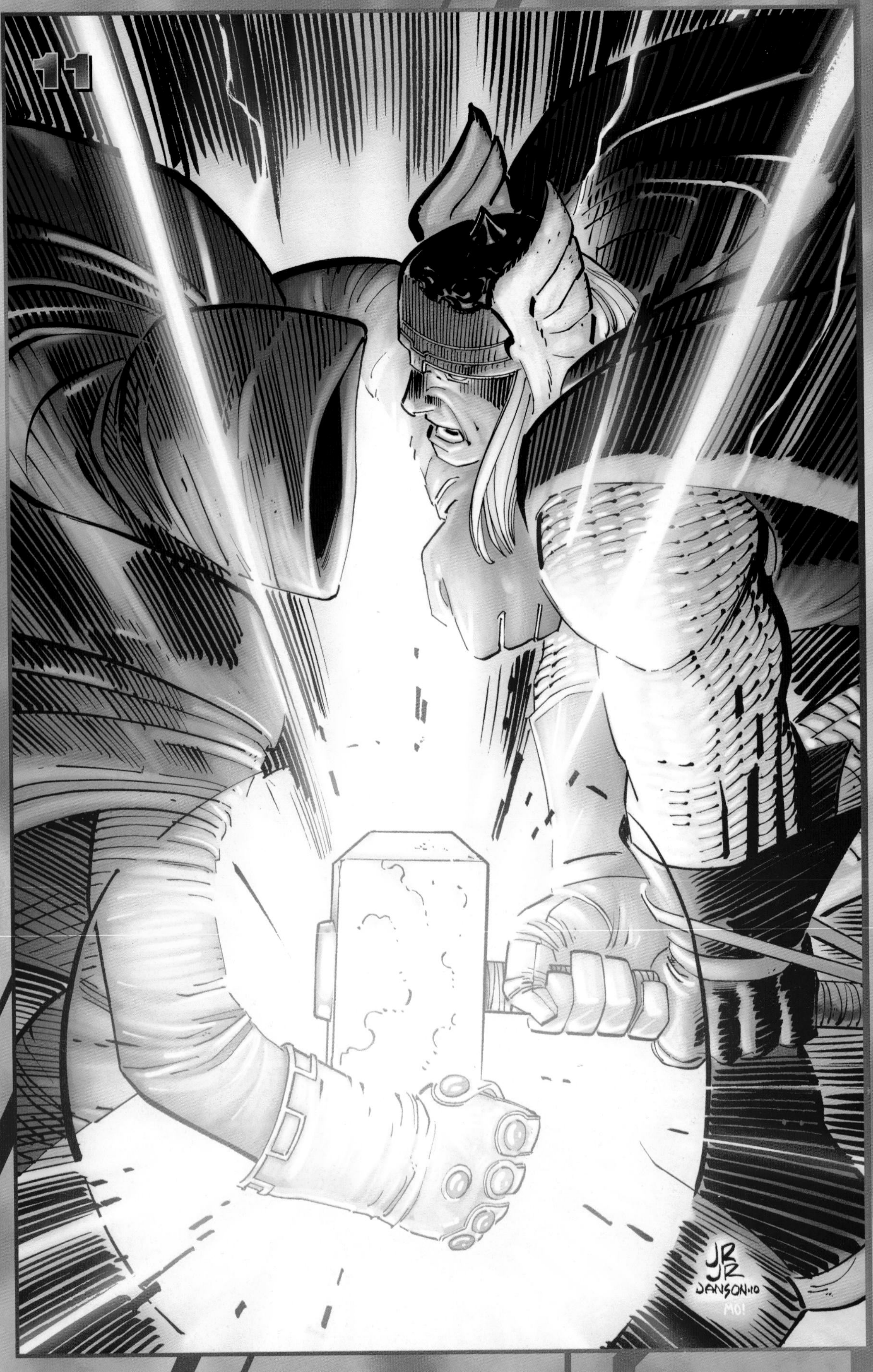
11
JR JR
JANSON·10
MO!

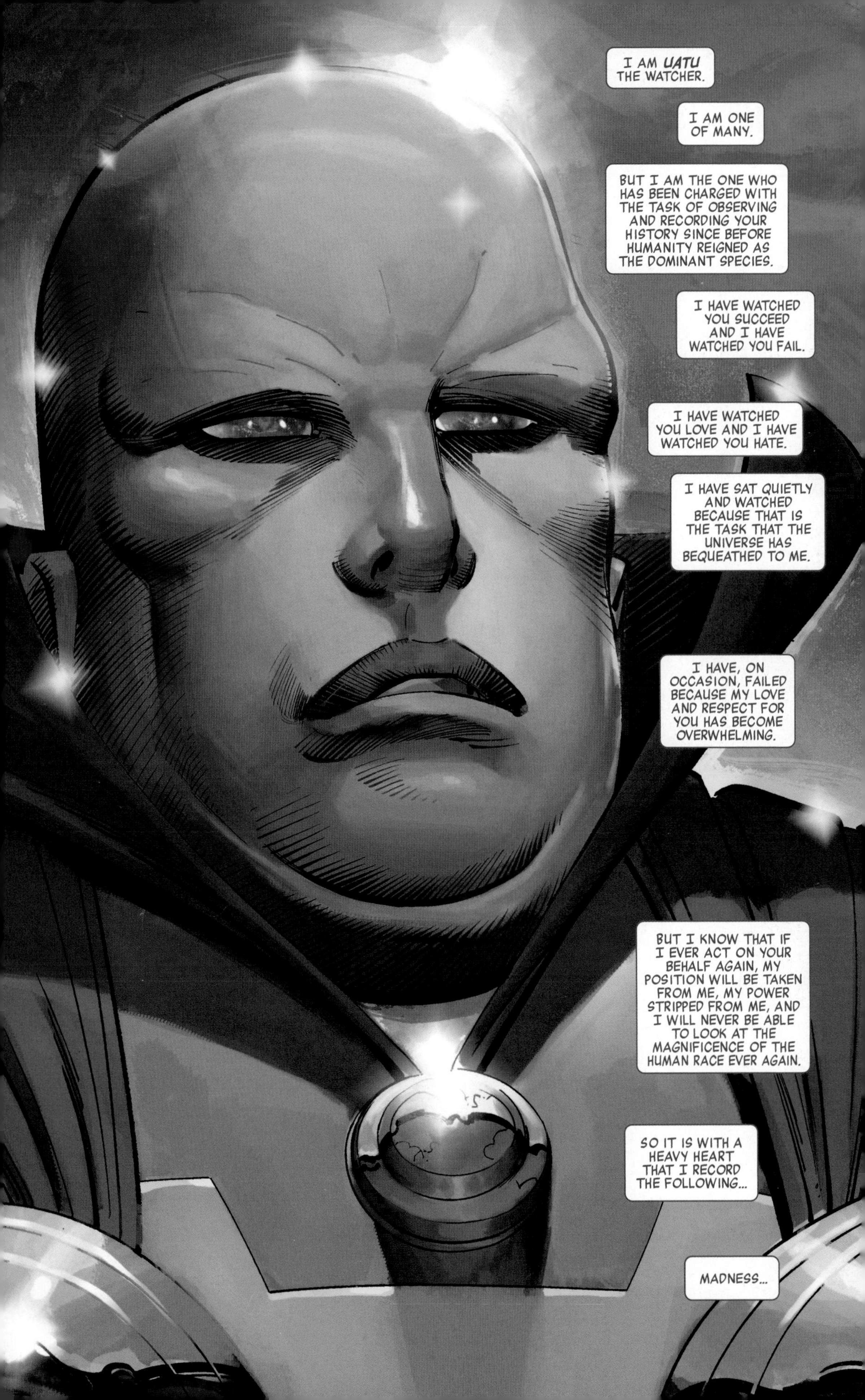
I AM *UATU* THE WATCHER.
I AM ONE OF MANY.
BUT I AM THE ONE WHO HAS BEEN CHARGED WITH THE TASK OF OBSERVING AND RECORDING YOUR HISTORY SINCE BEFORE HUMANITY REIGNED AS THE DOMINANT SPECIES.
I HAVE WATCHED YOU SUCCEED AND I HAVE WATCHED YOU FAIL.
I HAVE WATCHED YOU LOVE AND I HAVE WATCHED YOU HATE.
I HAVE SAT QUIETLY AND WATCHED BECAUSE THAT IS THE TASK THAT THE UNIVERSE HAS BEQUEATHED TO ME.
I HAVE, ON OCCASION, FAILED BECAUSE MY LOVE AND RESPECT FOR YOU HAS BECOME OVERWHELMING.
BUT I KNOW THAT IF I EVER ACT ON YOUR BEHALF AGAIN, MY POSITION WILL BE TAKEN FROM ME, MY POWER STRIPPED FROM ME, AND I WILL NEVER BE ABLE TO LOOK AT THE MAGNIFICENCE OF THE HUMAN RACE EVER AGAIN.
SO IT IS WITH A HEAVY HEART THAT I RECORD THE FOLLOWING...
MADNESS...

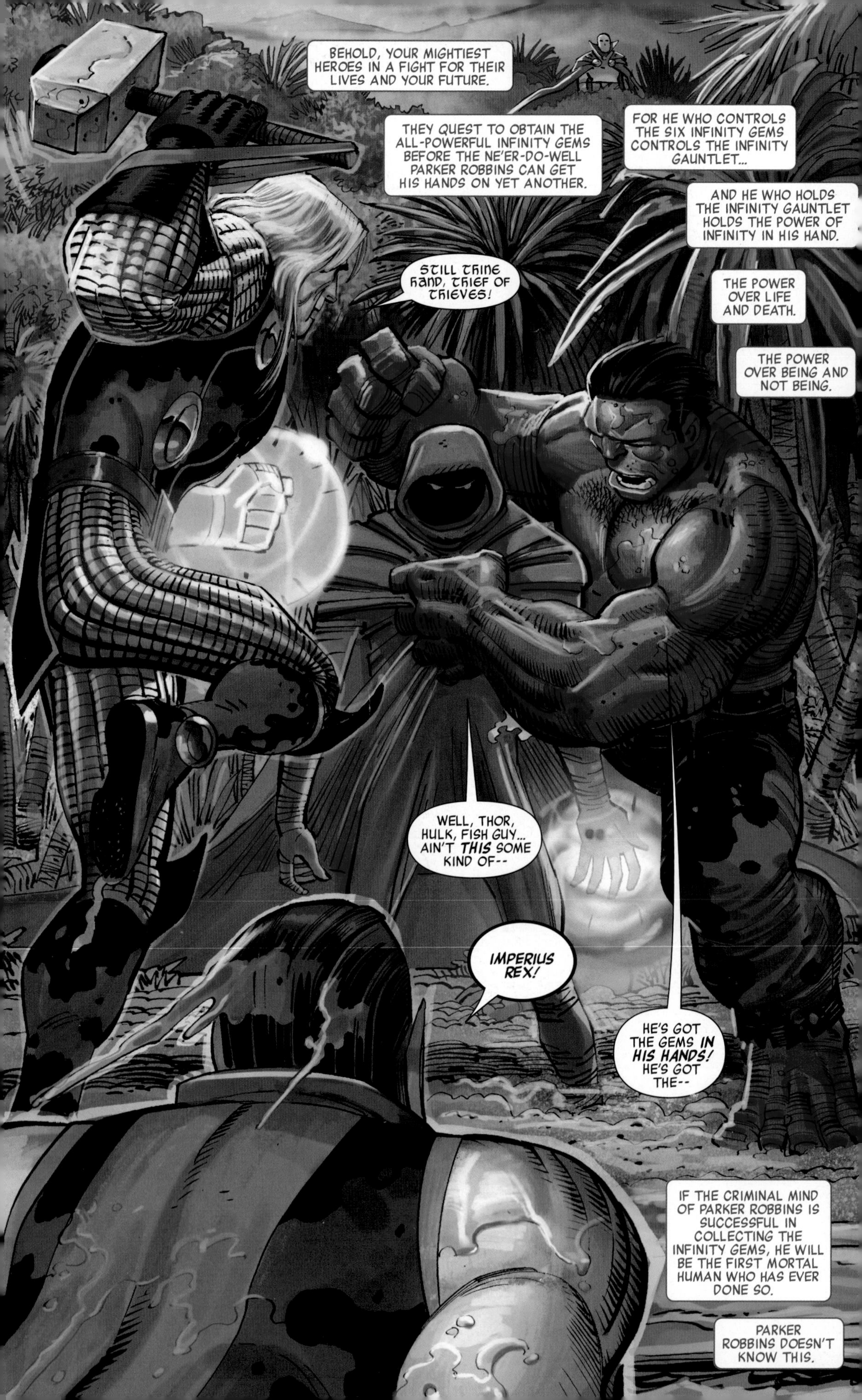
BEHOLD, YOUR MIGHTIEST HEROES IN A FIGHT FOR THEIR LIVES AND YOUR FUTURE.
THEY QUEST TO OBTAIN THE ALL-POWERFUL INFINITY GEMS BEFORE THE NE'ER-DO-WELL PARKER ROBBINS CAN GET HIS HANDS ON YET ANOTHER.
FOR HE WHO CONTROLS THE SIX INFINITY GEMS CONTROLS THE INFINITY GAUNTLET...
AND HE WHO HOLDS THE INFINITY GAUNTLET HOLDS THE POWER OF INFINITY IN HIS HAND.
STILL THINE HAND, THIEF OF THIEVES!
THE POWER OVER LIFE AND DEATH.
THE POWER OVER BEING AND NOT BEING.
WELL, THOR, HULK, FISH GUY... AIN'T THIS SOME KIND OF--
IMPERIUS REX!
HE'S GOT THE GEMS IN HIS HANDS! HE'S GOT THE--
IF THE CRIMINAL MIND OF PARKER ROBBINS IS SUCCESSFUL IN COLLECTING THE INFINITY GEMS, HE WILL BE THE FIRST MORTAL HUMAN WHO HAS EVER DONE SO.
PARKER ROBBINS DOESN'T KNOW THIS.

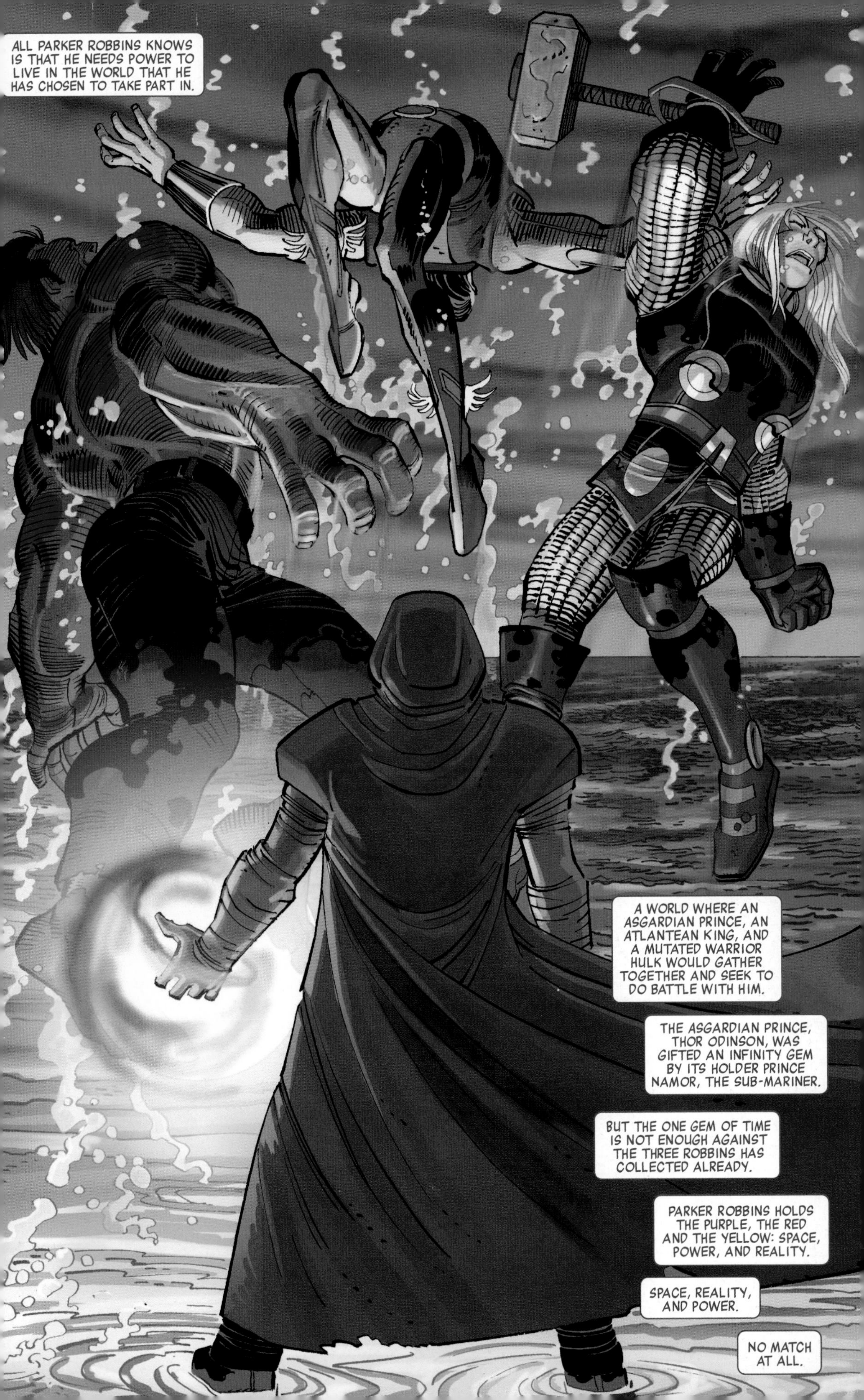
ALL PARKER ROBBINS KNOWS IS THAT HE NEEDS POWER TO LIVE IN THE WORLD THAT HE HAS CHOSEN TO TAKE PART IN.
A WORLD WHERE AN ASGARDIAN PRINCE, AN ATLANTEAN KING, AND A MUTATED WARRIOR HULK WOULD GATHER TOGETHER AND SEEK TO DO BATTLE WITH HIM.
THE ASGARDIAN PRINCE, THOR ODINSON, WAS GIFTED AN INFINITY GEM BY ITS HOLDER PRINCE NAMOR, THE SUB-MARINER.
BUT THE ONE GEM OF TIME IS NOT ENOUGH AGAINST THE THREE ROBBINS HAS COLLECTED ALREADY.
PARKER ROBBINS HOLDS THE PURPLE, THE RED AND THE YELLOW: SPACE, POWER, AND REALITY.
SPACE, REALITY, AND POWER.
NO MATCH AT ALL.

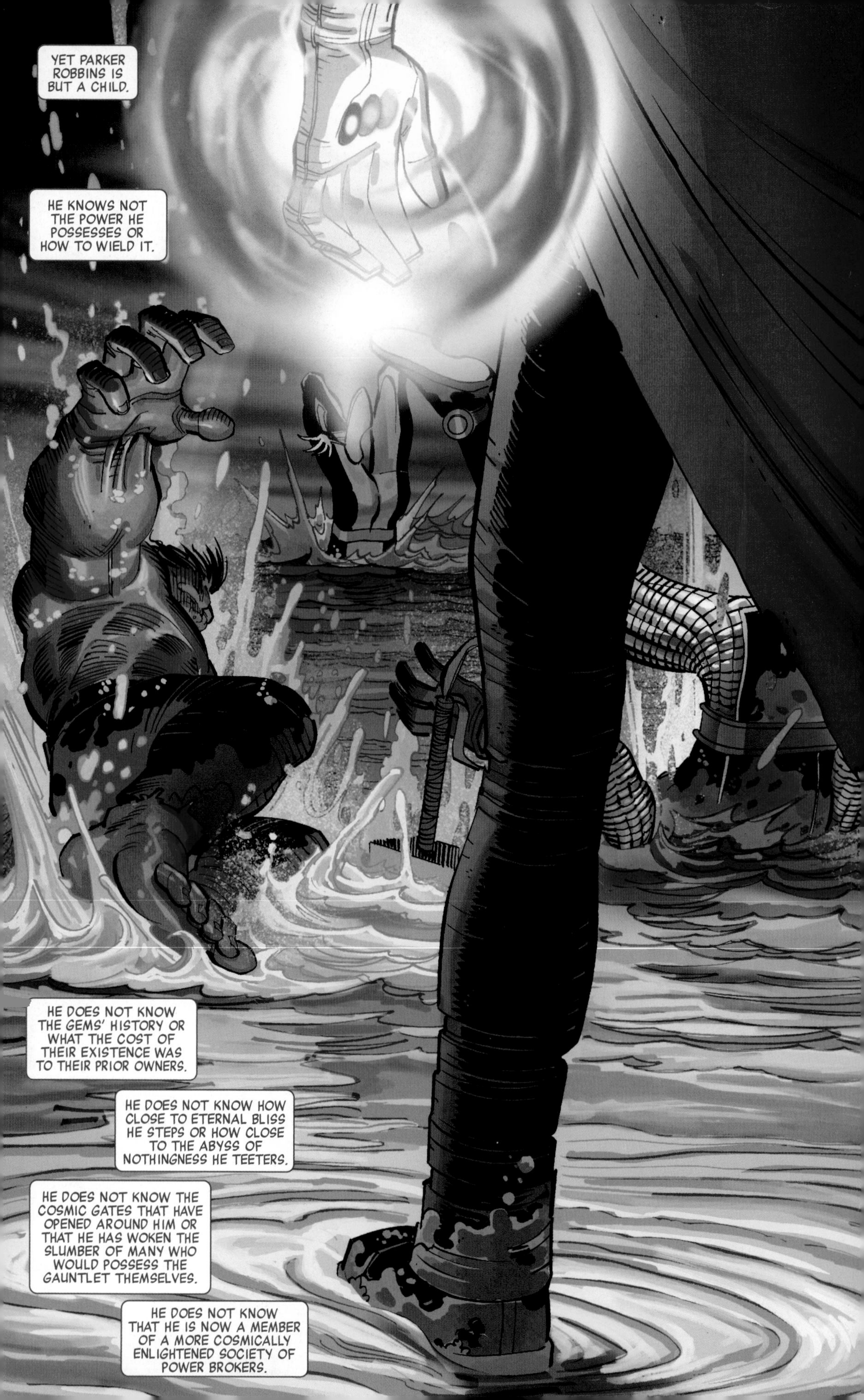
YET PARKER ROBBINS IS BUT A CHILD.
HE KNOWS NOT THE POWER HE POSSESSES OR HOW TO WIELD IT.
HE DOES NOT KNOW THE GEMS' HISTORY OR WHAT THE COST OF THEIR EXISTENCE WAS TO THEIR PRIOR OWNERS.
HE DOES NOT KNOW HOW CLOSE TO ETERNAL BLISS HE STEPS OR HOW CLOSE TO THE ABYSS OF NOTHINGNESS HE TEETERS.
HE DOES NOT KNOW THE COSMIC GATES THAT HAVE OPENED AROUND HIM OR THAT HE HAS WOKEN THE SLUMBER OF MANY WHO WOULD POSSESS THE GAUNTLET THEMSELVES.
HE DOES NOT KNOW THAT HE IS NOW A MEMBER OF A MORE COSMICALLY ENLIGHTENED SOCIETY OF POWER BROKERS.

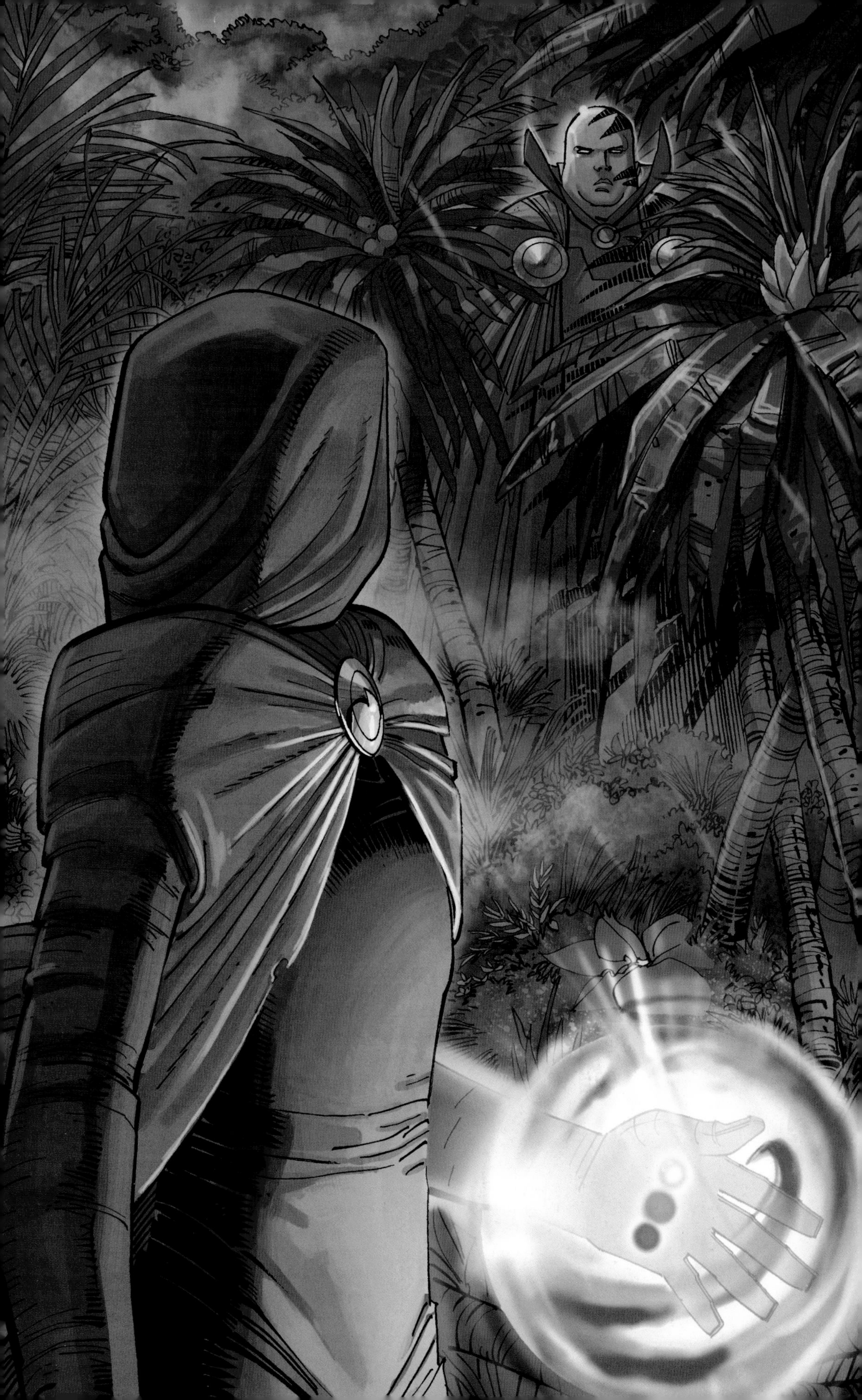

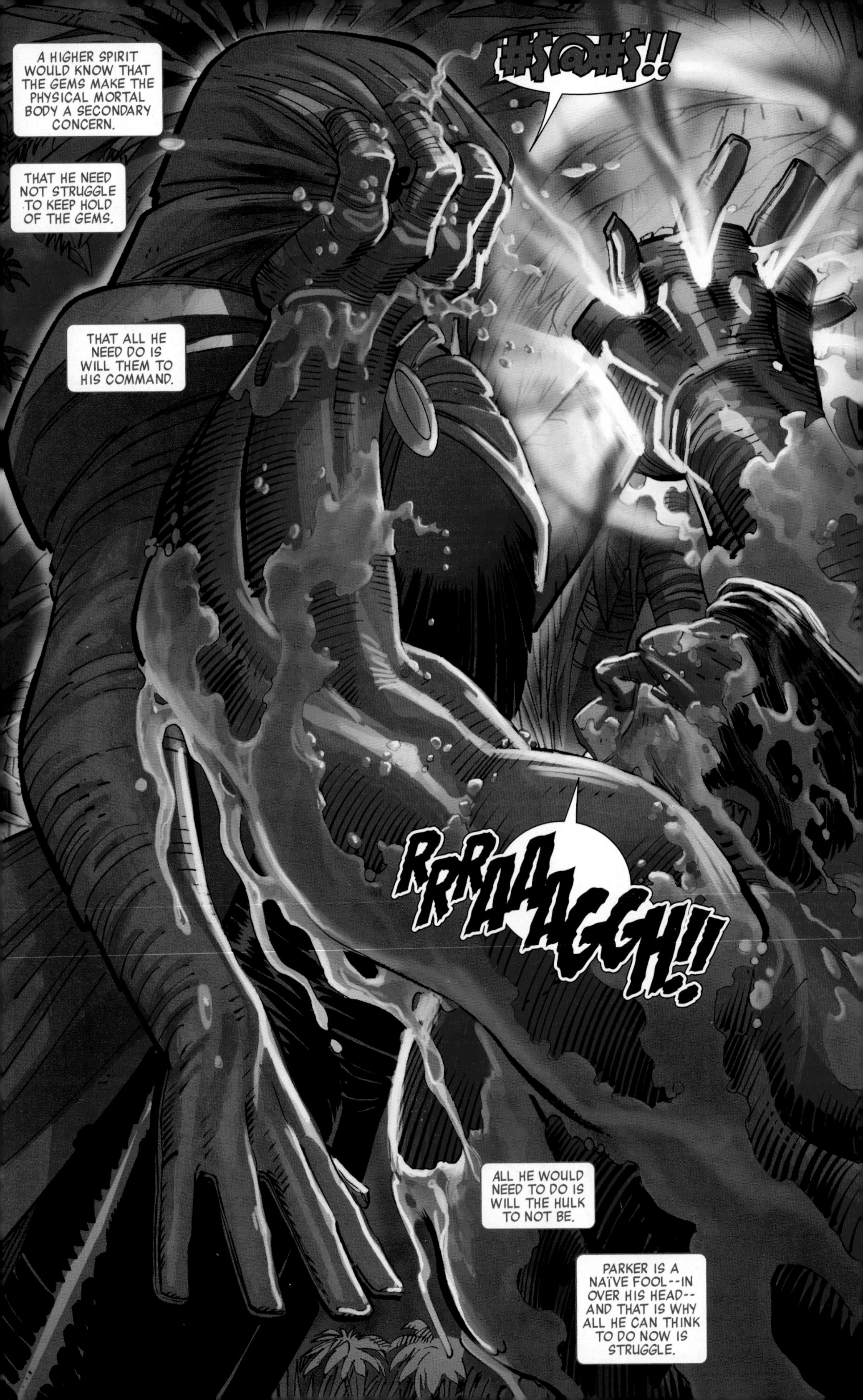

A HIGHER SPIRIT WOULD KNOW THAT THE GEMS MAKE THE PHYSICAL MORTAL BODY A SECONDARY CONCERN.
#$@#$!!
THAT HE NEED NOT STRUGGLE TO KEEP HOLD OF THE GEMS.
THAT ALL HE NEED DO IS WILL THEM TO HIS COMMAND.
RRRAAAGGH!!
ALL HE WOULD NEED TO DO IS WILL THE HULK TO NOT BE.
PARKER IS A NAÏVE FOOL--IN OVER HIS HEAD--AND THAT IS WHY ALL HE CAN THINK TO DO NOW IS STRUGGLE.

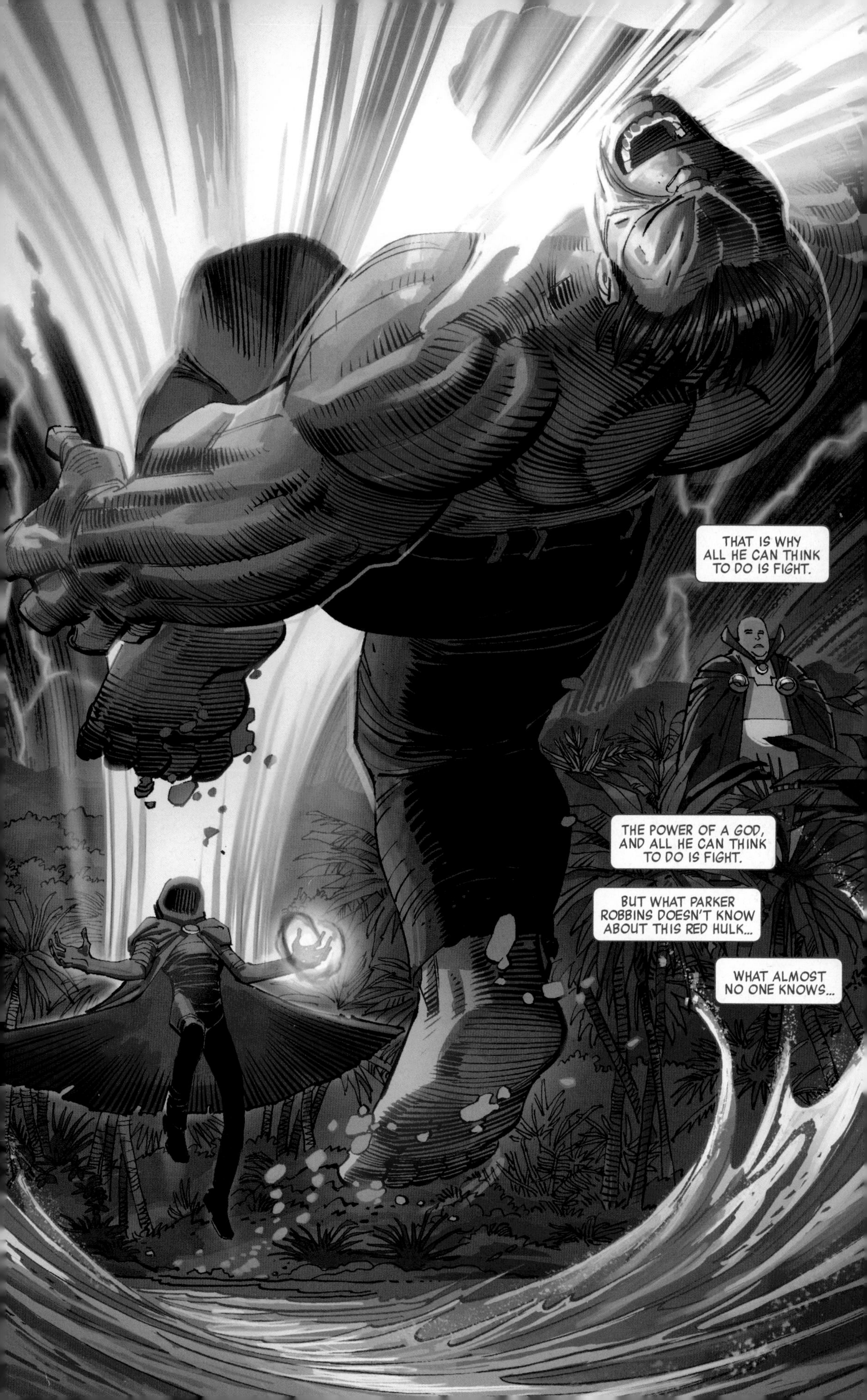
THAT IS WHY ALL HE CAN THINK TO DO IS FIGHT.
THE POWER OF A GOD, AND ALL HE CAN THINK TO DO IS FIGHT.
BUT WHAT PARKER ROBBINS DOESN'T KNOW ABOUT THIS RED HULK...
WHAT ALMOST NO ONE KNOWS...

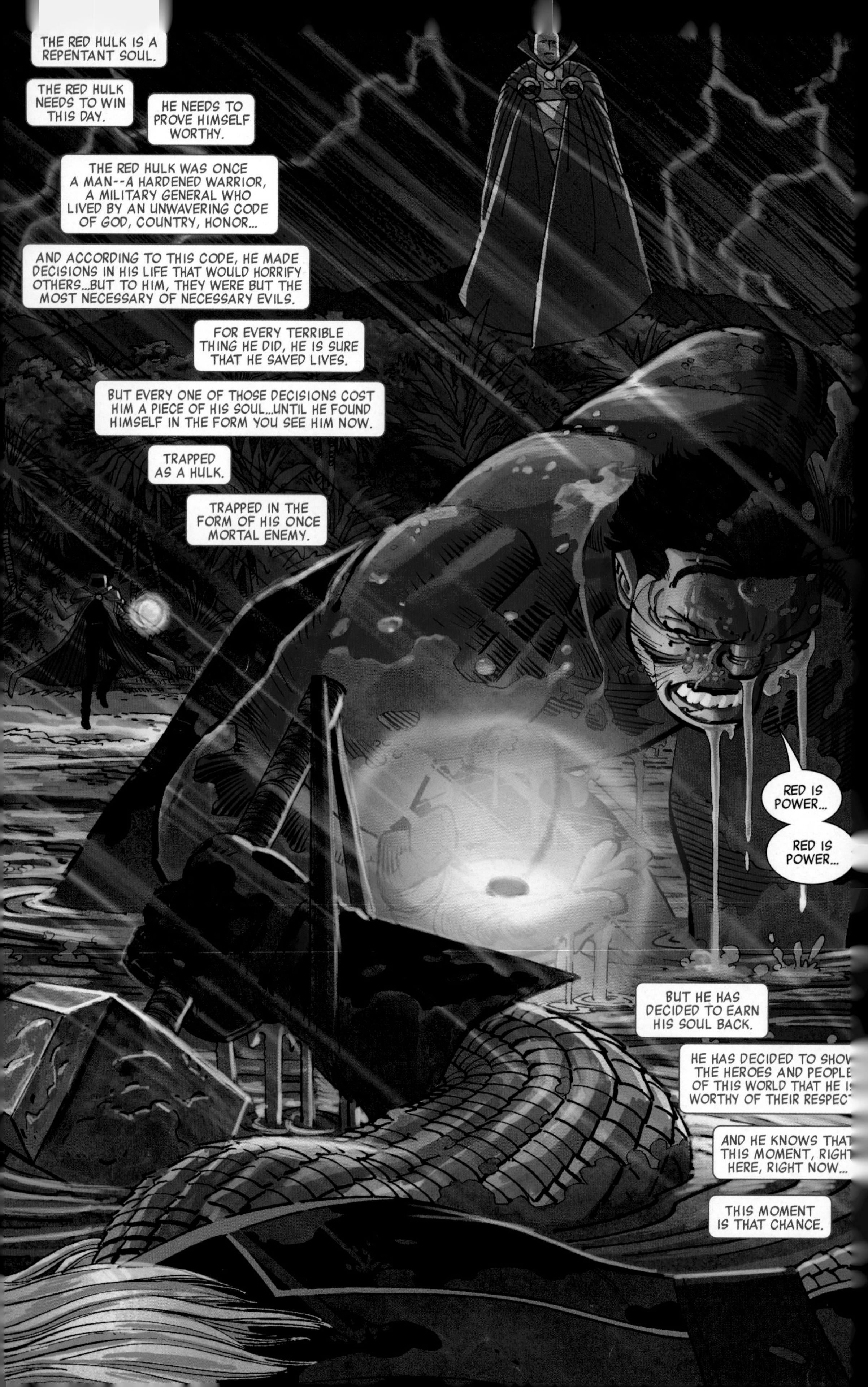
THE RED HULK IS A REPENTANT SOUL.
THE RED HULK NEEDS TO WIN THIS DAY.
HE NEEDS TO PROVE HIMSELF WORTHY.
THE RED HULK WAS ONCE A MAN--A HARDENED WARRIOR, A MILITARY GENERAL WHO LIVED BY AN UNWAVERING CODE OF GOD, COUNTRY, HONOR...
AND ACCORDING TO THIS CODE, HE MADE DECISIONS IN HIS LIFE THAT WOULD HORRIFY OTHERS...BUT TO HIM, THEY WERE BUT THE MOST NECESSARY OF NECESSARY EVILS.
FOR EVERY TERRIBLE THING HE DID, HE IS SURE THAT HE SAVED LIVES.
BUT EVERY ONE OF THOSE DECISIONS COST HIM A PIECE OF HIS SOUL...UNTIL HE FOUND HIMSELF IN THE FORM YOU SEE HIM NOW.
TRAPPED AS A HULK.
TRAPPED IN THE FORM OF HIS ONCE MORTAL ENEMY.
RED IS POWER...
RED IS POWER...
BUT HE HAS DECIDED TO EARN HIS SOUL BACK.
HE HAS DECIDED TO SHOW THE HEROES AND PEOPLE OF THIS WORLD THAT HE IS WORTHY OF THEIR RESPECT
AND HE KNOWS THAT THIS MOMENT, RIGHT HERE, RIGHT NOW...
THIS MOMENT IS THAT CHANCE.

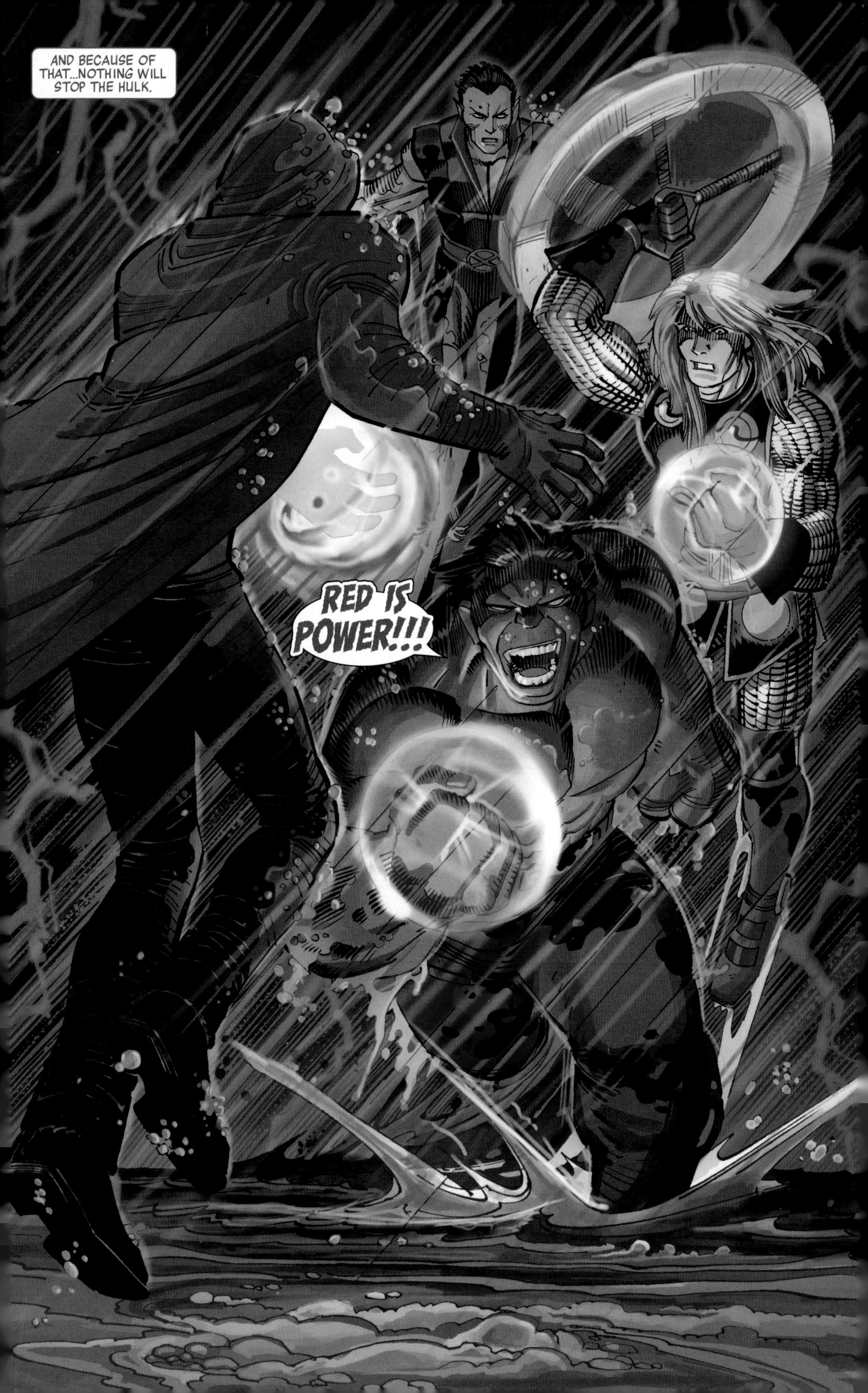
AND BECAUSE OF THAT...NOTHING WILL STOP THE HULK.
RED IS POWER!!!

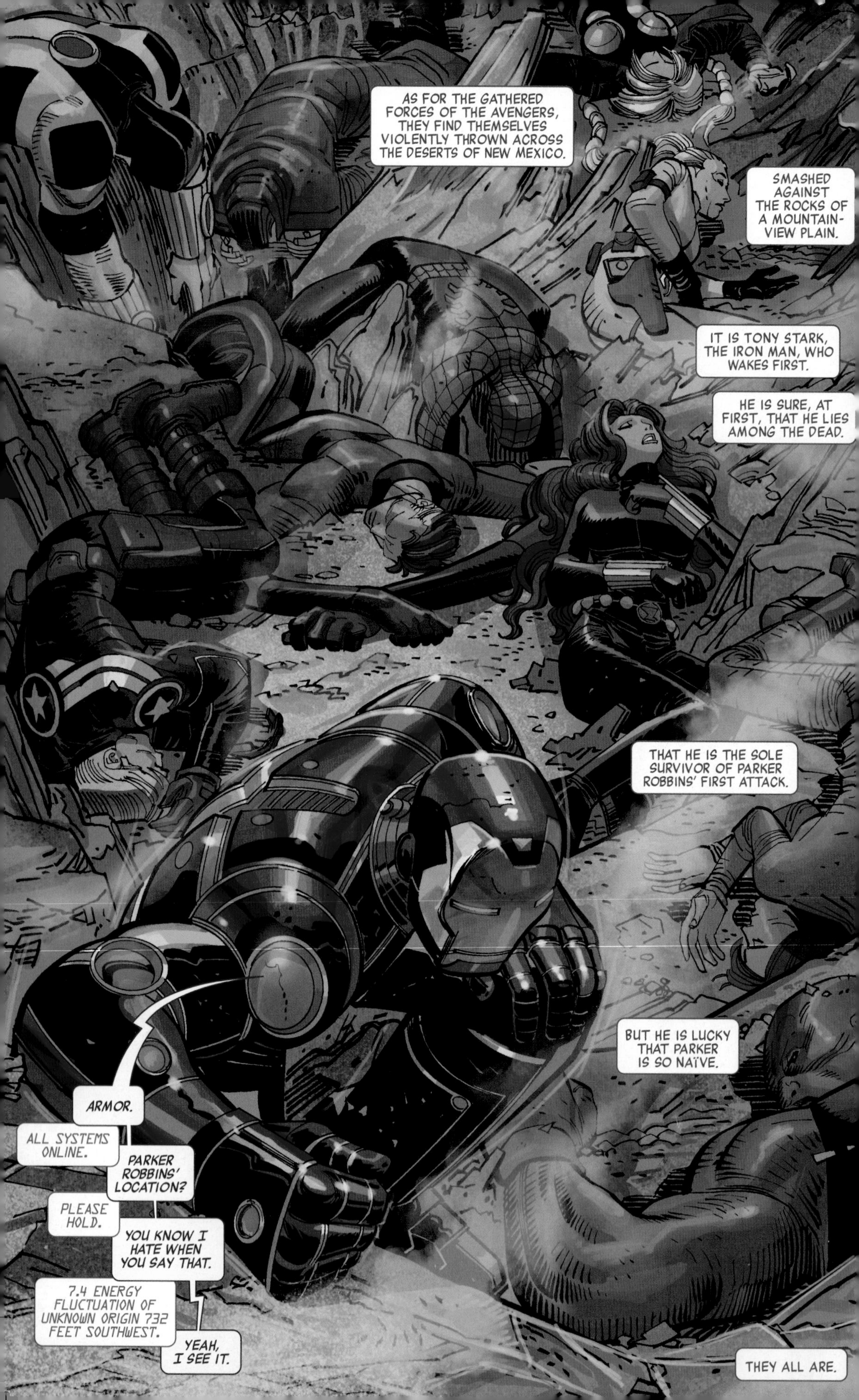
AS FOR THE GATHERED FORCES OF THE AVENGERS, THEY FIND THEMSELVES VIOLENTLY THROWN ACROSS THE DESERTS OF NEW MEXICO.
SMASHED AGAINST THE ROCKS OF A MOUNTAIN-VIEW PLAIN.
IT IS TONY STARK, THE IRON MAN, WHO WAKES FIRST.
HE IS SURE, AT FIRST, THAT HE LIES AMONG THE DEAD.
THAT HE IS THE SOLE SURVIVOR OF PARKER ROBBINS' FIRST ATTACK.
BUT HE IS LUCKY THAT PARKER IS SO NAÏVE.
ARMOR.
ALL SYSTEMS ONLINE.
PARKER ROBBINS' LOCATION?
PLEASE HOLD.
YOU KNOW I HATE WHEN YOU SAY THAT.
7.4 ENERGY FLUCTUATION OF UNKNOWN ORIGIN 732 FEET SOUTHWEST.
YEAH, I SEE IT.
THEY ALL ARE.

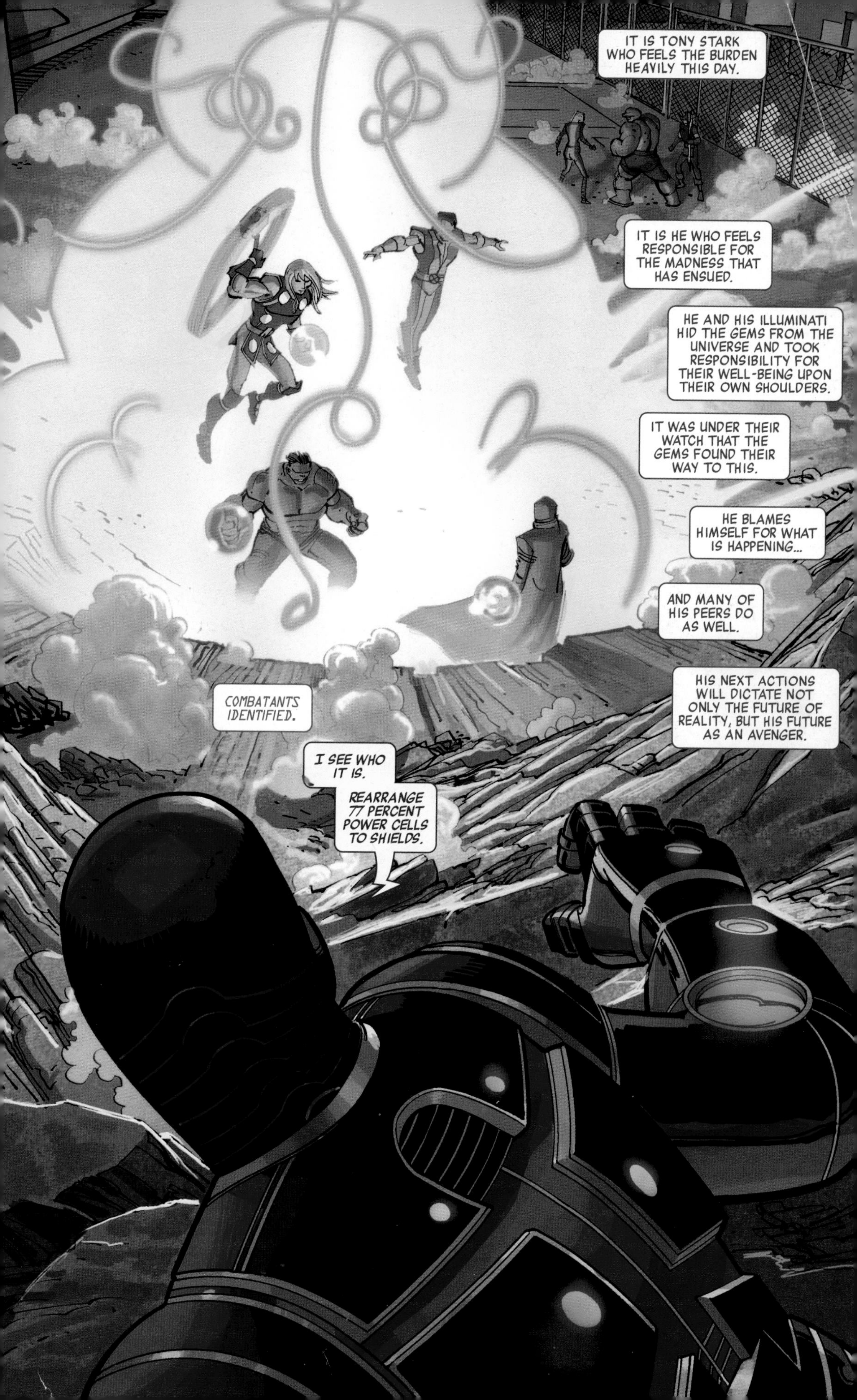
IT IS TONY STARK WHO FEELS THE BURDEN HEAVILY THIS DAY.
IT IS HE WHO FEELS RESPONSIBLE FOR THE MADNESS THAT HAS ENSUED.
HE AND HIS ILLUMINATI HID THE GEMS FROM THE UNIVERSE AND TOOK RESPONSIBILITY FOR THEIR WELL-BEING UPON THEIR OWN SHOULDERS.
IT WAS UNDER THEIR WATCH THAT THE GEMS FOUND THEIR WAY TO THIS.
HE BLAMES HIMSELF FOR WHAT IS HAPPENING...
AND MANY OF HIS PEERS DO AS WELL.
HIS NEXT ACTIONS WILL DICTATE NOT ONLY THE FUTURE OF REALITY, BUT HIS FUTURE AS AN AVENGER.
COMBATANTS IDENTIFIED.
I SEE WHO IT IS.
REARRANGE 77 PERCENT POWER CELLS TO SHIELDS.

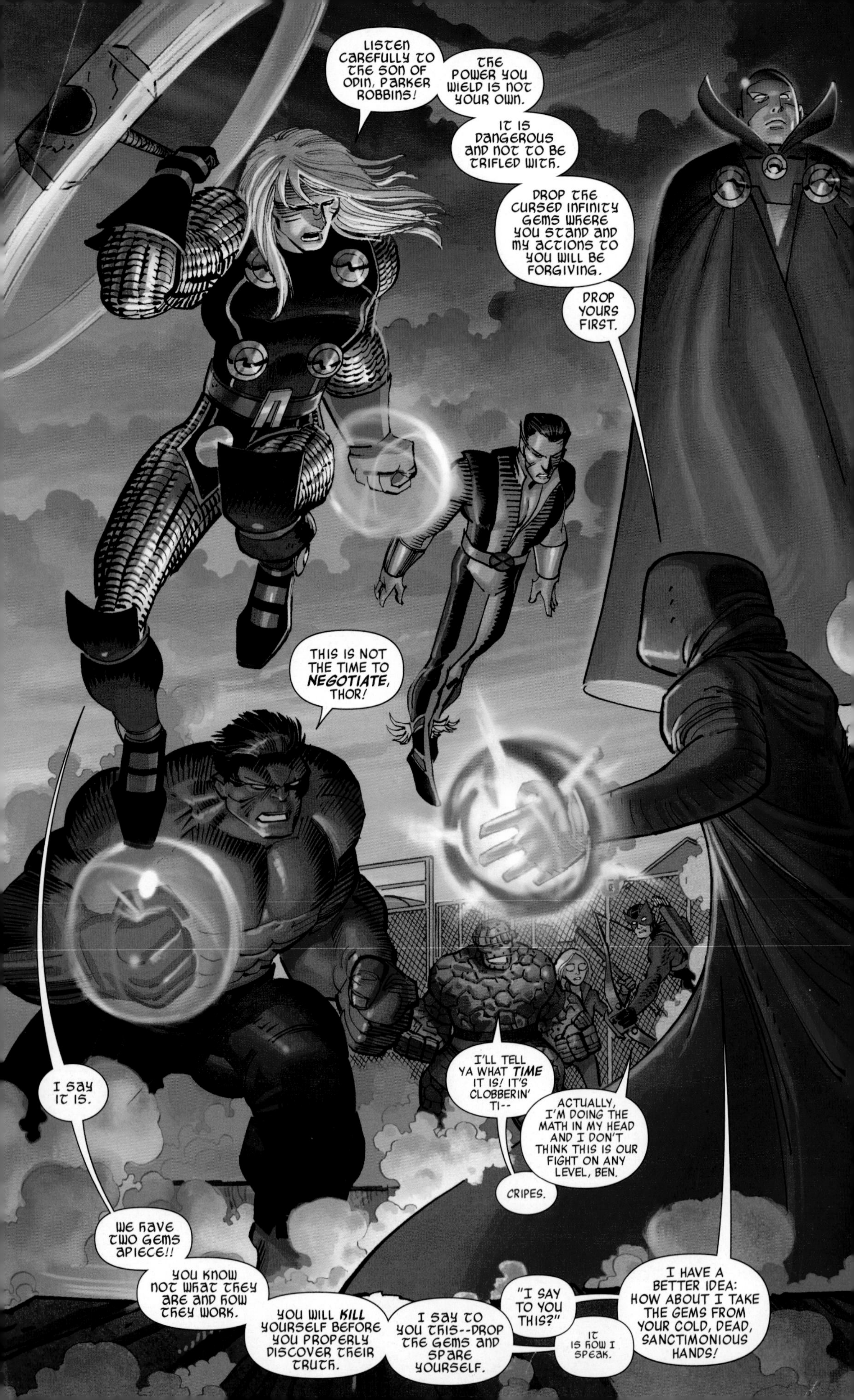
LISTEN CAREFULLY TO THE SON OF ODIN, PARKER ROBBINS!
THE POWER YOU WIELD IS NOT YOUR OWN.
IT IS DANGEROUS AND NOT TO BE TRIFLED WITH.
DROP THE CURSED INFINITY GEMS WHERE YOU STAND AND MY ACTIONS TO YOU WILL BE FORGIVING.
DROP YOURS FIRST.
THIS IS NOT THE TIME TO NEGOTIATE, THOR!
I SAY IT IS.
I'LL TELL YA WHAT TIME IT IS! IT'S CLOBBERIN' TI--
ACTUALLY, I'M DOING THE MATH IN MY HEAD AND I DON'T THINK THIS IS OUR FIGHT ON ANY LEVEL, BEN.
CRIPES.
WE HAVE TWO GEMS APIECE!!
YOU KNOW NOT WHAT THEY ARE AND HOW THEY WORK.
YOU WILL KILL YOURSELF BEFORE YOU PROPERLY DISCOVER THEIR TRUTH.
I SAY TO YOU THIS--DROP THE GEMS AND SPARE YOURSELF.
"I SAY TO YOU THIS?"
IT IS HOW I SPEAK.
I HAVE A BETTER IDEA: HOW ABOUT I TAKE THE GEMS FROM YOUR COLD, DEAD, SANCTIMONIOUS HANDS!

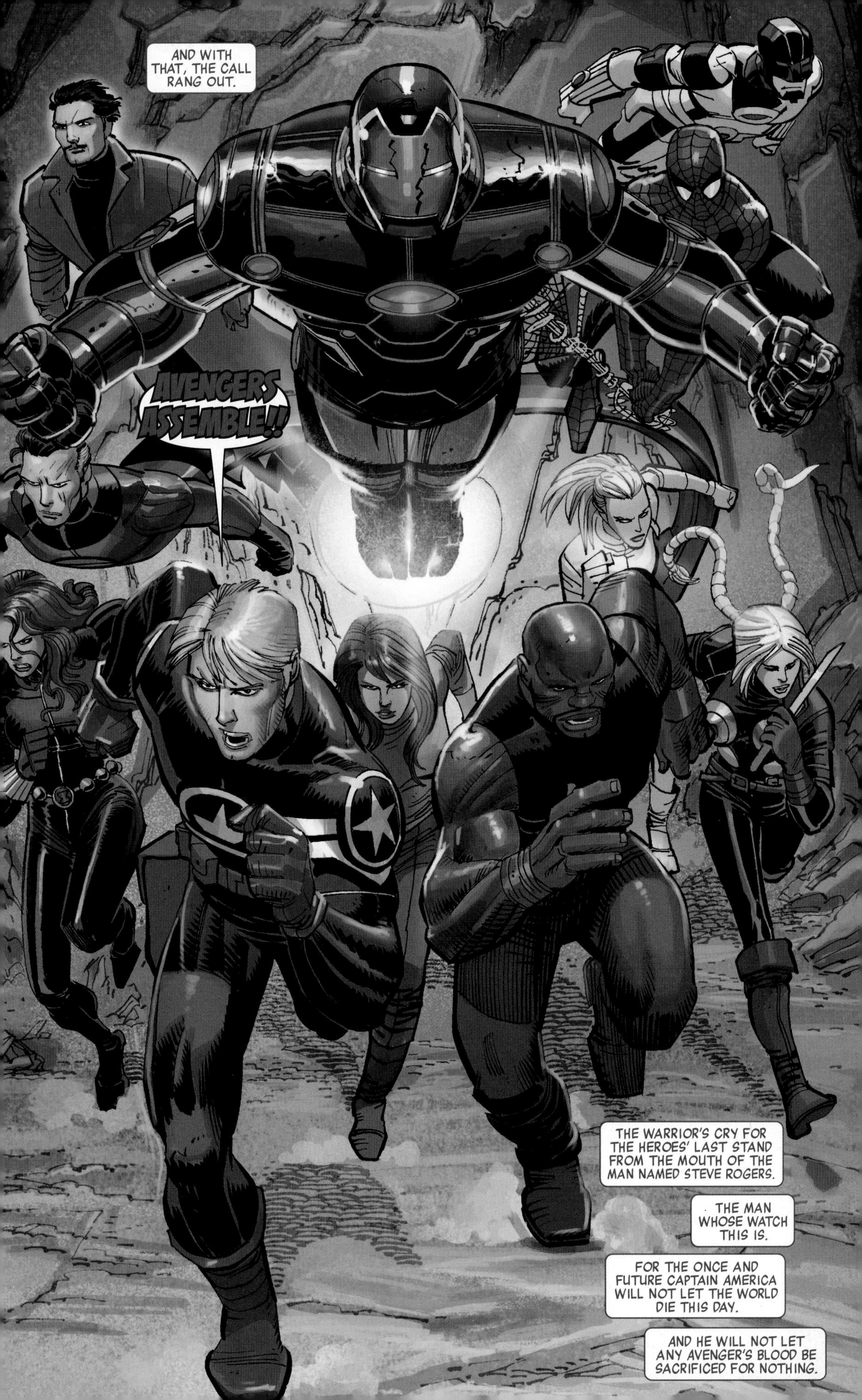
AND WITH THAT, THE CALL RANG OUT.
AVENGERS ASSEMBLE!!
THE WARRIOR'S CRY FOR THE HEROES' LAST STAND FROM THE MOUTH OF THE MAN NAMED STEVE ROGERS.
THE MAN WHOSE WATCH THIS IS.
FOR THE ONCE AND FUTURE CAPTAIN AMERICA WILL NOT LET THE WORLD DIE THIS DAY.
AND HE WILL NOT LET ANY AVENGER'S BLOOD BE SACRIFICED FOR NOTHING.

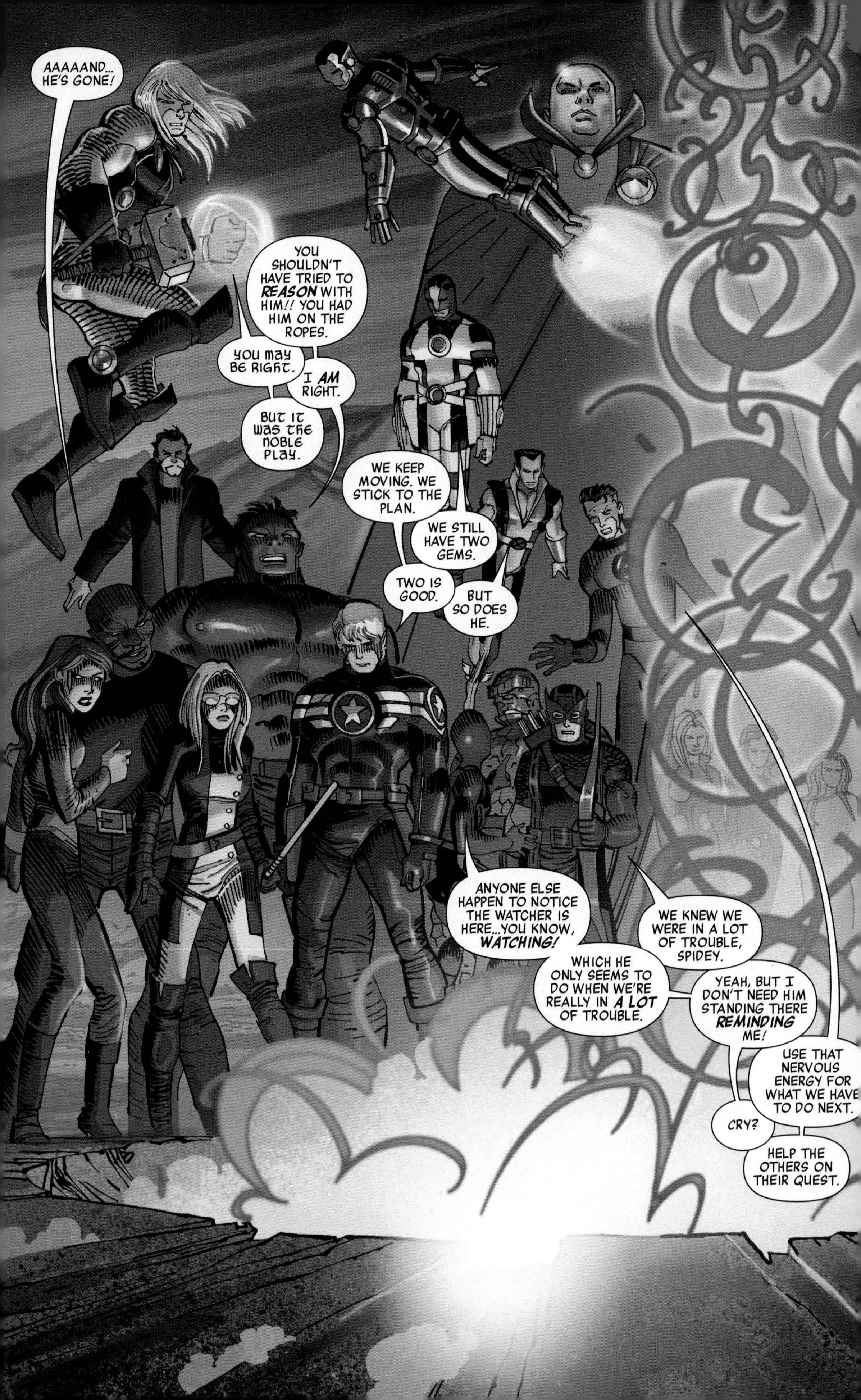
AAAAAND... HE'S GONE!
YOU SHOULDN'T HAVE TRIED TO REASON WITH HIM!! YOU HAD HIM ON THE ROPES.
YOU MAY BE RIGHT.
I AM RIGHT.
BUT IT WAS THE NOBLE PLAY.
WE KEEP MOVING. WE STICK TO THE PLAN.
WE STILL HAVE TWO GEMS.
TWO IS GOOD.
BUT SO DOES HE.
ANYONE ELSE HAPPEN TO NOTICE THE WATCHER IS HERE...YOU KNOW, WATCHING!
WE KNEW WE WERE IN A LOT OF TROUBLE, SPIDEY.
WHICH HE ONLY SEEMS TO DO WHEN WE'RE REALLY IN A LOT OF TROUBLE.
YEAH, BUT I DON'T NEED HIM STANDING THERE REMINDING ME!
USE THAT NERVOUS ENERGY FOR WHAT WE HAVE TO DO NEXT.
CRY?
HELP THE OTHERS ON THEIR QUEST.

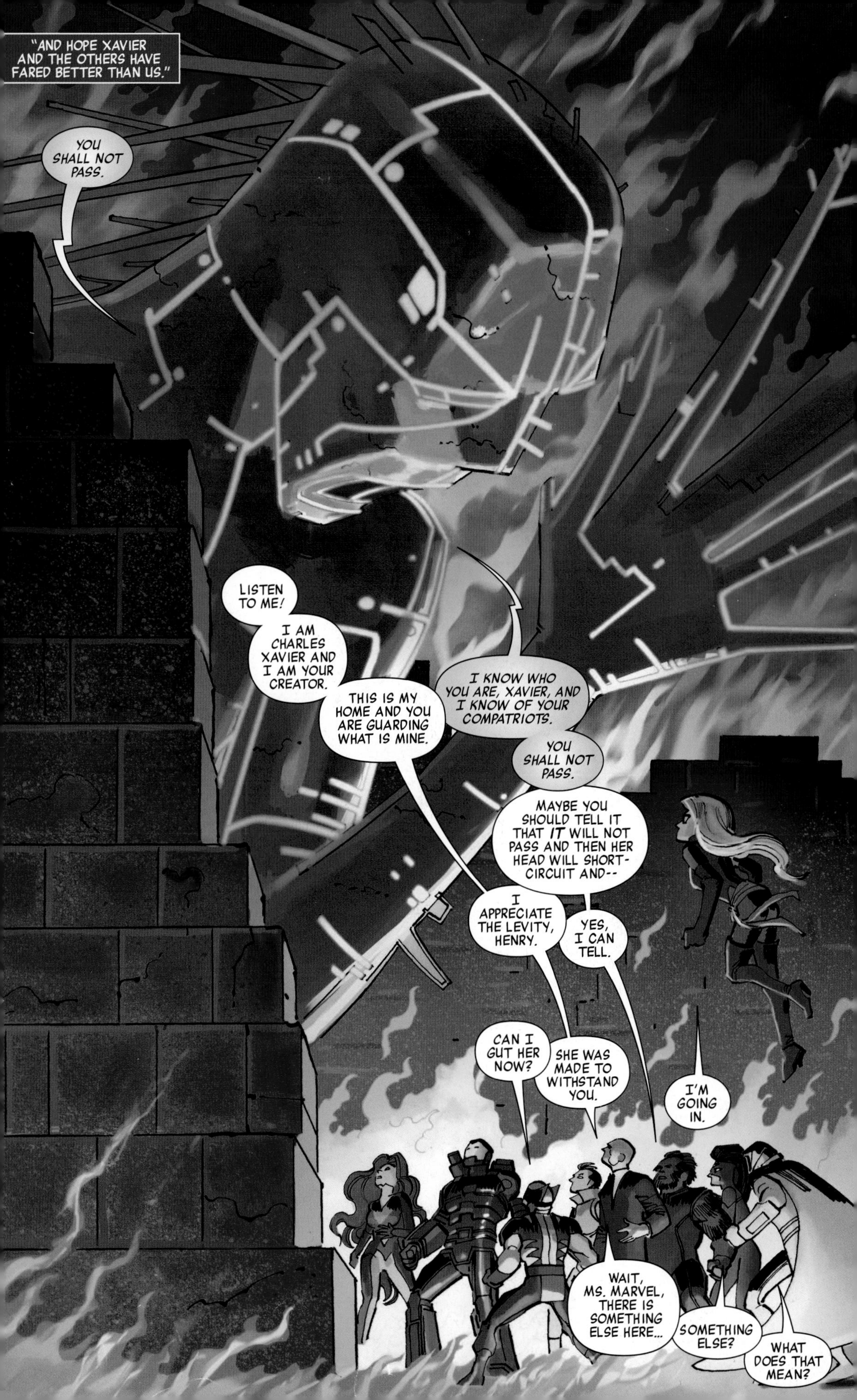
"AND HOPE XAVIER AND THE OTHERS HAVE FARED BETTER THAN US."
YOU SHALL NOT PASS.
LISTEN TO ME!
I AM CHARLES XAVIER AND I AM YOUR CREATOR.
THIS IS MY HOME AND YOU ARE GUARDING WHAT IS MINE.
I KNOW WHO YOU ARE, XAVIER, AND I KNOW OF YOUR COMPATRIOTS.
YOU SHALL NOT PASS.
MAYBE YOU SHOULD TELL IT THAT IT WILL NOT PASS AND THEN HER HEAD WILL SHORT-CIRCUIT AND--
I APPRECIATE THE LEVITY, HENRY.
YES, I CAN TELL.
CAN I GUT HER NOW?
SHE WAS MADE TO WITHSTAND YOU.
I'M GOING IN.
WAIT, MS. MARVEL, THERE IS SOMETHING ELSE HERE...
SOMETHING ELSE?
WHAT DOES THAT MEAN?

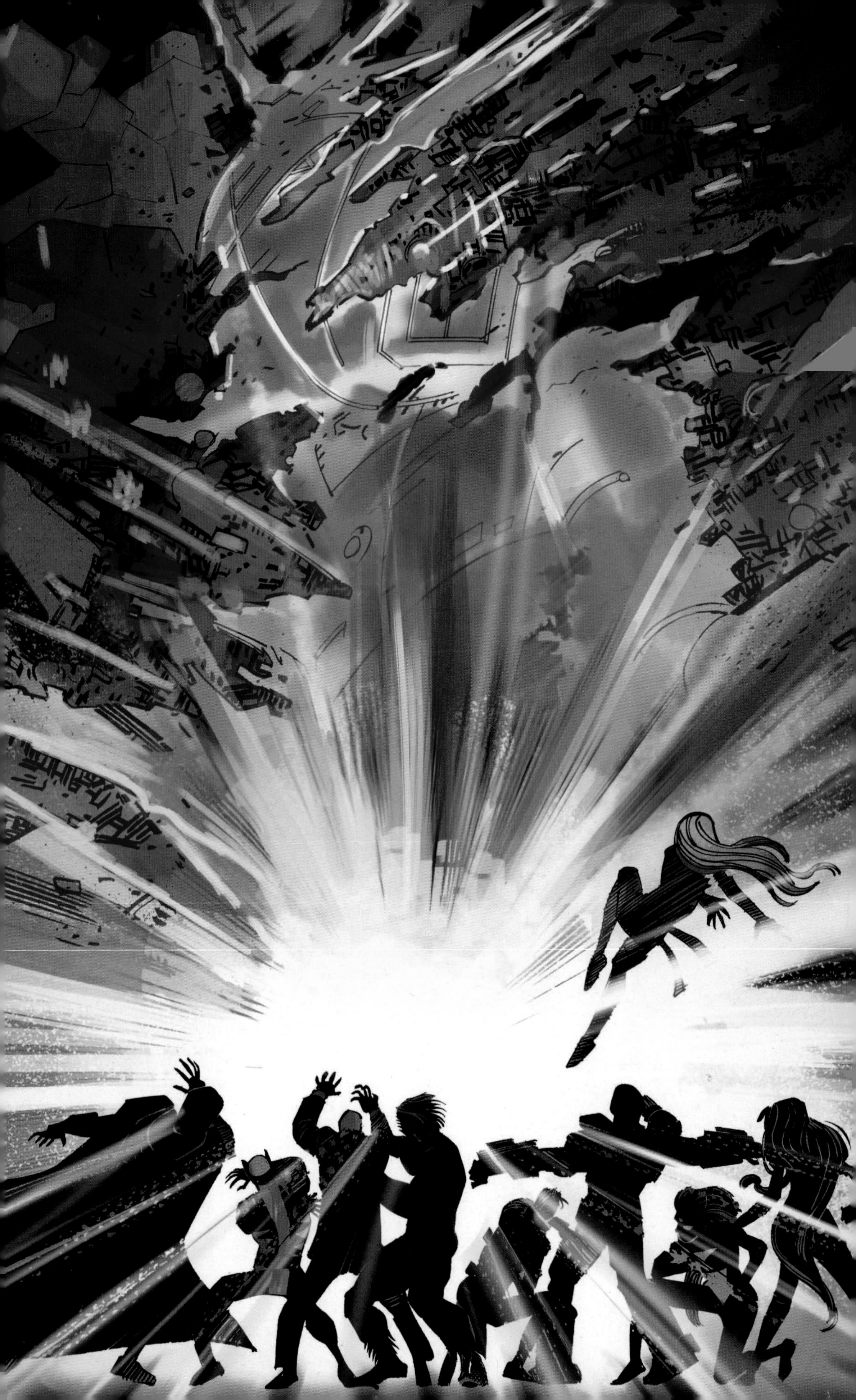

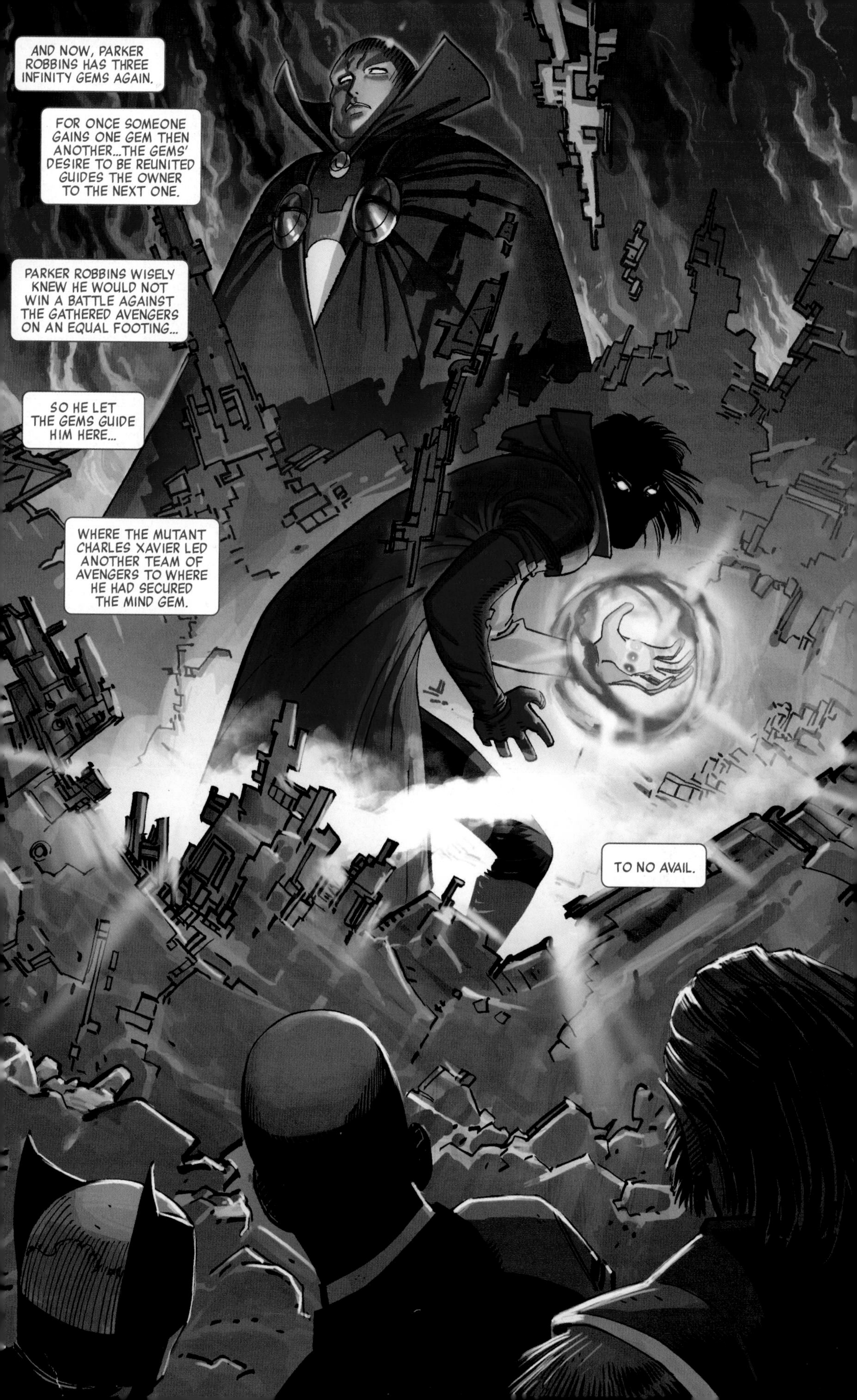
AND NOW, PARKER ROBBINS HAS THREE INFINITY GEMS AGAIN.
FOR ONCE SOMEONE GAINS ONE GEM THEN ANOTHER...THE GEMS' DESIRE TO BE REUNITED GUIDES THE OWNER TO THE NEXT ONE.
PARKER ROBBINS WISELY KNEW HE WOULD NOT WIN A BATTLE AGAINST THE GATHERED AVENGERS ON AN EQUAL FOOTING...
SO HE LET THE GEMS GUIDE HIM HERE...
WHERE THE MUTANT CHARLES XAVIER LED ANOTHER TEAM OF AVENGERS TO WHERE HE HAD SECURED THE MIND GEM.
TO NO AVAIL.

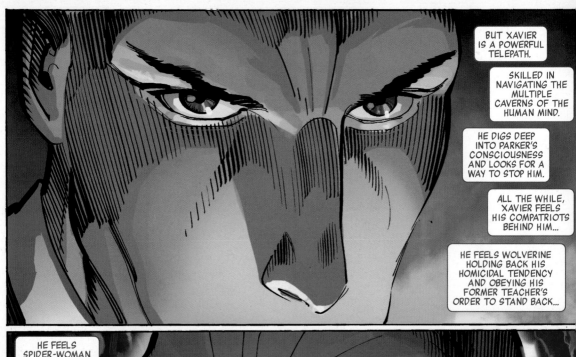

BUT XAVIER IS A POWERFUL TELEPATH.

SKILLED IN NAVIGATING THE MULTIPLE CAVERNS OF THE HUMAN MIND.

HE DIGS DEEP INTO PARKER'S CONSCIOUSNESS AND LOOKS FOR A WAY TO STOP HIM.

ALL THE WHILE, XAVIER FEELS HIS COMPATRIOTS BEHIND HIM...

HE FEELS WOLVERINE HOLDING BACK HIS HOMICIDAL TENDENCY AND OBEYING HIS FORMER TEACHER'S ORDER TO STAND BACK...

HE FEELS SPIDER-WOMAN BLASTING HER PHEROMONE POWER DIRECTLY AT PARKER, TRYING TO DO WHATEVER SHE CAN TO HELP CONFUSE HIM.

HE FEELS THE MAN WHO CALLS HIMSELF MOON KNIGHT WRESTLING WITH HIS DIFFERENT PERSONALITIES, DEVISING A PLAN OF ATTACK...

HE FEELS HIS FORMER STUDENT DR. HENRY McCOY, THE BEAST, DOING THE MATH IN HIS HEAD ON JUST HOW MUCH DAMAGE PARKER ROBBINS WILL DO TO THE WORLD, AND THE NUMBERS ARE NOT PROMISING.

CHARLES XAVIER IS BREAKING HIS OWN PERSONAL RULES NOW-- DIGGING INTO THE MIND OF A MAN WITHOUT HIS PERMISSION...

ATTEMPTING TO PLANT COMMANDS THAT ARE AGAINST PARKER ROBBINS' OWN WILL.

BUT XAVIER WAS PUT IN CHARGE OF THE BLUE INFINITY GEM.

THE MIND GEM.

IT ALLOWS THE HOLDER TO BOOST HIS MENTAL POWERS AND TO GAIN INSIGHT INTO THE THOUGHTS AND DREAMS OF ANYONE.

WITHOUT EVEN KNOWING HOW HE'S DOING IT, PARKER ROBBINS IS FIGHTING BACK AGAINST THE MOST POWERFUL TELEPATH ON THE PLANET.

AND XAVIER IS FIGHTING A BATTLE MORE POWERFUL THAN ANYTHING HE'S EVER COME UP AGAINST BEFORE.

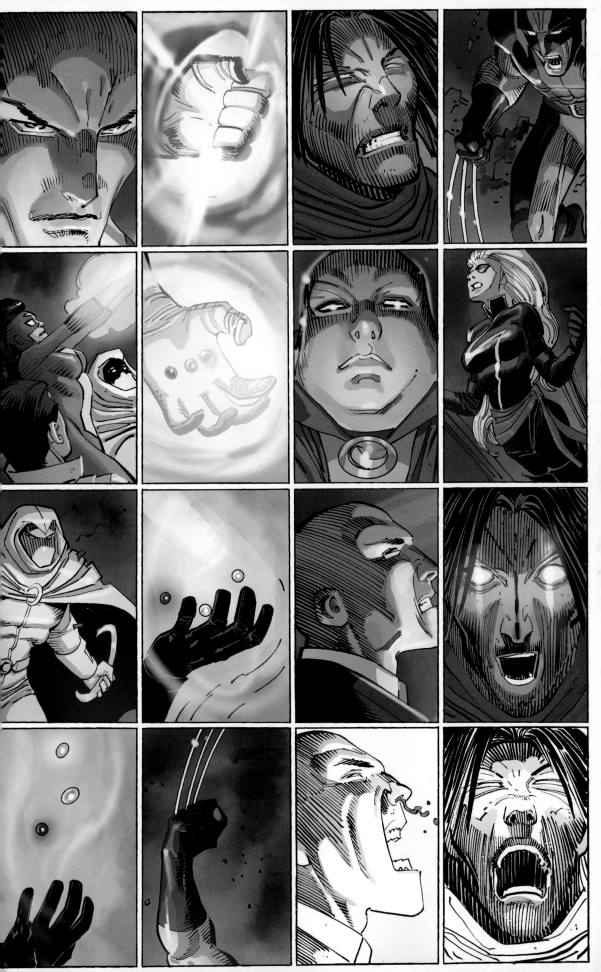

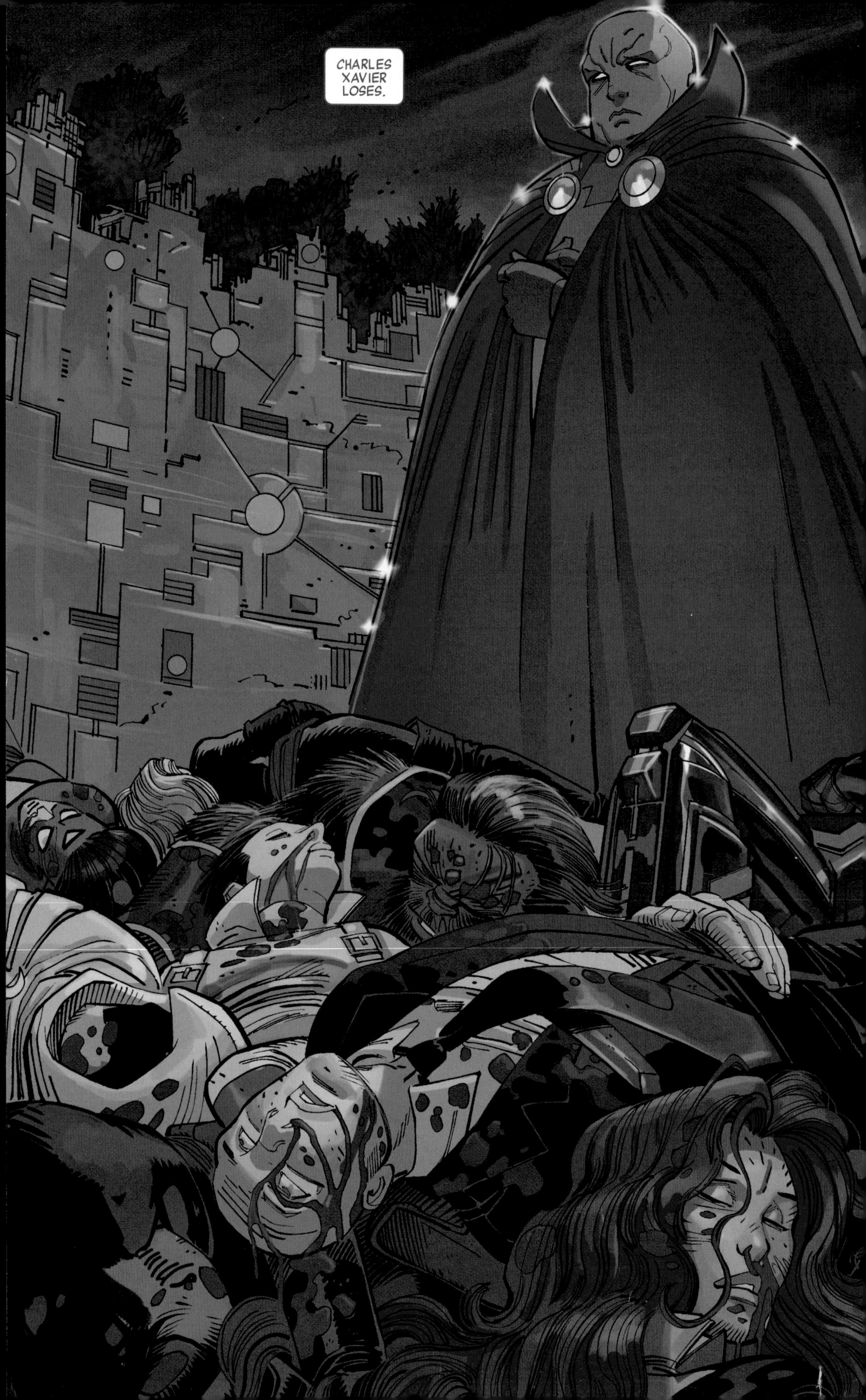
CHARLES XAVIER LOSES.

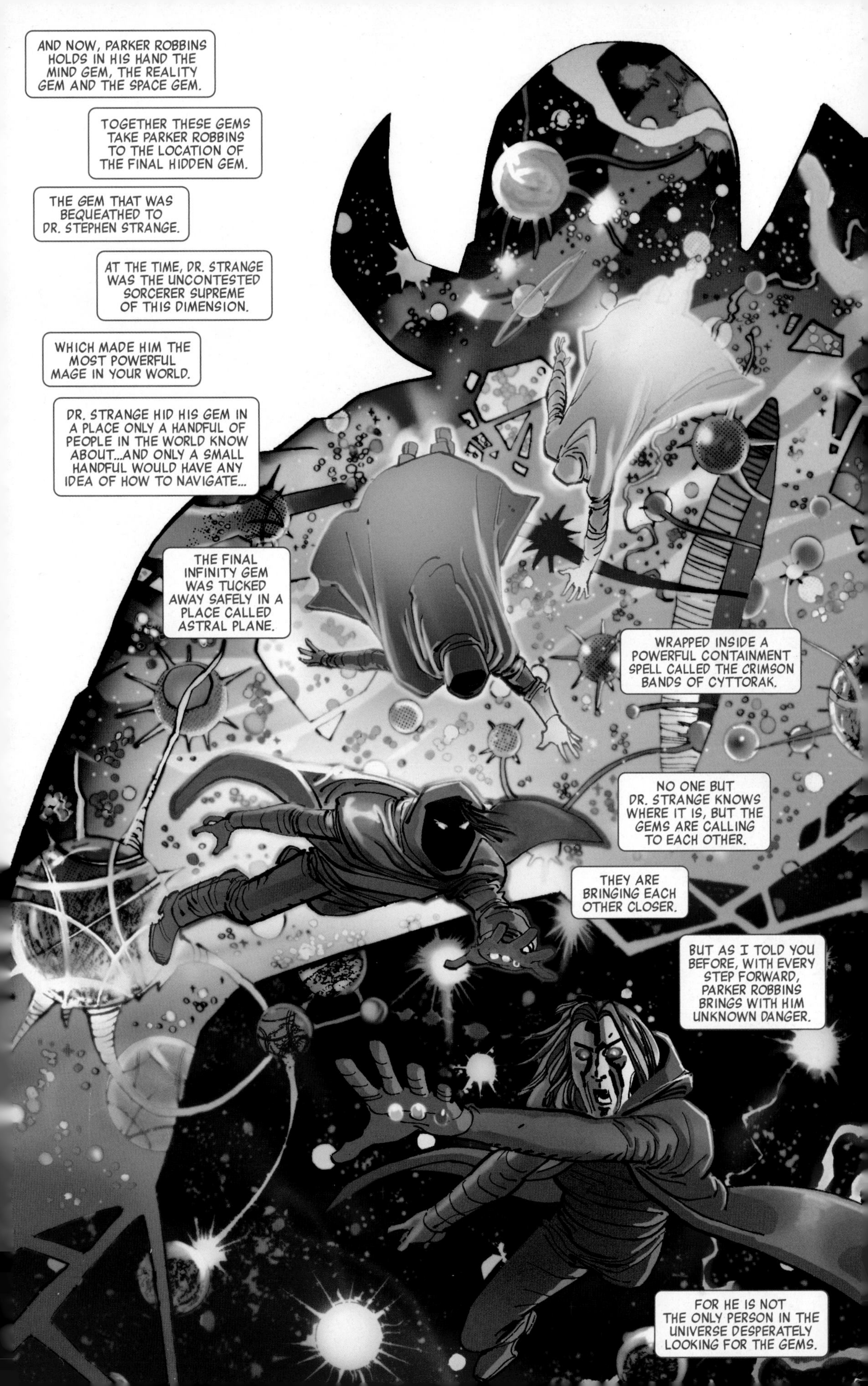
AND NOW, PARKER ROBBINS HOLDS IN HIS HAND THE MIND GEM, THE REALITY GEM AND THE SPACE GEM.
TOGETHER THESE GEMS TAKE PARKER ROBBINS TO THE LOCATION OF THE FINAL HIDDEN GEM.
THE GEM THAT WAS BEQUEATHED TO DR. STEPHEN STRANGE.
AT THE TIME, DR. STRANGE WAS THE UNCONTESTED SORCERER SUPREME OF THIS DIMENSION.
WHICH MADE HIM THE MOST POWERFUL MAGE IN YOUR WORLD.
DR. STRANGE HID HIS GEM IN A PLACE ONLY A HANDFUL OF PEOPLE IN THE WORLD KNOW ABOUT...AND ONLY A SMALL HANDFUL WOULD HAVE ANY IDEA OF HOW TO NAVIGATE...
THE FINAL INFINITY GEM WAS TUCKED AWAY SAFELY IN A PLACE CALLED ASTRAL PLANE.
WRAPPED INSIDE A POWERFUL CONTAINMENT SPELL CALLED THE CRIMSON BANDS OF CYTTORAK.
NO ONE BUT DR. STRANGE KNOWS WHERE IT IS, BUT THE GEMS ARE CALLING TO EACH OTHER.
THEY ARE BRINGING EACH OTHER CLOSER.
BUT AS I TOLD YOU BEFORE, WITH EVERY STEP FORWARD, PARKER ROBBINS BRINGS WITH HIM UNKNOWN DANGER.
FOR HE IS NOT THE ONLY PERSON IN THE UNIVERSE DESPERATELY LOOKING FOR THE GEMS.

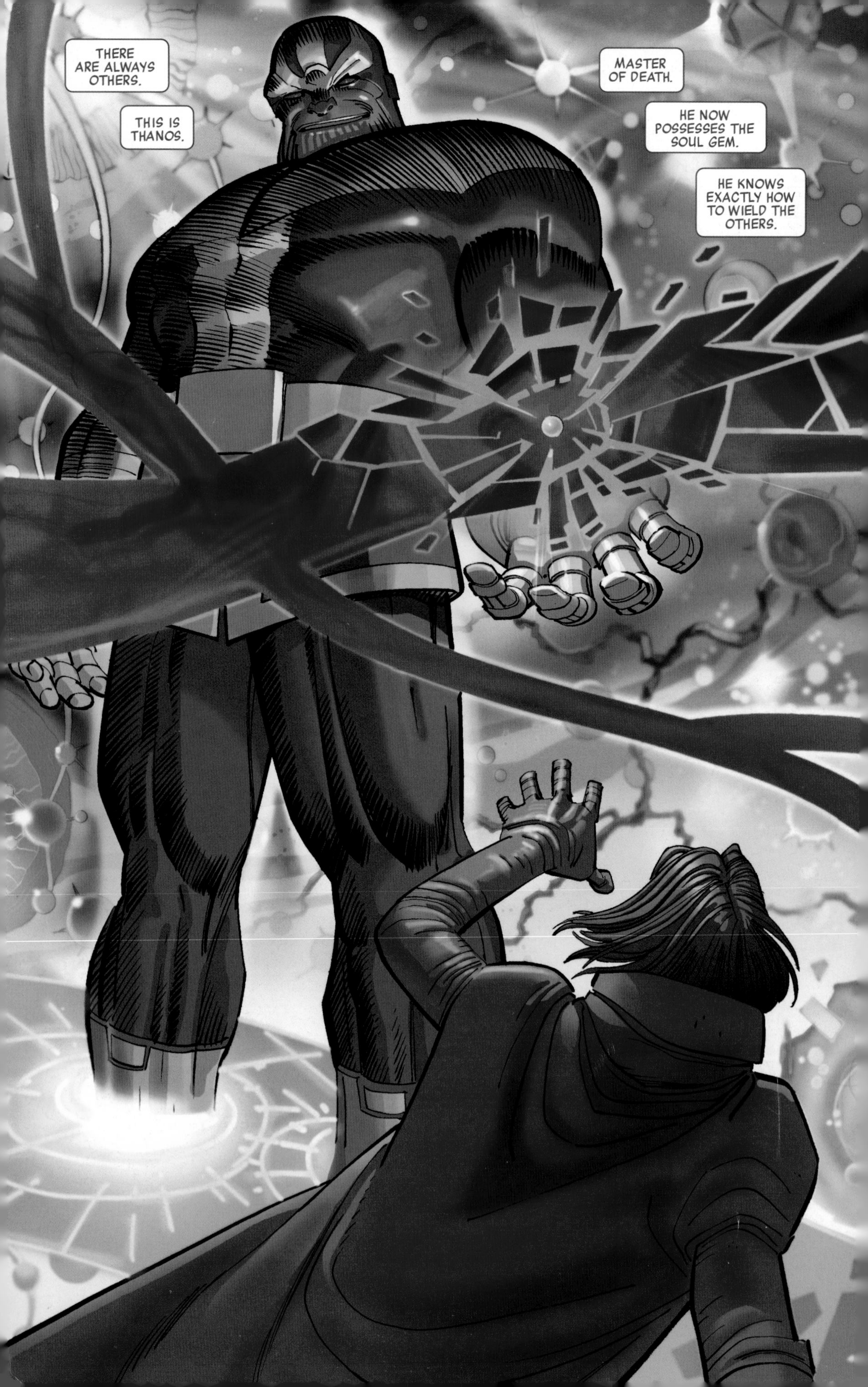
THERE ARE ALWAYS OTHERS.
THIS IS THANOS.
MASTER OF DEATH.
HE NOW POSSESSES THE SOUL GEM.
HE KNOWS EXACTLY HOW TO WIELD THE OTHERS.

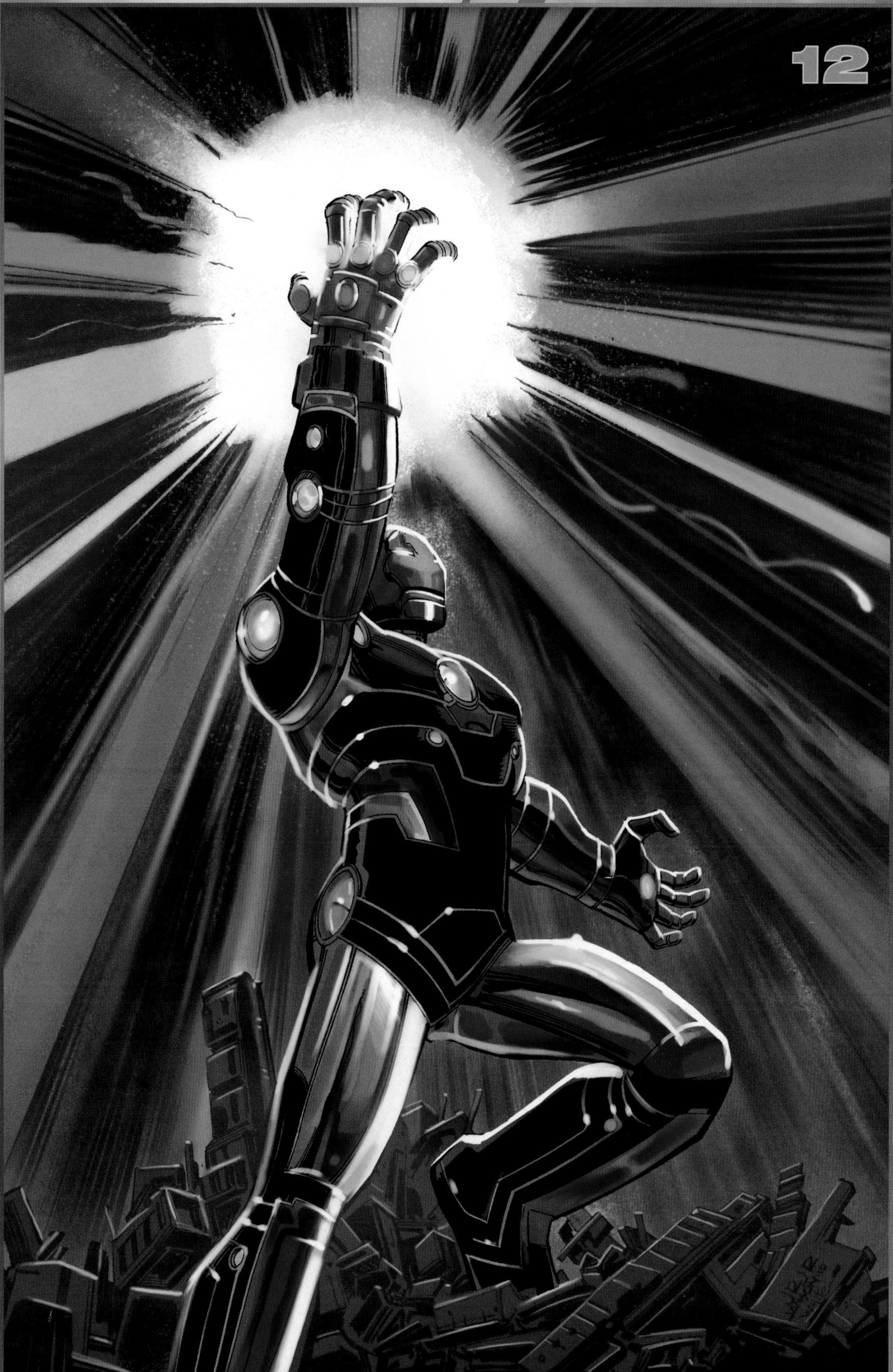
12

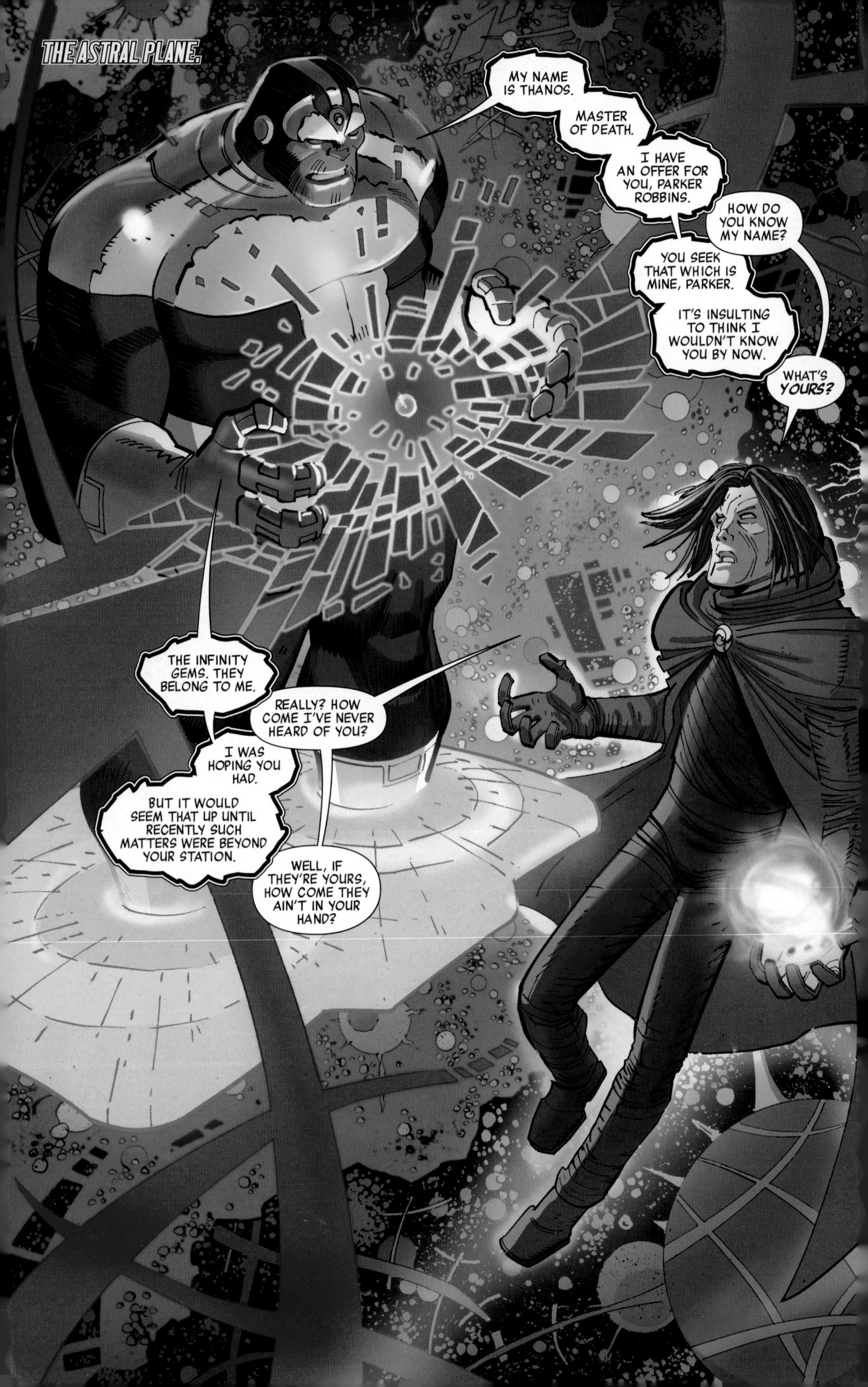
THE ASTRAL PLANE.
MY NAME IS THANOS.
MASTER OF DEATH.
I HAVE AN OFFER FOR YOU, PARKER ROBBINS.
HOW DO YOU KNOW MY NAME?
YOU SEEK THAT WHICH IS MINE, PARKER.
IT'S INSULTING TO THINK I WOULDN'T KNOW YOU BY NOW.
WHAT'S YOURS?
THE INFINITY GEMS. THEY BELONG TO ME.
REALLY? HOW COME I'VE NEVER HEARD OF YOU?
I WAS HOPING YOU HAD.
BUT IT WOULD SEEM THAT UP UNTIL RECENTLY SUCH MATTERS WERE BEYOND YOUR STATION.
WELL, IF THEY'RE YOURS, HOW COME THEY AIN'T IN YOUR HAND?

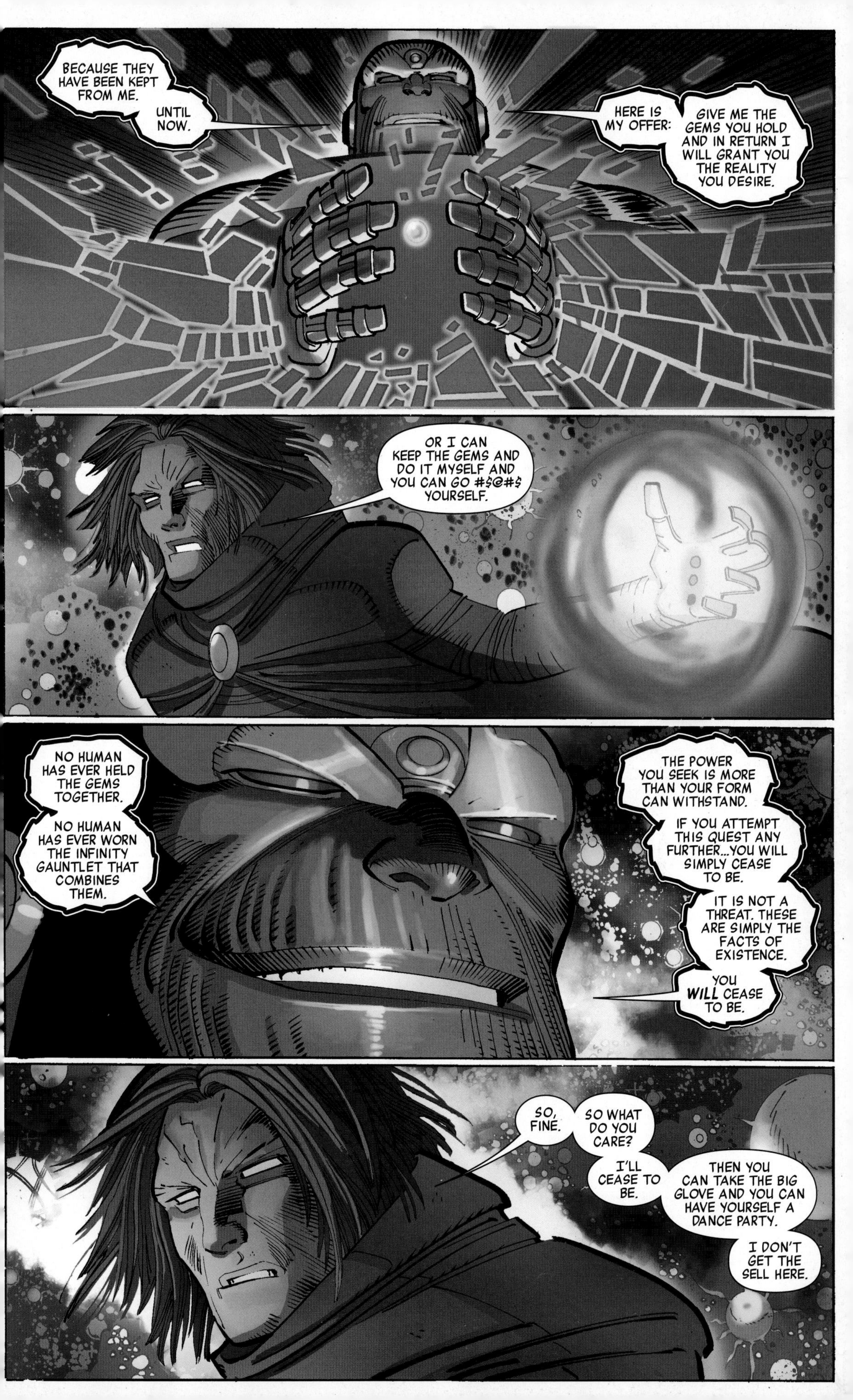
BECAUSE THEY HAVE BEEN KEPT FROM ME.
UNTIL NOW.
HERE IS MY OFFER:
GIVE ME THE GEMS YOU HOLD AND IN RETURN I WILL GRANT YOU THE REALITY YOU DESIRE.
OR I CAN KEEP THE GEMS AND DO IT MYSELF AND YOU CAN GO #$@#$ YOURSELF.
NO HUMAN HAS EVER HELD THE GEMS TOGETHER.
NO HUMAN HAS EVER WORN THE INFINITY GAUNTLET THAT COMBINES THEM.
THE POWER YOU SEEK IS MORE THAN YOUR FORM CAN WITHSTAND.
IF YOU ATTEMPT THIS QUEST ANY FURTHER...YOU WILL SIMPLY CEASE TO BE.
IT IS NOT A THREAT. THESE ARE SIMPLY THE FACTS OF EXISTENCE.
YOU **WILL** CEASE TO BE.
SO, FINE.
SO WHAT DO YOU CARE?
I'LL CEASE TO BE.
THEN YOU CAN TAKE THE BIG GLOVE AND YOU CAN HAVE YOURSELF A DANCE PARTY.
I DON'T GET THE SELL HERE.

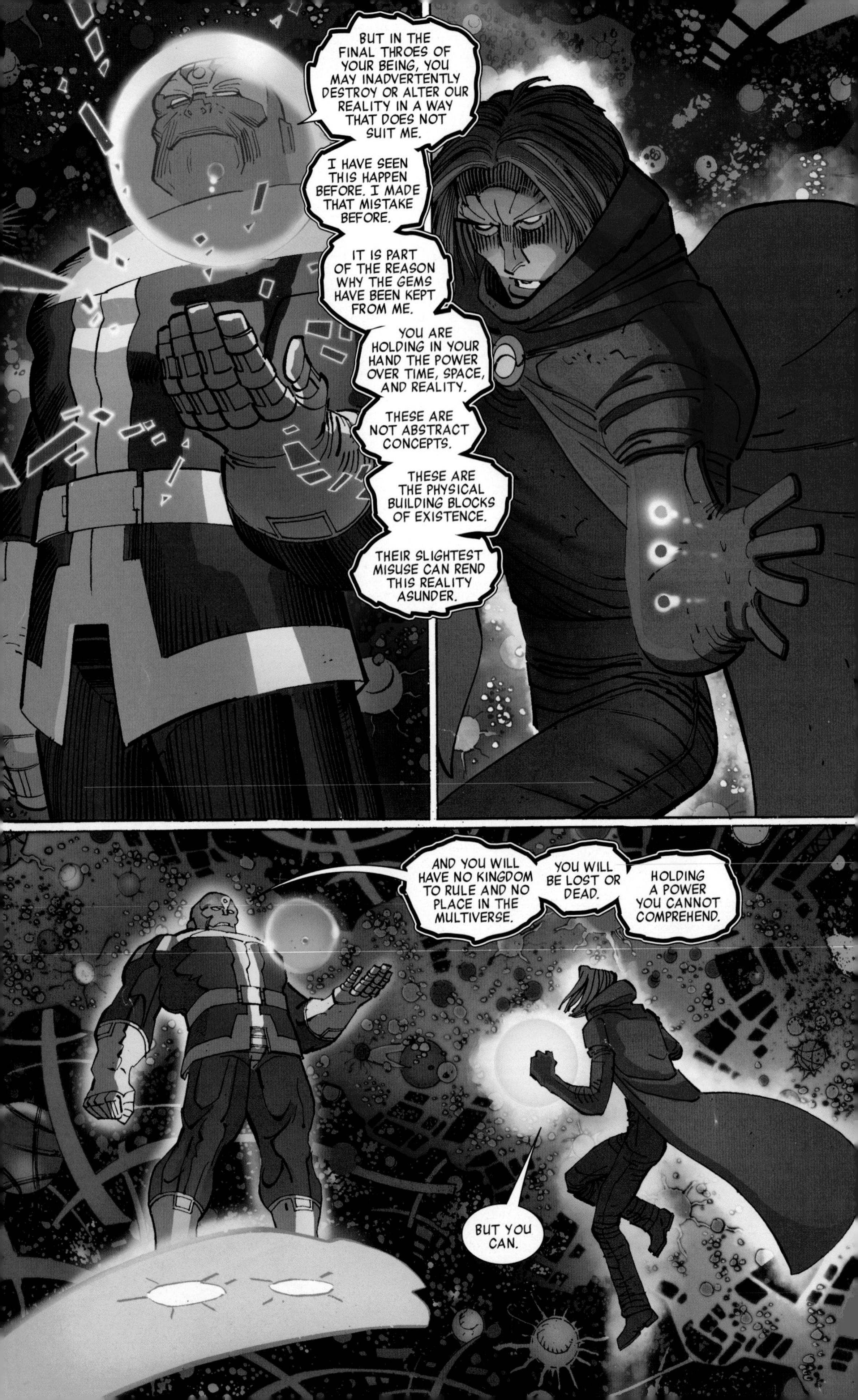
BUT IN THE FINAL THROES OF YOUR BEING, YOU MAY INADVERTENTLY DESTROY OR ALTER OUR REALITY IN A WAY THAT DOES NOT SUIT ME.
I HAVE SEEN THIS HAPPEN BEFORE. I MADE THAT MISTAKE BEFORE.
IT IS PART OF THE REASON WHY THE GEMS HAVE BEEN KEPT FROM ME.
YOU ARE HOLDING IN YOUR HAND THE POWER OVER TIME, SPACE, AND REALITY.
THESE ARE NOT ABSTRACT CONCEPTS.
THESE ARE THE PHYSICAL BUILDING BLOCKS OF EXISTENCE.
THEIR SLIGHTEST MISUSE CAN REND THIS REALITY ASUNDER.
AND YOU WILL HAVE NO KINGDOM TO RULE AND NO PLACE IN THE MULTIVERSE.
YOU WILL BE LOST OR DEAD.
HOLDING A POWER YOU CANNOT COMPREHEND.
BUT YOU CAN.

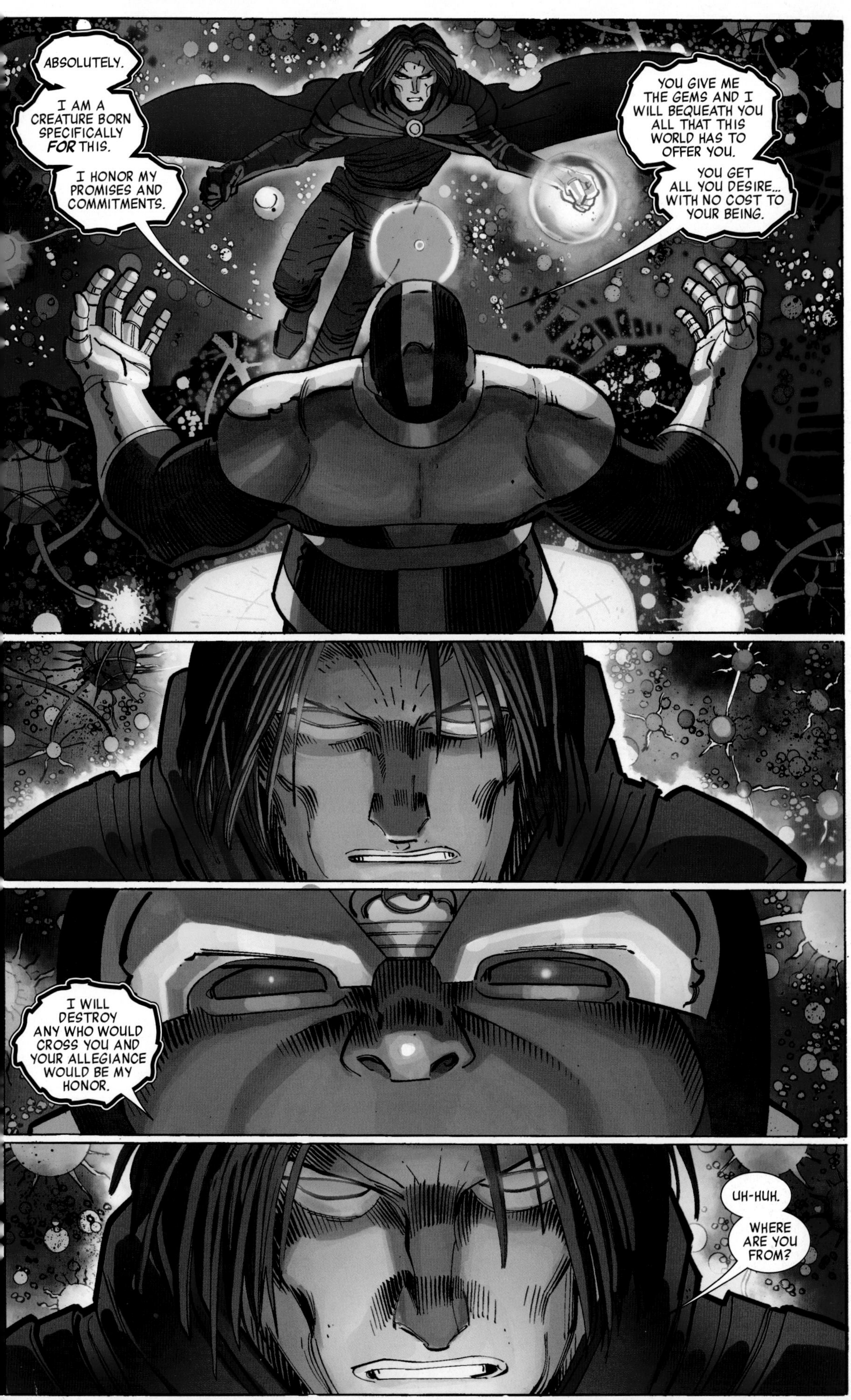
ABSOLUTELY.
I AM A CREATURE BORN SPECIFICALLY *FOR* THIS.
I HONOR MY PROMISES AND COMMITMENTS.
YOU GIVE ME THE GEMS AND I WILL BEQUEATH YOU ALL THAT THIS WORLD HAS TO OFFER YOU.
YOU GET ALL YOU DESIRE... WITH NO COST TO YOUR BEING.
I WILL DESTROY ANY WHO WOULD CROSS YOU AND YOUR ALLEGIANCE WOULD BE MY HONOR.
UH-HUH.
WHERE ARE YOU FROM?

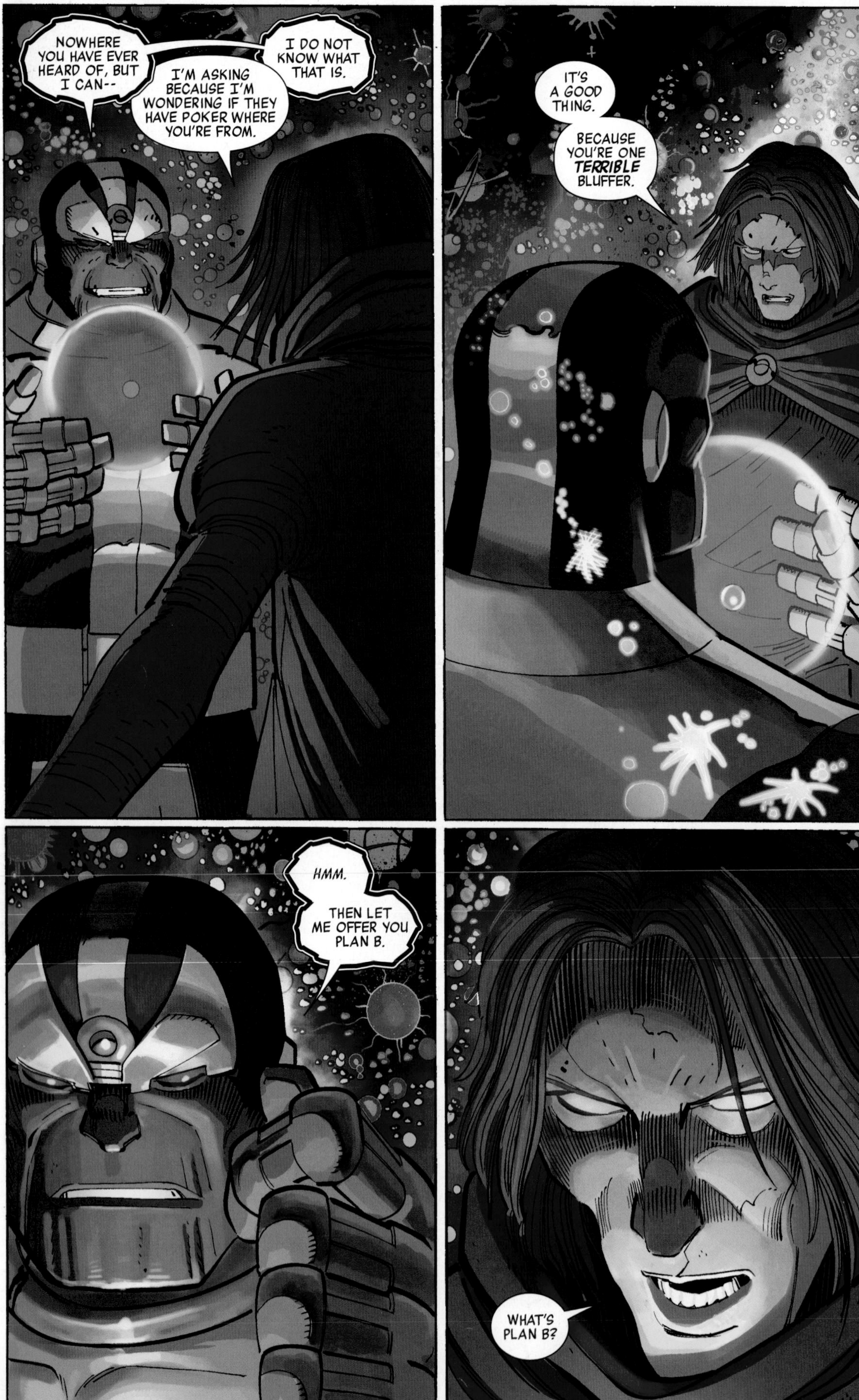
NOWHERE YOU HAVE EVER HEARD OF, BUT I CAN--
I DO NOT KNOW WHAT THAT IS.
I'M ASKING BECAUSE I'M WONDERING IF THEY HAVE POKER WHERE YOU'RE FROM.
IT'S A GOOD THING.
BECAUSE YOU'RE ONE TERRIBLE BLUFFER.
HMM.
THEN LET ME OFFER YOU PLAN B.
WHAT'S PLAN B?

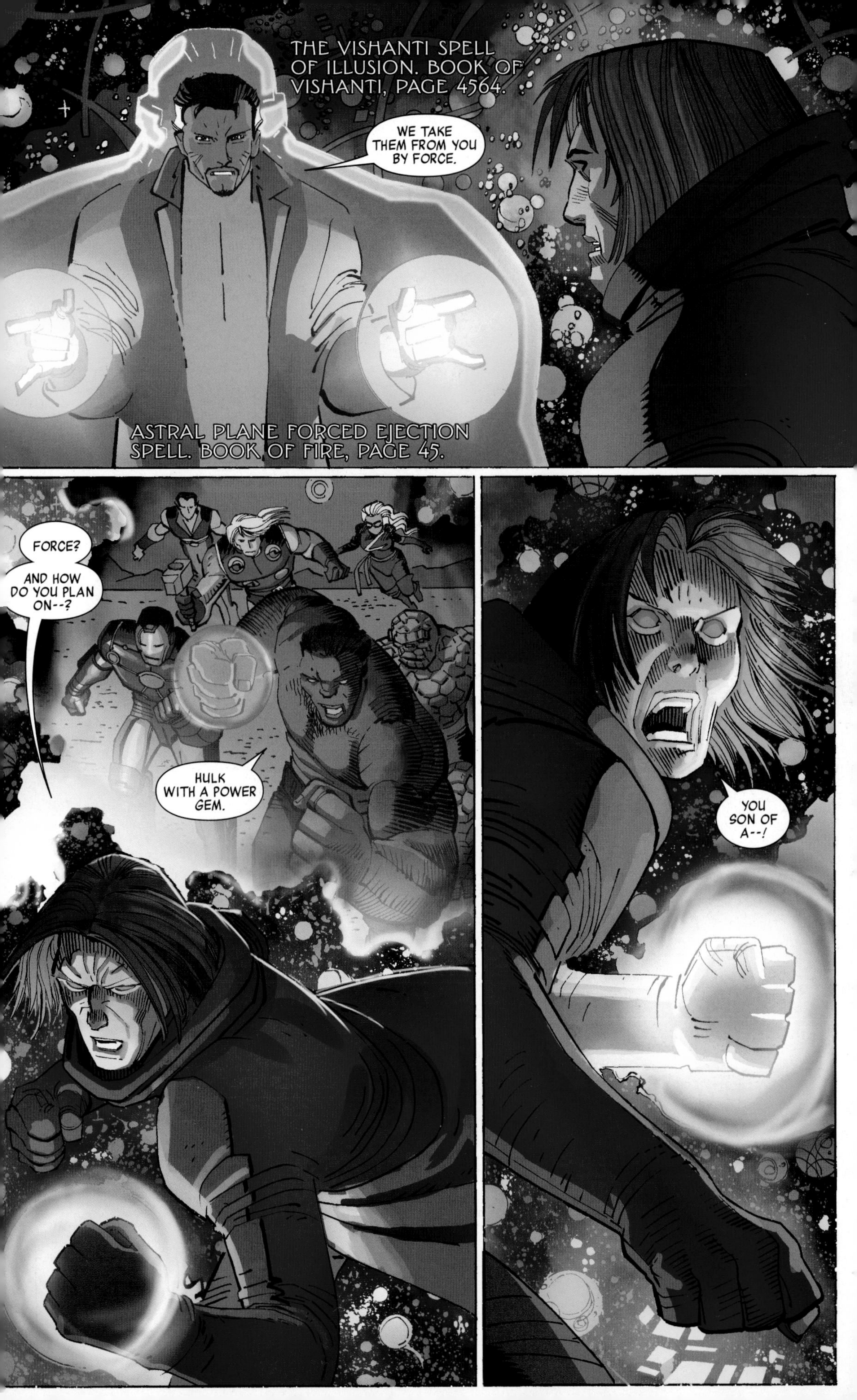
THE VISHANTI SPELL OF ILLUSION. BOOK OF VISHANTI, PAGE 4564.
WE TAKE THEM FROM YOU BY FORCE.
ASTRAL PLANE FORCED EJECTION SPELL. BOOK OF FIRE, PAGE 45.
FORCE?
AND HOW DO YOU PLAN ON--?
HULK WITH A POWER GEM.
YOU SON OF A--!

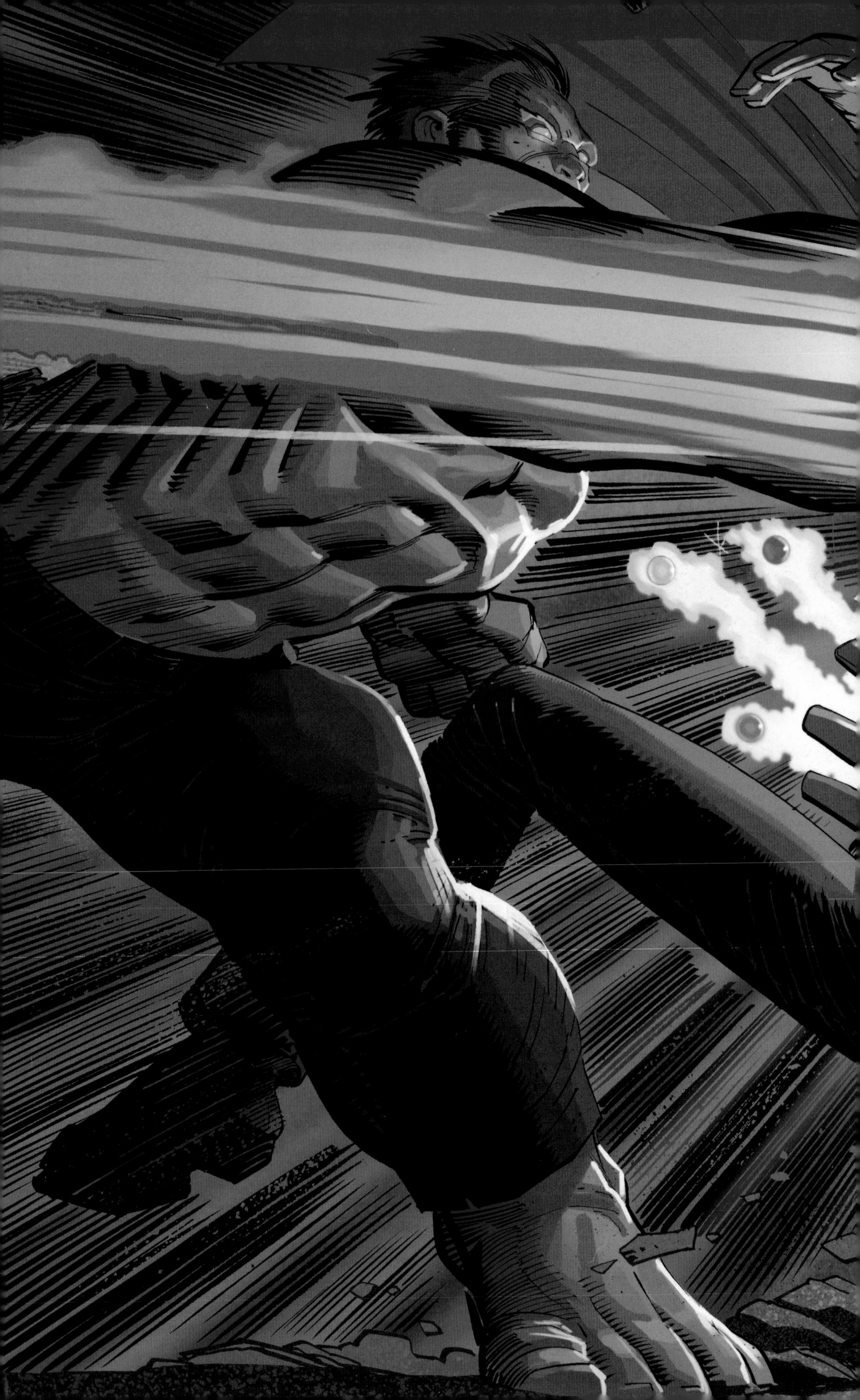

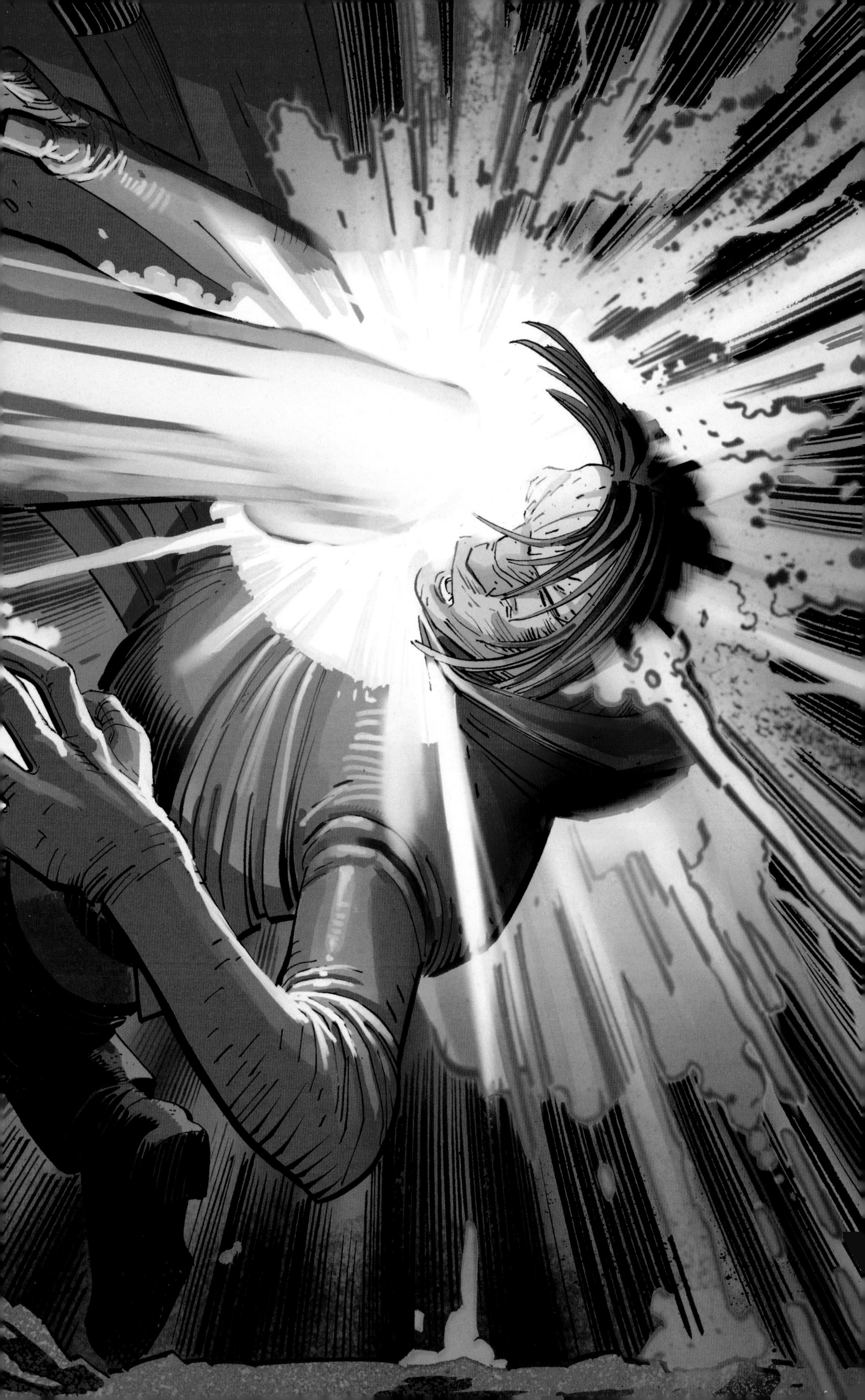

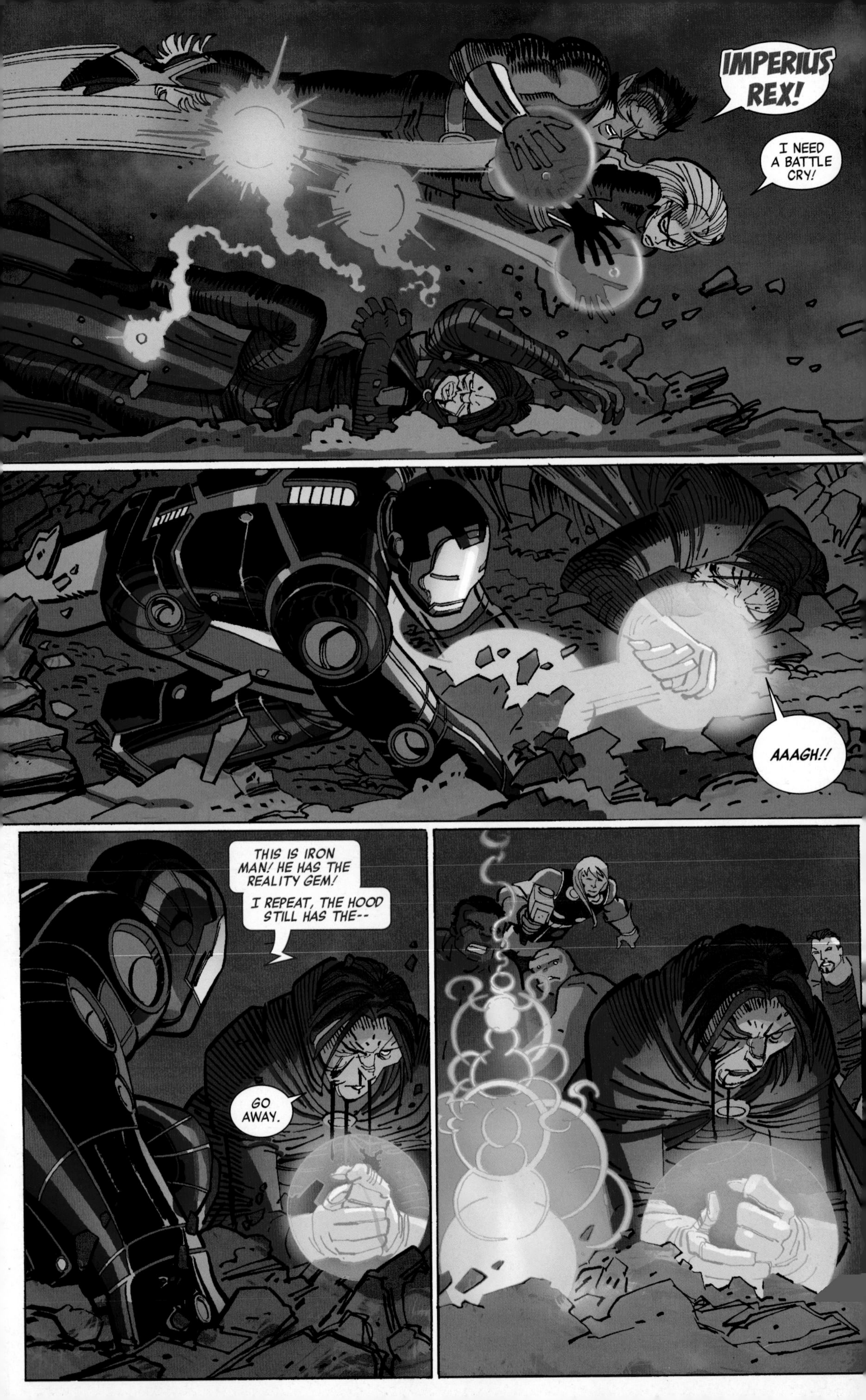
IMPERIUS REX!
I NEED A BATTLE CRY!
AAAGH!!
THIS IS IRON MAN! HE HAS THE REALITY GEM!
I REPEAT, THE HOOD STILL HAS THE--
GO AWAY.

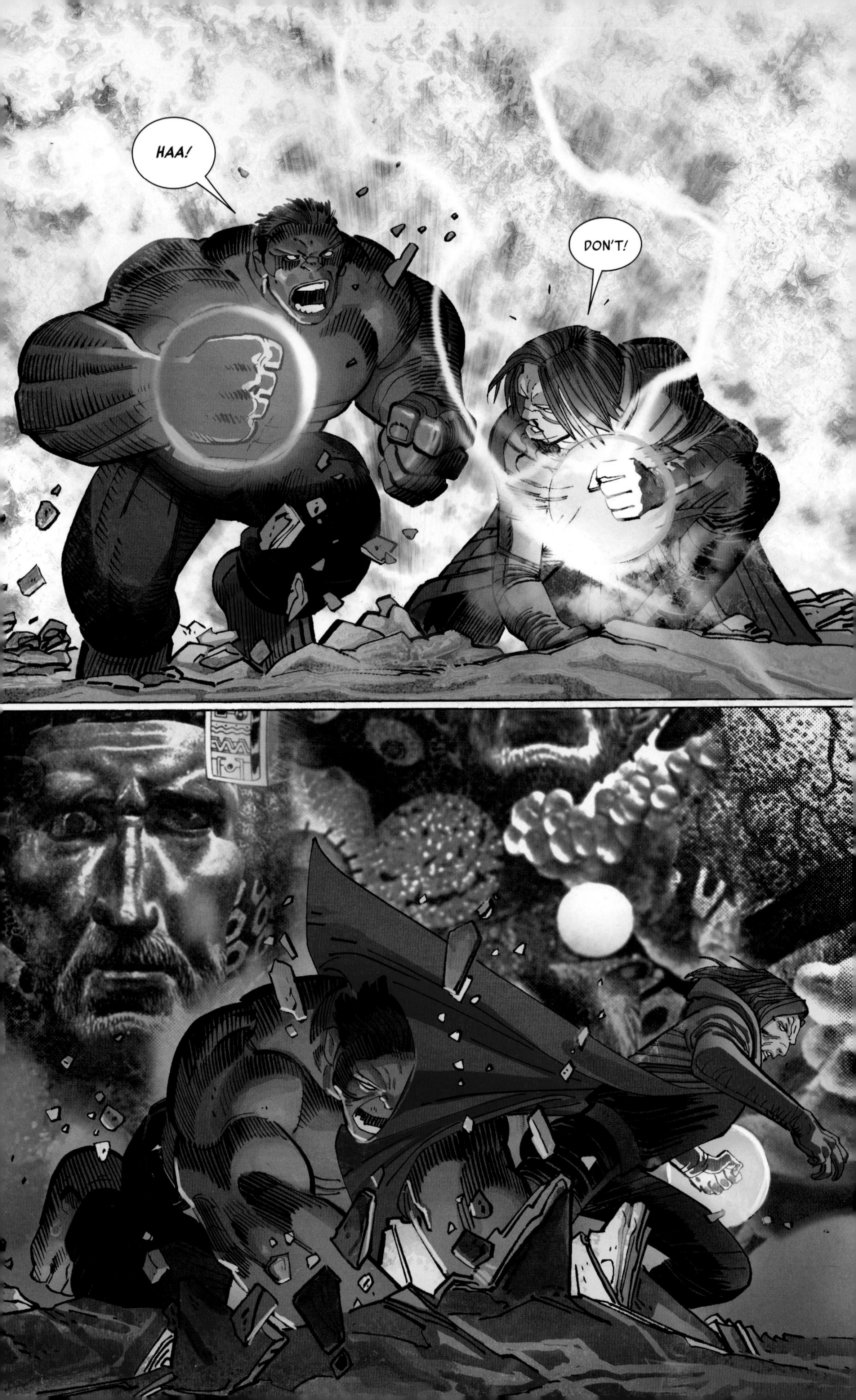
HAA!
DON'T!

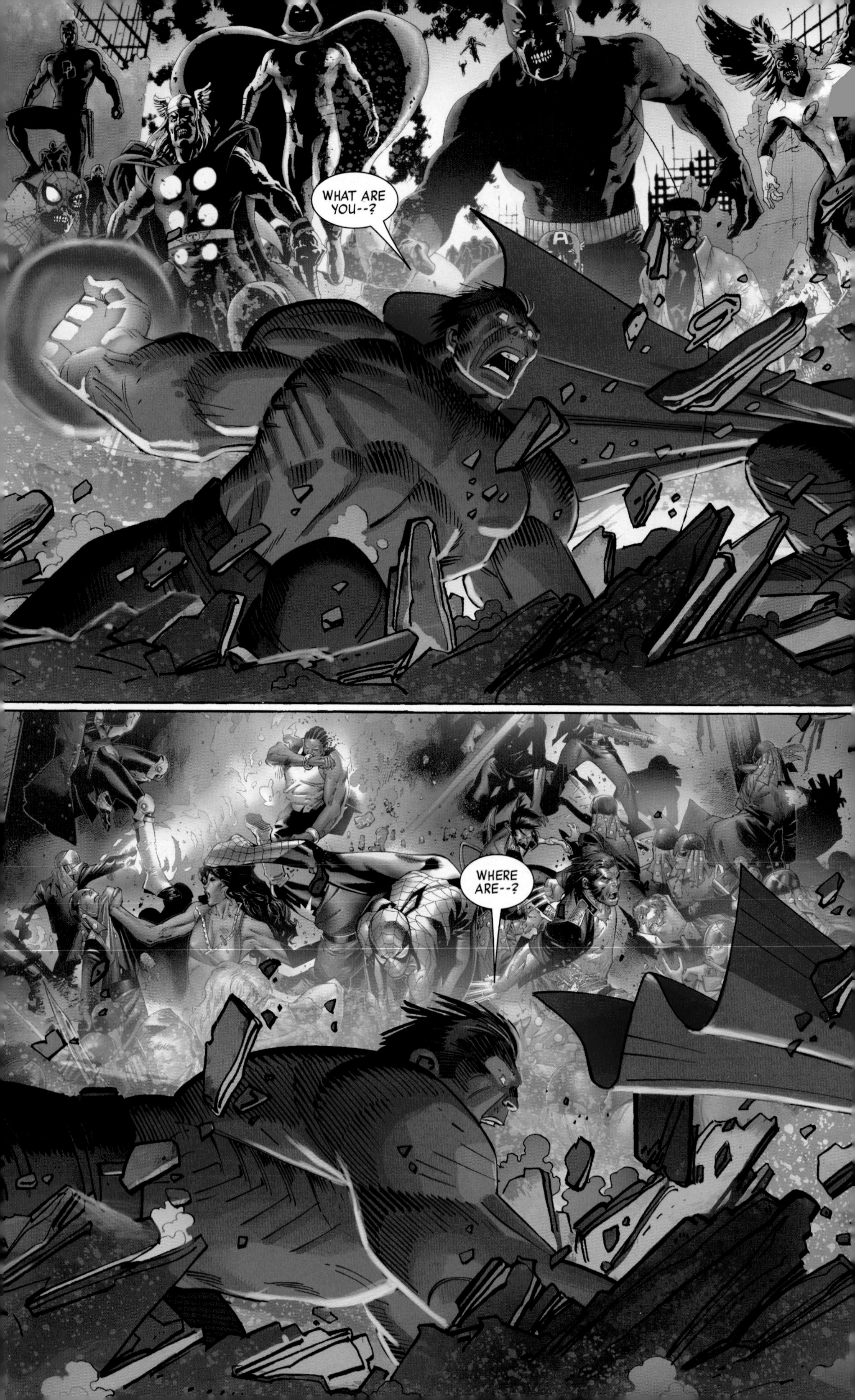
WHAT ARE YOU--?
WHERE ARE--?

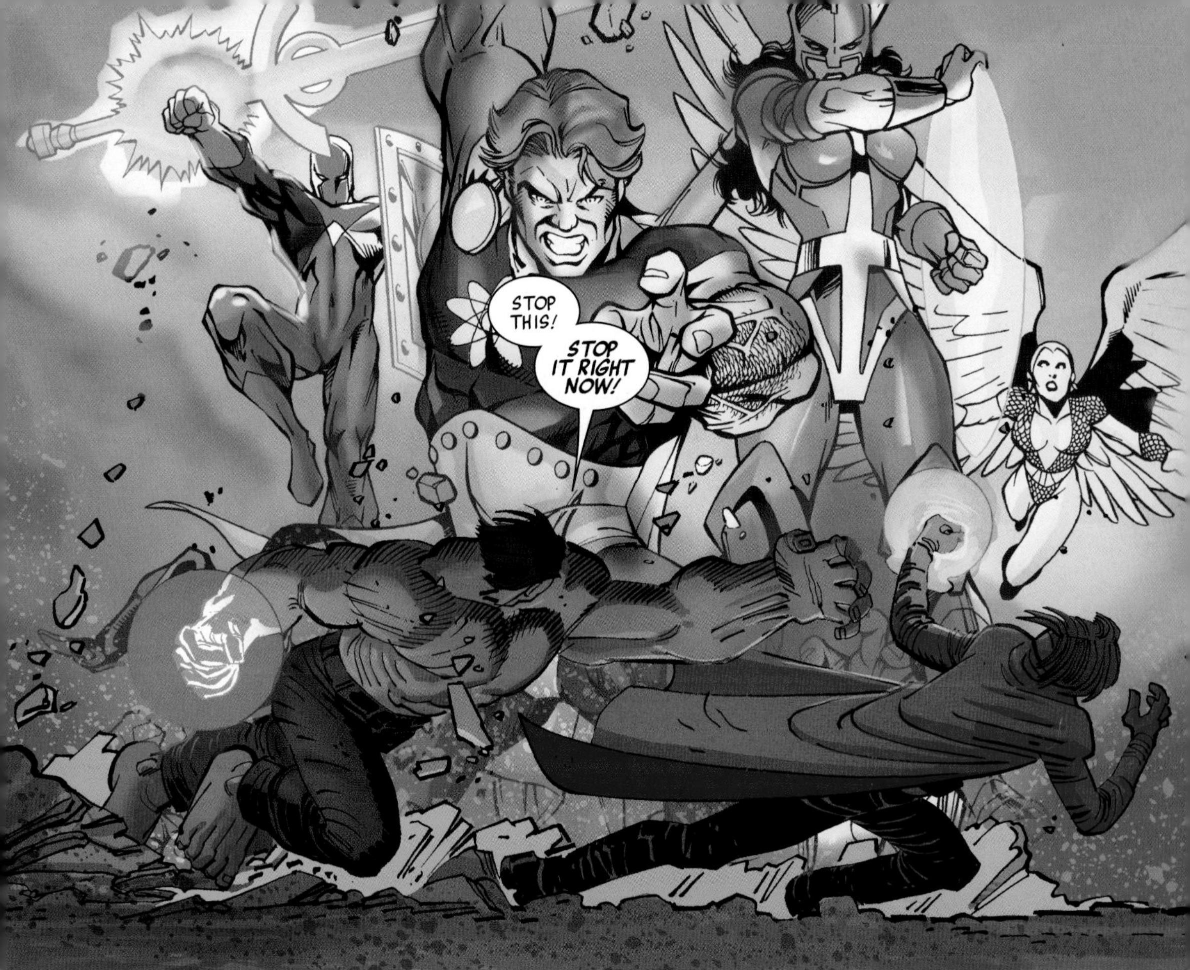
STOP THIS!
STOP IT RIGHT NOW!

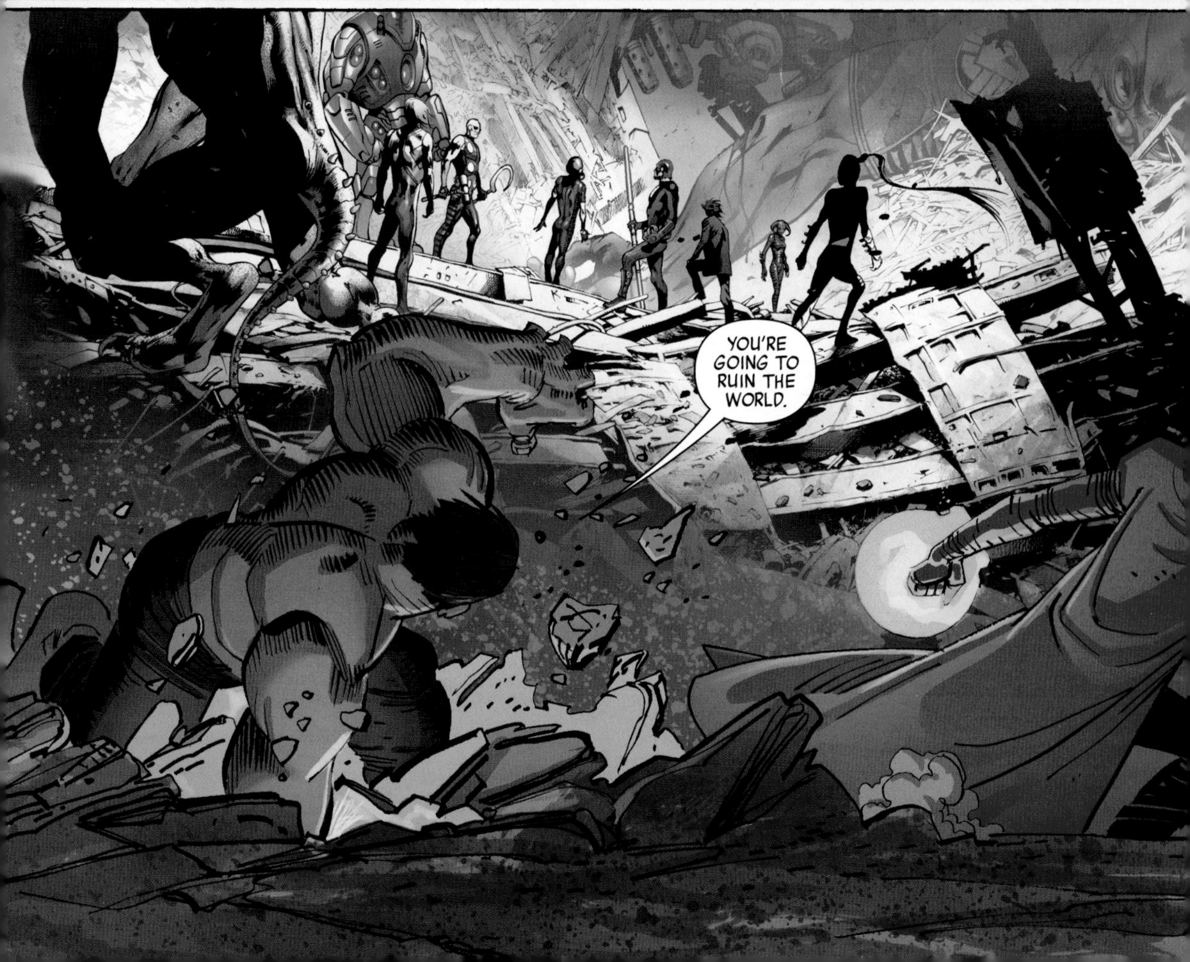
YOU'RE GOING TO RUIN THE WORLD.

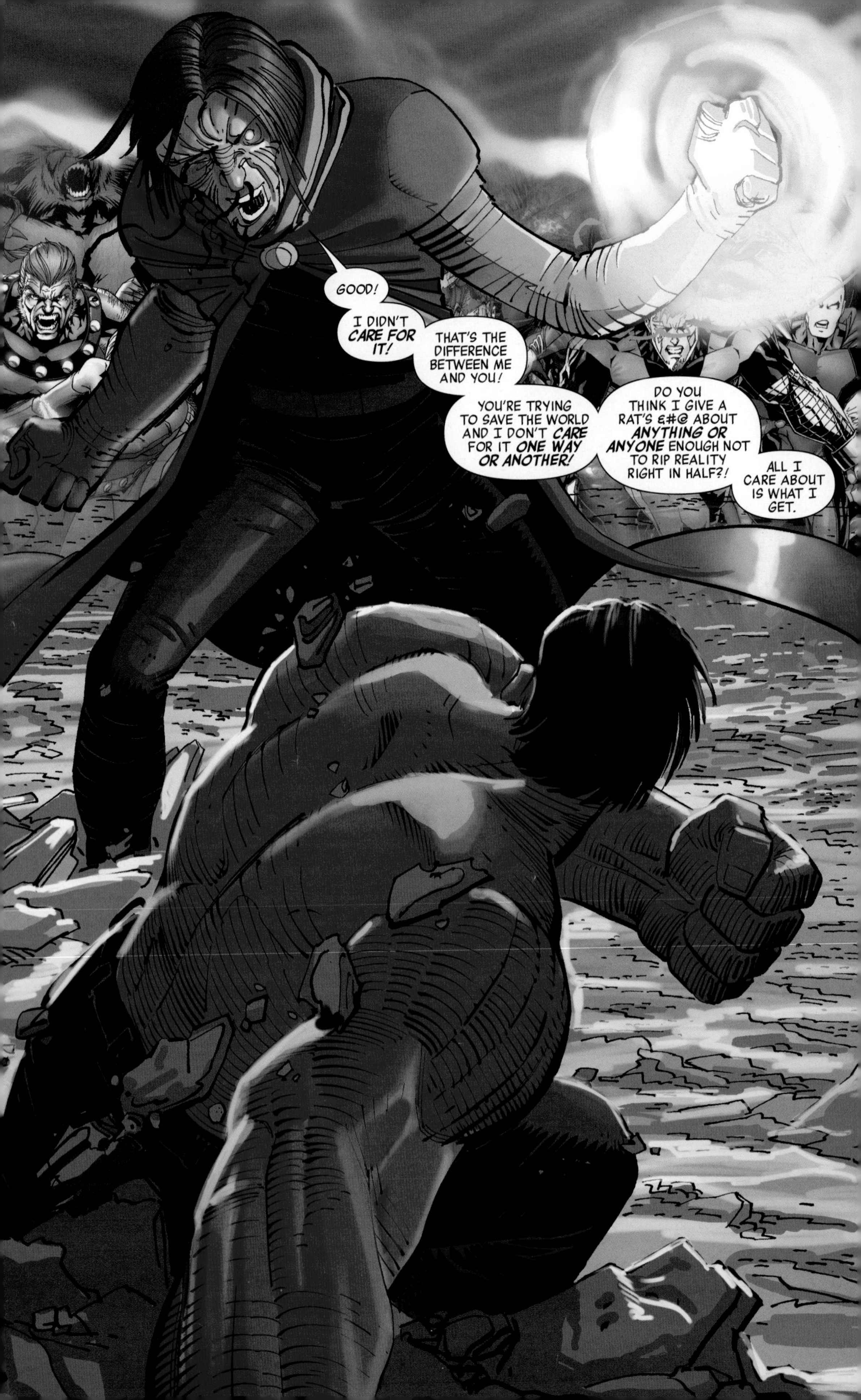
GOOD!
I DIDN'T CARE FOR IT!
THAT'S THE DIFFERENCE BETWEEN ME AND YOU!
YOU'RE TRYING TO SAVE THE WORLD AND I DON'T CARE FOR IT ONE WAY OR ANOTHER!
DO YOU THINK I GIVE A RAT'S &#@ ABOUT ANYTHING OR ANYONE ENOUGH NOT TO RIP REALITY RIGHT IN HALF?!
ALL I CARE ABOUT IS WHAT I GET.

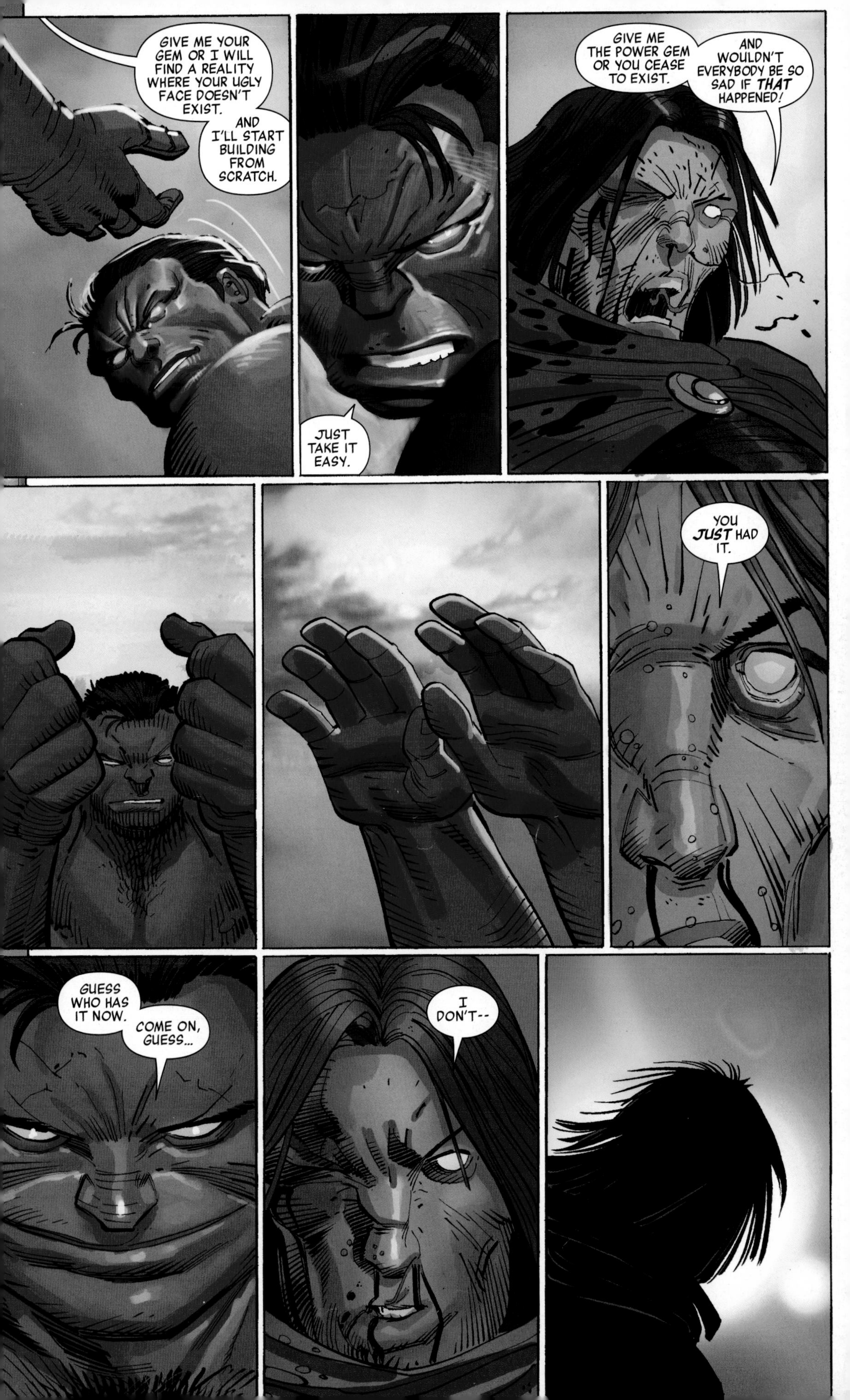
GIVE ME YOUR GEM OR I WILL FIND A REALITY WHERE YOUR UGLY FACE DOESN'T EXIST.
AND I'LL START BUILDING FROM SCRATCH.
JUST TAKE IT EASY.
GIVE ME THE POWER GEM OR YOU CEASE TO EXIST.
AND WOULDN'T EVERYBODY BE SO SAD IF THAT HAPPENED!
YOU JUST HAD IT.
GUESS WHO HAS IT NOW.
COME ON, GUESS...
I DON'T--

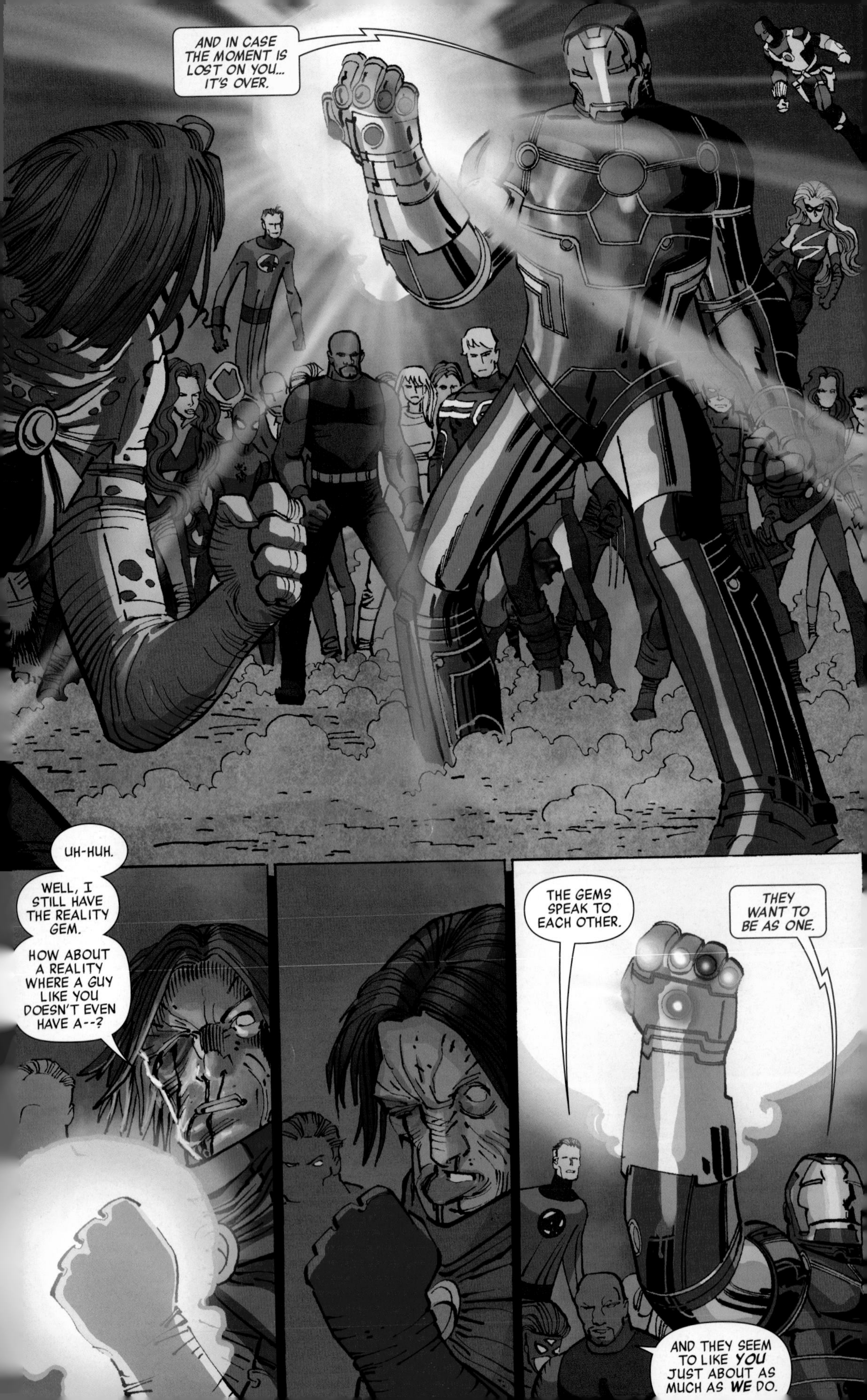
AND IN CASE THE MOMENT IS LOST ON YOU... IT'S OVER.
UH-HUH.
WELL, I STILL HAVE THE REALITY GEM.
HOW ABOUT A REALITY WHERE A GUY LIKE YOU DOESN'T EVEN HAVE A--?
THE GEMS SPEAK TO EACH OTHER.
THEY WANT TO BE AS ONE.
AND THEY SEEM TO LIKE *YOU* JUST ABOUT AS MUCH AS *WE* DO.

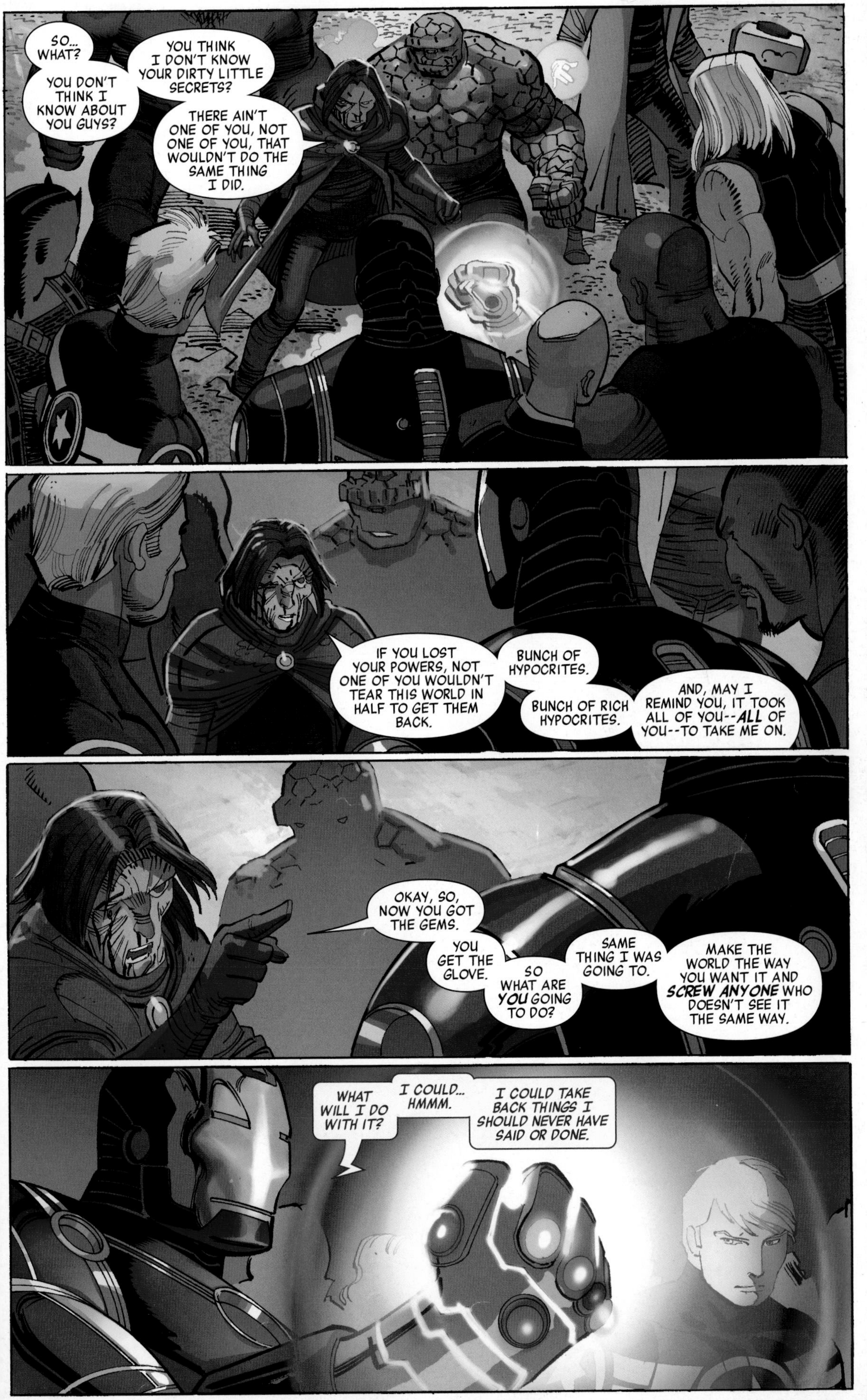
SO... WHAT?
YOU DON'T THINK I KNOW ABOUT YOU GUYS?
YOU THINK I DON'T KNOW YOUR DIRTY LITTLE SECRETS?
THERE AIN'T ONE OF YOU, NOT ONE OF YOU, THAT WOULDN'T DO THE SAME THING I DID.
IF YOU LOST YOUR POWERS, NOT ONE OF YOU WOULDN'T TEAR THIS WORLD IN HALF TO GET THEM BACK.
BUNCH OF HYPOCRITES.
BUNCH OF RICH HYPOCRITES.
AND, MAY I REMIND YOU, IT TOOK ALL OF YOU--ALL OF YOU--TO TAKE ME ON.
OKAY, SO, NOW YOU GOT THE GEMS.
YOU GET THE GLOVE.
SO WHAT ARE YOU GOING TO DO?
SAME THING I WAS GOING TO.
MAKE THE WORLD THE WAY YOU WANT IT AND SCREW ANYONE WHO DOESN'T SEE IT THE SAME WAY.
WHAT WILL I DO WITH IT?
I COULD... HMMM.
I COULD TAKE BACK THINGS I SHOULD NEVER HAVE SAID OR DONE.

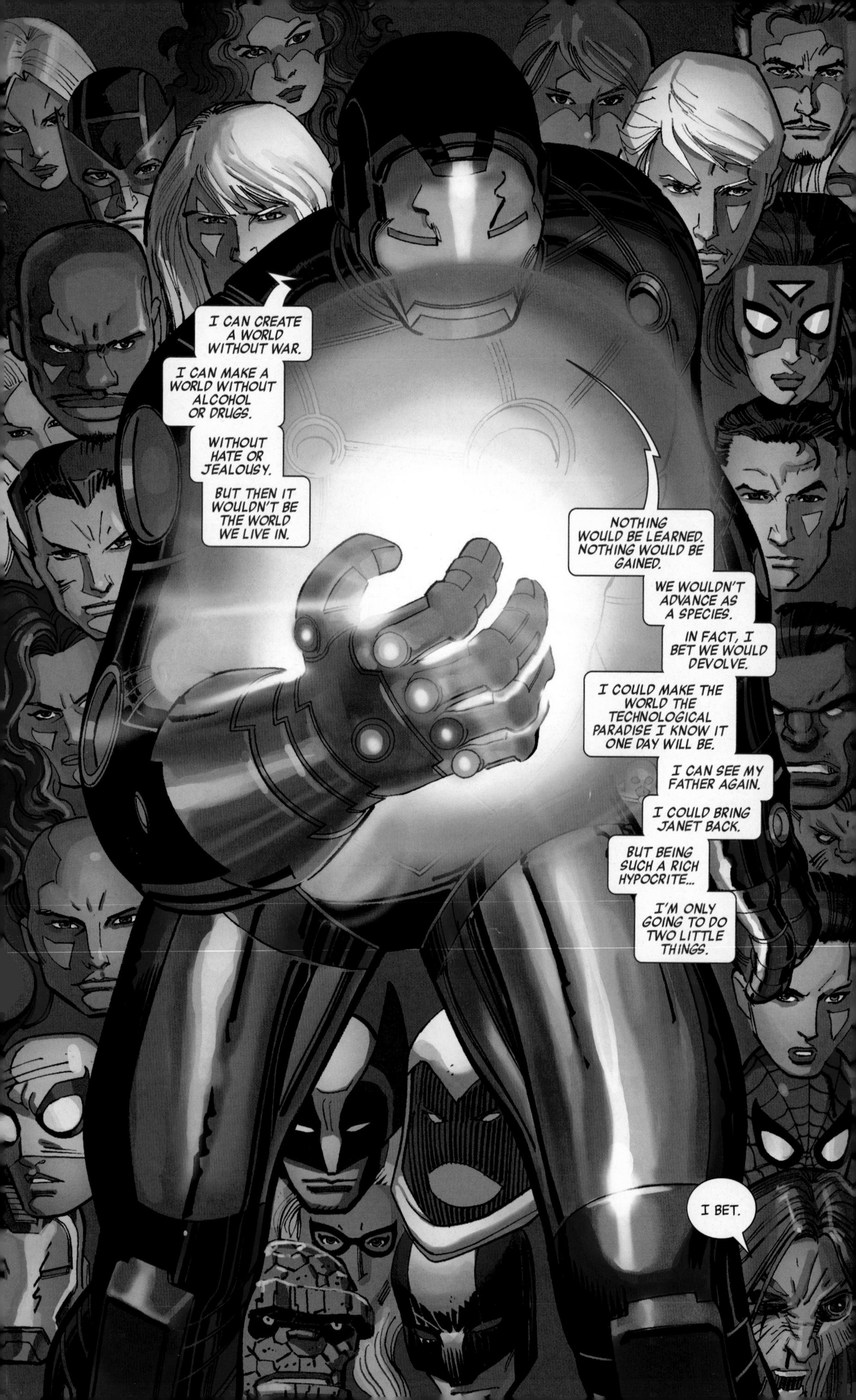
I CAN CREATE A WORLD WITHOUT WAR.
I CAN MAKE A WORLD WITHOUT ALCOHOL OR DRUGS.
WITHOUT HATE OR JEALOUSY.
BUT THEN IT WOULDN'T BE THE WORLD WE LIVE IN.
NOTHING WOULD BE LEARNED. NOTHING WOULD BE GAINED.
WE WOULDN'T ADVANCE AS A SPECIES.
IN FACT, I BET WE WOULD DEVOLVE.
I COULD MAKE THE WORLD THE TECHNOLOGICAL PARADISE I KNOW IT ONE DAY WILL BE.
I CAN SEE MY FATHER AGAIN.
I COULD BRING JANET BACK.
BUT BEING SUCH A RICH HYPOCRITE...
I'M ONLY GOING TO DO TWO LITTLE THINGS.
I BET.

FIRST, I PUT YOU BACK WHERE YOU BELONG.

NO.
NO NO
NO NO.

NOOOOO!!!

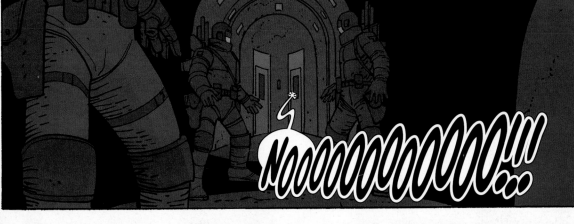

NOOOOOOOOOOOOO!!!...

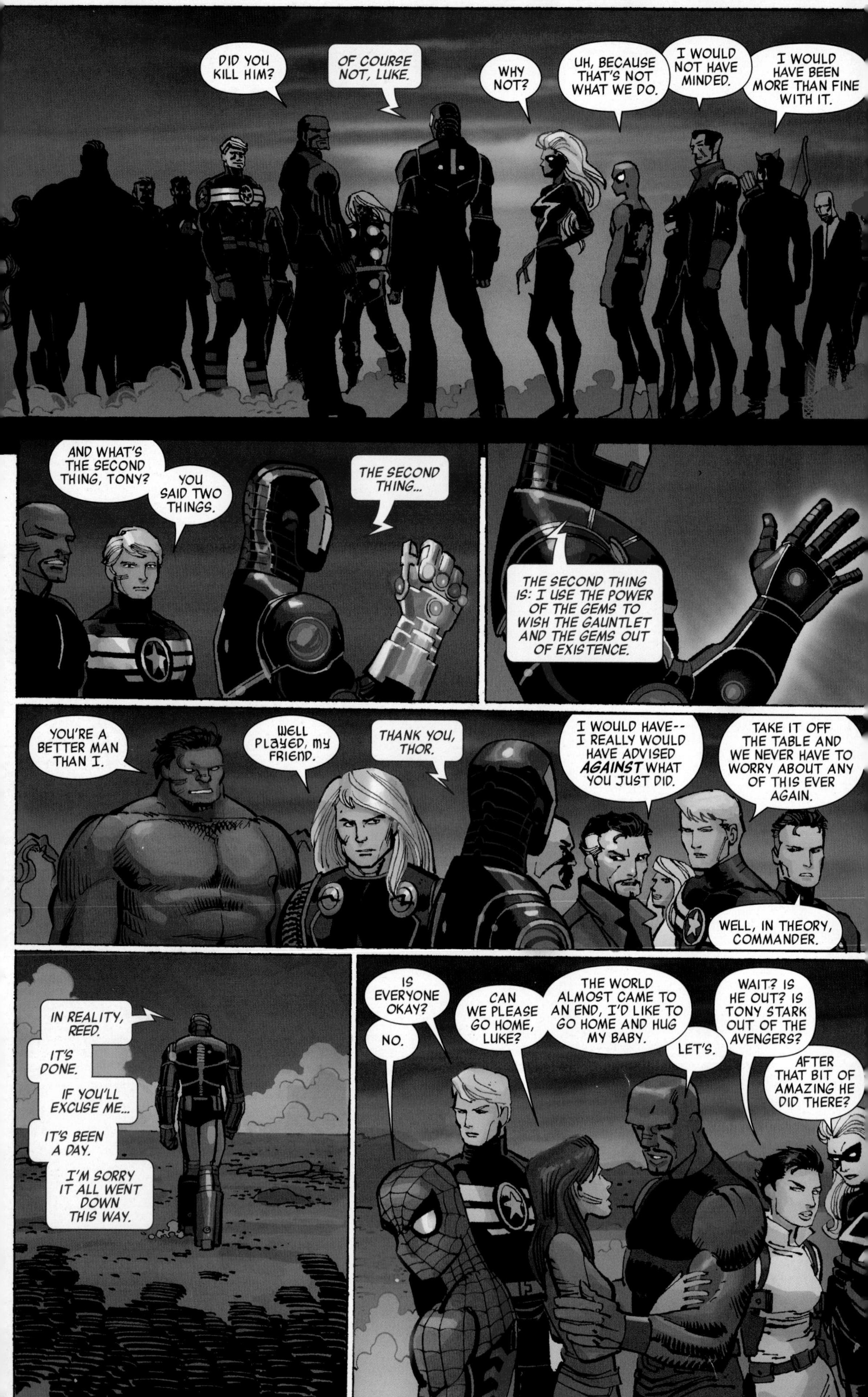
DID YOU KILL HIM?
OF COURSE NOT, LUKE.
WHY NOT?
UH, BECAUSE THAT'S NOT WHAT WE DO.
I WOULD NOT HAVE MINDED.
I WOULD HAVE BEEN MORE THAN FINE WITH IT.
AND WHAT'S THE SECOND THING, TONY?
YOU SAID TWO THINGS.
THE SECOND THING...
THE SECOND THING IS: I USE THE POWER OF THE GEMS TO WISH THE GAUNTLET AND THE GEMS OUT OF EXISTENCE.
YOU'RE A BETTER MAN THAN I.
WELL PLAYED, MY FRIEND.
THANK YOU, THOR.
I WOULD HAVE-- I REALLY WOULD HAVE ADVISED AGAINST WHAT YOU JUST DID.
TAKE IT OFF THE TABLE AND WE NEVER HAVE TO WORRY ABOUT ANY OF THIS EVER AGAIN.
WELL, IN THEORY, COMMANDER.
IN REALITY, REED.
IT'S DONE.
IF YOU'LL EXCUSE ME...
IT'S BEEN A DAY.
I'M SORRY IT ALL WENT DOWN THIS WAY.
IS EVERYONE OKAY?
NO.
CAN WE PLEASE GO HOME, LUKE?
THE WORLD ALMOST CAME TO AN END, I'D LIKE TO GO HOME AND HUG MY BABY.
LET'S.
WAIT? IS HE OUT? IS TONY STARK OUT OF THE AVENGERS?
AFTER THAT BIT OF AMAZING HE DID THERE?

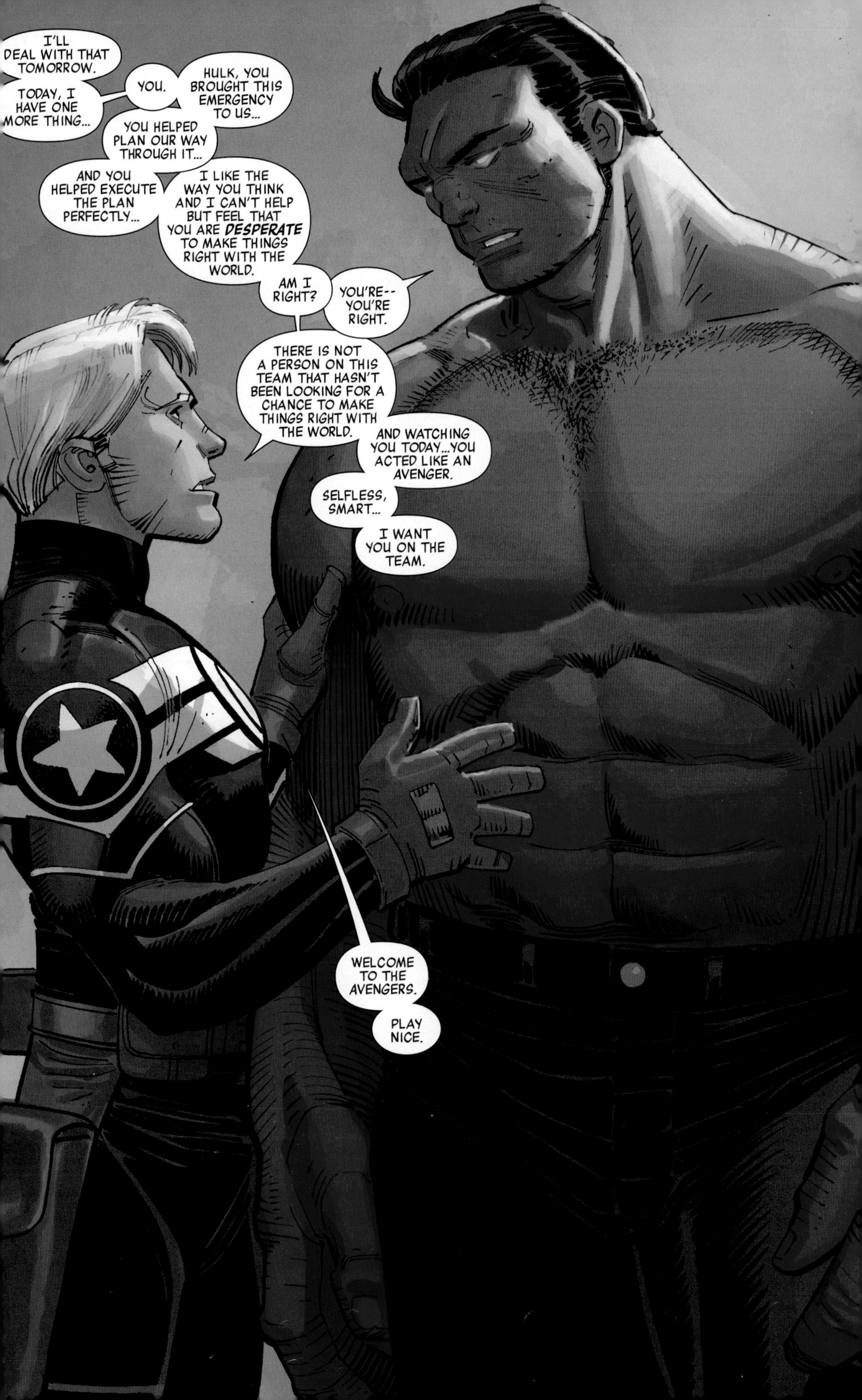
I'LL DEAL WITH THAT TOMORROW.
TODAY, I HAVE ONE MORE THING...
YOU.
HULK, YOU BROUGHT THIS EMERGENCY TO US...
YOU HELPED PLAN OUR WAY THROUGH IT...
AND YOU HELPED EXECUTE THE PLAN PERFECTLY...
I LIKE THE WAY YOU THINK AND I CAN'T HELP BUT FEEL THAT YOU ARE ***DESPERATE*** TO MAKE THINGS RIGHT WITH THE WORLD.
AM I RIGHT?
YOU'RE-- YOU'RE RIGHT.
THERE IS NOT A PERSON ON THIS TEAM THAT HASN'T BEEN LOOKING FOR A CHANCE TO MAKE THINGS RIGHT WITH THE WORLD.
AND WATCHING YOU TODAY...YOU ACTED LIKE AN AVENGER.
SELFLESS, SMART...
I WANT YOU ON THE TEAM.
WELCOME TO THE AVENGERS.
PLAY NICE.

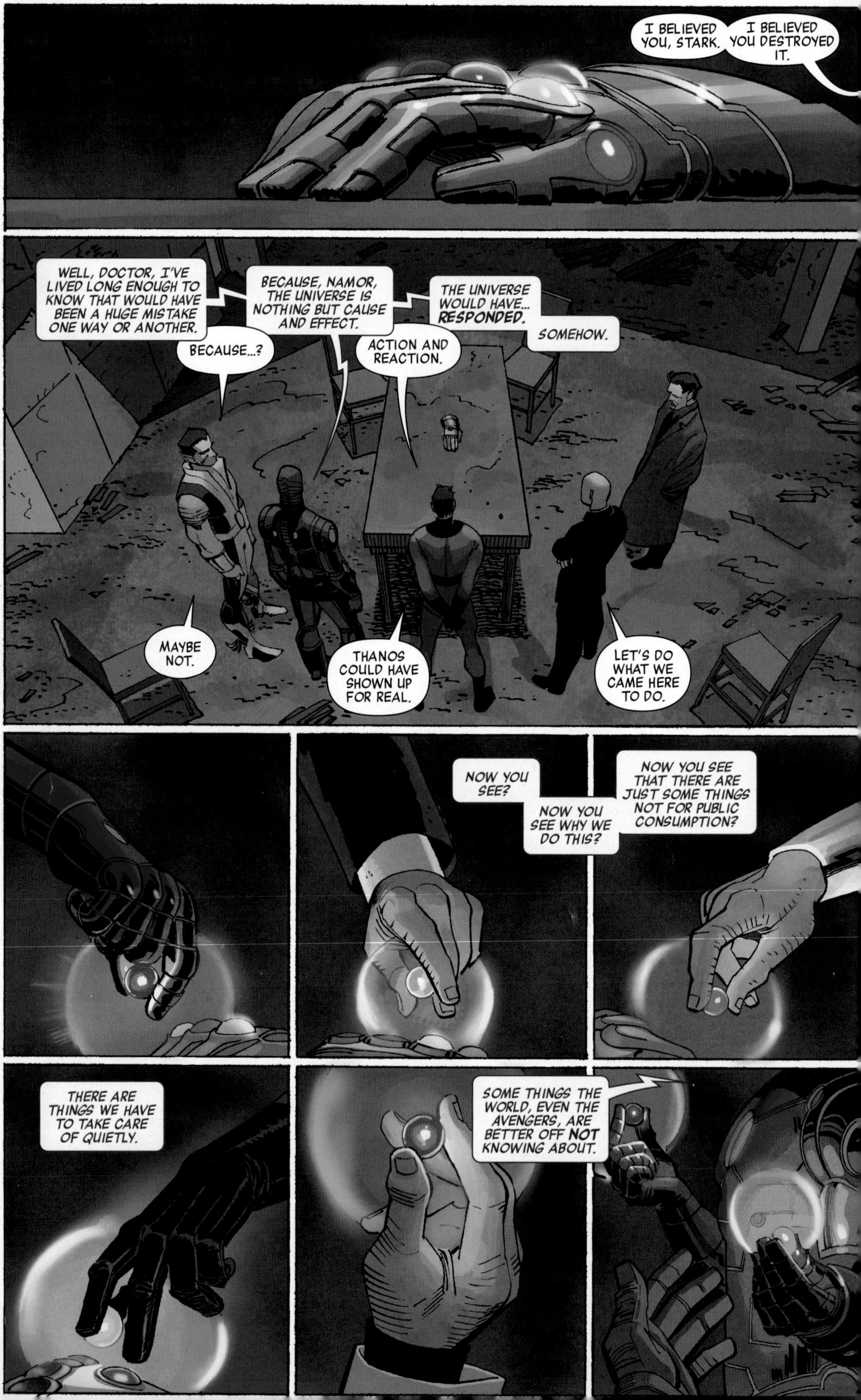

I BELIEVED YOU, STARK.
I BELIEVED YOU DESTROYED IT.
WELL, DOCTOR, I'VE LIVED LONG ENOUGH TO KNOW THAT WOULD HAVE BEEN A HUGE MISTAKE ONE WAY OR ANOTHER.
BECAUSE...?
BECAUSE, NAMOR, THE UNIVERSE IS NOTHING BUT CAUSE AND EFFECT.
ACTION AND REACTION.
THE UNIVERSE WOULD HAVE... **RESPONDED.**
SOMEHOW.
MAYBE NOT.
THANOS COULD HAVE SHOWN UP FOR REAL.
LET'S DO WHAT WE CAME HERE TO DO.
NOW YOU SEE?
NOW YOU SEE WHY WE DO THIS?
NOW YOU SEE THAT THERE ARE JUST SOME THINGS NOT FOR PUBLIC CONSUMPTION?
THERE ARE THINGS WE HAVE TO TAKE CARE OF QUIETLY.
SOME THINGS THE WORLD, EVEN THE AVENGERS, ARE BETTER OFF **NOT** KNOWING ABOUT.

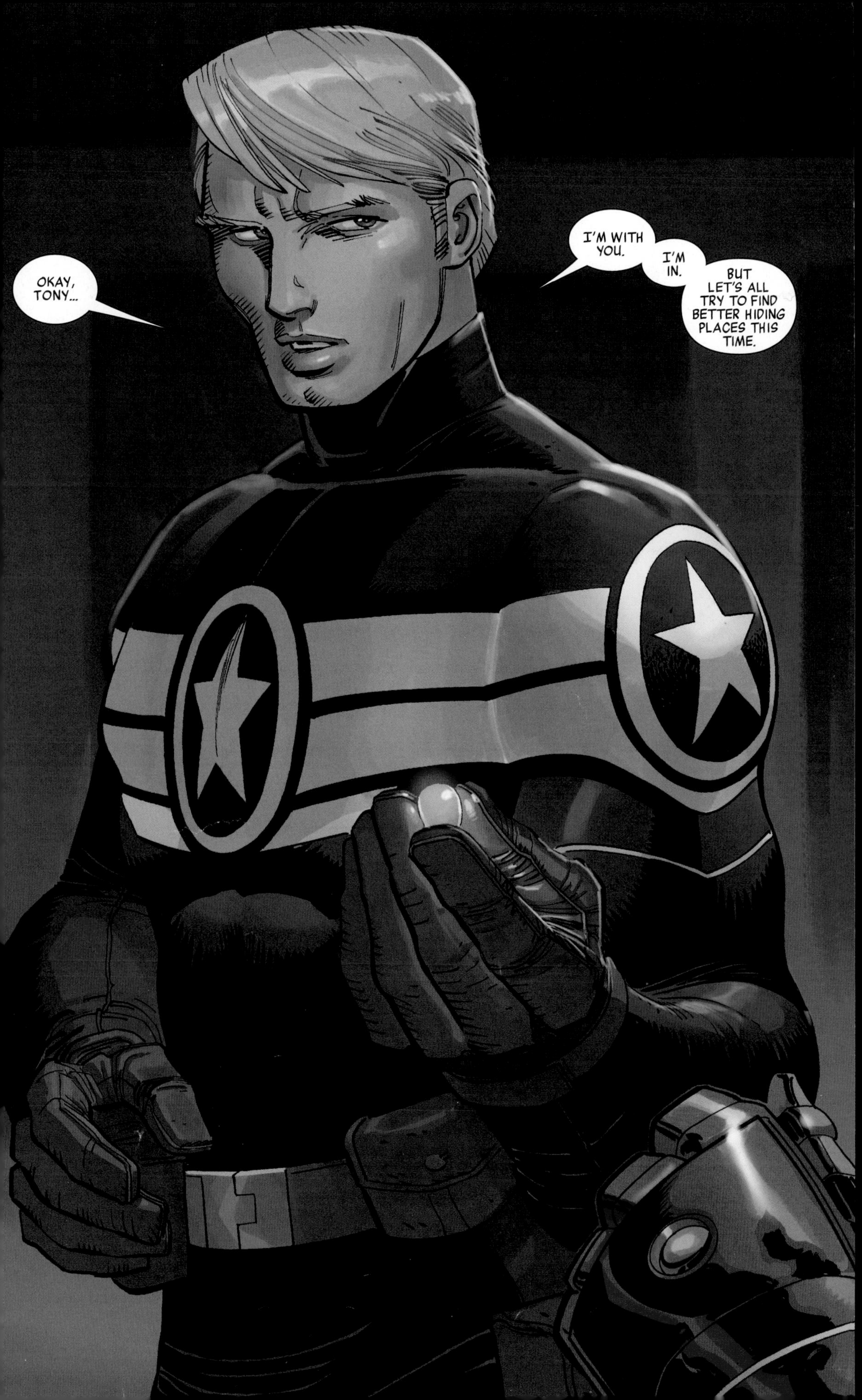
OKAY, TONY...
I'M WITH YOU.
I'M IN.
BUT LET'S ALL TRY TO FIND BETTER HIDING PLACES THIS TIME.

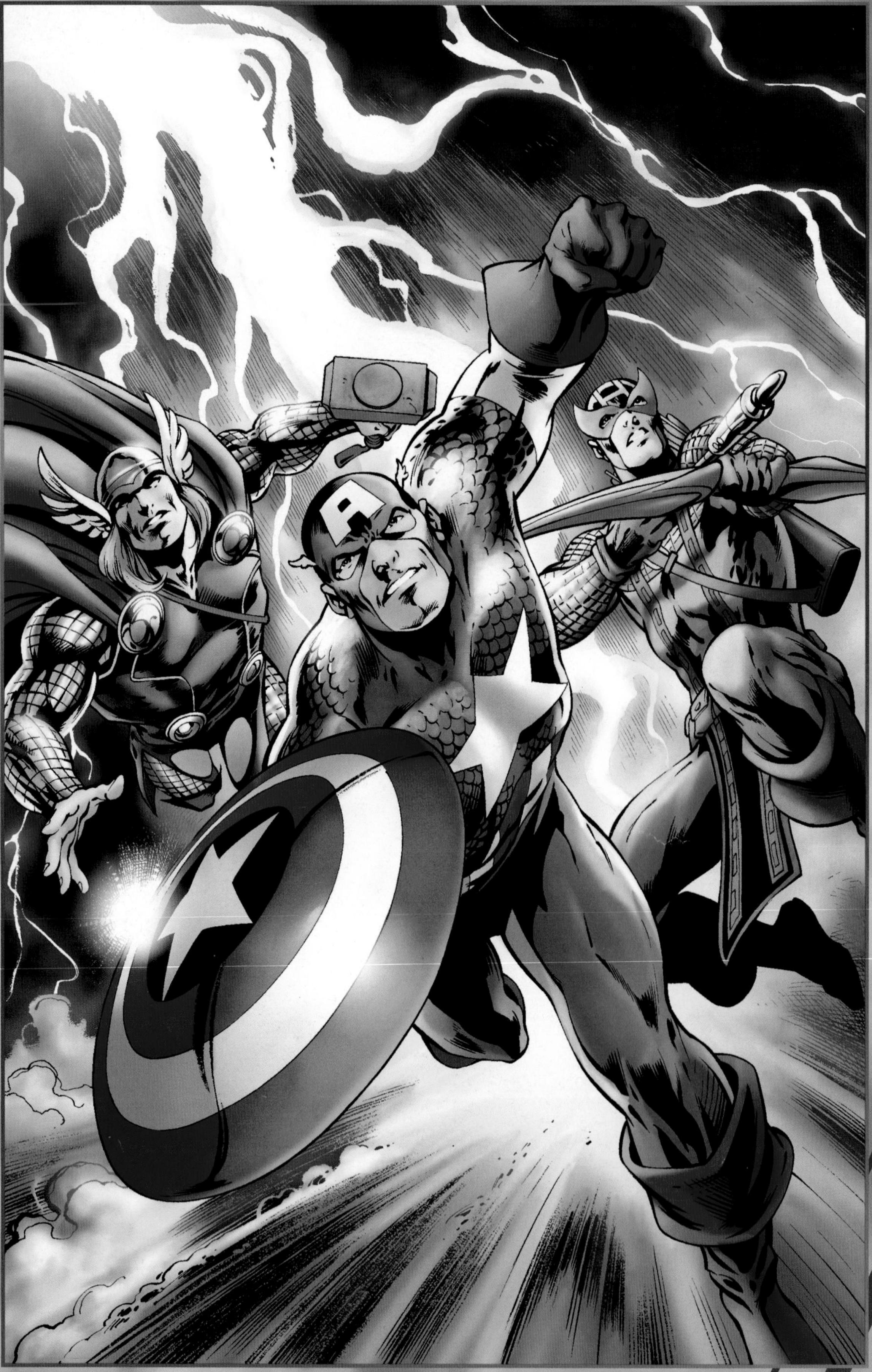

#11 VARIANT BY ALAN DAVIS, PAUL NEARY & PAUL MOUNTS

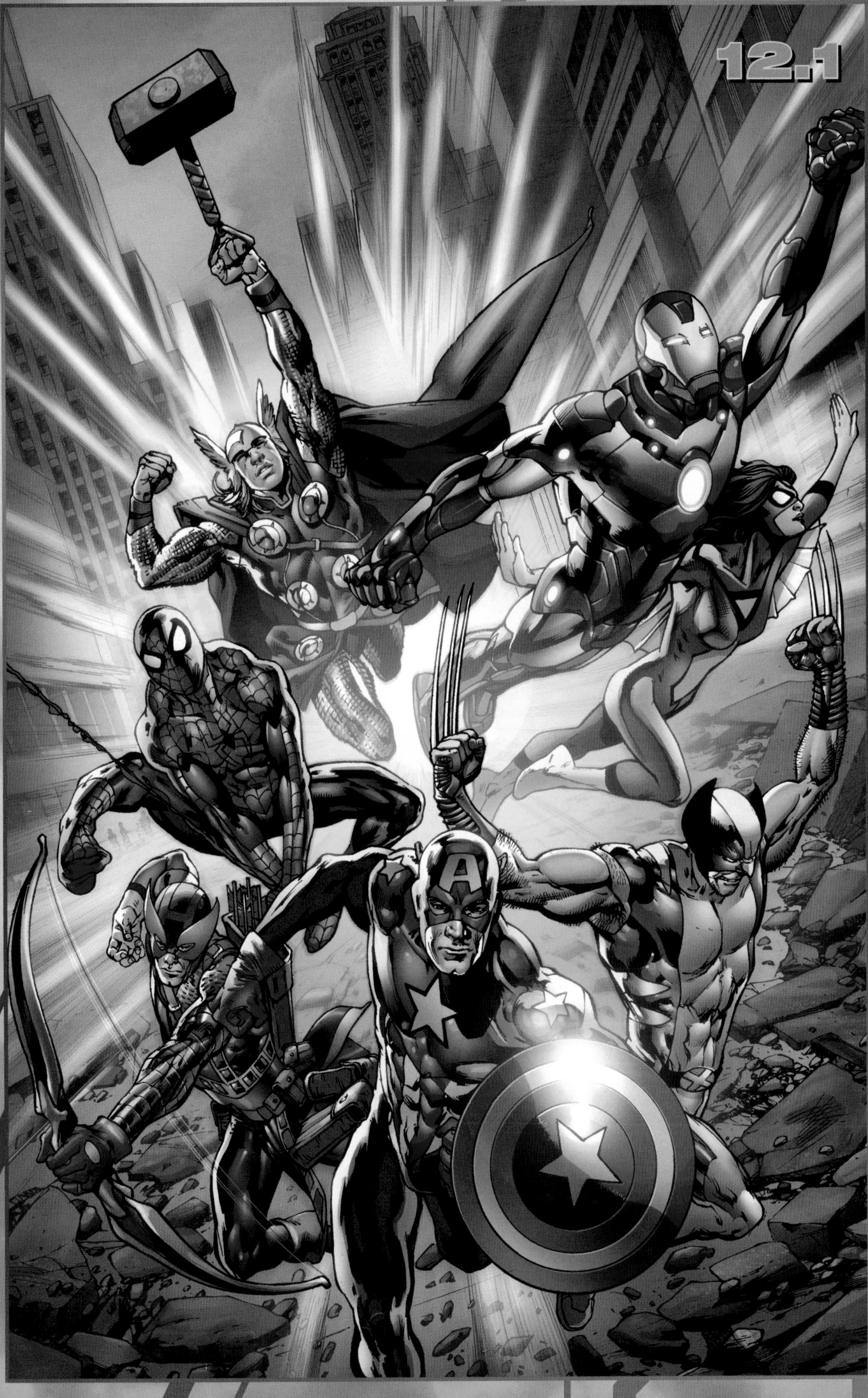
12.1

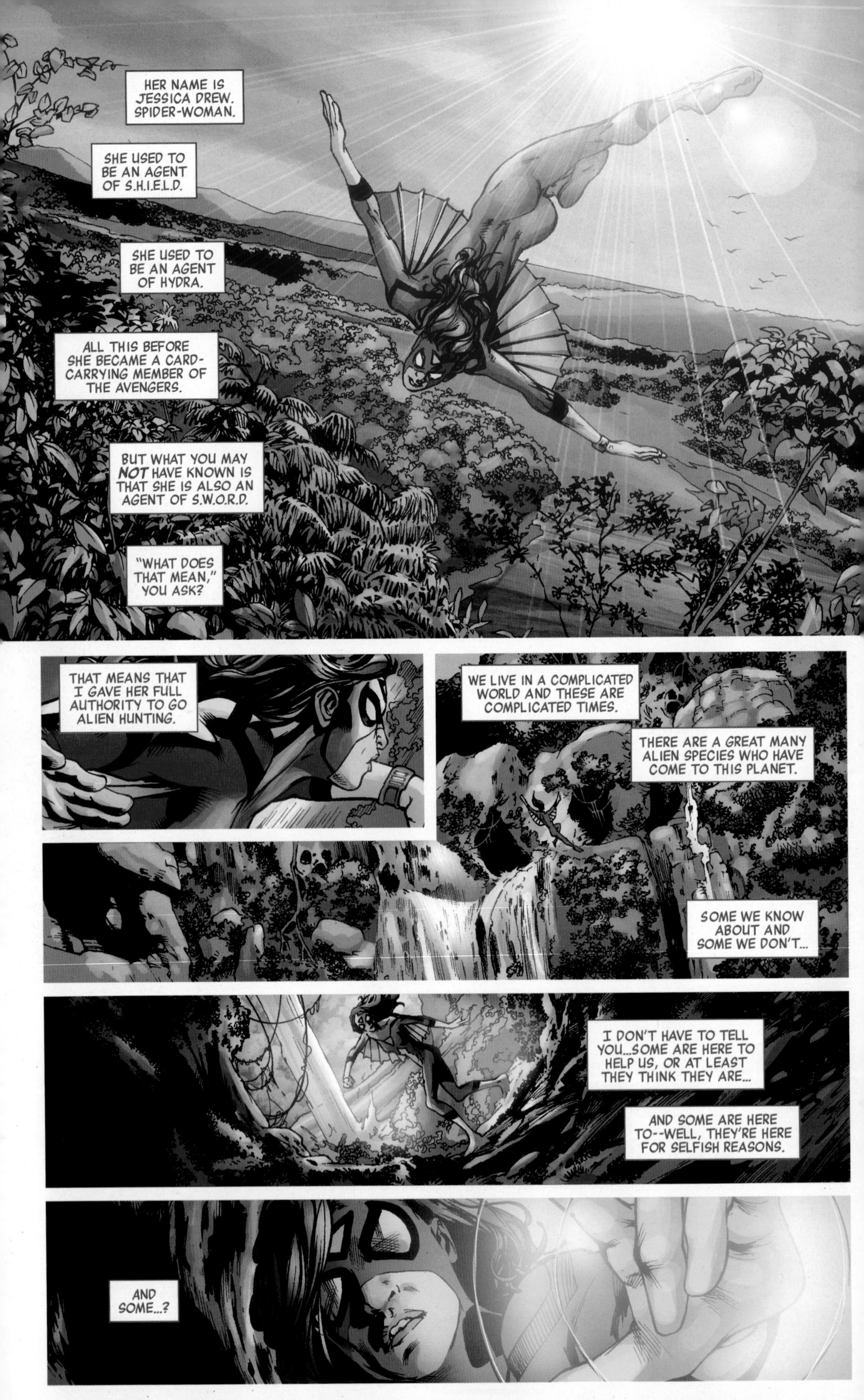
HER NAME IS JESSICA DREW. SPIDER-WOMAN.
SHE USED TO BE AN AGENT OF S.H.I.E.L.D.
SHE USED TO BE AN AGENT OF HYDRA.
ALL THIS BEFORE SHE BECAME A CARD-CARRYING MEMBER OF THE AVENGERS.
BUT WHAT YOU MAY **NOT** HAVE KNOWN IS THAT SHE IS ALSO AN AGENT OF S.W.O.R.D.
"WHAT DOES THAT MEAN," YOU ASK?
THAT MEANS THAT I GAVE HER FULL AUTHORITY TO GO ALIEN HUNTING.
WE LIVE IN A COMPLICATED WORLD AND THESE ARE COMPLICATED TIMES.
THERE ARE A GREAT MANY ALIEN SPECIES WHO HAVE COME TO THIS PLANET.
SOME WE KNOW ABOUT AND SOME WE DON'T...
I DON'T HAVE TO TELL YOU...SOME ARE HERE TO HELP US, OR AT LEAST THEY THINK THEY ARE...
AND SOME ARE HERE TO--WELL, THEY'RE HERE FOR SELFISH REASONS.
AND SOME...?

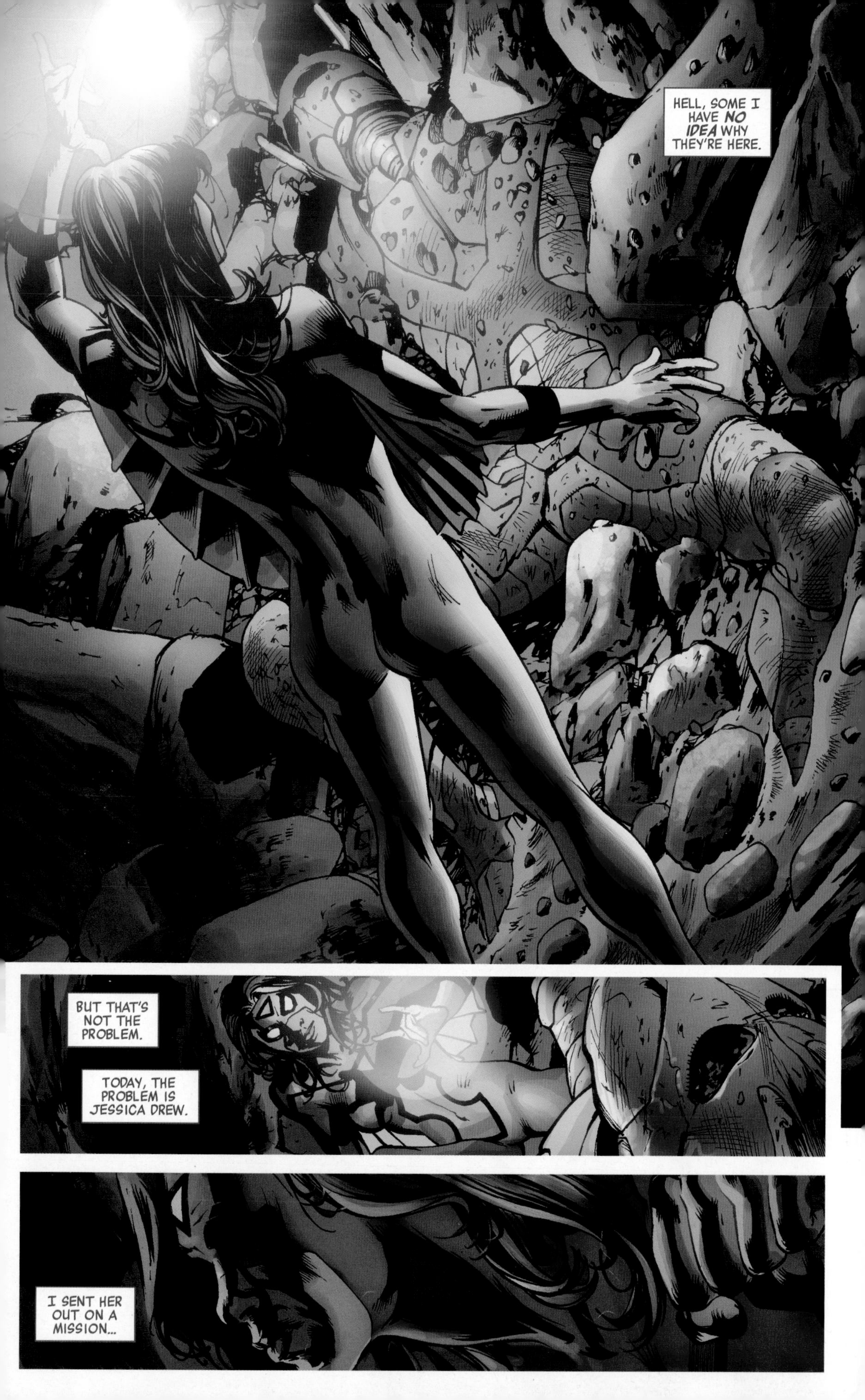
HELL, SOME I HAVE **NO IDEA** WHY THEY'RE HERE.
BUT THAT'S NOT THE PROBLEM.
TODAY, THE PROBLEM IS JESSICA DREW.
I SENT HER OUT ON A MISSION...

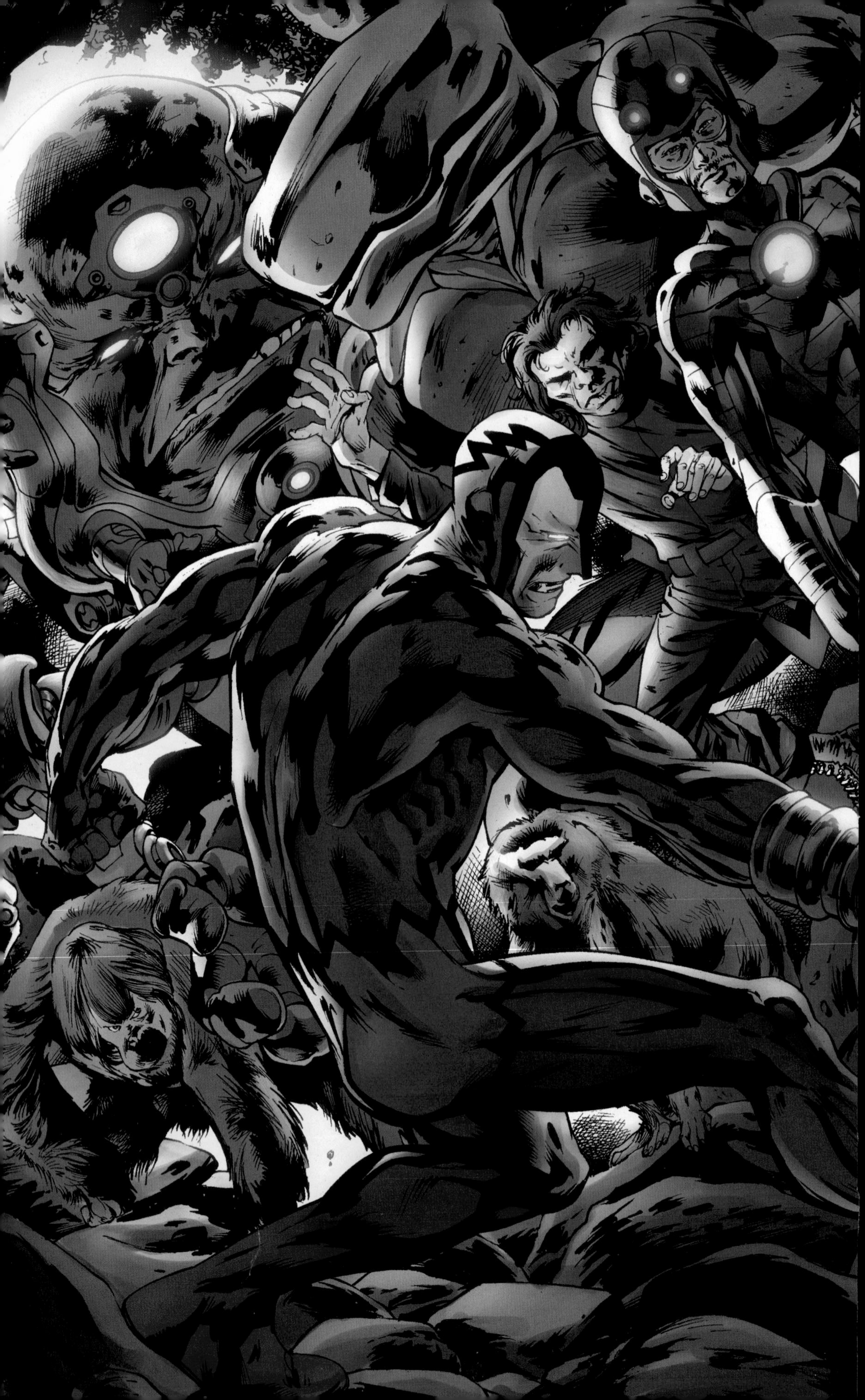

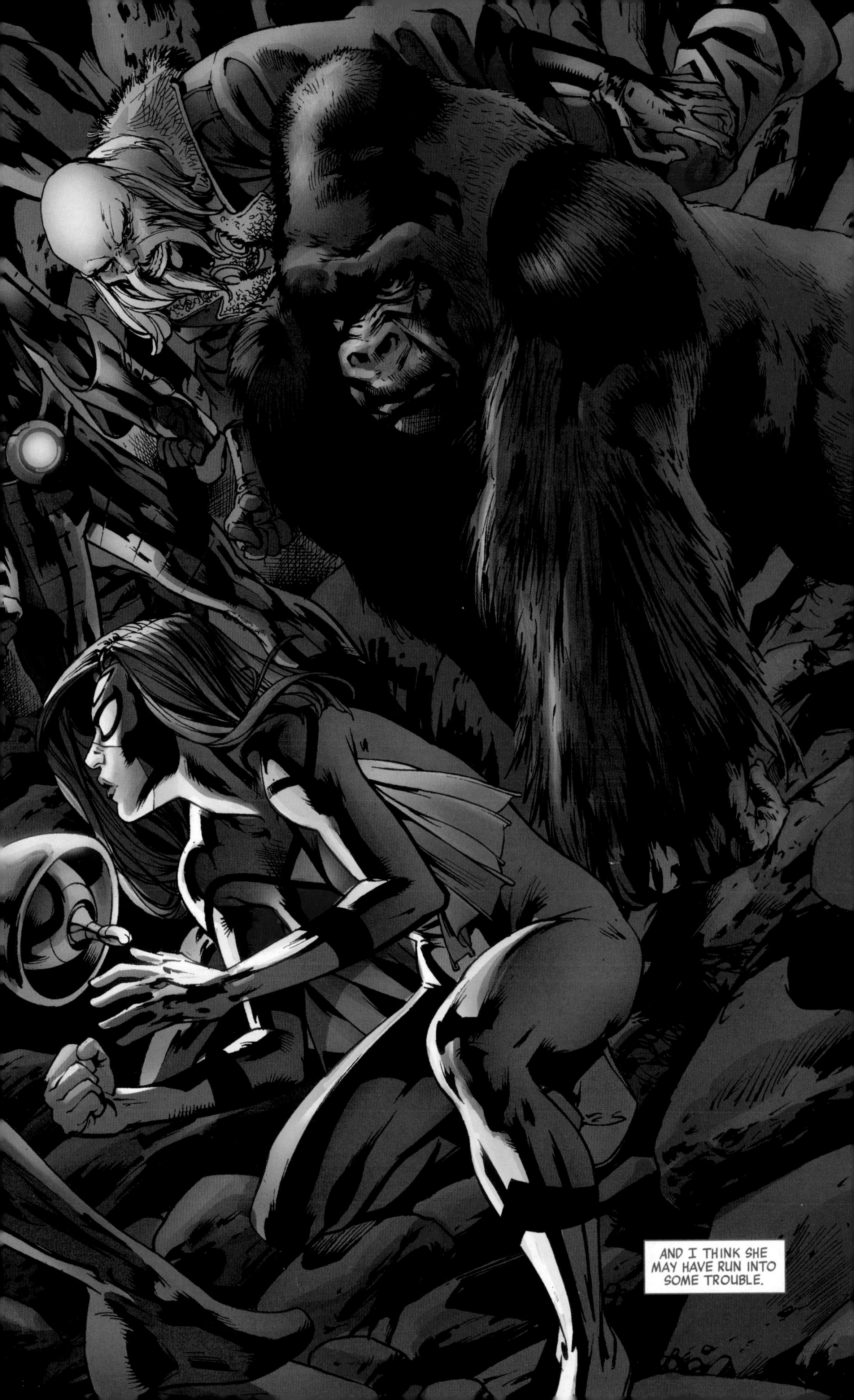
AND I THINK SHE
MAY HAVE RUN INTO
SOME TROUBLE.

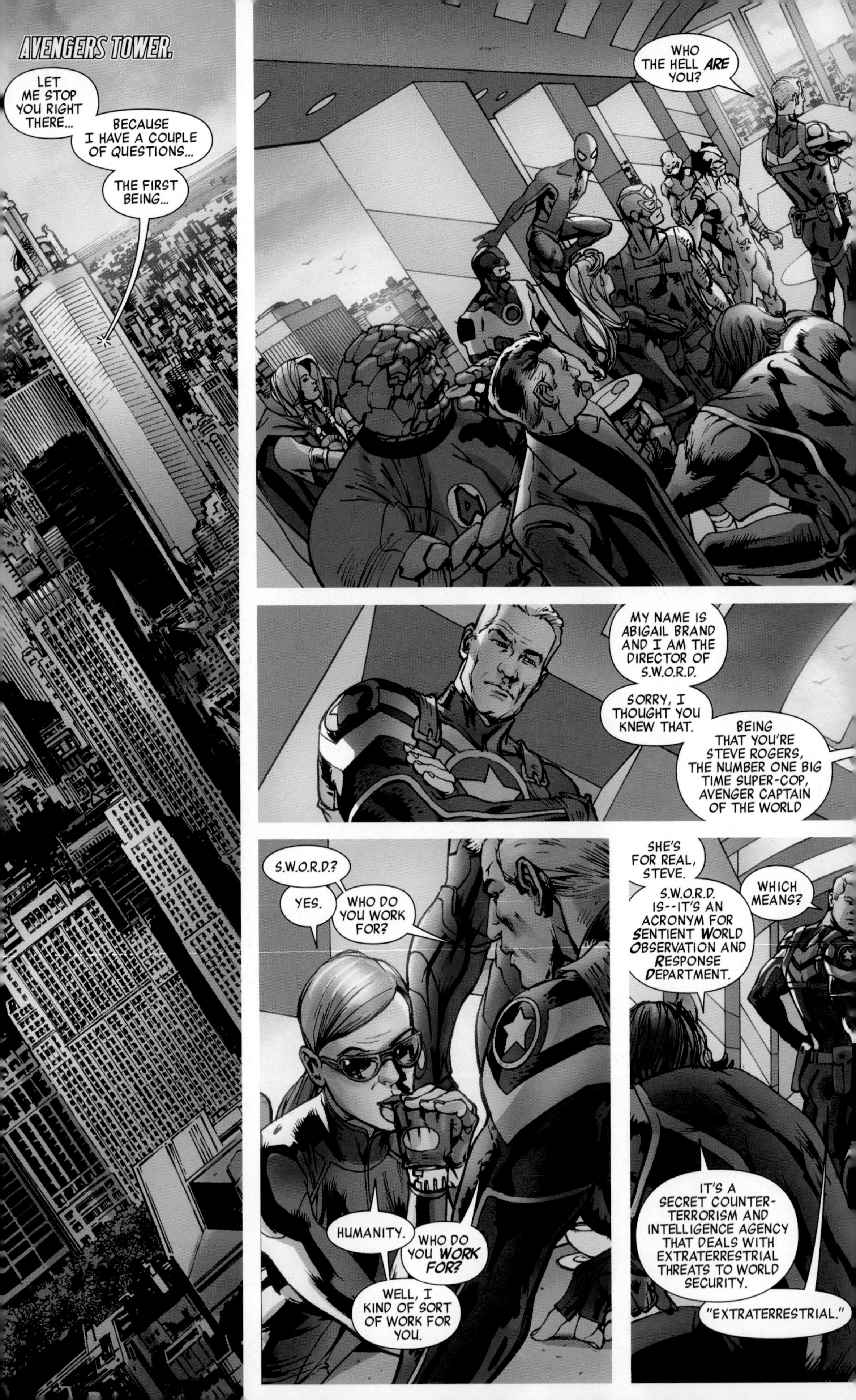
AVENGERS TOWER.
LET ME STOP YOU RIGHT THERE...
BECAUSE I HAVE A COUPLE OF QUESTIONS...
THE FIRST BEING...
WHO THE HELL ARE YOU?
MY NAME IS ABIGAIL BRAND AND I AM THE DIRECTOR OF S.W.O.R.D.
SORRY, I THOUGHT YOU KNEW THAT.
BEING THAT YOU'RE STEVE ROGERS, THE NUMBER ONE BIG TIME SUPER-COP, AVENGER CAPTAIN OF THE WORLD
S.W.O.R.D.?
YES.
WHO DO YOU WORK FOR?
HUMANITY.
WHO DO YOU WORK FOR?
WELL, I KIND OF SORT OF WORK FOR YOU.
SHE'S FOR REAL, STEVE.
S.W.O.R.D. IS--IT'S AN ACRONYM FOR SENTIENT WORLD OBSERVATION AND RESPONSE DEPARTMENT.
WHICH MEANS?
IT'S A SECRET COUNTER-TERRORISM AND INTELLIGENCE AGENCY THAT DEALS WITH EXTRATERRESTRIAL THREATS TO WORLD SECURITY.
"EXTRATERRESTRIAL."

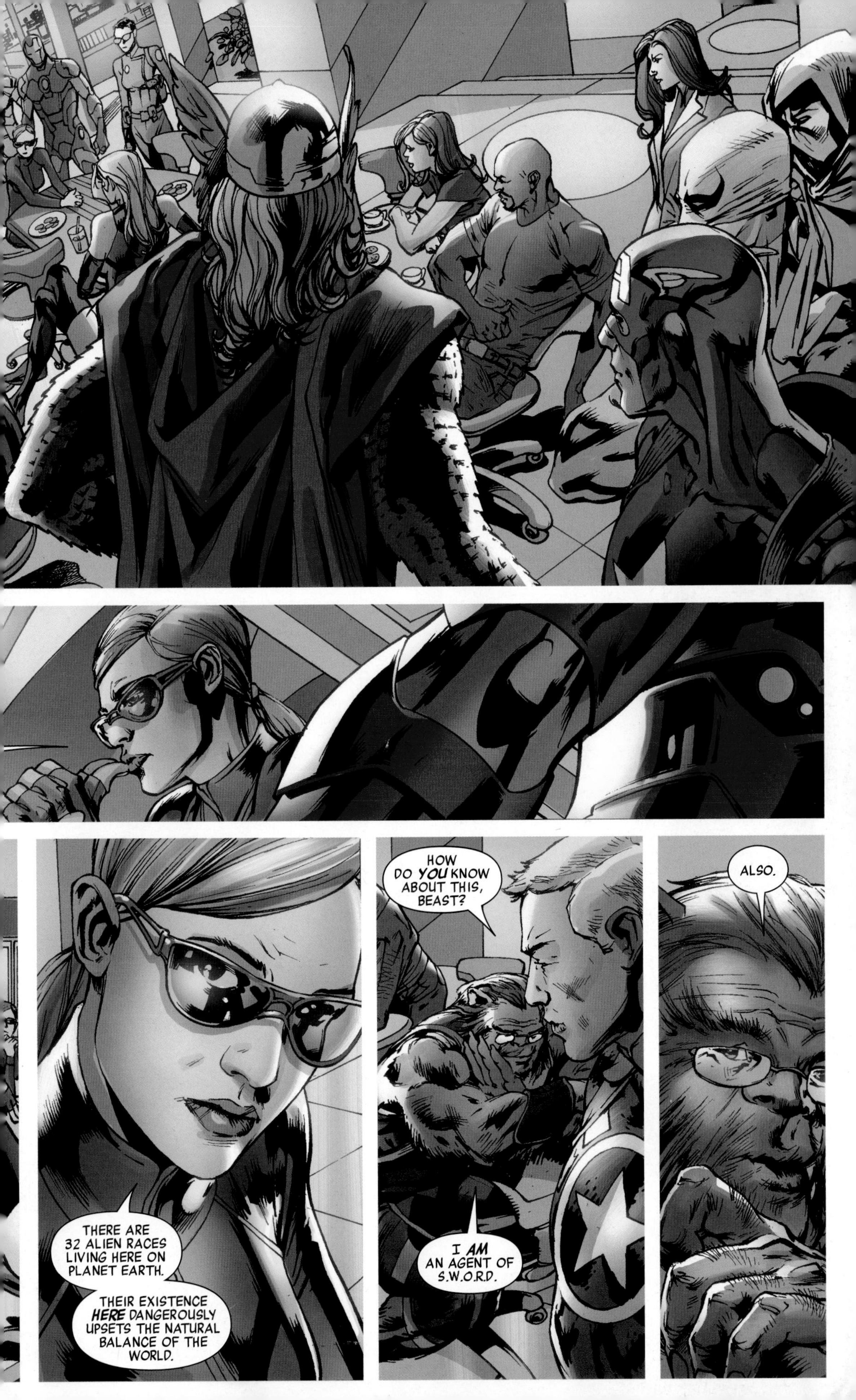
THERE ARE 32 ALIEN RACES LIVING HERE ON PLANET EARTH.
THEIR EXISTENCE HERE DANGEROUSLY UPSETS THE NATURAL BALANCE OF THE WORLD.
HOW DO YOU KNOW ABOUT THIS, BEAST?
I AM AN AGENT OF S.W.O.R.D.
ALSO.

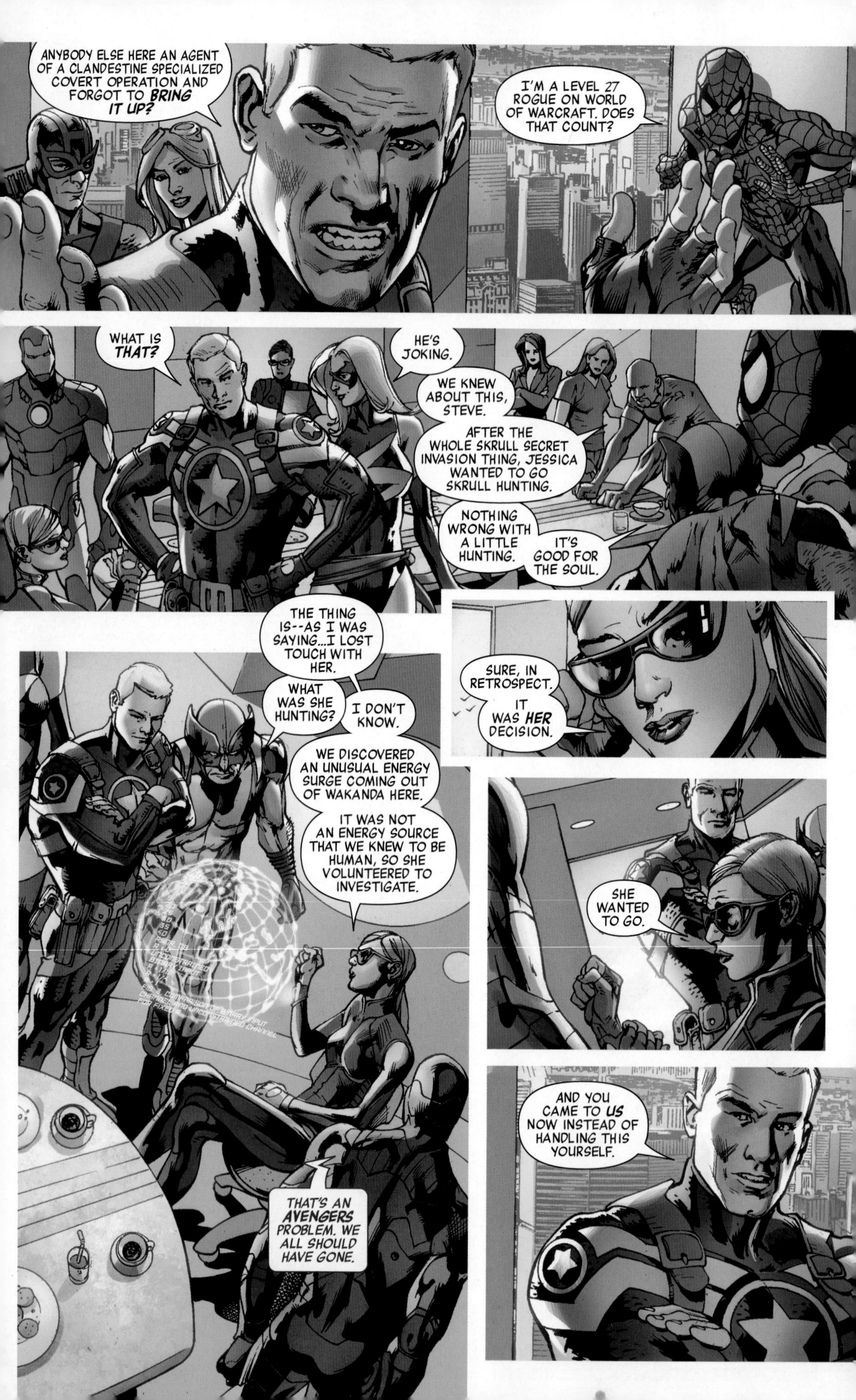

ANYBODY ELSE HERE AN AGENT OF A CLANDESTINE SPECIALIZED COVERT OPERATION AND FORGOT TO **BRING IT UP?**
I'M A LEVEL 27 ROGUE ON WORLD OF WARCRAFT. DOES THAT COUNT?
WHAT IS **THAT?**
HE'S JOKING.
WE KNEW ABOUT THIS, STEVE.
AFTER THE WHOLE SKRULL SECRET INVASION THING, JESSICA WANTED TO GO SKRULL HUNTING.
NOTHING WRONG WITH A LITTLE HUNTING.
IT'S GOOD FOR THE SOUL.
SURE, IN RETROSPECT.
IT WAS **HER** DECISION.
THE THING IS--AS I WAS SAYING...I LOST TOUCH WITH HER.
WHAT WAS SHE HUNTING?
I DON'T KNOW.
WE DISCOVERED AN UNUSUAL ENERGY SURGE COMING OUT OF WAKANDA HERE.
IT WAS NOT AN ENERGY SOURCE THAT WE KNEW TO BE HUMAN, SO SHE VOLUNTEERED TO INVESTIGATE.
SHE WANTED TO GO.
AND YOU CAME TO **US** NOW INSTEAD OF HANDLING THIS YOURSELF.
*THAT'S AN **AVENGERS** PROBLEM. WE ALL SHOULD HAVE GONE.*

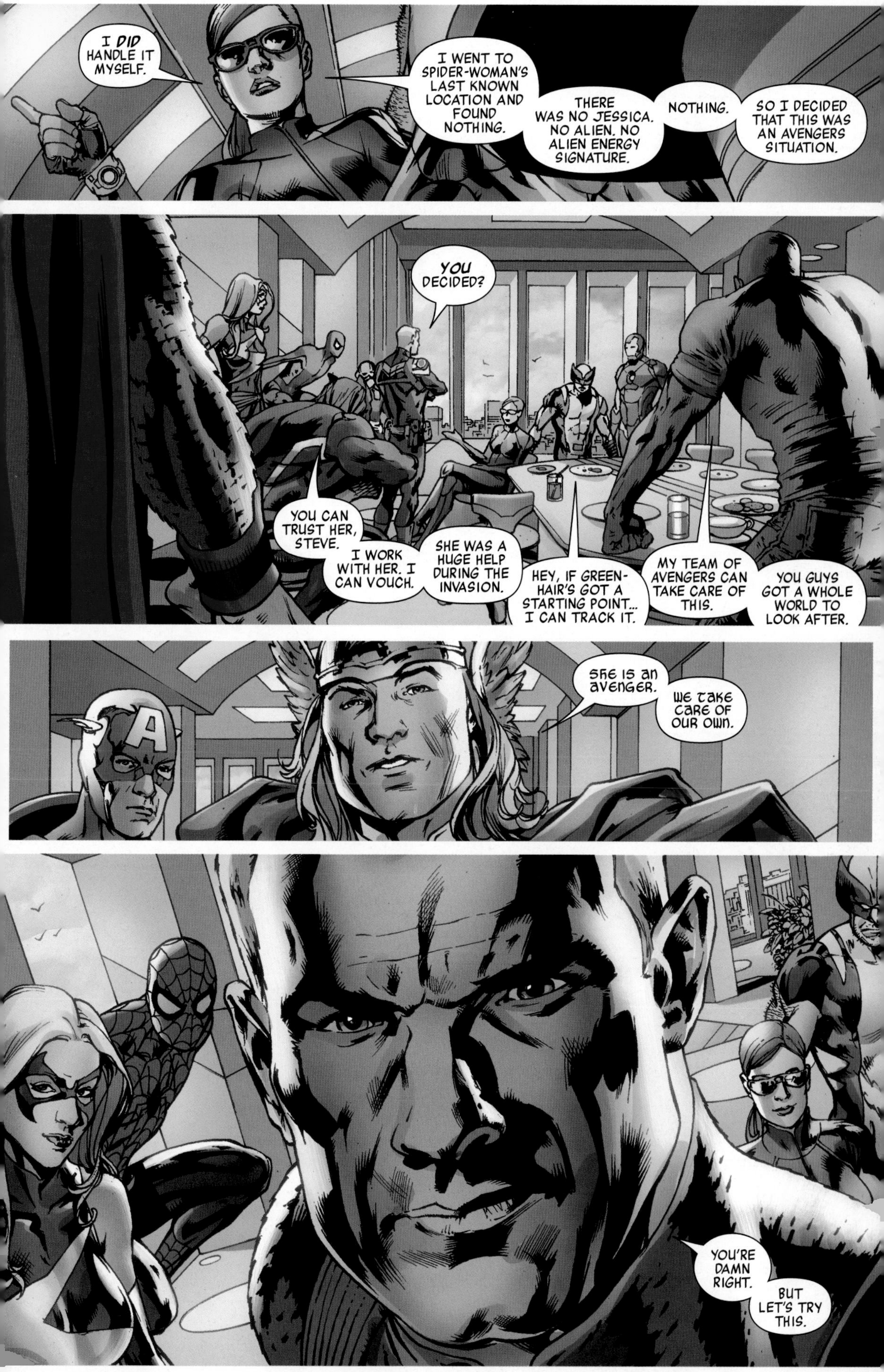
I DID HANDLE IT MYSELF.
I WENT TO SPIDER-WOMAN'S LAST KNOWN LOCATION AND FOUND NOTHING.
THERE WAS NO JESSICA. NO ALIEN. NO ALIEN ENERGY SIGNATURE.
NOTHING.
SO I DECIDED THAT THIS WAS AN AVENGERS SITUATION.
YOU DECIDED?
YOU CAN TRUST HER, STEVE.
I WORK WITH HER. I CAN VOUCH.
SHE WAS A HUGE HELP DURING THE INVASION.
HEY, IF GREEN-HAIR'S GOT A STARTING POINT... I CAN TRACK IT.
MY TEAM OF AVENGERS CAN TAKE CARE OF THIS.
YOU GUYS GOT A WHOLE WORLD TO LOOK AFTER.
SHE IS AN AVENGER.
WE TAKE CARE OF OUR OWN.
YOU'RE DAMN RIGHT.
BUT LET'S TRY THIS.

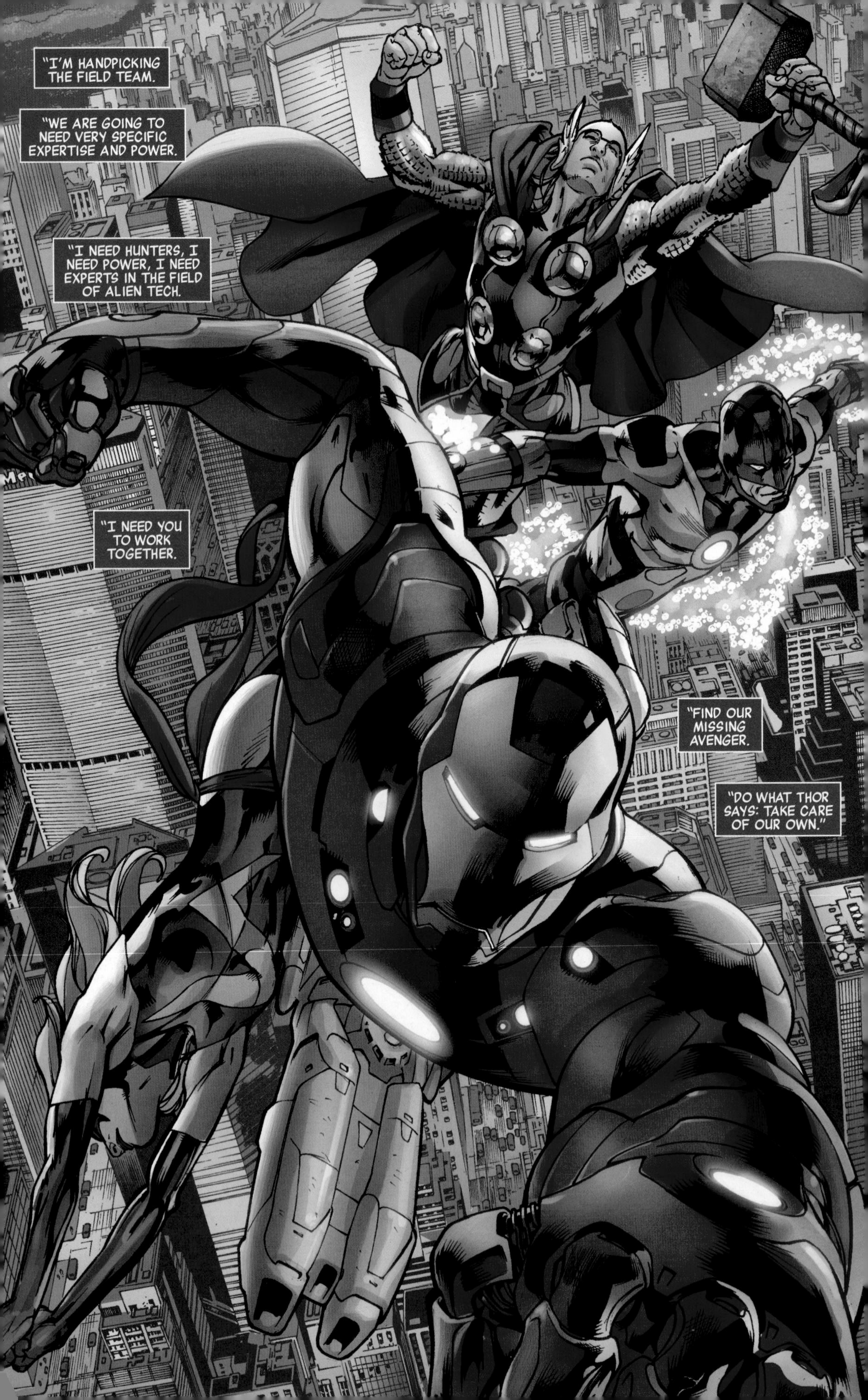
"I'M HANDPICKING THE FIELD TEAM.
"WE ARE GOING TO NEED VERY SPECIFIC EXPERTISE AND POWER.
"I NEED HUNTERS, I NEED POWER, I NEED EXPERTS IN THE FIELD OF ALIEN TECH.
"I NEED YOU TO WORK TOGETHER.
"FIND OUR MISSING AVENGER.
"DO WHAT THOR SAYS: TAKE CARE OF OUR OWN."

WHAT ARE YOU DOING?

HE'S PICKING UP A SCENT.

LET HIM DO HIS THING.

I HAVE SOME READINGS.

I HAVE SOMETHING TOO.

ENVIRONMENTAL SCAN UNDERWAY.

:SNFF:

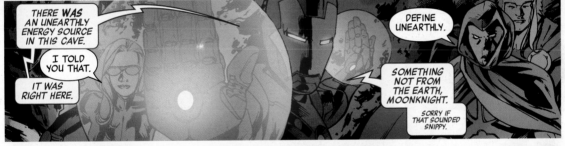

THERE *WAS* AN UNEARTHLY ENERGY SOURCE IN THIS CAVE.

I TOLD YOU THAT.

IT WAS RIGHT HERE.

DEFINE UNEARTHLY.

SOMETHING NOT FROM THE EARTH, MOONKNIGHT.

SORRY IF THAT SOUNDED SNIPPY.

SHE WAS RIGHT HERE.

CROUCHED DOWN.

SHE TURNED ON HER FOOT.

SEE THE MARKINGS IN THE DIRT?

NO.

SHE TURNED RIGHT HERE.

SOMEONE CAME UP BEHIND HER.

THERE...

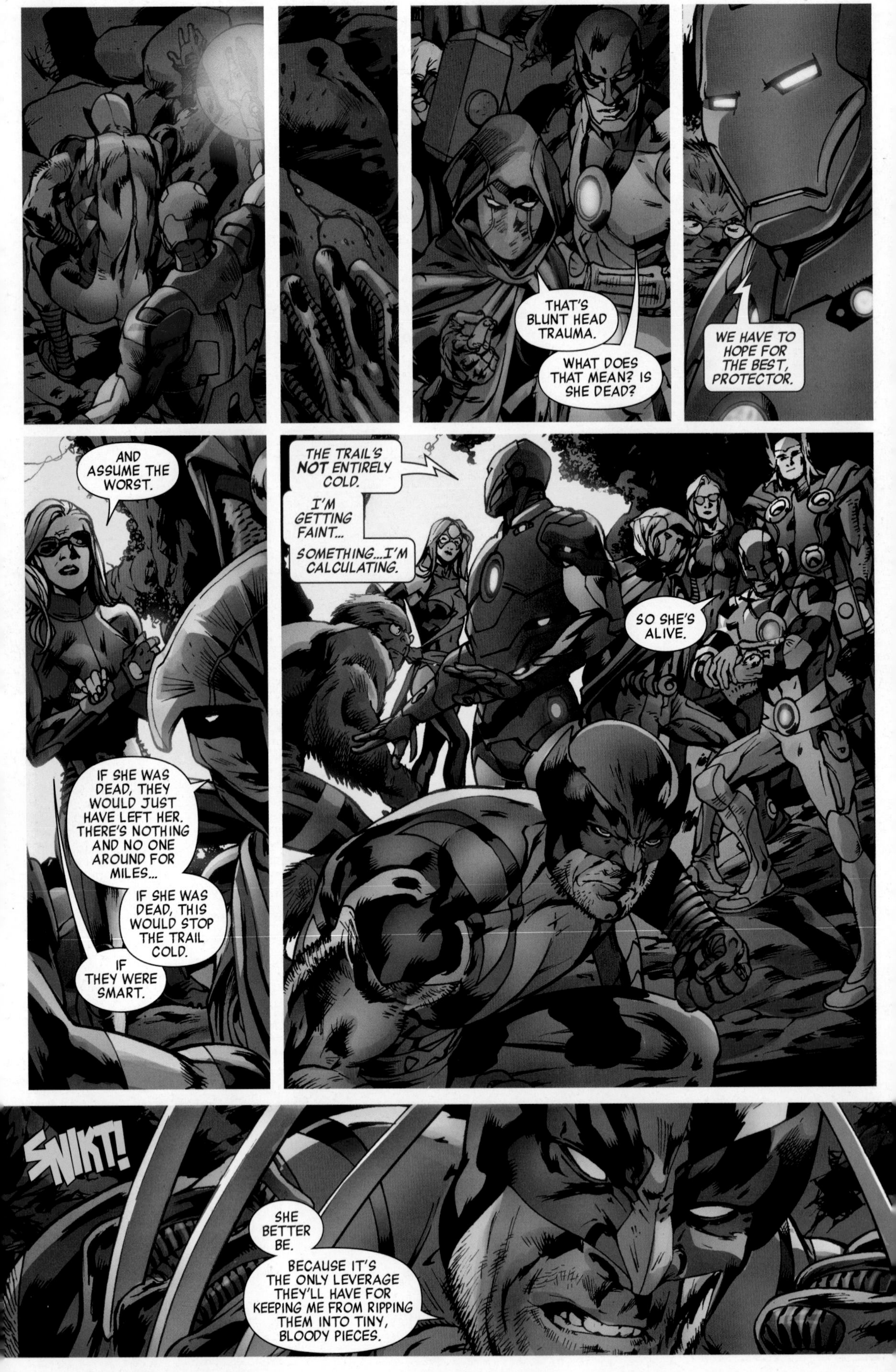
THAT'S BLUNT HEAD TRAUMA.
WHAT DOES THAT MEAN? IS SHE DEAD?
WE HAVE TO HOPE FOR THE BEST, PROTECTOR.
AND ASSUME THE WORST.
THE TRAIL'S **NOT** ENTIRELY COLD.
I'M GETTING FAINT...
SOMETHING...I'M CALCULATING.
SO SHE'S ALIVE.
IF SHE WAS DEAD, THEY WOULD JUST HAVE LEFT HER. THERE'S NOTHING AND NO ONE AROUND FOR MILES...
IF SHE WAS DEAD, THIS WOULD STOP THE TRAIL COLD.
IF THEY WERE SMART.
SNIKT!
SHE BETTER BE.
BECAUSE IT'S THE ONLY LEVERAGE THEY'LL HAVE FOR KEEPING ME FROM RIPPING THEM INTO TINY, BLOODY PIECES.

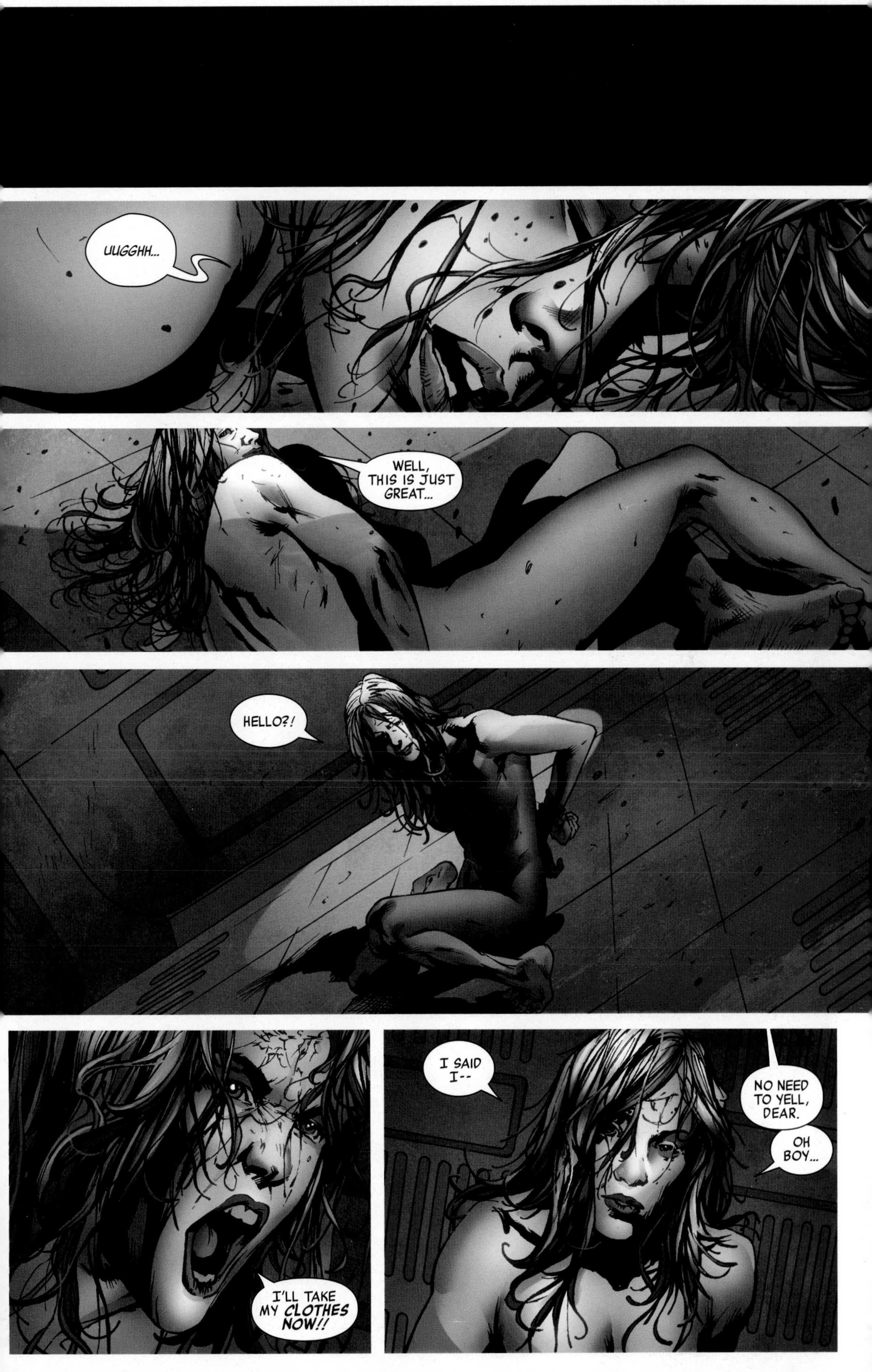
UUGGHH...
WELL, THIS IS JUST GREAT...
HELLO?!
I'LL TAKE MY CLOTHES NOW!!
I SAID I--
NO NEED TO YELL, DEAR.
OH BOY...

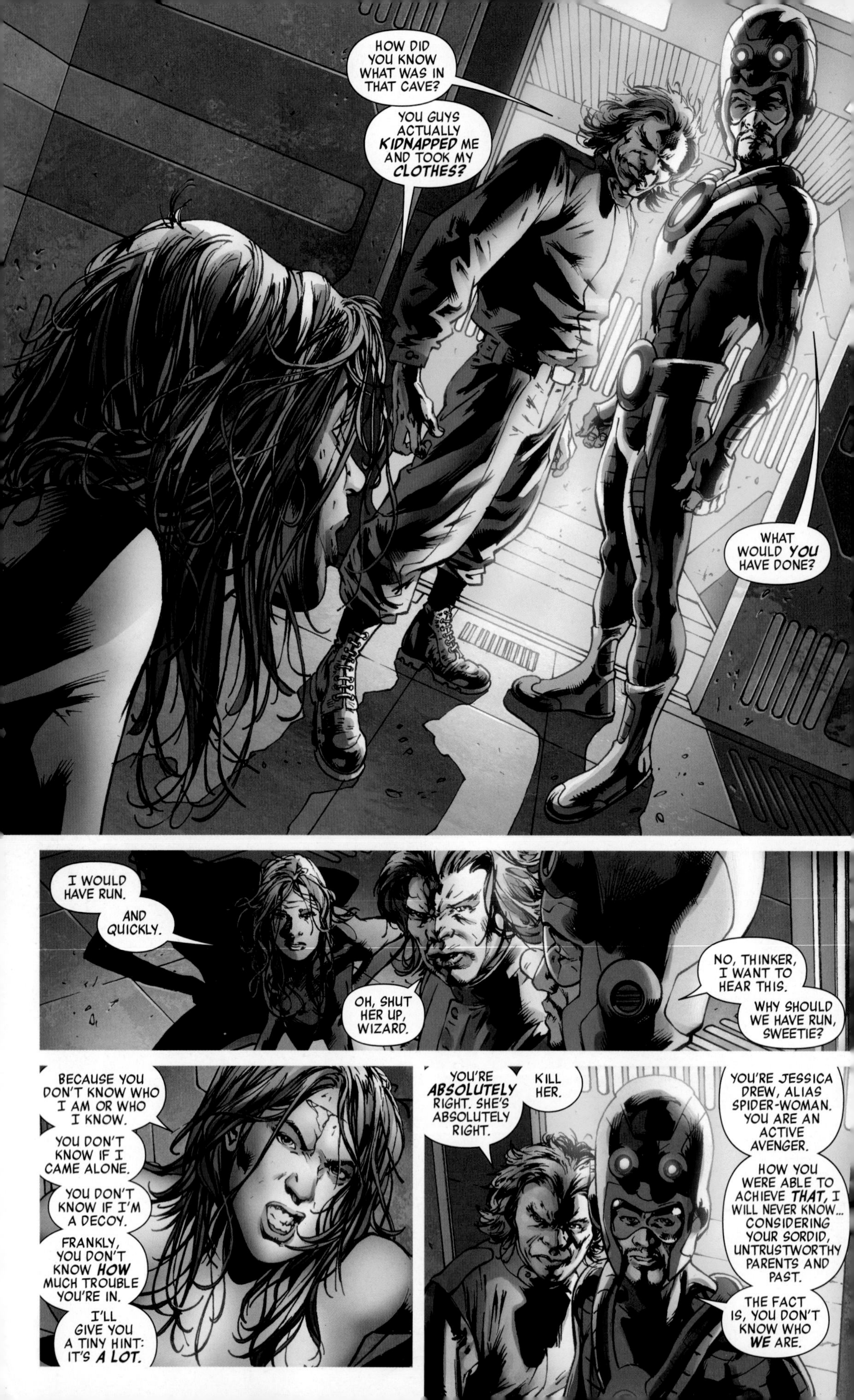
HOW DID YOU KNOW WHAT WAS IN THAT CAVE?
YOU GUYS ACTUALLY KIDNAPPED ME AND TOOK MY CLOTHES?
WHAT WOULD YOU HAVE DONE?
I WOULD HAVE RUN.
AND QUICKLY.
OH, SHUT HER UP, WIZARD.
NO, THINKER, I WANT TO HEAR THIS.
WHY SHOULD WE HAVE RUN, SWEETIE?
BECAUSE YOU DON'T KNOW WHO I AM OR WHO I KNOW.
YOU DON'T KNOW IF I CAME ALONE.
YOU DON'T KNOW IF I'M A DECOY.
FRANKLY, YOU DON'T KNOW HOW MUCH TROUBLE YOU'RE IN.
I'LL GIVE YOU A TINY HINT: IT'S A LOT.
KILL HER.
YOU'RE ABSOLUTELY RIGHT. SHE'S ABSOLUTELY RIGHT.
YOU'RE JESSICA DREW, ALIAS SPIDER-WOMAN. YOU ARE AN ACTIVE AVENGER.
HOW YOU WERE ABLE TO ACHIEVE THAT, I WILL NEVER KNOW... CONSIDERING YOUR SORDID, UNTRUSTWORTHY PARENTS AND PAST.
THE FACT IS, YOU DON'T KNOW WHO WE ARE.

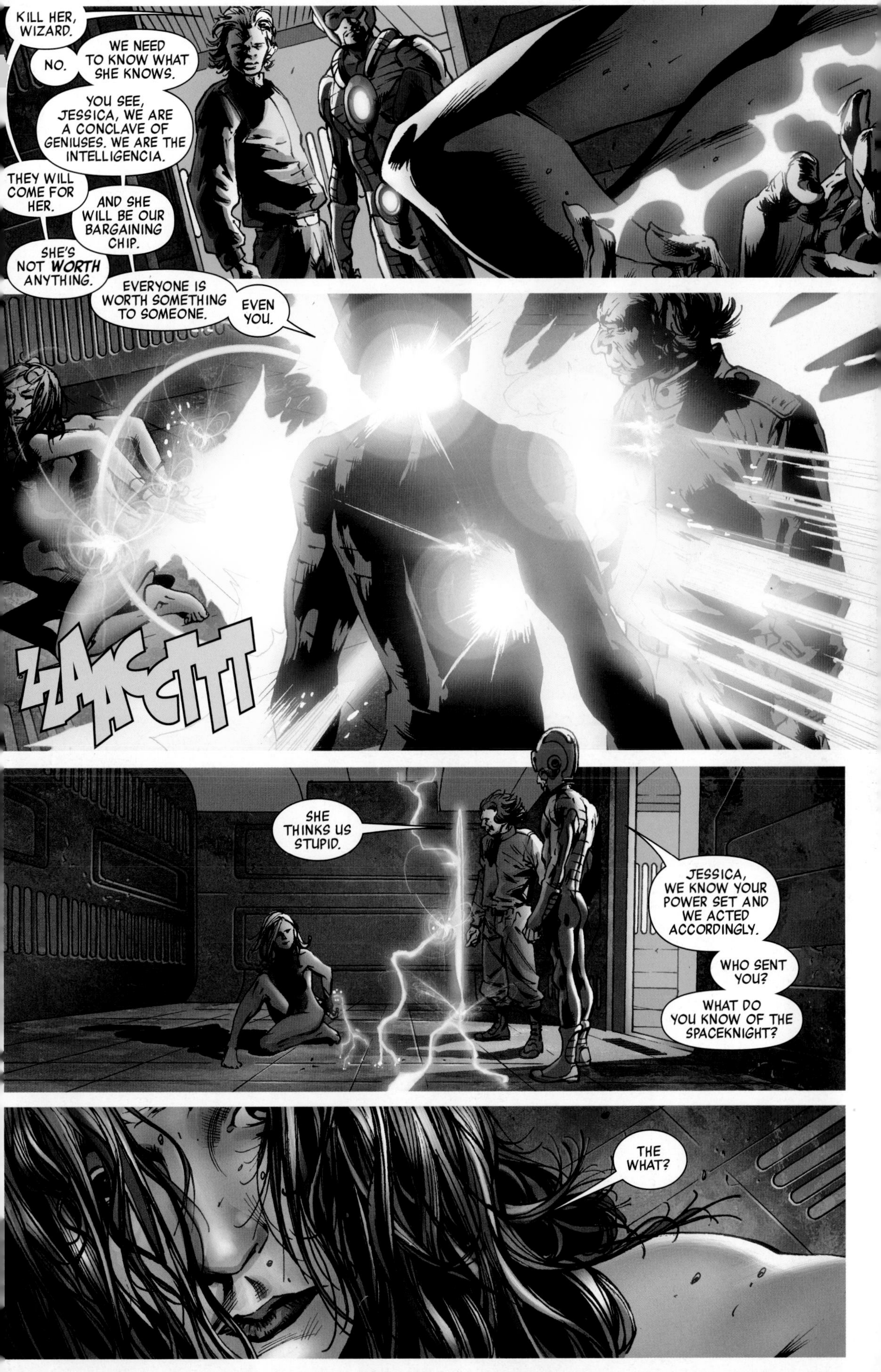
KILL HER, WIZARD.
NO.
WE NEED TO KNOW WHAT SHE KNOWS.
YOU SEE, JESSICA, WE ARE A CONCLAVE OF GENIUSES. WE ARE THE INTELLIGENCIA.
THEY WILL COME FOR HER.
AND SHE WILL BE OUR BARGAINING CHIP.
SHE'S NOT WORTH ANYTHING.
EVERYONE IS WORTH SOMETHING TO SOMEONE.
EVEN YOU.
ZZAACTTT
SHE THINKS US STUPID.
JESSICA, WE KNOW YOUR POWER SET AND WE ACTED ACCORDINGLY.
WHO SENT YOU?
WHAT DO YOU KNOW OF THE SPACEKNIGHT?
THE WHAT?

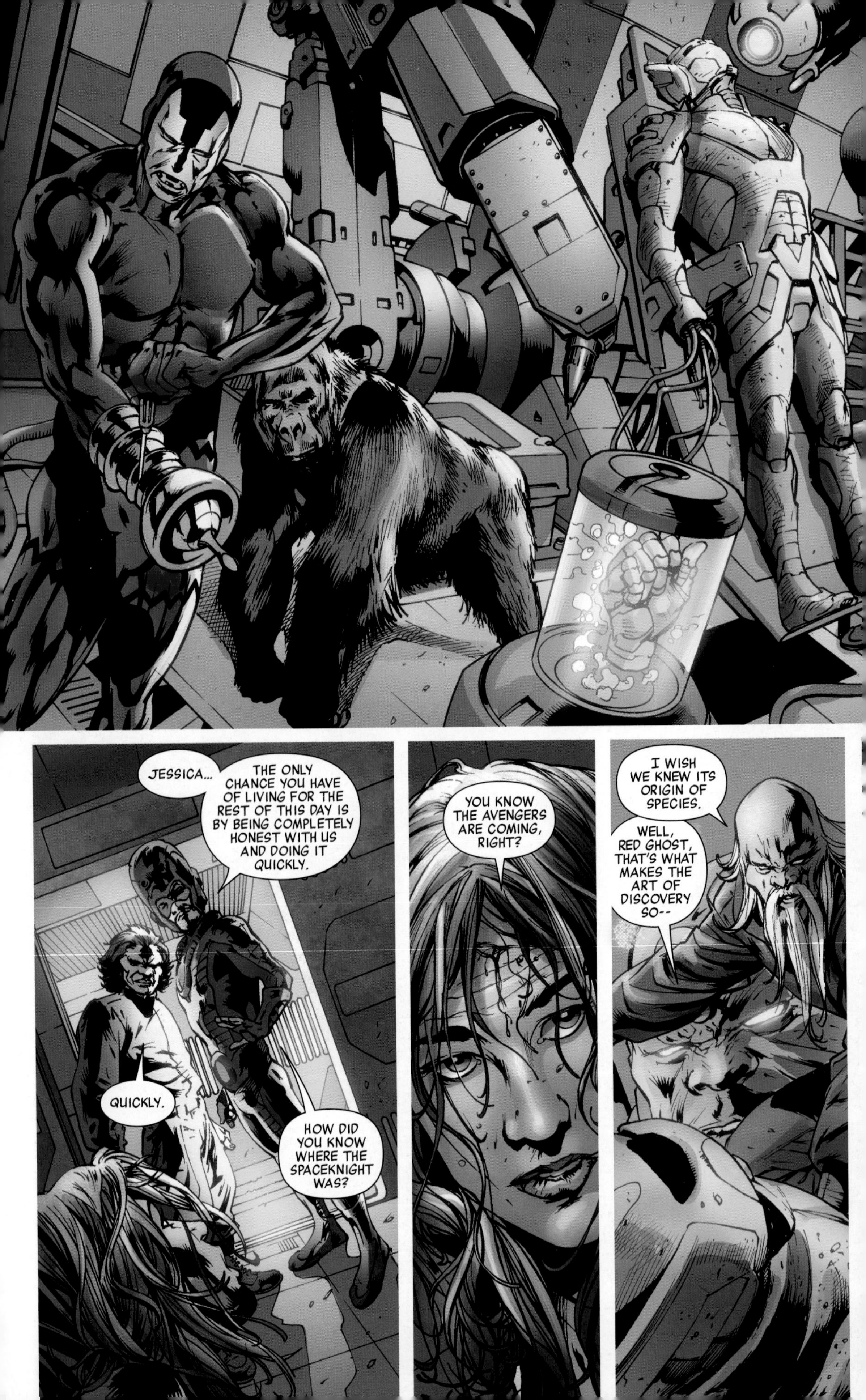
JESSICA...
THE ONLY CHANCE YOU HAVE OF LIVING FOR THE REST OF THIS DAY IS BY BEING COMPLETELY HONEST WITH US AND DOING IT QUICKLY.
QUICKLY.
HOW DID YOU KNOW WHERE THE SPACEKNIGHT WAS?
YOU KNOW THE AVENGERS ARE COMING, RIGHT?
I WISH WE KNEW ITS ORIGIN OF SPECIES.
WELL, RED GHOST, THAT'S WHAT MAKES THE ART OF DISCOVERY SO--

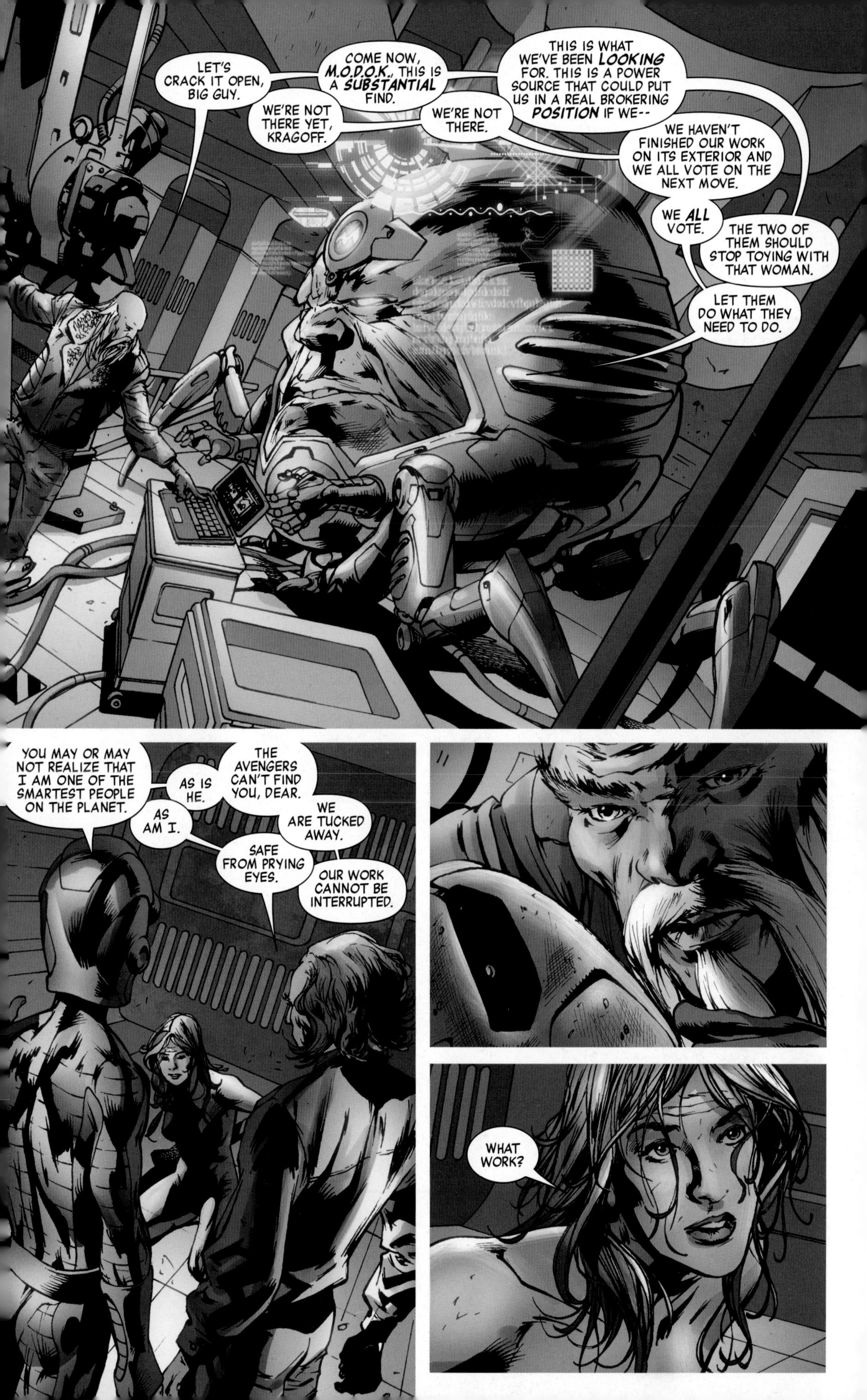

LET'S CRACK IT OPEN, BIG GUY.
COME NOW, M.O.D.O.K., THIS IS A SUBSTANTIAL FIND.
THIS IS WHAT WE'VE BEEN LOOKING FOR. THIS IS A POWER SOURCE THAT COULD PUT US IN A REAL BROKERING POSITION IF WE--
WE'RE NOT THERE YET, KRAGOFF.
WE'RE NOT THERE.
WE HAVEN'T FINISHED OUR WORK ON ITS EXTERIOR AND WE ALL VOTE ON THE NEXT MOVE.
WE ALL VOTE.
THE TWO OF THEM SHOULD STOP TOYING WITH THAT WOMAN.
LET THEM DO WHAT THEY NEED TO DO.
YOU MAY OR MAY NOT REALIZE THAT I AM ONE OF THE SMARTEST PEOPLE ON THE PLANET.
AS IS HE.
AS AM I.
THE AVENGERS CAN'T FIND YOU, DEAR.
WE ARE TUCKED AWAY.
SAFE FROM PRYING EYES.
OUR WORK CANNOT BE INTERRUPTED.
WHAT WORK?

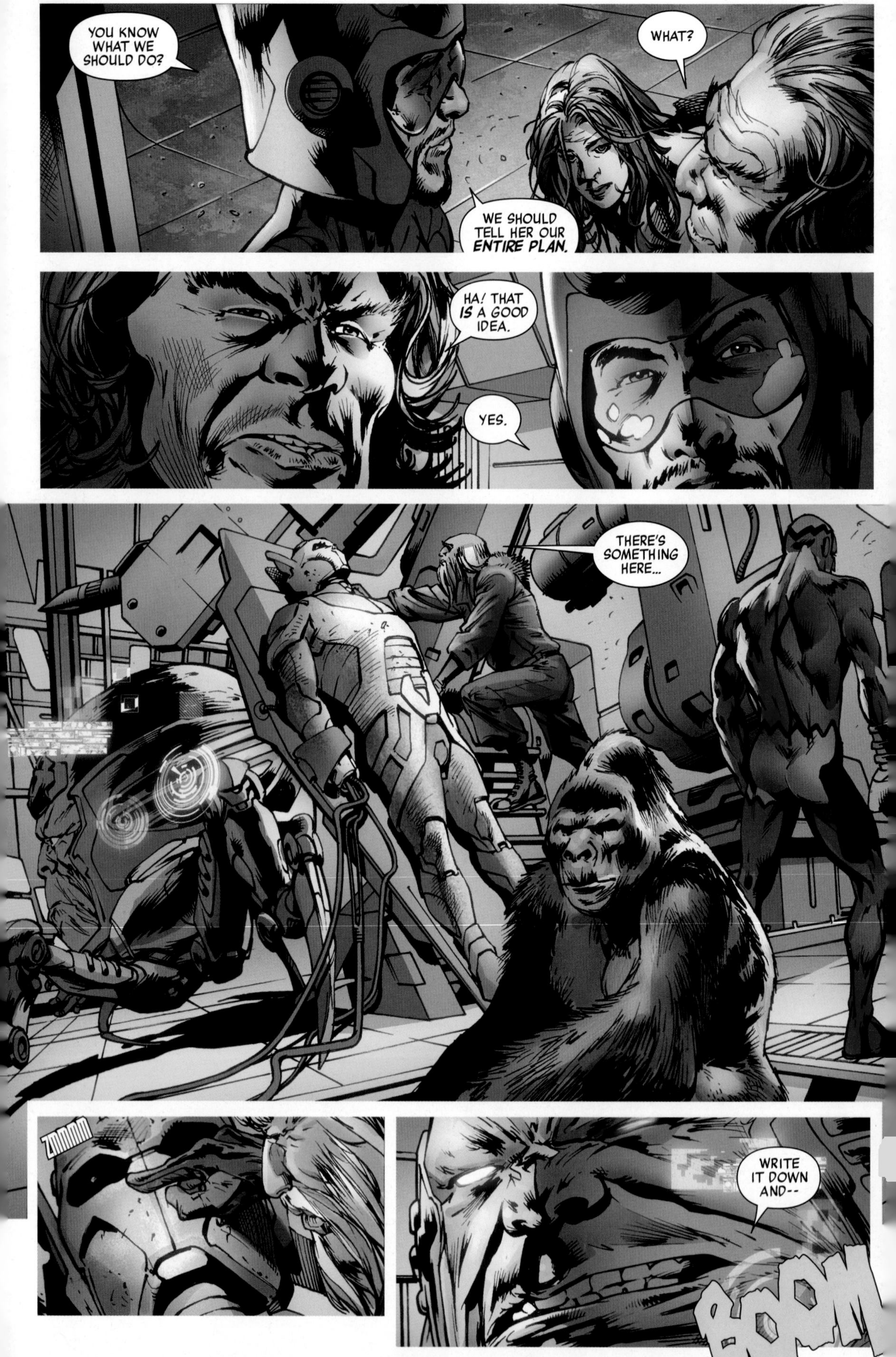
YOU KNOW WHAT WE SHOULD DO?
WHAT?
WE SHOULD TELL HER OUR ENTIRE PLAN.
HA! THAT IS A GOOD IDEA.
YES.
THERE'S SOMETHING HERE...
ZMMMM
WRITE IT DOWN AND--
BOOM

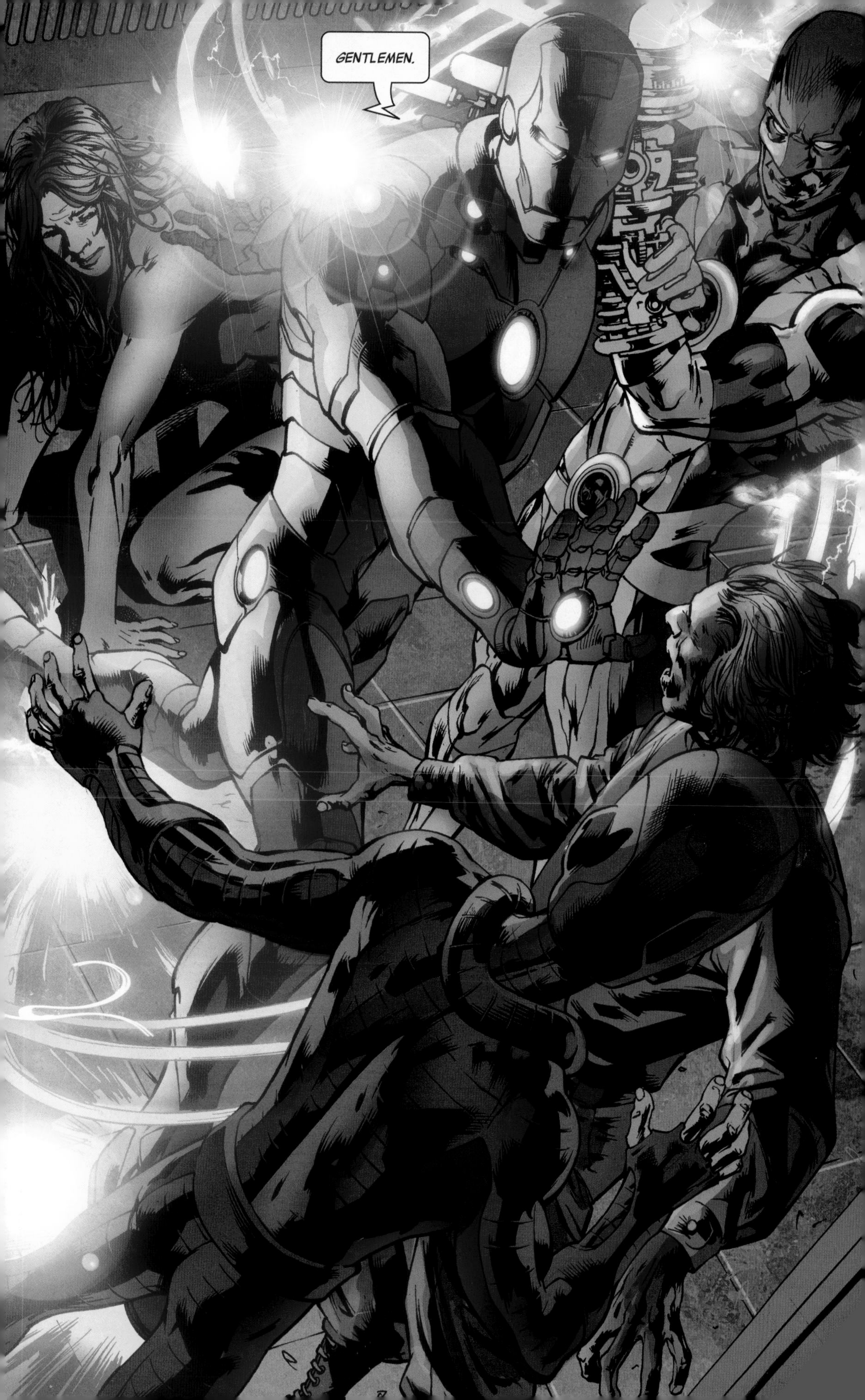
GENTLEMEN.

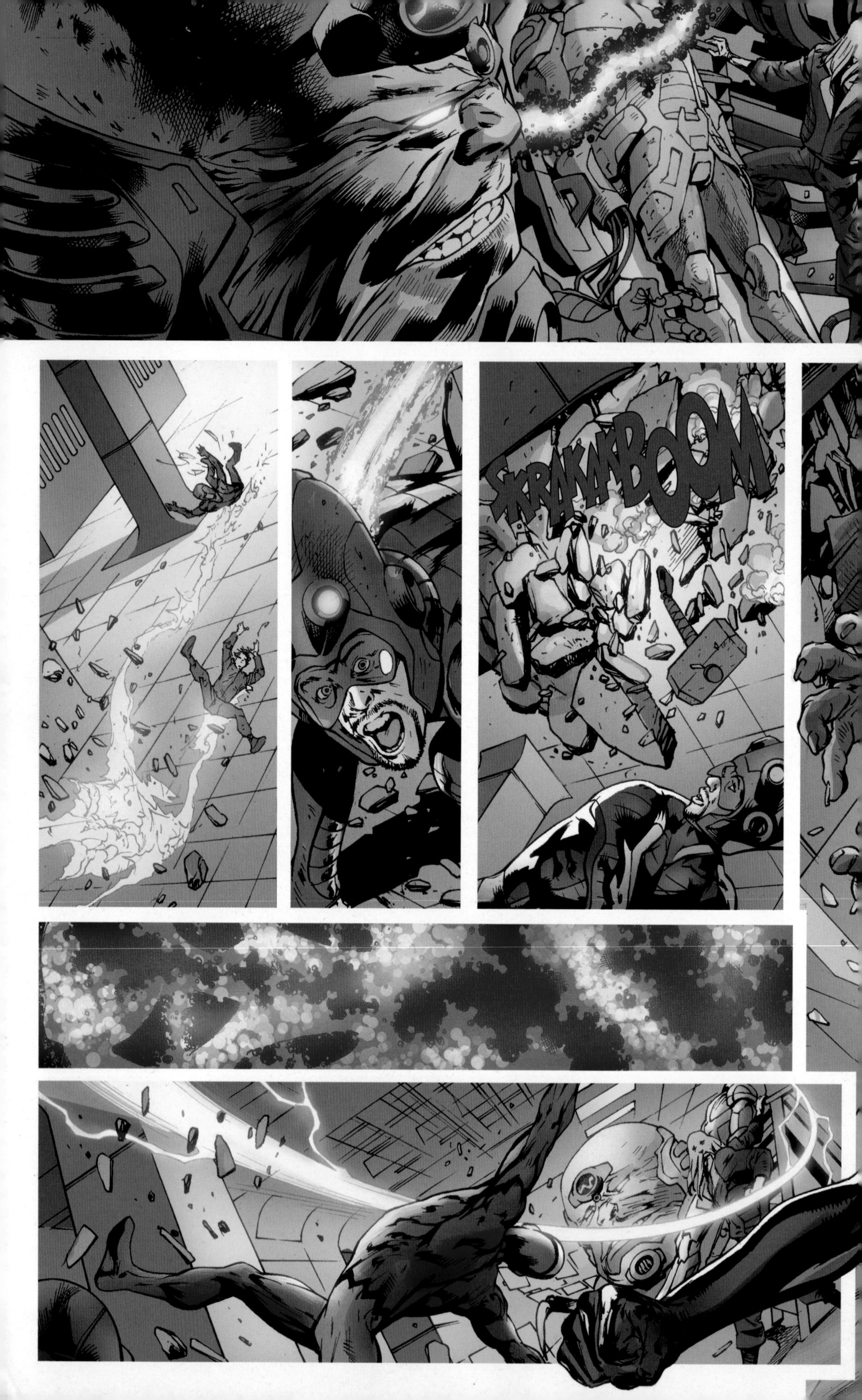
SKRAKAKBOOM

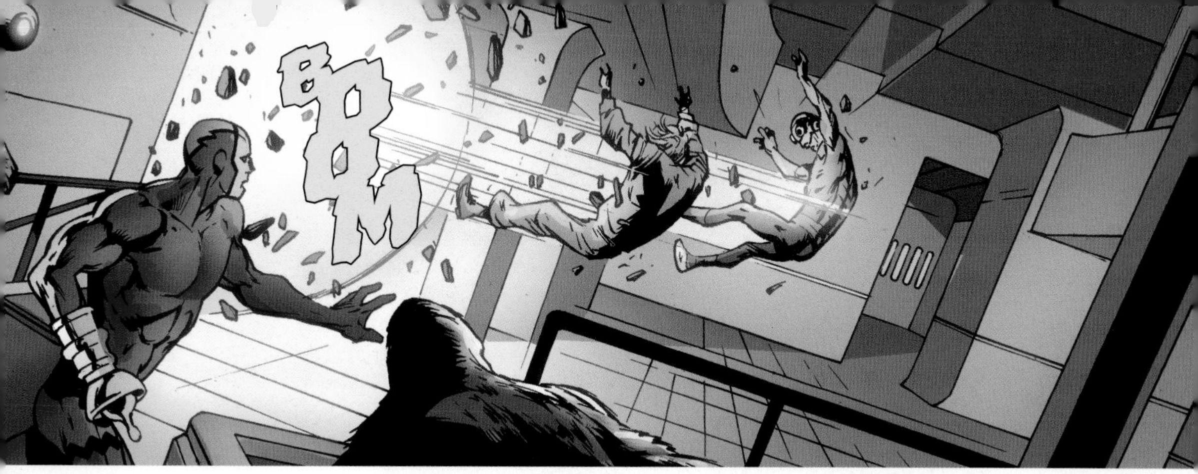
BOOM

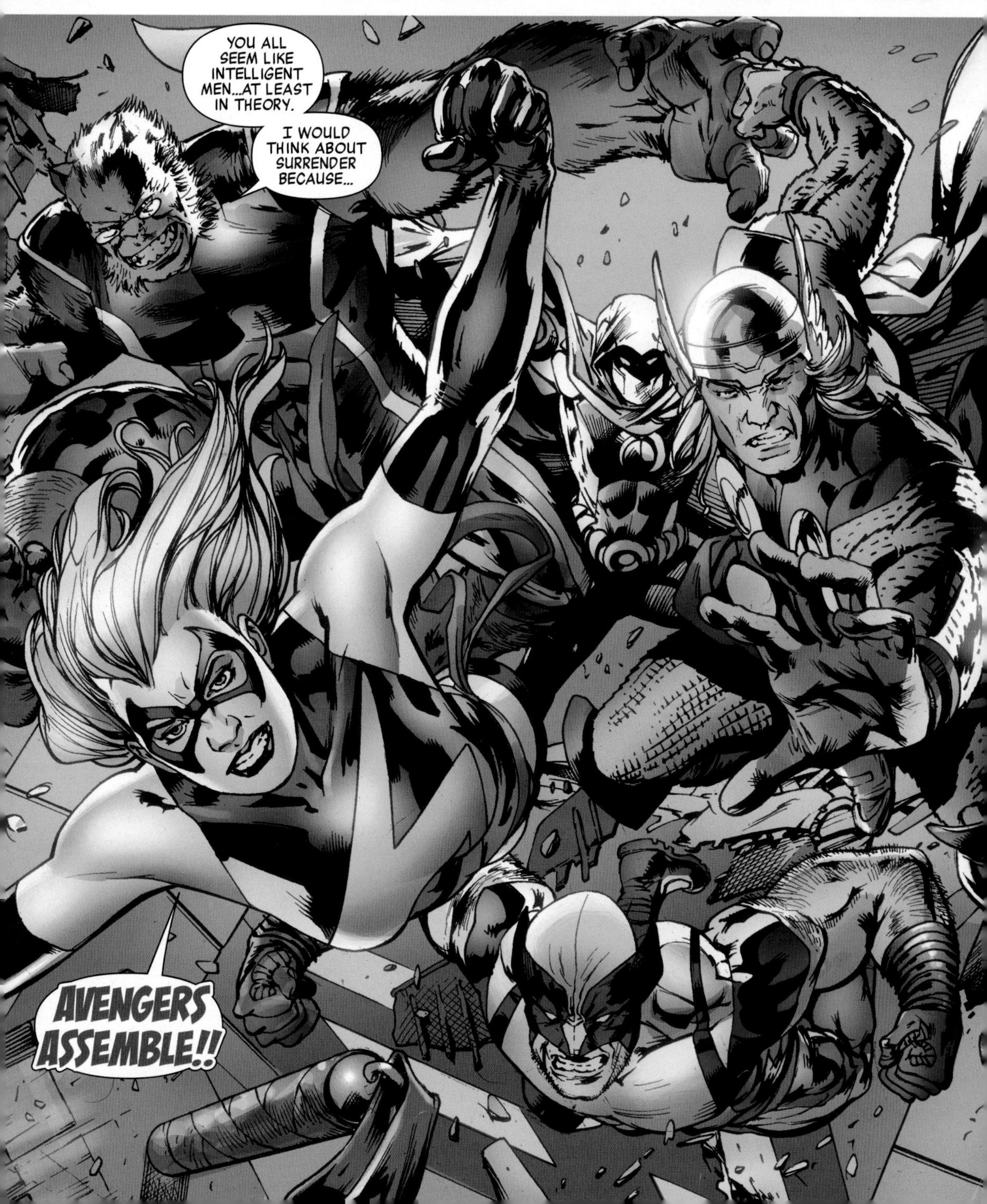
YOU ALL SEEM LIKE INTELLIGENT MEN...AT LEAST IN THEORY.
I WOULD THINK ABOUT SURRENDER BECAUSE...
AVENGERS ASSEMBLE!!

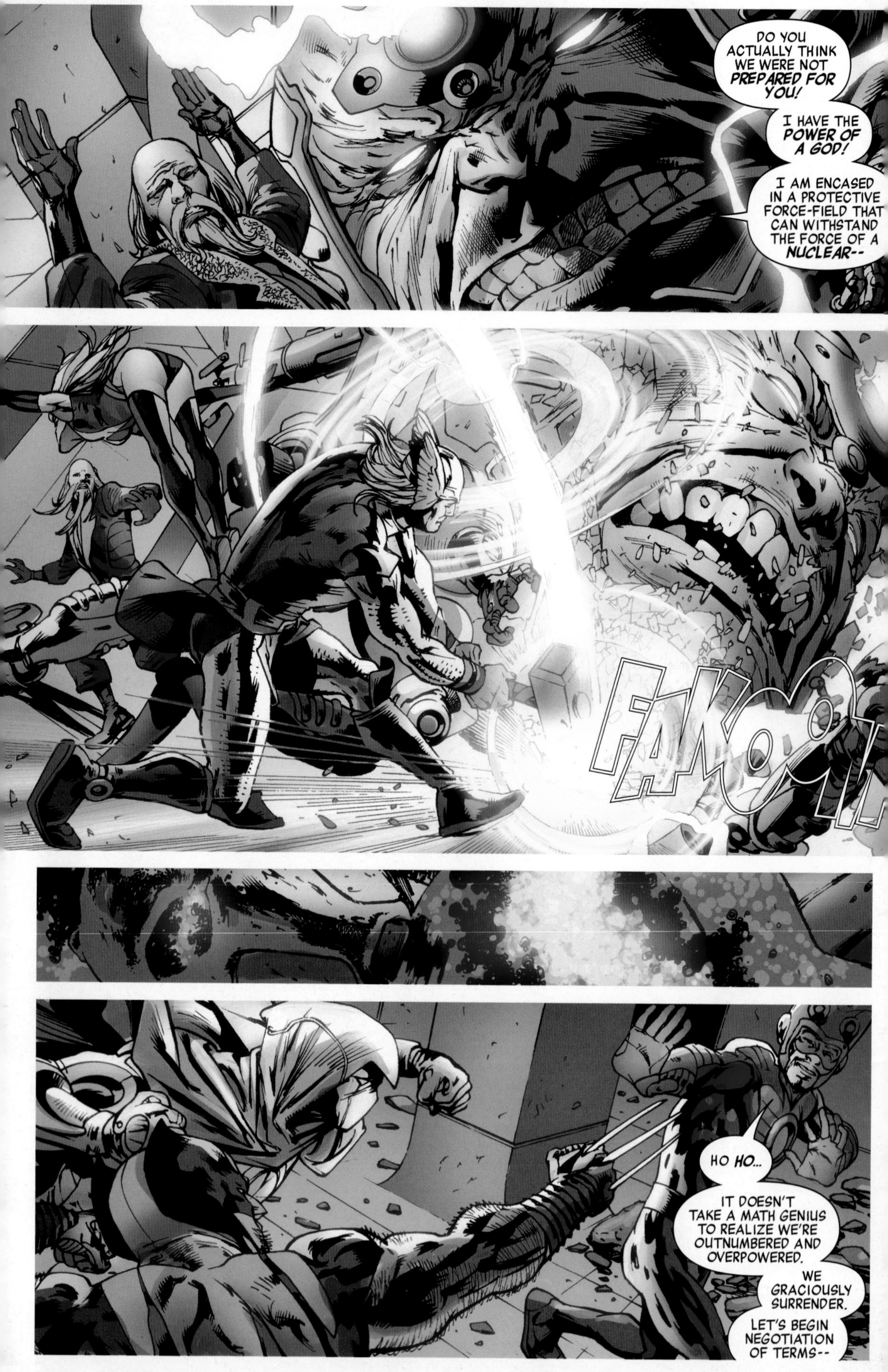

DO YOU ACTUALLY THINK WE WERE NOT PREPARED FOR YOU!
I HAVE THE POWER OF A GOD!
I AM ENCASED IN A PROTECTIVE FORCE-FIELD THAT CAN WITHSTAND THE FORCE OF A NUCLEAR--
FAKOOM!
HO HO...
IT DOESN'T TAKE A MATH GENIUS TO REALIZE WE'RE OUTNUMBERED AND OVERPOWERED.
WE GRACIOUSLY SURRENDER.
LET'S BEGIN NEGOTIATION OF TERMS--

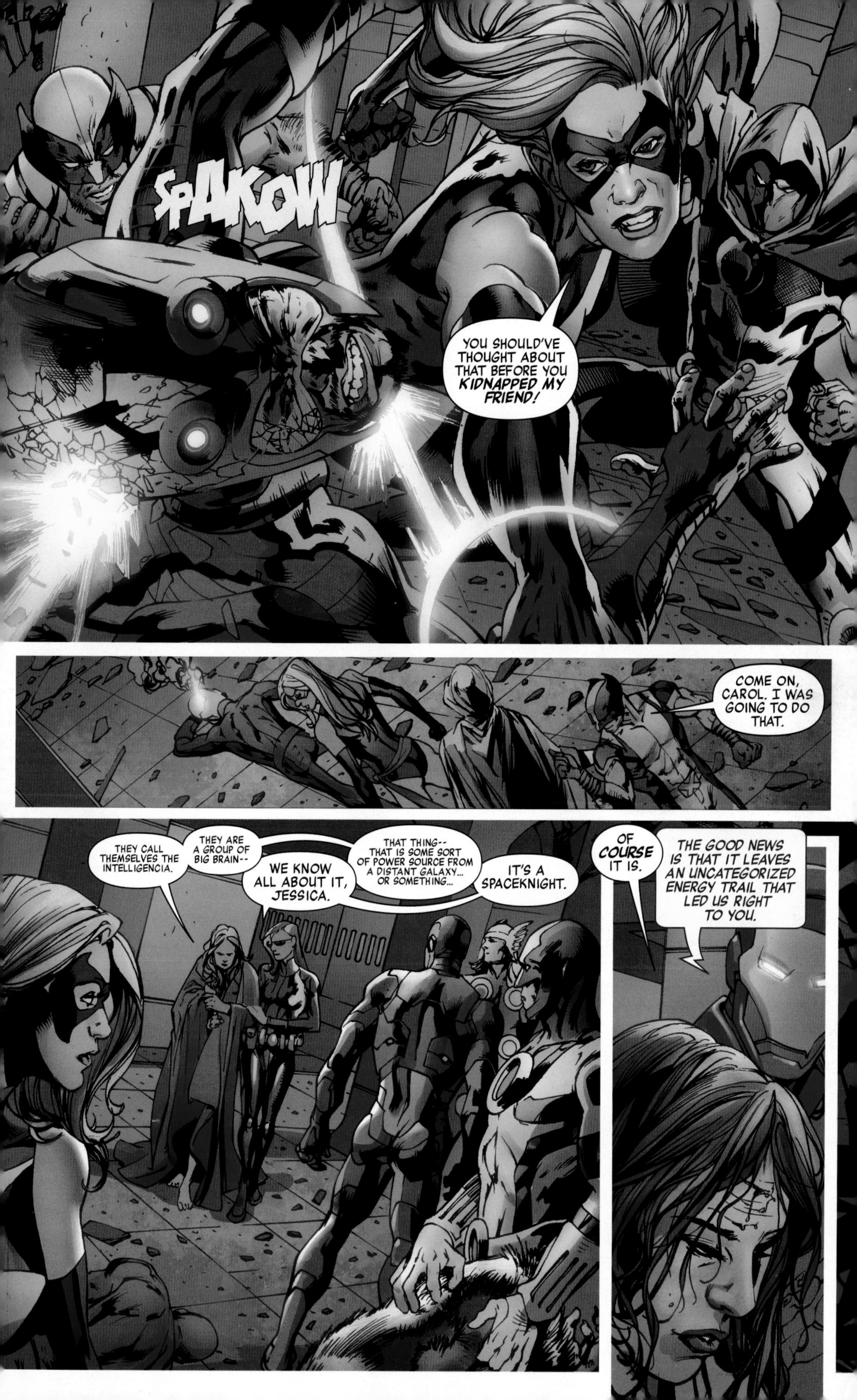
SPAKOW
YOU SHOULD'VE THOUGHT ABOUT THAT BEFORE YOU KIDNAPPED MY FRIEND!
COME ON, CAROL. I WAS GOING TO DO THAT.
THEY CALL THEMSELVES THE INTELLIGENCIA.
THEY ARE A GROUP OF BIG BRAIN--
WE KNOW ALL ABOUT IT, JESSICA.
THAT THING-- THAT IS SOME SORT OF POWER SOURCE FROM A DISTANT GALAXY... OR SOMETHING...
IT'S A SPACEKNIGHT.
OF COURSE IT IS.
THE GOOD NEWS IS THAT IT LEAVES AN UNCATEGORIZED ENERGY TRAIL THAT LED US RIGHT TO YOU.

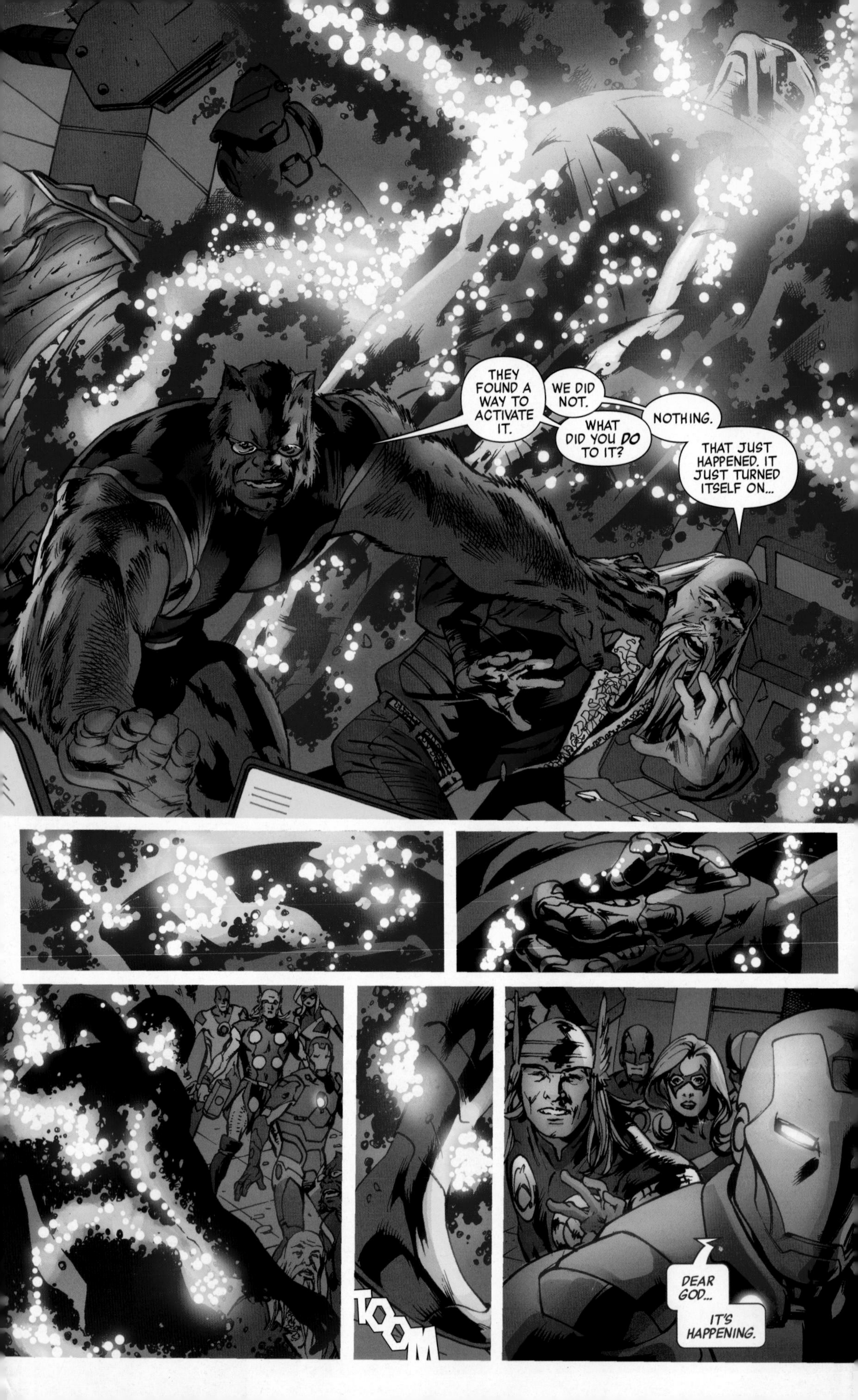
THEY FOUND A WAY TO ACTIVATE IT.
WE DID NOT.
WHAT DID YOU DO TO IT?
NOTHING.
THAT JUST HAPPENED. IT JUST TURNED ITSELF ON...
TOOM
DEAR GOD...
IT'S HAPPENING.

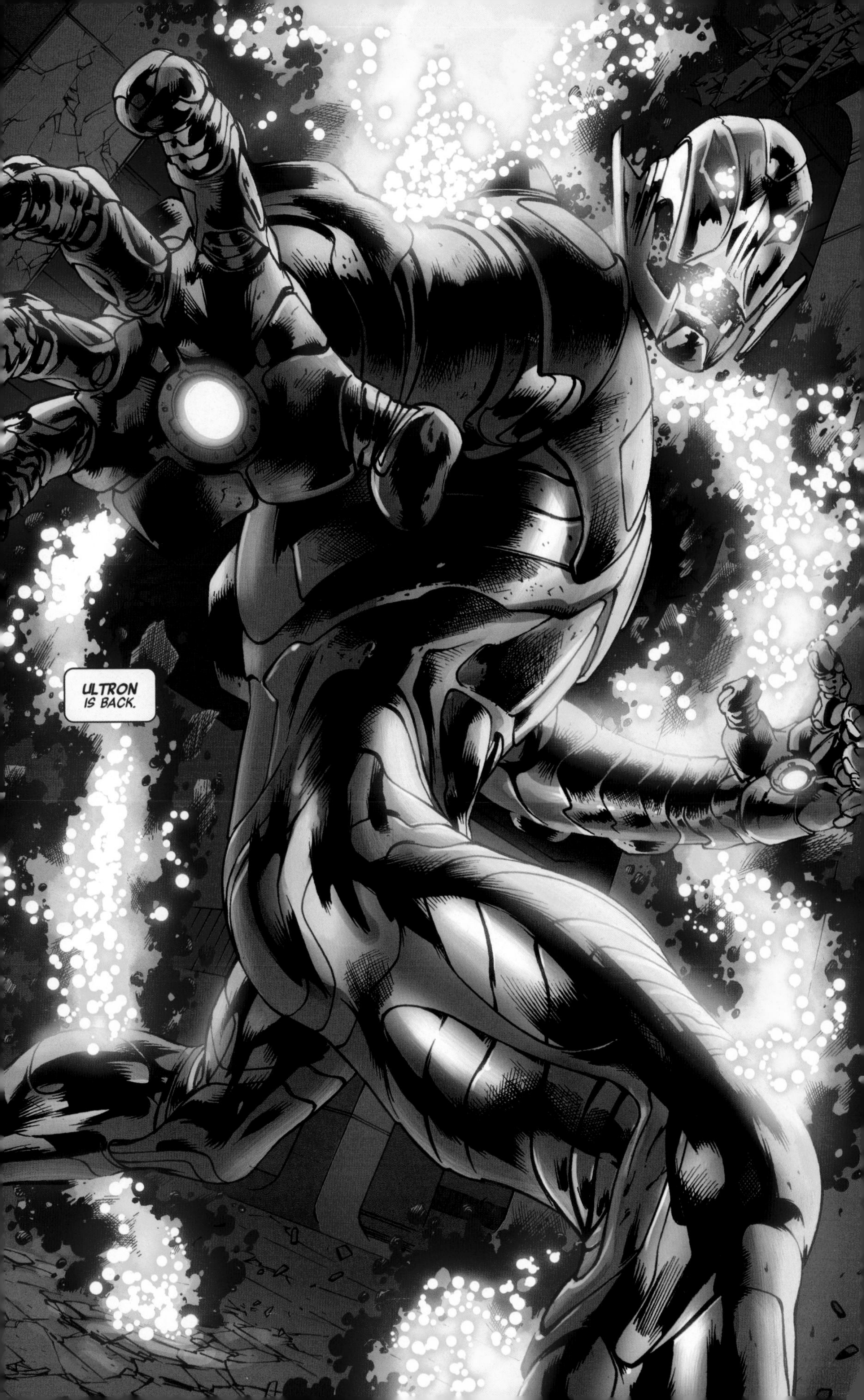
ULTRON IS BACK.

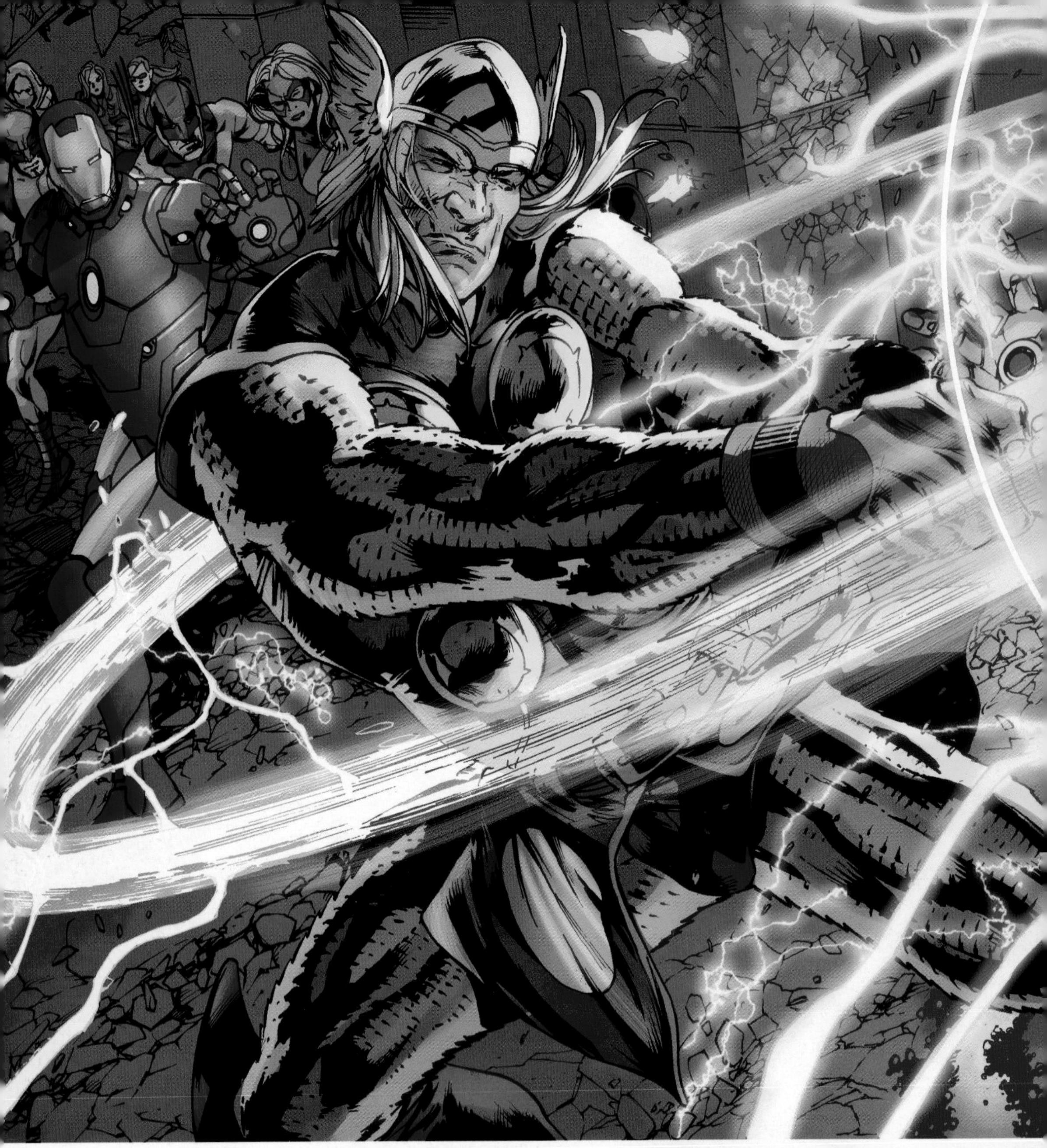

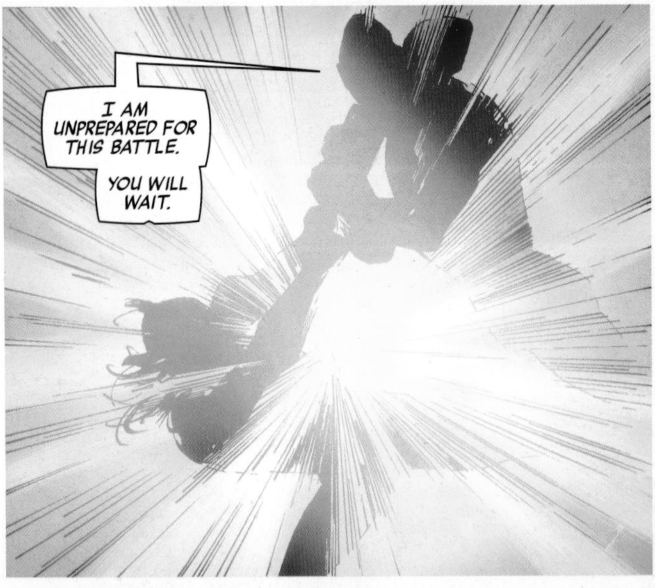
I AM UNPREPARED FOR THIS BATTLE.
YOU WILL WAIT.

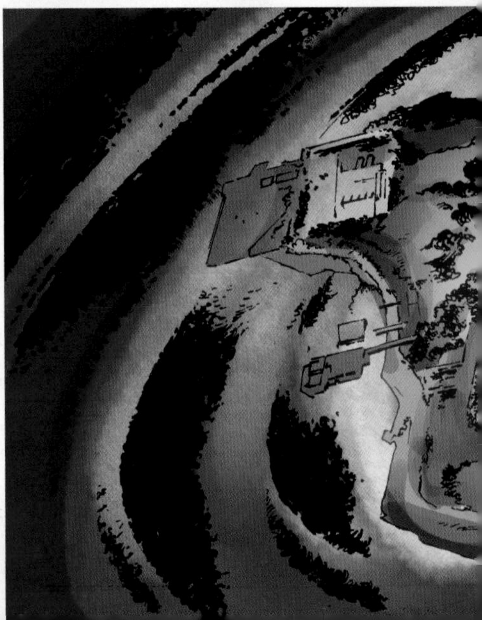

KRAKAROOM!!!

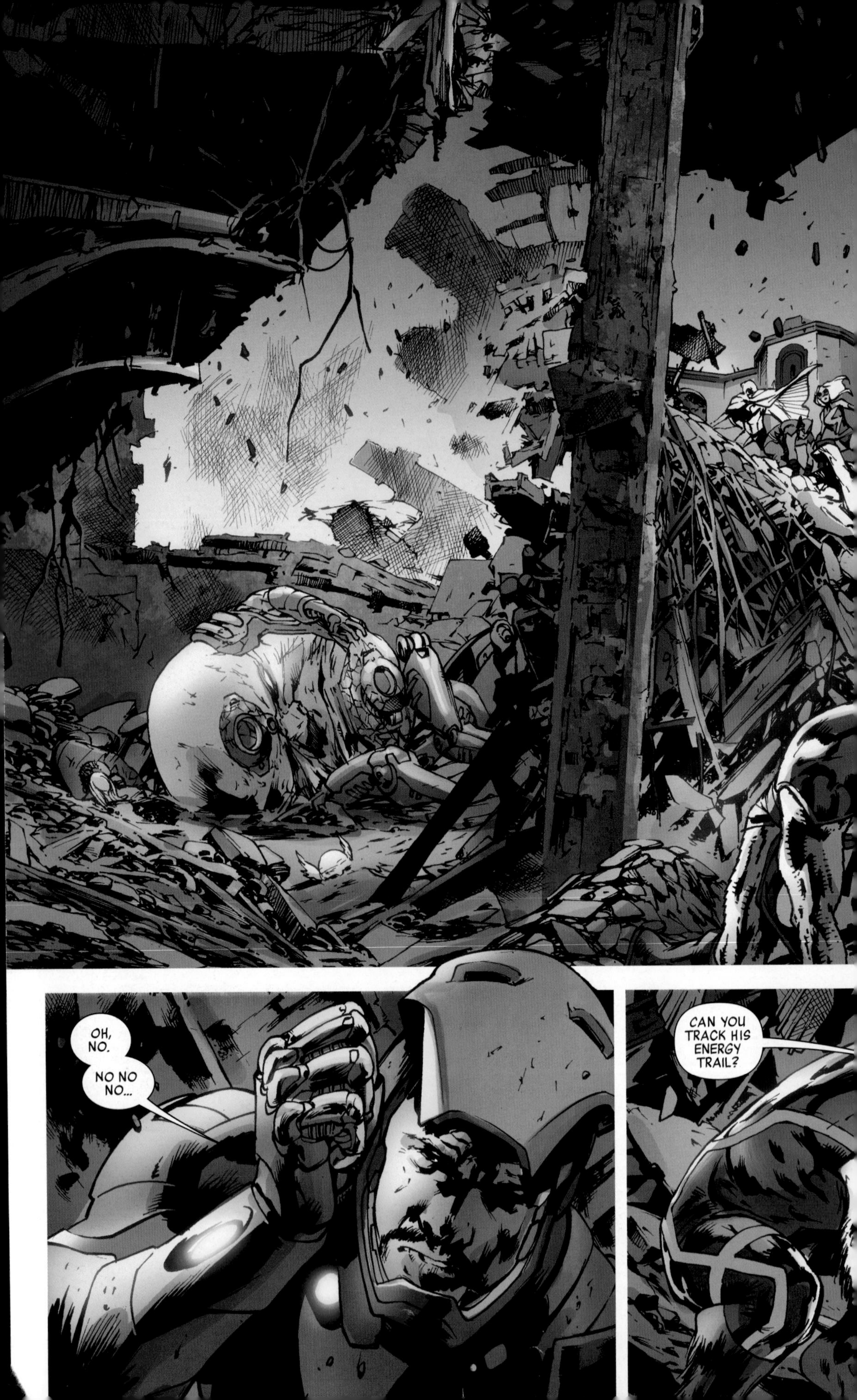
OH, NO.
NO NO NO...
CAN YOU TRACK HIS ENERGY TRAIL?

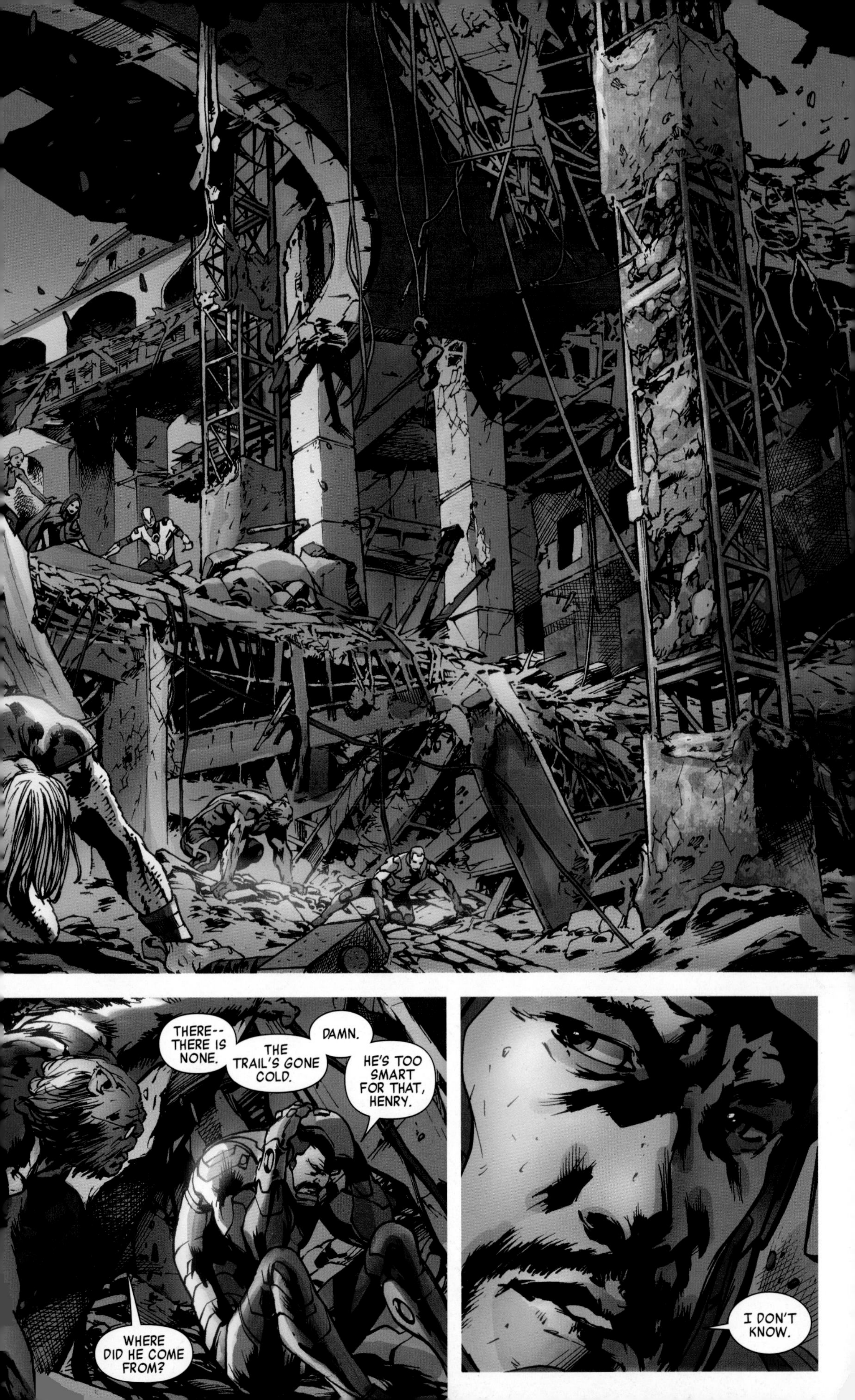
THERE-- THERE IS NONE.
THE TRAIL'S GONE COLD.
DAMN.
HE'S TOO SMART FOR THAT, HENRY.
WHERE DID HE COME FROM?
I DON'T KNOW.

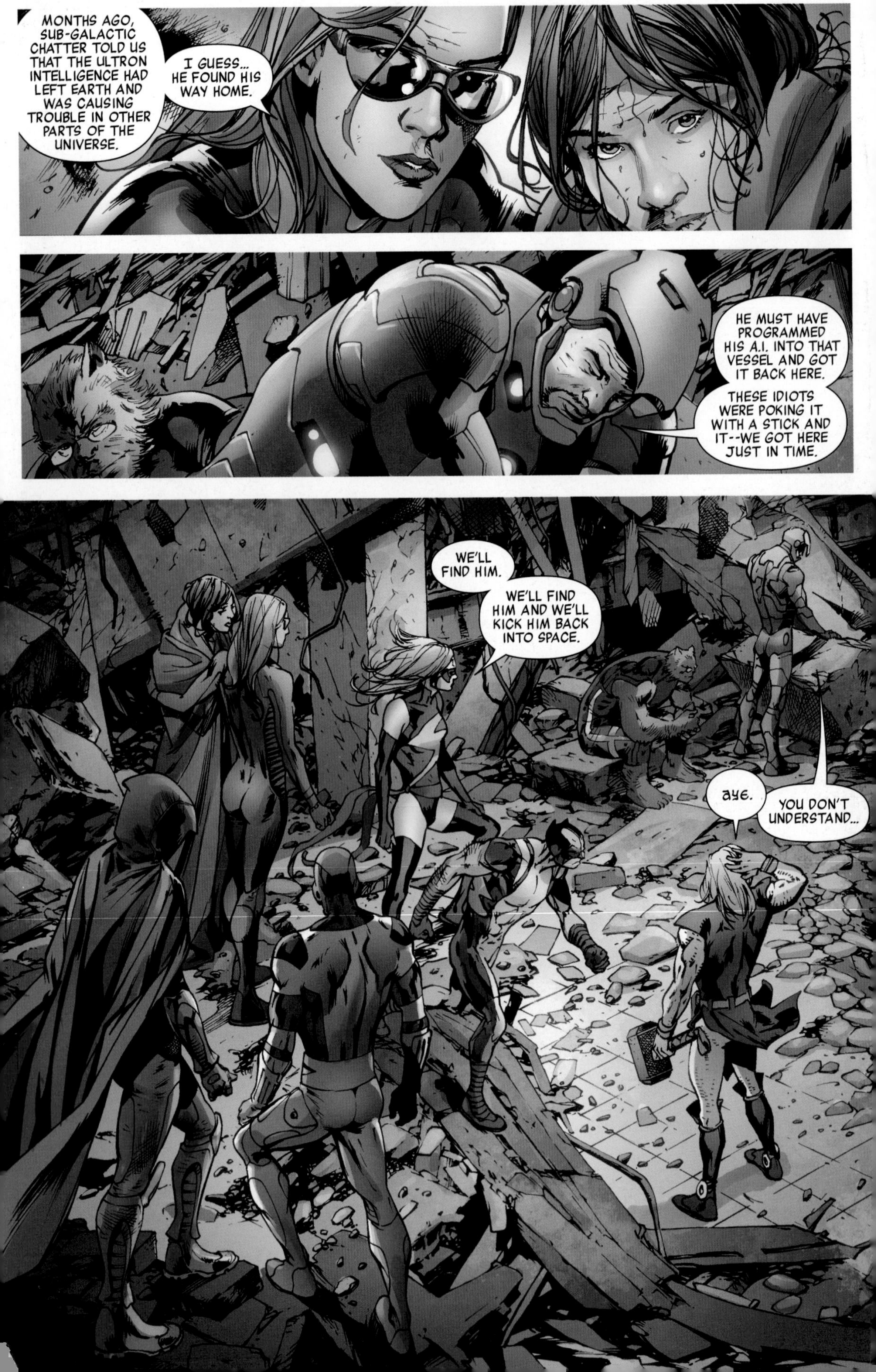
MONTHS AGO, SUB-GALACTIC CHATTER TOLD US THAT THE ULTRON INTELLIGENCE HAD LEFT EARTH AND WAS CAUSING TROUBLE IN OTHER PARTS OF THE UNIVERSE.
I GUESS... HE FOUND HIS WAY HOME.
HE MUST HAVE PROGRAMMED HIS A.I. INTO THAT VESSEL AND GOT IT BACK HERE.
THESE IDIOTS WERE POKING IT WITH A STICK AND IT--WE GOT HERE JUST IN TIME.
WE'LL FIND HIM.
WE'LL FIND HIM AND WE'LL KICK HIM BACK INTO SPACE.
aye.
YOU DON'T UNDERSTAND...

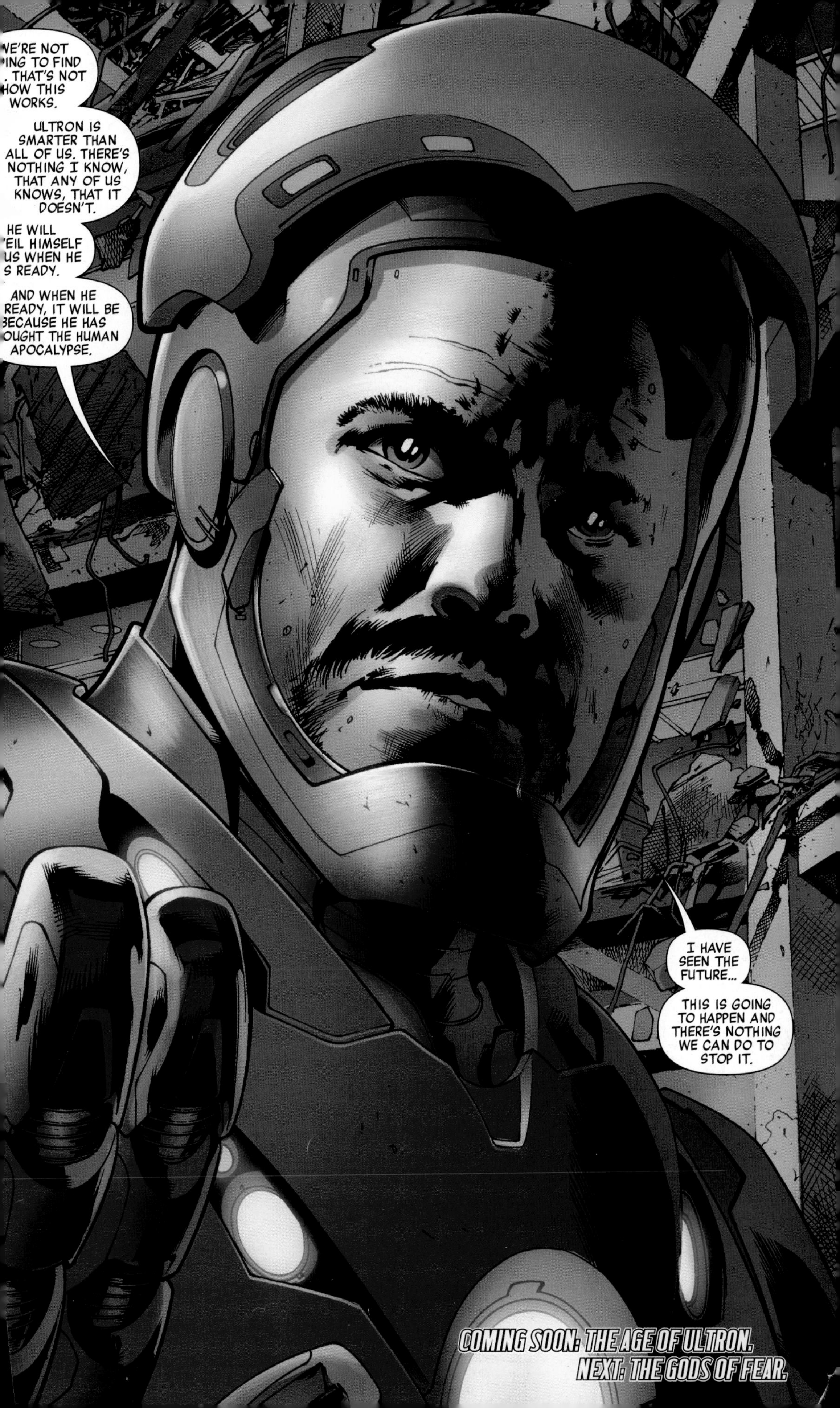

VE'RE NOT
ING TO FIND
. THAT'S NOT
HOW THIS
WORKS.
ULTRON IS SMARTER THAN ALL OF US. THERE'S NOTHING I KNOW, THAT ANY OF US KNOWS, THAT IT DOESN'T.
HE WILL
'EIL HIMSELF
US WHEN HE
S READY.
AND WHEN HE
READY, IT WILL BE
BECAUSE HE HAS
OUGHT THE HUMAN
APOCALYPSE.
I HAVE SEEN THE FUTURE...
THIS IS GOING TO HAPPEN AND THERE'S NOTHING WE CAN DO TO STOP IT.
COMING SOON: THE AGE OF ULTRON.
NEXT: THE GODS OF FEAR.

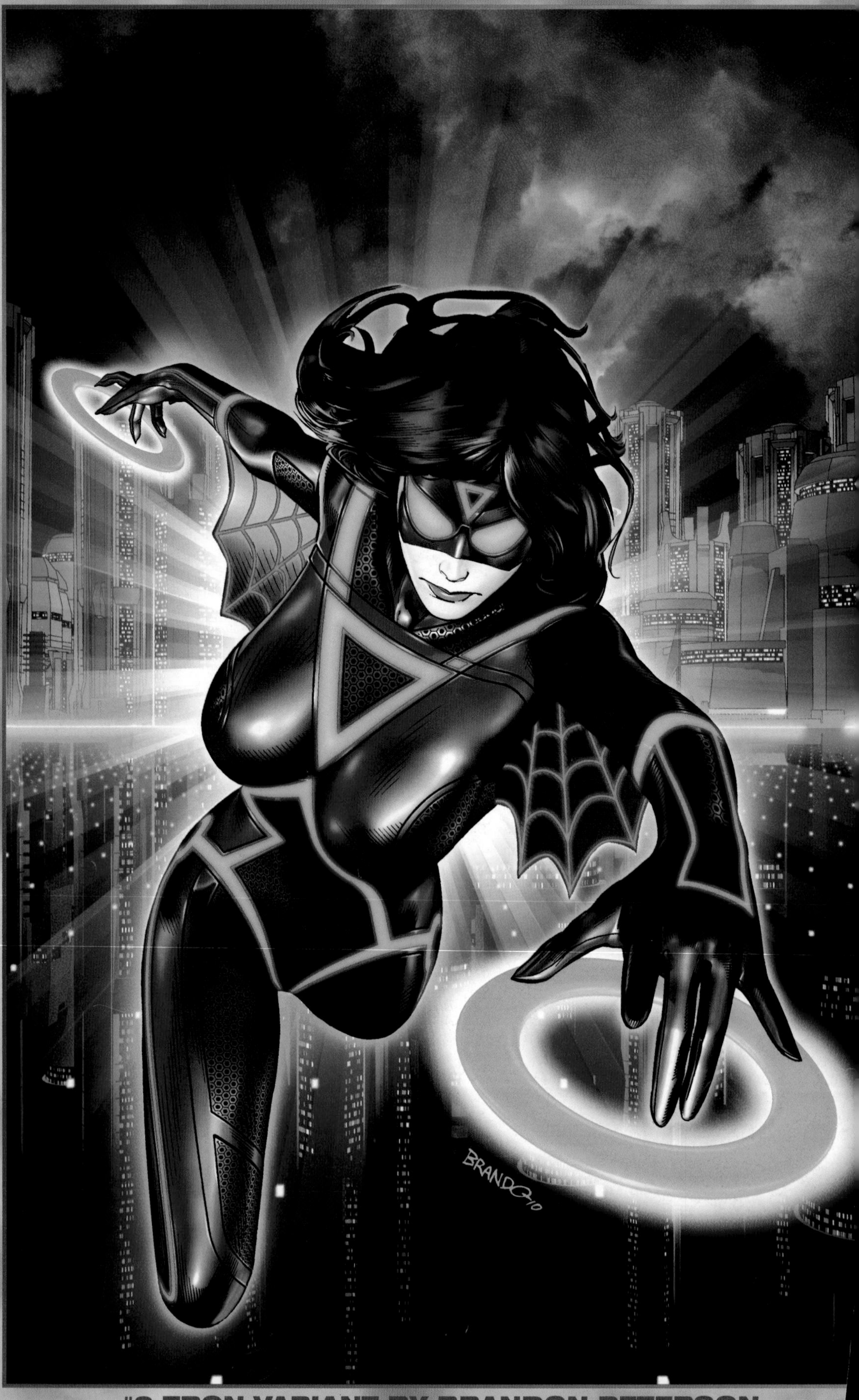
BRANDO'10

**#9 TRON VARIANT BY BRANDON PETERSON**